*The Principles
and Practice of
Educational Management*

Educational Management: Research and Practice
Series editor: Tony Bush

This book, *The Principles and Practice of Educational Management* is the reader for the MBA in Educational Management offered by the CELM, (previously EMDU), University of Leicester.

The modules in this course are:
Leadership and Strategic Management in Education
Managing Finance and External Relations
Human Resource Management in Schools and Colleges
Managing the Curriculum
Research Methods in Educational Management

For further information about the MBA in Educational Management, please contact the CELM at celm@le.ac.uk. For further information about the books associated with the course, contact Paul Chapman Publishing at www.paulchapmanpublishing.co.uk.

The Principles and Practice of Educational Management

Edited by
Tony Bush
and
Les Bell

P·C·P
Paul Chapman
Publishing

First published 2002

 Paul Chapman Publishing
A SAGE Publications Company
6 Bonhill Street
London EC2A 4PU

SAGE Publications Inc
2455 Teller Road
Thousand Oaks, California 91320

SAGE Publications India Pvt Ltd
32, M-Block Market
Greater Kailash - I
New Delhi 110 048

Library of Congress Control Number: 2002104048

A catalogue record for this book is available from the British
Library

ISBN 0 7619 4791 4
ISBN 0 7619 4792 2 (pbk)

Typeset by Dorwyn Ltd, Hampshire
Printed in Great Britain by The Cromwell Press, Wiltshire

Contents

Series Editor's Foreword

The effective management of education is increasingly regarded as a vital element in school and college improvement and in raising educational standards in many parts of the world. While the specific problems may be different, competent leadership and management are regarded as essential if institutional and system-wide objectives are to be achieved. The research on school effectiveness demonstrates conclusively that the quality of leadership is one of the major variables in delineating successful and less successful educational organisations, as the Commonwealth Secretariat (1996) and the English National College for School Leadership (2001) both acknowledge.

It is now widely accepted that managers in education require specific preparation if they are to be successful in leading schools and colleges. The development of effective leaders and managers requires a range of strategies, including high-quality courses and tuition, mentoring by experienced and successful principals, and opportunities to practise management at appropriate stages in professional careers. It also needs the support of literature which presents the major issues in clear, intelligible language while drawing on the best of theory and research. The aim of this series, and of this volume, is to develop a body of literature with the following characteristics:

- directly relevant to school and college management
- prepared by authors with national and international reputations
- an analytical approach based on empirical evidence but couched in intelligible language
- integrating the best of theory, research and practice.

The Principles and Practice of Educational Management is the eighth volume in the series and it aims to provide a comprehensive introduction to the main themes in educational management and leadership, including strategy, human resources, teaching and learning, finance, external relations and quality. The editors have attracted many of the best known authors on these topics and the chapters in this book provide a most valuable starting point for postgraduate students and practitioners. All successful educational organisations focus on improving student learning and this book should contribute to developing the management skills required to create the climate for effective teaching and learning.

Tony Bush
The University of Reading
October 2001

References

Commonwealth Secretariat (1996) *Better Schools: Resource Materials for Heads: Introductory Module*, London: Commonwealth Secretariat.

National College for School Leadership (2001) *First Corporate Plan: Launch Year 2001–2002*, Nottingham: National College for School Leadership.

Preface

This book is a sequel to *The Principles of Educational Management* (Bush and West-Burnham, 1994) which has made an important contribution to the literature in this field. Like its predecessor, it aims to provide a systematic and analytical introduction to the study of educational management. It offers an integrated and comprehensive review of the main theoretical perspectives and of their application to practice in schools and colleges.

University courses on educational leadership and management continue to be very popular and this volume is intended to be helpful for students on the master's and taught doctorate programmes now available in many countries. It is a set text for the University of Leicester's MBA in Educational Management and for the management strand of its Doctorate of Education.

Educational management, administration and leadership have become internationally significant as topics of theory, research and practice. As well as their academic importance, they have become the central elements of preparation programmes for school principals and other leaders in many countries, as a recent programme of study visits for the English National College for School Leadership demonstrated (Bush and Jackson, 2002).

The editors have chosen to focus on 'management' rather than leadership or administration in the title of the book. As we indicate in Chapter 1, this is partly because of a belief that 'management' represents a wider range of activities involved in running successful educational organisations than the alternative terms 'administration' and 'leadership'. We also agree with the Open University (1996: 11) that 'management [is] the overarching concept within which leadership is subsumed'.

The structure of the book reflects the main substantive areas of educational leadership and management and most of the major themes are covered in the volume's 19 chapters. Section I addresses the context of educational management. The opening chapter by Les Bell and Tony Bush sets the policy context for educational management. It emphasises that the contexts vary markedly between and within countries, for both economic and cultural reasons, and that these factors undoubtedly contribute to the marked differences in policy and practice despite apparent similarities in the issues facing schools and colleges.

In Chapter 2, Tony Bush discusses his well-known typology of educational management theory and applies it to practice in several international settings. He draws attention to different approaches to bureaucracy in contrasting educational systems and shows how the increasing demands for accountability are rooted in a bureaucratic perspective. He discusses the links between subjective theories and qualitative research and concludes by arguing that theory can improve practice through enabling school leaders and managers to diagnose problems effectively and to determine the most appropriate response.

The leading Australian writer, Brian Caldwell, presents concepts of autonomy in Chapter 3 and examines the evidence on the links between self-management and student outcomes. He reports on a large scale study of 39 countries which suggests that 'school autonomy in process and personnel decisions' are favourable to student performance. He concludes that self-management is likely to be successful if it is utilised to focus on learning outcomes.

Section II examines the linked themes of leadership and strategic management. Drawing on his experience in Hong Kong, Yin Cheng Cheong considers the relationship between leadership and strategy in Chapter 4. He reviews concepts of leadership, drawing on a wide range of international literature, and proposes a model linking affective, behavioural and cognitive domains to five dimensions of leadership.

In Chapter 5, Clive Dimmock and Allan Walker, whose collective academic experience includes Australia, England, Hong Kong and Singapore, present their innovative work on societal culture and link it to school leadership. They identify eight elements of leadership and provide a cross-cultural analysis illustrated by reference to several countries. They conclude that an appreciation of cultural differences makes it easier for leaders to understand practice in their own environment.

Successful leaders are expected to develop their 'vision', a clearly articulated notion of a more successful future for the organisation. Jacky Lumby examines this concept and relates it to strategic planning in Chapter 6. She points out that agreement on vision and values is an essential first step in planning but, given the dynamic nature of values, this will never be a straightforward process. She explains that strategic planning was problematic in English further education in the 1990s, for example, but it did produce a greater sense of purpose.

Section III focuses on the enduring topic of human resource management. People are the most important resource in any organisation, providing the knowledge and skill required to achieve desired outcomes. In Chapter 7, Ray Bolam argues that professional development is fundamental to organisational improvement. He points to a shift in the nature of professional development, with the needs of individual teachers subordinated to national and institutional requirements, with an inevitable impact on the nature of professionalism. He concludes by examining the implications of these trends for school leaders.

David Middlewood examines the twin concepts of appraisal and performance management in Chapter 8. He points to the emergence of performance appraisal in many countries and to the notion of linking financial rewards to such assessments. He outlines the process of appraisal and argues that it is likely to be most effective if carried out within the institution and by more than one person.

Chapter 9, by Marianne Coleman, addresses the increasingly important issue of equal opportunities in education. She points to the many characteristics which can lead to discrimination and recommends the establishment of a 'culture of equal opportunities'. She addresses the specific issues of recruitment and promotion and concludes that management of equal opportunities should be at the heart of all educational organisations.

Section IV looks at the central activities of teaching and learning, the aspects which so clearly differentiate educational institutions from other types of organisation. Schools and colleges are the ultimate learning organisations (Lumby, 1997) and they are assessed primarily by the extent to which they succeed in promoting learning. In Chapter 10, Margaret Preedy examines the management of the curriculum from the perspective of student learning. She points to the differences between the intended, offered and received curriculum and discusses the main curriculum management processes. She suggests that school curriculum decision-making is taking place within a tighter framework of control and accountability and shows the importance of the values underpinning the curriculum.

Ann Briggs focuses on monitoring and evaluation of learning in Chapter 11. She examines different approaches to learning and points to the need for educational organisations to be 'learner centred'. She considers different methods of evaluation and concludes by arguing that schools and colleges should evaluate what they value and not simply rely on those narrow indicators determined by external bodies.

In Section V, the focus switches to finance and resources. Given the emergence of self-management in many countries, the effective deployment of financial and real resources is critical if educational objectives are to be achieved. This is most likely to be achieved by ensuring that funding decisions are integrated with curriculum management. Rosalind Levačić, in Chapter 12, examines issues of efficiency and equity in autonomous schools. She differentiates between productive efficiency, for example examination results, and allocative efficiency, for example parental choice of school. She also considers the notion of equity, for example in respect of access to educational opportunities. She shows that self-managing schools use resources more efficiently.

Lesley Anderson examines resource allocation and acquisition within schools and colleges in Chapter 13. She presents a cyclical model of financial management which involves utilisation and evaluation of resources as well as allocation and acquisition She discusses the notion of cost-effectiveness and concludes by linking resource management to strategic planning.

Section VI focuses on the management of external relations. All educational institutions need to give attention to relationships with their stakeholders and this is particularly true of autonomous schools and colleges. Their reputations are likely to depend, in part, on how they are perceived within their local communities. In chapter 14, Ron Glatter addresses issues of governance, autonomy and accountability. He probes the concept of 'governance' and presents four models of school governance. He points out that increased autonomy is often accompanied by greater demands for accountability. Leaders may face conflicting demands for accountability and have to become effective at 'networking'.

Chapter 15, by Nick Foskett, discusses marketing in education and argues that its increasing importance for educational institutions is linked to the external scrutiny of their performance. He distinguishes between different definitions of markets and marketing and illustrates these notions with examples from several countries. He points to the importance of linking marketing with strategy and concludes that marketing requires managers to become more focused on the outside world.

Les Bell considers educational partnerships in Chapter 16 and focuses on the development of the role of parents, and on the links between education and business organisations. He argues that, in many countries, both forms of partnership are being mobilised to provide support for school improvement initiatives although, in some parts of the world, such partnerships concentrate on survival rather than improvement.

The final section of the book examines issues of quality. It is one of the 'buzzwords' of the new millennium, frequently advocated, widely used and rarely challenged. However, the concept lacks a clear definition and suffers from multiple and overlapping meanings. In Chapter 17, Hugh Busher focuses on the improvement of learning within a context of change. He points to the importance of the socio-political contexts within which schools operate and refers to the need for a culture of learning. He argues that leaders need to help teachers to cope with change.

Chapter 18 by Brian Fidler considers the twin issues of external evaluation and inspection. He points to the increased accountability pressures in education and links them to pressures for external evaluation. Its purposes are examined and he also reviews different types of evaluation. He presents case studies from England and Victoria, Australia, and concludes that the evaluation process should be systematic if it is to produce valid data about school performance.

The final chapter, by John West-Burnham, explores the concept of total quality and links it to educational leadership and management. He explains the genealogy of quality management and discusses competing definitions of quality. He examines several difficulties in applying the concept to education but concludes that schools and colleges should be 'fit for purpose' and that the perceptions of the client should be accorded status and significance.

The editors are grateful to all the authors for their scholarship and care in preparing their chapters for this volume. We also wish to express our thanks to Joyce Palmer who produced the manuscript. We hope and believe that their efforts have been rewarded by a book that will become a valuable contribution to the developing literature on educational leadership and management.

Tony Bush (The University of Reading)
and
Les Bell (University of Leicester)
October 2001

References

Bush, T. and Jackson, D. (2002) 'Preparation for school leadership: international perspectives', *Educational Management and Administration*, 30, (4).

Bush, T. and West-Burnham, J. (eds) (1994) *The Principles of Educational Management*, Harlow: Longman.

Lumby, J. (1997) 'The learning organisation', in T. Bush and D. Middlewood (eds), *Managing People in Education*, London: Paul Chapman Publishing.

Open University (1996) *E838 Effective Leadership and Management in Education: Study Guide*, Milton Keynes: Open University Press.

Notes on Contributors

Dr Lesley Anderson lectures in educational leadership and management at the Open University. She has particular interest in financial and resource management as well as policy relating to the organisation of schools and colleges. In respect of the former, her previous publications include *Managing Finance, Resources and Stakeholders in Education* (with A. R. J. Briggs and N. Burton) and *Managing Finance and Resources in Education* (with M. Coleman). Before joining the Open University, she was Director of the MBA in Educational Management by distance learning at the Centre for Educational Leadership and Management, University of Leicester, formerly the Educational Management Development Unit.

Les Bell is Professor of Educational Management and Director of the Doctorate of Education Programme at the Centre for Educational Leadership and Management, School of Education, University of Leicester. He trained as a teacher at Goldsmiths College, London and has taught in both primary and secondary schools in Grimsby and South London. He joined the Education Department at Coventry College of Education to teach Sociology of Education and subsequently became a member of the Education Department at the University of Warwick after the College merged with the University. In 1994 he left Warwick to become Director of the School of Education and Community Studies, and later Dean of Education, Health and Social Studies, at Liverpool John Moores University. He was appointed to the Chair of Educational Management at Leicester in 1999 and now teaches the Doctoral Programme in South East Asia and the UK. He has written extensively on educational management and his research interests include the impact of government education policy on primary school headteachers, the nature of schools as organisations and cultural diversity in educational management.

Ray Bolam is semi-retired and continues to work as Professor of Education in the School of Social Science at Cardiff University and as Visiting Professor at the Universities of Leicester and Bath. At Cardiff University, he was formerly Head of the School of Education and also Director of the National Professional Qualification for Headteachers (NPQH) Centre for Wales. From 1992 to 1994 he was Professor of Education at the University of Swansea and, prior to that, Senior Research Fellow at the University of Bristol where he was Director of the National Development Centre for School Management Training from 1983 to 1990. He has been a consultant for the OECD, the

British Council, the European Commission and for various national and international agencies in Africa, Asia, Europe and North America. His research interests and publications have focused on school leadership, professional development, school improvement and evidence-informed practice. His current research includes projects on 'Evidence-Informed Policy and Practice' and on 'Capacity-Building in Schools'.

Ann R. J. Briggs is a lecturer in Educational Management at the Centre for Educational Leadership and Management, University of Leicester. Her principal research interests are the management of learning and learning resources, and management in Further Education Colleges. She is co-editor with Marianne Coleman of *Research Methods in Educational Leadership and Management*.

Tony Bush is Professor of International and Comparative Education at the University of Reading. He was previously Professor of Educational Management and Director of the Educational Management Development Unit, now the Centre for Educational Leadership and Management, at the University of Leicester from 1992 until 2000. He has been a visiting professor, external examiner, consultant or keynote speaker in China, Greece, Hong Kong, New Zealand, Portugal, Singapore and South Africa. He has represented the English National College for School Leadership in both Canada and the United States, and been an adviser to the Teacher Training Agency and the Learning and Skills Research Centre. He has published more than 80 books, articles and chapters on aspects of educational leadership and management, including educational management theory, self-managing schools, preparation for school principals, and international and comparative education.

Dr Hugh Busher is a senior lecturer in the School of Education, University of Leicester, where he is deputy director of the international Doctorate of Education programme. He has had extensive experience of teaching in secondary schools and in universities. Long-standing research interests include: leadership and change processes in educational organisations to improve teaching and learning; the professional development and identities of teachers and other staff in schools; the interaction of policy and community contexts with the internal micropolitics and cultures of educational organisations; social justice and the creation of inclusive education.

Brian J. Caldwell is Professor and Dean of Education at the University of Melbourne, Australia. He was previously at the University of Tasmania, where he also served as Dean of Education, and at the University of Alberta, Canada. He is co-author with Jim Spinks of three books on self-managing schools that have helped shape developments in several nations: *The Self-Managing School* (1988), *Leading the Self-Managing School* (1992) and *Beyond the Self-*

Managing School (1998). His interest in self-management spans more than 25 years, commencing with studies of pioneering initiatives in Canada in the mid-1970s. His research agenda includes a continuation of studies that explore the impact of self-management on learning. He is currently engaged in a three-year project to develop a new concept of public education for the twenty-first century. He continues his teaching at the postgraduate level in the area of strategic leadership. He has undertaken research, served as consultant or made presentations, in 28 nations, including assignments for OECD, UNESCO, UNICEF, World Bank and Asia Development Bank. He has held Visiting Professorships at the Chinese University of Hong Kong, University of Nottingham, University of Southern California and the National College of School Leadership in England, and has served as Invitational Research Fellow of the Japanese Society for the Promotion of Science.

Professor Yin Cheong Cheng is Director of the Centre for Research and International Collaboration of the Hong Kong Institute of Education. He is also the Head of the Asia-Pacific Centre for Education Leadership and Education Quality. He serves as a full member of the University Grants Committee and a panel member of the Research Grants Council of the Hong Kong SAR Government. Previously, he was the associate director of the Hong Kong Institute of Educational Research and a professor in the Department of Educational Administration and Policy of the Chinese University of Hong Kong. Professor Cheng has published eight books and nearly 150 book chapters and academic journal articles in different parts of the world. Some of his English publications have been translated into Chinese, Hebrew, Korean, Spanish and Thai. His research has won him a number of international awards and recognition including the Awards for Excellence from the Literati Club in UK in 1994, 1996–98 and 2001. He has been invited to attend as a keynote speaker at numerous international and regional conferences in education.

Dr Marianne Coleman is a senior lecturer at the Institute of Education, London University and was previously at the School of Education, University of Leicester. She has written and researched extensively in the field of educational management and has a particular research interest in women in educational management and leadership.

Clive Dimmock is Professor of Educational Management and Director of the Centre for Educational Leadership and Management, the University of Leicester, UK. He has held positions at Cardiff University, the University of Western Australia and the Chinese University of Hong Kong. His research interests focus on cross-cultural and comparative educational leadership and management, particularly with regard to Chinese and Anglo-American societies, school leader preparation and training, and school design for improvement. He has been a consultant to many governments, including those in Australia and Hong Kong. His publications include many journal articles and books, one of which is *Designing the Learning-Centred School: A Cross-Cultural Perspective*, Falmer Press, 2000.

Brian Fidler teaches and researches at the University of Reading. He is professor of education management and course leader for the MSc Managing School Improvement. His main interest and recent writing has been on strategic management. His latest book is *Strategic Management for School Development* from Paul Chapman Publishing. He is editor of *School Leadership and Management*, the international journal specialising in school leadership and school development, and a past treasurer of the British Educational Leadership, Management and Administration Society.

Nick Foskett is Professor of Education and Head of the Research and Graduate School of Education at the University of Southampton. He is also Director of the university's Centre for Research in Education Marketing (CREM). His research is in the field of educational policy and management, with a particular focus on markets and marketing in education and training. He taught in schools and colleges before moving into higher education teaching and research. Recent research has included national projects on young people's choice processes and their interaction with institutional strategies, and recent publications have included *Managing External Relations in Schools and Colleges* (with Jacky Lumby) and *Choosing Futures* (with Jane Hemsley-Brown).

Ron Glatter is Professor in the Centre for Educational Policy and Management (CEPAM), which he directed for some years, at the Open University, UK. He has contributed to numerous Open University courses and readers. He worked previously at the University of London Institute of Education. He was the founding Honorary Secretary of what is now the British Educational Leadership, Management and Administration Society (BELMAS), later became its national Chair and is currently a Vice-President. His major interests and publications are in the fields of educational leadership development and the effects of choice and diversity in education. He is currently conducting research on the governance of education.

Rosalind Levačić is Professor of Economics and Finance of Education at the Institute of Education, University of London. Her research is concerned with the allocation of resources to and within schools and the management of finance and resources in schools. She is research associate at the DfES-funded Centre for the Economics of Education where she is working on projects concerning the relationship between school resources and student outcomes. She has written widely on school finance and the local management of schools.

Her books include *Local Management of Schools: Analysis and Practice* (Open University Press, 1995) and *Needs Based Resource Allocation in Education via Formula Funding of Schools* edited with Ken Ross (International Institute of Educational Planning, 1999). She has worked on two EU PHARE projects on the decentralisation of school finance in Poland and is a governor of a secondary school and a first school in Milton Keynes.

Jacky Lumby is Professor of Educational Leadership at the International Institute for Educational Leadership, at the University of Lincoln. She was previously Deputy Director of the Educational Management Development Unit, with a special responsibility for teaching and learning. She has taught in a range of educational settings, including schools, community and further education. Her special interest is the management of further/technical education. International research has included the management of vocational education in China, Hong Kong and South Africa and in schools in South Africa. She has also researched and published on the management of both general further education and sixth form colleges in the learning and skills sector in England.

David Middlewood is Deputy Director of the Centre for Educational Leadership and Management of the University of Leicester. Prior to joining the University in 1990, he was headteacher of a secondary comprehensive school for nine years and had taught in a range of schools previously. David has edited and contributed to volumes on topics such as strategic management, home–school links, recruitment and selection and staff development, and he is co-author of *Practitioner Research in Education* (1999). He has published on and researched performance appraisal in the UK, New Zealand and South Africa and has produced the first book (with Carol Cardno) looking at international practice in this field *Managing Teacher Appraisal and Performance: A Comparative Approach* (Routledge/Falmer 2001). David is also co-editor of the UK journals *Headship Matters* and *Primary Headship*.

Margaret Preedy is a lecturer in the Faculty of Education and Language Studies at the Open University.

Allan Walker is a Professor in the Department of Educational Administration and Policy at the Chinese University of Hong Kong. His teaching and research interests include the influence of societal culture on educational administration and leadership and the needs assessment of principals undergoing professional development.

John West-Burnham is Professor of Educational Leadership at the International Leadership Centre, University of Hull. John worked in schools, adult and further education for 15 years before moving into higher education.

He has worked at Crewe and Alsager College, the University of Leicester and the University of Lincolnshire and Humberside. He was also Development Officer for Teacher Performance for Cheshire LEA. John is author of *Managing Quality in Schools*, co-author of *Effective Learning in Schools* and *Leadership and Professional Development in Schools*. He has edited and written 13 other books and over 30 articles. He has also worked in Australia, Hong Kong, Israel, New Zealand, South Africa and the USA. John's research interests centre on the nature of leadership and leadership development and the emergence of the science of learning and its implications for school organisation. He has recently published research reports on performance management and the relationship between schools and their communities.

Section I
The Context of Educational Management

1

The Policy Context

Les Bell and Tony Bush

Introduction: educational management and leadership

As editors, we have deliberately chosen *The Principles and Practice of Educational Management* as the title of this book. This is partly because of a belief that 'management' represents a wider range of activities involved in running successful educational organisations than the alternative terms 'administration' and 'leadership'. Educational administration, as used in the United States and Australia, for example, refers to courses very similar to educational management programmes in Britain and many countries in Europe, Asia and Africa. However, in Britain administration has a much narrower meaning, referring to the work of civil servants and local officers rather than to institutional management, except those involved in routine clerical and financial functions.

The field of educational management has tended to include the notion of leadership: 'Management [is] the overarching concept within which leadership is subsumed' (Open University, 1996: 11). Both these terms imply an emphasis on vision, mission and purpose coupled with a capacity to inspire others to work towards the achievement of these aims. Operational management, in relation to budgeting, staff issues, teaching and learning and relationships with parents and the community, are then linked to these strategic aims. Recently, in England and Wales, official bodies have made a firmer distinction between the two concepts and given much greater emphasis to leadership. The former chief executive of the Teacher Training Agency (TTA), for example, stated that: 'the central issue we need to tackle is leadership, in particular how the qualities of leadership can be identified and fostered' (Millett, 1996). This stance leads to a prescriptive approach to what leaders should do and to the production of lists that foster atomised thinking, because they separate and fragment the work of leaders into categories and create a false dichotomy between leadership and management. The dichotomy is false because effective schools require good leadership *and* good management. As the American writers Bolman and Deal, emphasise: 'The challenge of modern organisations requires the objective perspective of the manager as well as the flashes of brilliance of vision and commitment wise leadership provides' (Bolman and Deal, 1991: xiii–xiv).

Assuming a sharp difference between leadership and management is dangerous also because it can lead to allegations of 'managerialism', an emphasis on implementation or the technical aspects of management with little regard for the values and purposes of education. Seeking to promote leadership and management as integrated and complementary aspects of effective organisations helps to ensure that operational management is linked closely to the aims and values of education: 'Erecting this kind of dichotomy between something pure called "leadership" and something "dirty" called "management", or between values and purposes on the one hand and methods and skills on the other, would be disastrous' (Glatter, 1997: 189).

Bell (1999) argues that the prevailing dichotomy between leadership and management is inappropriate because these activities are inextricably linked in all schools and colleges. At its most strategic, management involves formulating a vision for the school based on strongly held values about the aims and purposes of education, and translating this into action in specific institutions. Leadership involves the embodiment and articulation of this vision and its communication to others.

The fundamental flaw in this conceptualisation of educational leadership and management is that it overemphasizes the role of the headteacher or principal. If management at the strategic level involves translating the vision into broad aims and long-terms plans, then it is at the organisational level that the strategic view is converted into medium-term objectives supported by the allocation of appropriate resources and the delegation of responsibility for decision-making, implementation, review and evaluation. In turn, at the operational level, resources are utilised, tasks are completed, and activities are co-ordinated and monitored

These three levels of management, strategic, organisational and operational, must work in harmony towards a common purpose, especially if site-based management is to work effectively. This can happen only if the values and vision are shared by all members of the community. Each level of management depends on the other two. Organisational and operational management can be aimless without clear values and purposes but even the most inspiring leadership will fail if it does not lead to effective implementation. Combining these three levels is the prime function of management.

Integrating theory, research and practice

This book sets out to explore the relationship between research and practice in educational management. Management is essentially a practical activity. Determining aims and strategies, making and implementing plans, managing teaching and learning, people, budgets and external relations, and evaluating practice, all require action. However, the action needs to be underpinned by educational values. These provide a set of guidelines about how to behave as leaders and managers. The values, in turn, are linked to principles or theories of management. For example, a commitment to full participation of teachers and school governors in the decision-making process represents a belief in collegiality whether or not the managers have an explicit awareness of this model. Similarly, the assumptions underpinning educational reform, in England and Wales, and elsewhere, are based on a de facto rational model: 'Governing bodies and headteachers are expected to link their financial planning to their educational policies in an overtly rational process' (Bush, 1999: 247).

As well as being grounded in an explicit awareness of theory, it is important that management practice should be based on research evidence. In many countries, there is an explicit relationship between theory, research, policy and practice. This is evident in Ontario, Canada, for example, where aspiring school principals follow a course which is underpinned by research on school leadership, notably that of the Ontario Institute for the Study of Education (OISE). The work of leading academics, such as Leithwood et al. (1999), is mediated and applied by experienced school principals who, in turn, are regular participants in OISE seminars on school leadership (Bush and Jackson, 2002). In addition, the course requires participants to research their own practice as a key element of the process of evaluation and review.

In the early years of the new millennium, there is increasing interest in research on educational leadership and management in England and Wales. Participants in the National Professional Qualification for Headteachers (NPQH) are expected to conduct in-school enquiries as part of their assessment. The Department for Education and Skills (DfES) has a funded teacher-researcher scheme while the National College for School Leadership (NCSL) has appointed a Director of Research and School Improvement and is involved in several initiatives to link research with school leadership and management practice.

The underlying message from these initiatives is that teaching and management should be research-based professions. Practice without theory and research neglects previous findings and experience and risks repeating the mistakes of the past. An explicit awareness of theory and research provides the potential for informed decision-making: 'Managers in all organisations . . . can increase their effectiveness and their freedom through the use of multiple vantage points. To be locked into a single path is likely to produce error and self-imprisonment' (Bolman and Deal, 1984: 4).

In searching for solutions to problems, or identifying ways of tackling complex issues, educational leaders need to be aware of research findings to see what has worked well in similar situations. Research findings often lead to 'grounded theories' (Glaser and Strauss, 1967) which can provide the conceptual frameworks for managers seeking ways of responding to difficult events or situations. These frameworks may be drawn from education or from commerce and industry.

Management within and outside education

Educational management as a field of study and practice was derived from management principles first applied to industry and commerce, mainly in the United States. Dependence on imported ideas, from other countries and other management settings, has reduced as educational management has become an established discipline with its own theories and some empirical data to test their validity in education. This transition has been accompanied by lively argument about the extent to which education should be regarded as simply another field for the application of general principles of management or be seen as a separate field with its own body of knowledge.

One view is that there are general principles of management which can be applied to all organisational settings (Handy, 1984). This 'general principles' case rests largely upon the functions thought to be common to different types of organisation. These include strategic planning, financial management, human resource management and relationships with the organisation's clients and the wider community. The alternative argument is that the management of education is sufficiently different to merit separate provision for the development of school and college managers. The case for distinctive treatment is based on the difficulty of defining, and measuring the achievement of, educational objectives, the presence of children and young people as the 'outputs' of schools and colleges, and the special role of teachers as professionals (Bush, 1995).

The debate about the most appropriate relationship between general management and that specific to education has been rekindled since 1995 with the Teacher Training Agency's clear emphasis on the need to take account of 'best practice outside education' in devising professional development programmes for head teachers in England. This stance is partly driven by political imperatives; satisfying the ideologically driven view that the private sector has much to teach, and little to learn, from education. It fails to recognise that many chief executives of business companies do not work with as much complexity as educational leaders, and that many would find it challenging to run a school. However, it does rest on the valid assumption that management in education should be able to benefit from good practice wherever it occurs.

While taking account of 'best practice' appears sensible, identifying it is not a straightforward, rational process. Who decides what good, let alone 'best', practice is? How is such good practice to be adapted for use in training school leaders? Is good practice a universal trait, or does it depend on the specific school setting as well as the broader organisational context? Glatter (1997: 187) shows that this issue is highly problematic: 'It is not always very clear what constitutes best practice in management outside education. As in education itself, there are different approaches and contending schools of thought.'

This issue has returned to the forefront of debate at a time when research on school effectiveness and school improvement (Stoll, 1996) is emphasising the need for leaders to focus most strongly on the specifically educational topics of learning and teaching rather than the generic tasks of managing staff, finance and external relations. This suggests that schools, rather than industry and commerce, should remain the main focus of management learning for educational leaders. As Bell notes in his chapter for this volume, however, the relationship between education and industry has now become more complex. Industrial and commercial organisations are now being encouraged to become full partners in the educational enterprise. This partnership can take several different forms. Education Action Zones in England are based on the involvement of business organisations while most schools in China operate their own businesses to generate income and those in Hungary have developed partnerships with industry in order to survive.

This volume seeks to stimulate an awareness of theory and practice in schools and colleges based on research in a wide range of educational settings in different countries and cultures. However, much management practice is grounded in educational principles which are sometimes fully articulated but often only implicit in action. There may also be tensions between those educational principles and both the policy context and the wider societal systems within which schools and colleges are located. This may be particularly true when Western management practices are applied to other cultures and contexts.

Culture and context

This book is intended for an international audience in recognition that many of the major themes of educational management have global significance. Notions of bureaucracy, autonomy and control, accountability and quality, for example, are evident in many different countries. However, it is vital to be aware of the powerful differences between countries and not to overestimate their similarities. Some of the problems may be the same but their solutions often depend more on local circumstances than on importing ready-made answers from very different contexts. Ron Glatter, in this volume, cautions against over-simplification of international issues: 'It is easy to become over-impressed by apparent similarities between "reforms" in various countries and to neglect deep differences at the level of implementation and practice' (Glatter, 2002: 225).

Crossley and Broadfoot (1992: 100) urge a respect for context and state that: 'policies and practice cannot be translated intact from one culture to another since the mediation of different cultural contexts can quite transform the former's salience'. Hughes makes a similar point in noting the need to focus on the unique qualities of different contexts in assessing educational management practice: 'The uncritical transportation of theories and methodologies across the world, without regard to the qualities and circumstances of different communities, can no longer be regarded as acceptable' (Hughes 1990: 3).

It may also be unwise to assume that educational issues are common even *within* countries let alone between them. It was evident in conducting research on school management in China, for example, that there were considerable differences between urban and rural schools (Bush et al., 1998). Similarly, the new South Africa is still coming to terms with the institutionalised differences in its schools arising from the apartheid era. Comparing the former 'white' schools in the major cities with deep rural schools provides as sharp a contrast as the differences between developed and developing countries (Bush and Heystek, forthcoming).

Some of the differences between educational systems can be attributed to economics. Many developing countries do not have the resources to ensure universal education, even at primary level, or to provide buildings, equipment or staffing of the quality which is taken for granted in the developed world. These countries are caught in a vicious circle. They lack the resources to develop all their children to their full potential. This contributes to a continuing economic weakness because they do not have the skills to compete effectively in high-tech industries or in the global service sector. As a result, the tax base is too weak to fund a really effective educational system.

Although the economic issues should not be underestimated, the main differences between countries may be cultural. Dimmock and Walker, in this volume, provide an extended discussion of societal culture and it will suffice here to note that cultural differences play an important part in explaining the varied approaches to apparently similar issues in many different countries. One example relates to attitudes to bureaucracy in different countries. As Bush notes in Chapter 3, it is the preferred model in many countries, including Eastern Europe, China and South America. In some Western countries, however, it is associated with inefficiency and excessive centralisation and may be linked to managerialism, as we noted earlier. The differences may be explained by alternative perspectives on the nature of authority with those favouring bureaucracy more willing to defer to those holding positional power than people who feel constrained by it.

Differences in culture and context should be uppermost in the minds of international researchers seeking to explain why educational systems and institutions have developed in such diverse ways.

Autonomy and control

Many developed countries have transformed their educational systems since the end of the 1980s. The reforms have often involved the devolution of financial and staff management direct to schools and colleges, leading to institutional self-management. This includes local management of schools (LMS) in England and Wales, where school governing bodies receive their own budgets, and Charter schools in the United States, where parents are empowered to establish their own schools with public funding (Yancey, 2000).

Charter schools also provide an important example of another aspect of these reforms, enhanced parental choice of school. Parents are cast in the role of consumer with the right to select the most appropriate educational experience for their children. Similarly, open enrolment in England and Wales gives parents the opportunity to express a preference for the school their children will attend. They do not have an absolute choice because demand sometimes exceeds the supply of places. The roles may then be reversed with schools choosing children in accordance with their, often diverse, admissions policies.

The main assumption underpinning self-management is that decisions for individual units within the educational system should be made by people within those schools rather than by national or local politicians or officials. The argument is that principals, staff and governors are able to tailor spending to the perceived requirements of their pupils while national and local decision-makers, however well intentioned, can only determine priorities on the basis of perceived national or local need (Bush, 1999). An OECD synthesis of studies in nine countries gives a cautious welcome to self-management and concludes that it is likely to be beneficial:

> Greater autonomy in schools . . . [leads] to greater effectiveness through greater flexibility in and therefore better use of resources; to professional development selected at school level; to more knowledgeable teachers and parents, so to better financial decisions; to whole school planning and implementation with priorities set on the basis of data about student [outcomes] and needs. (Quoted in Thomas and Martin, 1996: 28)

This judgement suggests that the theoretical case for self-management has been borne out in practice but there are sceptics who take a different view. They argue that it is a way of deflecting criticism from governments for policies emanating from the centre but implemented, in their detail, by school governors and managers (Ball, 1994; Smyth, 1996). The latter claims, from an Australian perspective, that self-management has several limitations:

- It is a mandated form of self-management; schools have no choice.
- It is occurring in a context of sharply reduced central provision of resources for public education.

● The supposed decentralisation of power is illusory and the reality is an intensification of central control.

The bureaucratic structures that have traditionally supported the work of teaching are progressively dismantled and schools are converted to stand-alone institutions in which there is only an illusion of a shift in power and control. (Smyth, 1996)

Ball (1994: 78) argues that the presence of the National Curriculum in England and Wales means that there is no real autonomy. 'Self-management is a mechanism for delivering reform rather than a vehicle for institutional initiative and innovation'. Ball expresses concern about the changes in the working conditions of staff and concludes with an attack on 'the textual apologists of self-management'. These texts are firmly imbricated in the construction of new forms of control (Ball, 1994: 83).

Ball's comment goes to the heart of the debate about self-management; what is the most appropriate balance between autonomy and control in twenty-first century educational systems? Despite the negative views of Smyth (1996) and Ball (1994), there is a strong case for devolution of powers to school level so that decisions can be made at the 'point of delivery' rather than in offices remote from students and teachers. The bureaucratic centralism which still characterises many educational systems often leads to a compliance model rather than one which favours initiative and local decision-making. In South America, for example, educational systems are fundamentally bureaucratic:

> Among the most outstanding characteristics of the Spanish American educational systems . . . is the high degree of centralisation . . . all decisions relating to educational matters [are] taken by suitably qualified civil servants and the teaching institutions throughout the land . . . fall under their control. In addition, governmental power tends to be very concentrated. (Newland, 1995: 103)

Newland (1995) states that most Spanish American countries are administered through a similar structure headed by a ministry of education and an education council whose members are appointed by the government. He refers to several problems arising from this bureaucratic framework:

1 Educational programmes were too uniform and failed to respect regional and rural differences, giving priority to city schools.
2 Bureaucracy discouraged innovations in teaching and learning.
3 Parents were prevented from taking part in basic educational decisions.
4 There are serious inefficiencies, including high levels of absenteeism, for example 20 per cent in Buenos Aires, which are tolerated by the bureaucracies.
5 Security of tenure, and the power of teacher unions, makes it impossible to remove incompetent teachers.

Self-managing school systems avoid some of these problems but there is little doubt that school autonomy remains conditional. Curricula and pedagogy may be prescribed, leading to a reduction in professional discretion and limited teacher autonomy. The literacy and numeracy hours in English and Welsh primary schools are good examples of prescription in respect of both content and delivery, leaving only limited opportunity for professionals to use their expertise in teaching these core subjects.

Evaluating the effectiveness of school autonomy is difficult also because it takes on different forms and its nature can vary within and between educational systems. It is easy to present a simplistic view of autonomy as one of two alternative forms of governance in which all matters of importance are delegated to the school. The other alternative in this oversimplified model is where nothing is delegated and all decisions are taken by a central authority. The reality is much more complex. Autonomy can vary along a number of different dimensions. One of the first and most widely respected discussions of this concept provides the following definition of those elements that might be delegated to autonomous schools:

- knowledge (decisions relating to curriculum, including decisions relating to the goals or ends of schooling)
- technology (decisions relating to the means of teaching and learning)
- power (authority to make decisions)
- material (decisions relating to the use of facilities, supplies and equipment)
- people (decisions relating to the allocation of people in matters relating to teaching and learning, and the support of teaching and learning)
- time (decisions relating to the allocation of time)
- finance (decisions related to the allocation of money) (Caldwell and Spinks, 1988: 5).

Thomas and Martin (1996) suggest four items which might be included in this list:

- funding (decisions over fees to be charged for the admission of pupils and other income generating matters)
- admission arrangements (decisions over which pupils are to be admitted to the school).
- assessment (decisions over how pupils are to be assessed)
- information (decisions over the selection of data to be published about the school's performance).

One further factor might be added:

- school governance (decisions over the power and composition of the governing body).

11

Post-apartheid South Africa provides an interesting example of the ways in which these decisions might be allocated. Knowledge, material, time and assessment are largely controlled by the national or provincial governments. Schools are able to determine their own admission arrangements. These are supposed to avoid discrimination on the grounds of race or class but in practice such devices as advertising in the 'white' press, and charging high fees, restrict the access of poorer children, most of them black. Schools also decide their own 'top up' fees, subject to the agreement of parents. Technology and time are also devolved but the former depends on the facilities available to schools, and these vary substantially, as noted earlier. There is only limited devolution of power and 'people' but there is provision for elections to school governing bodies (Bush and Heystek, forthcoming).

Autonomy is a complex notion, as the South African example demonstrates, but it seems likely that this will become an increasingly attractive dimension of educational systems. It provides the potential for schools to be more responsive to their parents and local communities which may want greater involvement in decision-making, particularly if they are required to contribute to school funding, which is now the case in many countries. Although governments wish to retain control of many aspects of educational institutions, they may also acknowledge that effective implementation of national policies depends on devolving sufficient power to ensure that all involved in the school community are motivated to participate in meaningful decision-making for the benefit of pupils and students.

Conclusion: educational management in the twenty-first century

Educational systems are being restructured in many parts of the world. This is often because governments are seeking to improve the quality of educational outputs to increase competitiveness in the global economy. A highly educated workforce is seen as a major way of promoting flexibility in an era of technological change, and developed countries seek to retain their strong economies by investing heavily in education to prepare workers with basic and advanced skills. Education is also a priority in developing nations but here the emphasis is often to ensure that there is a universal system of primary education with some progression to secondary education and a limited university sector. The lack of resources to invest in education serves to widen the divide between the advanced and developing economies.

The restructuring often takes the form of greater decentralisation of powers to schools or local administrative bodies to enhance responsiveness to the needs of local communities. While the pressures of the global economy may drive such systemic changes, the nature of the innovations need to be grounded in local traditions and 'culture' if they are to achieve their objectives. Importing ready-made solutions from other contexts is unlikely to work well. Global problems require local responses.

The huge expectations imposed on educational establishments has led to a significant change in the nature and scale of accountability. Increasingly, leaders have to meet nationally imposed targets and face penalties, including dismissal, if they do not succeed. This has led to an increase in negative stress, resulting in resignations and early retirements in some developed countries, including England. Such systemic pressures need to be matched by enhanced support mechanisms if the negative consequences of reform are not to outweigh the intended benefits.

Senior educational managers, including principals and headteachers, are particularly vulnerable to such negative effects and need to construct and sustain working frameworks and processes that recognise that leadership and management skills are needed at many points in the organisation. Promoting team work helps in developing such capabilities and also provides the potential for supportive networks for all managers, teachers, staff and students. The demands on educational institutions have never been so great and schools and colleges need to find new ways of working that meet the challenges of the twenty-first century.

Further reading

Bell, L. (1999) 'Back to the Future: the development of educational policy in England', *Journal of Educational Administration*, 37 (3 and 4): 200–28.

Bush, T. (1999) 'Crisis or crossroads: the discipline of educational management in the late 1990s', *Educational Management and Administration*, 27 (3): 239–52.

Glatter, R. (1997) 'Context and capability in educational management', *Educational Management and Administration*, 25 (2): 181–92.

References

Ball, S. (1994) *Education Reform: A Critical and Post-Structural Approach*, Buckingham: Open University Press.

Bell, L. (1999) 'Back to the future: the development of educational policy in England', *Journal of Educational Administration*, 37 (3 and 4): 200–28.

Bolman, L. and Deal, T. (1984) *Modern Approaches to Understanding and Managing Organisations*, San Francisco: Jossey-Bass.

Bolman, L. and Deal, T. (1991) *Reframing Organisations: Artistry, Choice and Leadership*, San Francisco: Jossey-Bass.

Bush, T. (1995) *Theories of Educational Management: Second Edition*, London: Paul Chapman Publishing.

Bush, T. (1999) 'Crisis or crossroads: the discipline of educational management in the late 1990s', *Educational Management and Administration*, 27 (3): 239–52.

Bush, T. and Heystek, J. (forthcoming) 'School governance in South Africa', *Compare*.

Bush, T. and Jackson, D. (2002) 'Preparation for school leadership: international perspectives', *Educational Management and Administration*, 30 (4).

Bush, T., Qiang, H. and Fang, J. (1998) 'Educational management in China: an overview', *Compare*, 28 (2): 133–40.

Caldwell, B. and Spinks, J. (1988) *The Self-Managing School*, Lewes: Falmer Press.

Crossley, M. and Broadfoot, P. (1992) 'Comparative and international research in education: scope, problems and potential', *British Educational Research Journal*, 18: 99–112.

Glaser, B. and Strauss, A. (1967) *The Discovery of Grounded Theory*, London: Weidenfeld and Nicolson.

Glatter, R. (1997) 'Context and capability in educational management', *Educational Management and Administration*, 25 (2): 181–92.

Glatter, R. (2002) 'Governance, autonomy and accountability in education', in T. Bush and L. Bell (eds), *The Principles and Practice of Educational Management*, London: Paul Chapman Publishing.

Handy, C. (1984) *Taken for Granted? Looking at Schools as Organisations*, York: Longman.

Hughes, M. (1990) 'Improving education and training for educational administrators: urgent needs', paper presented to UNESCO International Congress, Planning and Management of Educational Development, Mexico.

Leithwood, K., Jantzi, D. and Steinbach, R. (1999) *Changing Leadership for Changing Times*, Buckingham: Open University Press.

Millett, A. (1996) 'A head is more than a manager', *Times Educational Supplement*, 15 July.

Newland, C. (1995) 'Spanish American elementary education 1950–1992: bureaucracy, growth and decentralisation', *International Journal of Educational Development*, 15(2): 103–14.

Open University (1996) *E838 Effective Leadership and Management in Education: Study Guide*, Buckingham: Open University Press.

Smyth, J. (1996) 'The socially just alternative to the self-managing school', in K. Leithwood, J. Chapman, D. Corson, P. Hallinger and A. Hart (eds), *International Handbook of Educational Leadership and Administration*, Boston: Kluwer.

Stoll, L. (1996) 'Linking school effectiveness and school improvement: issues and possibilities', in J. Gray, D. Reynolds, C. Fitz-Gibbon and D. Jesson (eds), *Merging Traditions: The Future of Research on School Effectiveness and School Improvement*, London: Cassell.

Thomas, H. and Martin, J. (1996) *Managing Resources for School Improvement*, London: Routledge.

Yancey, P. (2000) *Parents Founding Charter Schools: Dilemmas of Empowerment and Decentralisation*, New York: Peter Lang.

2

Educational Management: Theory and Practice
Tony Bush

Introduction: theory and practice

Theory is an unfashionable notion in education, particularly in England and Wales. It is regarded by some politicians and administrators as irrelevant to the practice of teaching and management in schools. The shift of teacher education from a predominantly university-based activity to a prescribed training programme largely taking place in schools has been accompanied by a cacophony of dismissive comments about the alleged over-theoretical bias of university education departments. Similarly, the National Professional Qualification for Headship (NPQH) in England and Wales has been developed by practitioners and is atheoretical (Fidler, 1998). Ouston (1998: 319) criticises this approach and argues for 'inclusion of some aspects of organisational theory . . . [to] provide a framework for professional reflection and for the development of personal practice and understanding'.

The purpose of this chapter is to provide an overview of organisational and management theory and, more ambitiously, to demonstrate its relevance to contemporary practice.

Why is theory important?

Theory and practice are often regarded as separate aspects of educational management. Academics develop and refine theory while teachers and managers engage in practice. Theory may be perceived as esoteric and remote from practice and this may be its greatest weakness. The acid test of theory in an applied discipline such as educational management is its relevance to practice:

> Theories are most useful for influencing practice when they suggest new ways in which events and situations can be perceived. Fresh insight may be provided by focusing attention on possible interrelationships that the practitioner has failed to notice, and which can be further explored and tested through empirical research . . . Theory cannot then be dismissed as irrelevant. (Hughes and Bush, 1991: 234)

Theory provides the framework for managerial decisions. What practitioners may regard as 'just common sense' is often based on their assumptions about good practice. Such 'implicit theories' often provide the rationale for decision-making. However, managerial effectiveness is likely to be 'enhanced by an *explicit* awareness of the theoretical framework underpinning practice in educational institutions' (Bush, 1995: 18).

There are three main arguments supporting the view that managers have much to learn from an appreciation of theory, providing that it is grounded firmly (Glaser and Strauss, 1967) in the realities of practice:

- Reliance on facts as the sole guide to action is unsatisfactory because all evidence requires *interpretation*. Theory provides the framework for interpreting events. It provides 'mental models' (Leithwood et al., 1999: 75) to help in understanding the nature and effects of practice.
- Dependence on personal *experience* in interpreting facts and making decisions is narrow because it discards the knowledge of others. Grounded theory emerges by assessing a wide range of practice and developing models which seem to help in explaining events and behaviour. Theory also helps by reducing the likelihood of mistakes occurring while experience is being acquired.
- Experience is likely to prove particularly unhelpful when the practitioner begins to operate in a different *context*. Practice in one institution may have little relevance in the new environment. Awareness and understanding of organisational culture, for example, are likely to be valuable in interpreting events in the new context.

Explicit attention to theory is likely to be valuable for postgraduate students who need to plan their research, or interpret their findings, using an appropriate conceptual framework.

What do we mean by 'theory' in educational management?

There is no single all-embracing theory of educational management. This is because it comprises a series of perspectives rather than an all-embracing 'scientific' truth. The existence of several different, and competing, perspectives, creates what Bolman and Deal (1984) describe as 'conceptual pluralism'. Most theories have something to offer but each tends to provide only a partial explanation of educational management practice:

> Theories and explanations of organisational life are based on metaphors that lead us to see and understand organisations in distinctive yet partial ways . . . the use of metaphor provides a way of thinking and a way of seeing that pervades how we understand our world . . . metaphor . . . always produces this kind of

one-sided insight. In highlighting certain interpretations it tends to force others into a background role. (Morgan, 1986: 12–13)

Many different perspectives drawn from organisation and management theory appear in the diverse and expanding body of literature on educational leadership and management. These perspectives may be presented as six distinct theories of educational management (Bush, 1995). We turn now to examine these six theories.

Bureaucracy

The concept of bureaucracy is associated with the work of the German sociologist Max Weber. It has become the most powerful and pervasive theory of educational management and is the preferred model in many countries, including the Czech Republic (Svecova, 2000), China (Bush et al., 1998), Greece (Bush, 2001; Persianis, 1998), Israel (Gaziel, 1998), Poland (Klus-Stanska and Olek, 1998), South Africa (Sebakwane, 1997), Slovenia (Becaj, 1994) and much of South America (Newland, 1995).

> The purely bureaucratic type of administrative organisation . . . is, from a technical point of view, capable of attaining the highest degree of efficiency and is in this sense formally the most rational means of carrying out imperative control over human beings. It is superior to any other form in precision, in stability, in the stringency of its discipline, and in its reliability. (Weber, 1989: 16)

This positive assessment contradicts the widely held 'common sense' view that bureaucracy is associated with inefficiency and excessive centralisation.

Main features of bureaucracy

- There is a *hierarchical authority structure* which is often vertical with staff being accountable to their superordinate in the hierarchy. In schools, teachers are accountable to the principal, often through a middle manager such as a head of department. The 'ethos of top-down management' (Johnson, 1995: 224) is evident in South African schools: 'It [is] important to bear in mind the nature of power relations within the schools. In most cases power resides with the principal who has legal authority and is legally accountable' (Johnson, 1995: 225).
- Schools and colleges are *goal oriented*. Staff are expected to work towards achieving those aims set by school leaders.
- There is a *division of labour* with staff specialising on the basis of expertise. This is evident in the departmental structure of secondary schools and colleges and in primary schools in many countries, including Hong Kong and Singapore. This aspect of bureaucracy does not apply to British primary schools which usually operate with a class teacher model.

- Decisions and behaviour are governed by *rules and regulations* rather than personal initiative. Schools usually have rules for children's behaviour and handbooks to guide the behaviour of staff. These rules may extend to the central issues of curriculum and pedagogy. In South Africa, 'the teachers . . . were . . . subjected to tight bureaucratic regulation, especially in the matter of the curriculum' (Sebakwane, 1997: 397). In Greece, bureaucratic control extends to prescribing the textbooks to be used by teachers (Bush, 2001).

  The threat to professionalism implicit in these examples is one of the most powerful criticisms of bureaucracy. When curricula are tightly defined, teachers have limited scope to use their professional judgement to tailor provision to the specific needs of the pupils in their class. This criticism may also apply to the National Curriculum in England and Wales and to the government's literacy and numeracy strategies.
- Decisions are made through a *rational process* (see below).
- Leaders are *accountable* to external bodies for the operation of their schools (see below).

Rational decision-making

In bureaucratic models, it is assumed that decisions are made through a rational process involving a clear and logical relationship between problems and solutions. The process of rational decision-making is thought to have the following sequence:

1 Perception of a problem or a choice opportunity.
2 Analysis of the problem, including data collection.
3 Formulation of alternative solutions or choices.
4 Choice of the most appropriate solution to meet the goals of the organisation.
5 Implementation of the chosen alternative.
6 Monitoring and evaluation of the effectiveness of the chosen strategy (Bush, 1995: 38).

The process is essentially iterative in that the evaluation may lead to a redefinition of the problem or a search for an alternative solution (see Figure 2.1).

The introduction of self-management in many countries has been accompanied by an explicit assumption that school management operates within a rational framework. Levačić (1995: 61), referring to local management of schools in England and Wales, describes rational management processes as 'the official leitmotif of local management'. She discusses the prescribed model in language remarkably similar to the process described above:

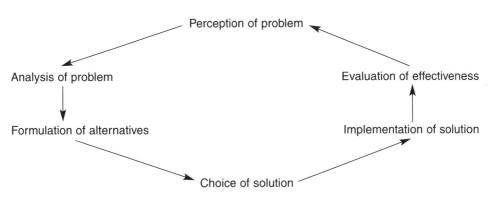

Figure 2.1 The rational process
(Bush, 1995:39)

> The model of good management practice ... is essentially a rational one. It
> advocates a system for allocating resources which is directed at the explicit
> achievement of institutional objectives. This requires clarity in the specification
> of objectives, gathering and analysing information on alternative ways of attain-
> ing the objectives, evaluating the alternatives and selecting those actions judged
> most likely to maximise achievement of the objectives. (Levačić, 1995: 62)

Similar considerations underpin the management of post-incorporation further education colleges in England and Wales. Management is assumed to be
'rooted in a rational-scientific model that proposes the creation of a SMP
[strategic management process] that is sequential, linear and controllable
(Watson and Crossley, 2001: 114).

The rational model places a strong emphasis on 'value for money'.
Inspectors appointed by the Office for Standards in Education (Ofsted) are
required to make a specific judgement on this criterion when reporting on
their findings in English and Welsh schools.

In practice, rational approaches may be difficult to sustain, particularly in
periods of rapid and multiple change, as we shall discuss later in this chapter.

Bureaucracy and public accountability

The hierarchical dimension of bureaucracy applies to the school's external
links as well as to internal relationships between staff. Principals are accountable to their external superordinate for the operation of their school. In most
cases, this responsibility is to a senior official in local, regional or national government. This person has a legitimate right to hold the principal to account
for events at the school (Kogan, 1986).

A significant aspect of bureaucracy is that accountability to officials is
regarded as more important than responsibility to clients such as students or
parents. This is powerfully illustrated in Becaj's (1994) discussion of Slovenia:

Heads know that parents and children are important but in fact they have been used to accepting the superior institutions and authorities as the real and powerful 'customers' on which they are really dependent. At the same time, parents and children have been used to see the school and its teachers as authorities who should be obeyed . . . This kind of relationship between heads and parents also suits and supports bureaucratic organisation and head centred leadership very well. (Becaj, 1994: 11)

Public accountability is the most obvious external manifestation of a bureaucratic education system.

Collegiality

Collegiality is an attractive model for educational organisations because it provides for the participation of teachers, in particular, in those decisions which affect their working lives. The assumption is that schools and colleges determine policies and make decisions through a process of discussion leading to consensus. Power is shared amongst some or all of the members of the organisation who are thought to have a mutual understanding about the aims of the school (Bush, 1995).

There are three main arguments in favour of a collegial approach to management:

- There is ample evidence that teachers wish to be involved in decision-making. For example, several projects in South Africa (Poo and Hoyle, 1995; Steyn and Squelch, 1997) show that teachers want greater participation.
- The quality of decision-making may be better when educators participate in the process. Staff involvement increases the quantum of expertise brought to bear on problems although the time spent in meetings may elongate the decision process and frustrate participants (Bush, 1995).
- Effective implementation of decisions is more likely if teachers 'own' the outcomes through their participation. Poo and Hoyle's (1995: 86) research in South Africa shows that 'collective responsibility for decision-making would make teachers more keen to see that decisions are carried out'.

Main features of collegiality

- Collegiality assumes an *authority of expertise* in contrast to the positional authority associated with bureaucracy. Teachers have specific expertise as subject specialists as well as general competence as education professionals.
- Teachers have a *common set of values* emanating from the socialisation which occurs during training and professional practice. These common values are thought to lead to shared aims.

- Decisions are reached through a process of discussion leading to *consensus*. The belief that there are common values and shared aims leads to a view that it is both desirable and feasible to resolve issues by agreement.

Collegiality in practice

Collegiality has been strongly advocated in England and Wales and has become closely associated with school improvement (Campbell and Southworth, 1993). In practice, only a modified version of collegiality has operated, as we shall see later.

Collegiality is a Western concept and is thought to have emanated from the colleges of Oxford and Cambridge universities. However, a similar notion, the 'jiaoyanzu', operates in Chinese schools (Bush et al., 1998; Paine and Ma, 1993). Paine and Ma (1993) refer to the 'assumption that teachers would work together in virtually every aspect of their work' and explain how the jiaoyanzu operate: 'Many decisions about curriculum and instruction are made jointly through the jiaoyanzu . . . teachers have a structured time to work together . . . teachers work together . . . in an office that belongs to their jiaoyanzu' (Paine and Ma, 1993: 679).

A remarkable example of extended collegiality occurs in Spain where head-teachers are effectively appointed by the teachers and other stakeholders. From 1985 until 1995, the head was elected by the School Council from the ranks of ordinary teachers and served for a three-year period. The School Council comprises teachers and representatives of other stakeholders, including parents. The process was modified in 1995 to allow only teachers accredited by the Administration to be elected, and to extend the period of headship to five years (Ruiz Vera, 1997). However, this arrangement remains significant because it seems evident that the head's primary accountability must be to the appointing body, including the teachers, rather than to the administrative apparatus.

Contrived or controlled collegiality

Collegiality is an attractive notion because it provides for the involvement of teachers in decisions which affect their professional lives. However, it has several limitations, notably in the time often taken to make decisions and in the optimistic assumption that outcomes will be determined by consensus rather than conflict. It also depends on the willingness of both heads and teachers to make it work. Heads may prefer to rely on their own professional judgement while teachers may not wish to commit the time required to participate in the meetings required to implement collegiality.

Hargreaves (1994) makes a more fundamental criticism, arguing that collegiality is being espoused or 'contrived' by official groups in order to secure the implementation of national or school policy. Contrived collegiality has the following features:

- administratively regulated rather than spontaneous
- compulsory rather than discretionary
- geared to the implementation of the mandates of government or principal
- fixed in time and place
- designed to have predictable outcomes (Hargreaves, 1994: 195–6).

The literacy and numeracy hours in England and Wales illustrate contrived collegiality. Teachers are expected to discuss *how* to implement these initiatives, which prescribe pedagogy as well as curriculum content, but not *whether* to do so. Brundrett (1998: 313) argues that collegiality may be just another vehicle for control, 'the handmaiden of an . . . increasingly centralised bureaucracy'.

Micropolitics

The concept of micropolitics refers to political activity which takes place inside schools or colleges. It may be contrasted with macropolitics which relate to debate and disagreement within the wider policy-making process. A micropolitical approach assumes that policy and decisions emerge through a process of negotiation and bargaining. Interest groups develop and form alliances in pursuit of particular policy aims. Conflict is viewed as a natural phenomenon and power accrues to dominant coalitions rather than being the preserve of formal leaders (Bush, 1995).

Main features of micropolitics

- The focus is on *group activity* rather than the whole institution. In education, the main unit of analysis is the department and its sectional approach to decision-making.
- Micropolitics are concerned with *interests* and *interest groups*. Individuals have a variety of interests which they pursue within the organisation. Individual interests may lead to collaboration and the formation of interest groups, which may be temporary or enduring.
- Micropolitics stress the prevalence of *conflict* in organisations. Individuals and interest groups pursue their different aims, leading to conflict between them. 'I take schools . . . to be riven with actual or potential conflict between members; to be poorly co-ordinated, to be ideologically diverse . . . if we are to understand the nature of schools as organisations, we must achieve some understanding of these conflicts (Ball, 1987: 19). Bishop and Mulford (1999: 179) refer to teacher resistance to externally imposed change in Victoria, Australia, as a manifestation of conflict in schools.

- Decisions emerge after a complex process of *bargaining* and *negotiation*. Interests are promoted in committees, and during informal meetings, and differences may be resolved only after a long and multi-stage process.
- The concept of *power* is central to micropolitics. The decision-making process is likely to be resolved according to the relative power of the participants. 'Divergent interests give rise to conflicts, visible and invisible, that are resolved or perpetuated by various kinds of power play' (Morgan, 1986: 148).

Micropolitics and resource allocation

The concept of micropolitics has been applied to the process of resource allocation by several authors (Bush, 2000; Levačić, 1995; Simkins, 1998). 'Resource management is . . . a micropolitical process, providing an arena within which participants compete for . . . resources' (Simkins, 1998: 71). As with other aspects of decision-making, the budgetary process is likely to be resolved by the relative power of the participants.

The main resource allocation approach likely to involve micropolitical activity is a bidding system. Bidding involves individuals or groups applying for resources, usually against set criteria. This is a political exercise because applicants have to decide whether, and how much, to inflate bids: 'This approach encourages departments to inflate their estimates . . . it tends to undervalue the modest and realistic departments against the pushy and wily ones; and it still leaves unsolved the problem of the final decision' (Knight, 1983: 118).

The main merit of a micropolitical approach to resource allocation is that it is likely to satisfy a higher proportion of participants than many other methods, notably the zero-based approach (Bush, 2000), which is designed to change the status quo and is bound to offend certain interest groups.

School governing bodies and micropolitics

School governing bodies provide a significant example of micropolitical activity in education because they arise from the interaction of officially sanctioned interest groups. Forums designed to constitute the framework for community participation and local democracy also provide the platform for conflict between different representative groups. Governing bodies may then become political arenas where competing interests jostle for supremacy. The most dramatic example in England occurred at Stratford school in East London. There was a series of disputes between the head and the governing body over staff appointments, community use of premises and the conduct of assemblies. The head was suspended by the governing body and only reinstated following a series of court actions and after parent governor elections altered the balance of power (Bush et al., 1993; Snelling, 2001).

The new governing bodies in post-apartheid South Africa also provide evidence of micropolitical activity. Political actions during the years of struggle have continued in certain governing bodies. South Africa is unusual in including learners as members of governing bodies but Phakoa and Bisschoff (2001) show that they are frustrated because they cannot vote on financial matters and because they disagree with the provision for parents to constitute a majority on governing bodies. Many learners are much older than in other countries, because their education was interrupted during the struggle, and they resent being treated as minors.

All forums set up to facilitate participation, including governing bodies, are likely to become micropolitical arenas, at certain times and for particular decisions. They provide a legitimate opportunity to promote interests and also offer the prospect of regulating and resolving conflict between groups.

Subjective theories

Subjective theories focus on individuals within organisations. Each person is assumed to have a unique and subjective perception of the organisation with events having different meanings for each participant. Organisations are portrayed as the manifestations of the values and beliefs of individuals, rather than the concrete realities of bureaucracy.

Subjective theories became prominent as a result of the work of Greenfield (1973) who was very critical of conventional (largely bureaucratic) theory:

> Most theories of organisation grossly simplify the nature of the reality with which they deal. The drive to see the organisation as a single kind of entity with a life of its own apart from the perceptions and beliefs of those involved in it blinds us to its complexity and the variety of organisations people create around themselves. (Greenfield, 1973: 571)

Main features of subjective theories

- They focus on the beliefs and perceptions of *individual* members of organisations. In schools and colleges, individual teachers, support staff and pupils have different values and aspirations according to their own background and motivation. The school is not the same reality for all its participants.
- They are concerned with the *meanings* placed on events by individual participants. The focus is on individual interpretation of behaviour rather than the situations and actions themselves.
- They treat *structure* as essentially a product of human interaction rather than being predetermined or fixed.
- They emphasise the significance of *individual purposes* and deny the existence of organisational aims. 'What is an organisation that it can have such a thing as a goal?' (Greenfield, 1973: 553).

24

Subjective theories and qualitative research

Subjective theories relate to a mode of research which is predominantly inter-pretive or qualitative. This approach to enquiry is based on the subjective experience of individuals. The main aim is to seek understanding of the ways in which individuals create, modify and interpret the social world which they inhabit. It is concerned with meanings as much as with facts and this is one of the major differences between qualitative and quantitative research. The link between qualitative research and subjective theories is evident in Cohen and Manion's (1994) definition: '[Qualitative research] stresses the importance of the subjective experience of individuals in the creation of the social world . . . The principal concern is with an understanding of the way in which he or she finds himself or herself . . . The approach now takes on a qualitative . . . aspect' (Cohen and Manion, 1994: 8).

Just as researchers seek the individual perceptions of participants, notably in using unstructured and semi-structured interviews, managers have to be aware of the individual needs of their colleagues. A recognition of the differ-ent values and motivations of the people who work in organisations, 'what makes them tick', is an essential element if they are to be led and managed effectively.

Ambiguity theories

Ambiguity theories stress uncertainty and unpredictability in organisations. The emphasis is on the instability and complexity of institutional life. These approaches assume that organisational aims are problematic and that institu-tions experience difficulty in ordering their priorities. March (1982) explains that ambiguity theories were developed to provide a better way of explaining the nature of complex organisations:

> Theories of choice underestimate the confusion and complexity surround-ing actual decision making. Many things are happening at once; technologies are changing and poorly understood; alliances, preferences and perceptions are changing; problems, solutions, opportunities, ideas, people and outcomes are mixed together in a way that makes their interpretation uncertain and their connections unclear. (March, 1982: 36)

Main features of ambiguity theories

- There is a lack of clarity about the *aims* of the organisation. 'It may not be at all clear what the goals of the school are. Different members of the school may perceive different goals or attribute different priorities to the same goals, or even be unable to define goals which have any operational meaning' (Bell, 1989: 134).

- Organisations are characterised by *fragmentation* and *loose coupling* (Weick, 1976). Schools are divided into groups which have an internal coherence based on common values and goals. Links between groups are more tenuous and unpredictable.
- *Organisational structure* is regarded as problematic. There is uncertainty over the relative power of the different parts of institution. Committees have rights and responsibilities which overlap with each other and with the authority assigned to individual managers. The more complex the structure, the greater the potential for ambiguity. Noble and Pym's (1989: 33) classic study of 'the receding locus of power' shows how difficult it can be to establish which body is responsible for decision-making. 'There was a widespread feeling of powerlessness, a feeling that decisions were really taken elsewhere'.
- There is *fluid participation* as members move in and out of decision-making situations. 'The participants . . . vary among themselves in the amount of time they devote to the organisation; individual participants vary from one time to another' (Cohen and March, 1986: 114). An interesting example of *fluid participation* was noted by Yancey (2000: 64) in respect of parental involvement in Charter schools in California: 'The parent group was never particularly cohesive, even from the beginning. Parents would come to a flurry of meetings, disappear for a month or so and then reappear . . . people would pull in and out all the time'.

Rational and irrational decision-making

We noted earlier in this chapter that bureaucracy assumes a rational decision-making process. Ambiguity theory challenges this assumption and claims that the absence of clear goals makes it problematic to link decisions to institutional aims. This argument is illustrated in respect of budgeting by Levačić (1995) and Bush (2000). Because purposes are unclear, it is difficult to link budgeting to aims and the notion of an optimum choice is also contentious. Budgetary decisions are likely to be characterised by a lack of clarity.

> The rational model is undermined by ambiguity, since it is so heavily dependent on the availability of information about relationships between inputs and outputs – between means and ends. If ambiguity prevails, then it is not possible for organisations to have clear aims and objectives . . . This state of affairs would explain why decision-making, particularly in the public sector, does not in fact follow the rational model, but is characterised by incrementalism. (Levačić, 1995: 82)

In practice, educational organisations tend to operate with a mix of rational and irrational processes. The ambiguity tends to increase at times of external turbulence and this makes it more difficult to adhere to rational approaches. 'Rationalistic approaches will always be blown off course by the contingent, the unexpected and the irrational' (Hoyle, 1986: 72).

Organisational culture

Culture has become increasingly important as a way of describing and under-standing social and educational issues. The concept of *societal* culture is examined by Dimmock and Walker in Chapter 5 of this volume. The purpose of this section is to assess the significance of *organisational* culture for schools and colleges. Culture may be regarded as one of several alternative means of conceptualising organisations, or as a holistic way of understanding them. This chapter adopts the first approach, consistent with the notion of 'concep-tual pluralism' noted earlier.

The concept of organisational culture emphasises the informal aspects of organisations rather than their official elements. It focuses on the values, beliefs and norms of people in the organisation and on how these individual perceptions coalesce into shared organisational meanings. 'An increasing num-ber of writers . . . have adopted the term "culture" to define that social and phenomenological uniqueness of a particular organisational community' (Beare et al., 1989: 173).

Main features of organisational culture

- The central focus is on the *values* and *beliefs* of members of organisations. These values underpin the behaviour and attitudes of individuals within schools and colleges, but they may not always be explicit. 'Many beliefs are indeed so deeply buried that individuals do not even know what they are' (Nias et al., 1989: 11).
- There is an assumption that individual values will coalesce and lead to *shared norms and meanings* which gradually become cultural features of the school or college, 'the way we do things around here'. Alternatively, and particu-larly in larger schools and colleges, several sub-cultures may develop, reflect-ing the different value systems of departments and other sub-units.
- Culture is typically expressed through *rituals* and *ceremonies* which are used to support and celebrate beliefs and norms. Educational organisations are rich in such symbols as assemblies, prize-givings, religious occasions and graduation ceremonies.
- Culture assumes the existence of *heroes* and *heroines* who embody the val-ues and beliefs of the organisation. These heroes might be successful in sport, music, drama, business or politics but they bring credit on the organ-isation through their achievements. Schools are likely to give prominence to those people whose triumphs match the aspirations of the school. The importance of sport in South Africa is reflected in schools' choice of heroes. One Durban school visited by the author in 2001, for example, had chosen South Africa's cricket captain, Shaun Pollock, a former student, to open its newest building.

27

Managing organisational culture

Effective leadership is increasingly linked to the generation or adaptation of culture (Bush, 1998). One way of generating culture is to focus on the aims of the school or college. The statement of aims, and their espousal in action, serve to reinforce the values and beliefs of the organisation. Clearly articulated aims should help in creating a strong culture. However, this may be problematic if leaders are seeking to generate a culture at odds with the prevailing norms. Turner (1990: 11), for example, doubts that 'something as powerful as culture can be much affected by the puny efforts of top managers'.

A dramatic example of the difficulty of disturbing an entrenched culture is provided by the continuing lack of a culture of teaching and learning in the new South Africa. The years of struggle against apartheid inevitably affected schools, particularly those in townships. Both students and teachers used to 'strike' and demonstrate against the policies of the white government. A culture of teaching and learning was difficult to sustain in such a hostile climate. The shift to majority government has produced only limited and patchy improvement in this situation. 'The crisis in black education, including what has come to be referred to as the "breakdown" in the "culture of learning", . . . continues unabated' (Badat, 1995: 143).

South African principals surveyed by the author (Bush and Anderson, forthcoming) are adopting four overlapping strategies to address this problem:

- instilling in the minds of learners that 'education is their future'
- showing the importance of education within and outside the school
- providing a conducive educational environment
- developing a culture of learning.

Despite these strategies, however, it seems likely that the development of a genuine culture of learning will be slow and dependent on the quality of leadership in individual schools (Bush and Anderson, forthcoming).

Understanding organisational culture is an important aspect of leadership in schools and colleges. Externally imposed innovation often fails because it is out of tune with the values of the teachers who have to implement it. 'Since organisation ultimately resides in the heads of the people involved, effective organisational change implies cultural change' (Morgan, 1986: 138).

Conclusion: applying theory to practice

Conceptual pluralism

Bolman and Deal's (1984) notion of 'conceptual pluralism', discussed earlier, offers a framework for the analysis of educational management theory. The six theories discussed in this chapter each provide important insights into school and college management but they are all uni-dimensional. Individually, they are partial and selective but taken together they represent a powerful means of analysing and explaining events and behaviour in education: 'Managers . . . can increase their effectiveness and their freedom through the use of multiple vantage points. To be locked into a single path is likely to produce error and self-imprisonment' (Bolman and Deal, 1984: 4).

Theory and national culture

The concept of national or societal culture, discussed in Chapter 5, provides one way of understanding the relevance of theories in different contexts. The values and beliefs of leaders and managers have been moulded by their cultural backgrounds and this makes them more comfortable with certain approaches than with other theories. The norms and expectations of society predispose managers to operate within a particular conceptual framework.

Managers in China, and other predominantly Chinese societies, tend to operate within the bureaucratic framework. The notion of 'adoring authority' is one of the main aspects of traditional authority in China (Bush and Qiang, 2000). Just as children are required to comply with the requirements of adults without question, so teachers are expected to follow the policies of principals, who hold positional authority within an essentially bureaucratic system. It is not culturally acceptable for teachers to question school leaders who expect and receive compliance with their decisions. Even the jiaoyanzu, which provides the potential for collegiality as we noted earlier, is subject to the overall responsibility of the teaching dean, a senior manager within the school's hierarchy (Bush et al., 1998).

In post-apartheid South Africa, a commitment to democratic values means that notions of collegiality are beginning to permeate a previously bureaucratic model of management. The principle of democratic governance is expected to influence all levels of society and is reflected in both increased teacher empowerment and the involvement of all stakeholders in school policy-making, notably through the governing bodies. The recent history of South Africa means that 'the notion of participation is currently in vogue' (Sayed and Carrim, 1997: 94).

Using theory to improve practice

The ultimate test of theory is whether it improves practice and the *potential* for it to do so is clear. Managers generally engage in a process of implicit theorising in deciding how to formulate policy or respond to developments. 'Practice is never theory-free, for it is always guided by an image of what one is trying to do. The real issue is whether or not we are aware of the theory guiding our action' (Morgan, 1986: 336). Theory provides the explanatory framework which helps managers to ascertain the real meaning of events.

29

Explicit use of theory helps in two specific ways:

- *diagnosis*: assessing the situation and highlighting the main issues to be addressed
- *evaluation*: determining the most appropriate response to the problem.

These skills are consistent with the concept of the 'reflective practitioner', whose managerial approach incorporates both learning from experience and a distillation of theory based on wide reading and engagement with academics and practitioners. This might also involve small-scale research to establish the relevance of theory in the leader's professional context. A combination of theory and experience is likely to lead to more effective practitioners than relying on experience alone.

Further reading

Bush, T. (1995) *Theories of Educational Management: Second Edition*, London: Paul Chapman Publishing.

Hoyle, E. (1986) *The Politics of School Management*, Sevenoaks: Hodder and Stoughton.

Levačić, R. (1995) *Local Management of School: Analysis and Practice*, Buckingham: Open University Press.

References

Badat, S. (1995) 'Educational politics in the transition period', *Comparative Education*, 31 (2): 141–59.

Ball, S. (1987) *The Micropolitics of the School: Towards a Theory of School Organisation*, London: Methuen.

Beare, H., Caldwell, B. and Millikan, R. (1989) *Creating an Excellent School: Some New Management Techniques*, London: Routledge.

Becaj, J. (1994) 'Changing bureaucracy to democracy', *Educational Change and Development*, 15 (1): 7–14.

Bell, L. (1989) 'Ambiguity models and secondary schools: a case study', in T. Bush, (ed.), *Managing Education: Theory and Practice*, Buckingham: Open University Press.

Bishop, P. and Mulford, B. (1999) 'When will they ever learn?: another failure of centrally-imposed change', *School Leadership and Management*, 19 (2): 179–87.

Bolman, L. and Deal, T. (1984) *Modern Approaches to Understanding and Managing Organisations*, San Francisco: Jossey-Bass.

Brundrett, M. (1998) 'What lies behind collegiality, legitimation or control?: an analysis of the purported benefits of collegial management in education', *Educational Management and Administration*, 26 (3): 305–16.

Bush, T. (1995) *Theories of Educational Management: Second Edition*, London: Paul Chapman Publishing.

Bush, T. (1998) 'Organisational culture and strategic management', in D. Middlewood and J. Lumby (eds), *Strategic Management in Schools and Colleges*, London: Paul Chapman Publishing.

Bush, T. (2000) 'Management styles: impact on finance and resources', in M. Coleman and L. Anderson (eds), *Managing Finance and Resources in Education*, London: Paul Chapman Publishing.

Bush, T. (2001) 'School organisation and management: international perspectives', paper presented at the Federation of Private School Teachers' Annual Conference, Athens, May.

Bush, T. and Anderson, L. (forthcoming) 'Organisational culture', in T. Bush, M. Coleman and M. Thurlow (eds), *Leadership and Strategic Management in South African Schools*.

Bush, T. and Qiang, H. (2000) 'Leadership and culture in Chinese education', *Asia Pacific Journal of Education*, 20 (2): 58–67.

Bush, T., Coleman, M. and Glover, D. (1993) *Managing Autonomous Schools: The Grant-Maintained Experience*, London: Paul Chapman Publishing.

Bush, T., Coleman, M. and Si, X. (1998) 'Managing secondary schools in China', *Compare*, 28 (2): 183–96.

Campbell, P. and Southworth, G. (1993) 'Rethinking collegiality: teachers views', in N. Bennett, M. Crawford and C. Riches (eds), *Managing Change in Education: Individual and Organisational Perspectives*, London: Paul Chapman Publishing.

Cohen, L. and Manion, L. (1994) *Research Methods in Education*, London: Routledge.

Cohen, M. and March, J. (1986) *Leadership and Ambiguity: The American College President*, Boston: Harvard Business School Press.

Fidler, B. (1998) 'Editorial', *School Leadership and Management*, 18 (3): 309–15.

Gaziel, H. (1998) 'School-based management as a factor in school effectiveness', *International Review of Education*, 44 (4): 319–33.

Glaser, B. and Strauss, A. (1967) *The Discovery of Grounded Theory*, London: Weidenfeld and Nicolson.

Greenfield, T. (1973) 'Organisations as social inventions: rethinking assumptions about change', *Journal of Applied Behavioural Science*, 9 (5): 551–74.

Hargreaves, A. (1994) *Changing Teachers, Changing Times: Teachers' Work and Culture in the Postmodern Age*, London: Cassell.

Hoyle, E. (1986) *The Politics of School Management*, Sevenoaks: Hodder and Stoughton.

Hughes, M. and Bush, T. (1991) 'Theory and research as catalysts for change', in W. Walker, R. Farquhar and M. Hughes (eds), *Advancing Education: School Leadership in Action*, London: Falmer Press.

Johnson, D. (1995) 'Developing an approach to educational management development in South Africa', *Comparative Education*, 31 (2): 223–41.

Klus-Stanska, D. and Olek, H. (1998) 'Private education in Poland: breaking the mould', *International Review of Education*, 44 (2–3): 235–49.

Knight, B. (1983) *Managing School Finance*, London: Heinemann.

Kogan, M. (1986) *Education Accountability: An Analytic Overview*, London: Hutchinson.

Leithwood, K., Jantzi, D. and Steinbach, R. (1999) *Changing Leadership for Changing Times*, Buckingham: Open University Press.

Levačić, R. (1995) *Local Management of Schools: Analysis and Practice*, Buckingham: Open University Press.

March, J. (1982) 'Theories of choice and making decisions', *Society*, 20 (1).

Morgan, G. (1986) *Images of Organization*, Newbury Park, CA: Sage.

Newland, C. (1995) 'Spanish American elementary education 1950–1992: bureaucracy, growth and decentralisation', *International Journal of Educational Development*, 15 (2): 103–14.

Nias, J., Southworth, G. and Yeomans, R. (1989) *Staff Relationships in the Primary School*, London: Cassell.

Noble, T. and Pym, B. (1989) 'Collegial authority and the receding locus of power', in T. Bush (ed.), *Managing Education: Theory and Practice*, Buckingham: Open University Press.

Ouston, J. (1998) 'Introduction', *School Leadership and Management*, 18 (3): 317–20.

Paine, L. and Ma, L. (1993) 'Teachers working together: a dialogue on organisational and cultural perspectives of Chinese teachers', *International Journal of Educational Research*, 19: 675–97.

Persianis, P. (1998) 'Compensatory legitimation in Greek educational policy: an explanation for the abortive educational reforms in Greece in comparison with those in France', *Comparative Education*, 33 (1): 71–84.

Phakoa, T. and Bisschoff, T. (2001) 'The status of minors in governing bodies of public secondary schools', Education Management Association of South Africa Conference, Durban, March.

Poo, B. and Hoyle, E. (1995) 'Teacher involvement in decision-making', in D. Johnson (ed.), *Educational Management and Policy: Research, Theory and Practice in South Africa*, Bristol: University of Bristol.

Ruiz Vera, L. (1997) 'The selection of headteachers in Spain', *European Forum on Educational Administration Newsletter*, 1: 1 and 11.

Sayed, Y. and Carrim, N. (1997) 'Democracy, participation and equity in educational governance', *South African Journal of Education*, 17 (3): 91–100.

Sebakwane, S. (1997) 'The contradictions of scientific management as a mode of controlling teachers' work in black secondary schools: South Africa', *International Journal of Educational Development*, 17 (4): 391–404.

Simkins, T. (1998) 'Autonomy, constraint and the strategic management of resources', in D. Middlewood and J. Lumby (eds), *Strategic Management in Schools and Colleges*, London: Paul Chapman Publishing.

Snelling, A. (2001) 'Stratford GM school: a policy and its impact', unpublished Ed.D. thesis, University of Leicester.

Steyn, G. and Squelch, J. (1997) 'Exploring the perceptions of teacher empowerment in South Africa: a small-scale study', *South African Journal of Education*, 17 (1): 1–6.

Svecova, J. (2000) 'Privatisation of education in the Czech republic', *International Journal of Educational Development*, 20: 127–33.

Turner, C. (1990) *Organisational Culture*, Blagdon: Mendip Papers.

Watson, G. and Crossley, M. (2001) 'Beyond the rational: the strategic management process, cultural change and post-incorporation further education', *Educational Management and Administration*, 29 (1): 113–25.

Weber, M. (1989) 'Legal authority in a bureaucracy', in T. Bush (ed.), *Managing Education: Theory and Practice*, Buckingham: Open University Press.

Weick, K. (1976) 'Educational organisations as loosely coupled systems', *Administrative Science Quarterly*, 21 (1): 1–19.

Yancey, P. (2000) *Parents Founding Charter Schools: Dilemmas of Empowerment and Decentralisation*, New York: Peter Lang.

3

Autonomy and Self-Management: Concepts and Evidence

Brian J. Caldwell

Introduction

Debates on the merits of school-based management, local management and self-management have been robust and inconclusive for most of the last two decades since these elements of school reform made their appearance in a small number of nations. It is now apparent that these phenomena are a feature of school reform in virtually every nation that is seeking to improve the quality of learning. In most instances, adoption appears irreversible, with most stakeholders not wishing to return to more centralised approaches. There has been a pause in some instances, and a few steps back have been taken in others, but the trend is inexorable. Critics have referred to the absence of evidence of impact on learning. There is a range of implementation issues, not least of which is the fact that implementation has occurred at the same time as the costs of providing a quality education have increased, leading to a more demanding regime of accountability, for learning outcomes and for the use of public funds.

The purpose of this chapter is to explain the concept of self-management, noting that it has been distinguished in the past from the concept of autonomy. A brief account is provided of developments in a number of countries, including developing countries, with acknowledgement that several are now moving or proposing to move beyond self-management towards autonomy. Evidence of impact is reviewed, with findings from particular nations as well as from the Third International Mathematics and Science Study (TIMSS) in 39 nations that identified a number of 'policy settings' for optimising outcomes on a range of organisational characteristics. These settings included a high level of self-management within a centrally determined framework of goals, policies, curriculum, assessment and accountabilities.

The chapter concludes with the view that the merits of self-management have been established, but the focus of implementation must shift to making the connections between empowerment at the school level and strategies to achieve improved learning outcomes for students.

The concepts

This writer is co-author of three books on the self-managing school (Caldwell and Spinks, 1988; 1992; 1998). Conceptualization was consistent and along the following lines. A self-managing school is a school in a system of education to which there has been decentralized a significant amount of authority and responsibility to make decisions related to the allocation of resources within a centrally determined framework of goals, policies, standards and accountabilities. Resources are defined broadly to include knowledge, technology, power, material, people, time, assessment, information and finance.

A self-managing school is not an autonomous school nor is it a self-governing school, for each of these kinds of schools involves a degree of independence that is not provided in a centrally determined framework. The existence of a centrally determined framework implies that a self-managing school is part of a system of schools, so the concept applies most readily to systems of government or public schools, or to systems of non-government or private schools where there has been decentralisation, such as in systems of Catholic schools in some countries. Truly independent, non-systemic schools would ordinarily be considered self-governing or autonomous schools.

The concept of autonomous schools has moved to centre stage with the release of a White Paper that contains the plans of the Blair government for its second term (Department for Education and Skills, 2001). Self-management, or local management, was one of several thrusts in the 1988 Education Reform Act of the Thatcher government, extending to all schools in Britain a practice that had been successfully pioneered in several authorities as local financial management. The Blair government went further by requiring local education authorities to decentralise a larger part of their education budgets to the school level (now approaching 90 per cent across all authorities). The Blair government had previously abandoned the contentious reform of the Thatcher government that created a number of grant-maintained schools, moving beyond self-management to self-government. These schools had a degree of autonomy and higher levels of funding that could be secured on the majority vote of parents in favour of a change in status.

Announcing the intentions of the Blair government, paragraph 5.5 in the White Paper (Summary Document) declares that 'the best schools will earn greater autonomy'. The following excerpts illustrate how the process will work:

> We propose to free the best secondary schools from constraints which stand in the way of yet higher standards. We will legislate to allow them to opt out of parts of the National Curriculum, for example to lead the development of thinking about Key Stage 4. And we will allow them flexibility over some elements of teachers' pay and conditions, for example to allow schools to agree to a more flexible working day and year. Important elements of pay and conditions will remain common to all teachers. (Ibid.: para. 5.5)

But schools also need freedom to rethink the teacher's role. Qualified teachers need to be allowed to concentrate on using their professional skills to raise standards, delegating other tasks to support staff where this is practicable. We will therefore legislate to give schools more freedom to innovate – sharing good teachers, for example. (ibid.: para. 7.7)

Central to achieving higher standards is the confident, well-managed school, setting its own targets and accountable for its performance. Within the framework of accountability we have established, we want schools to have as much freedom as possible. (Ibid.: para. 8.1)

We want to reduce and simplify regulations that schools find burdensome. For example, we will make it easier for governors to provide childcare and loosen legislative constraints so that schools can more easily share resources and expertise, for example sharing an excellent team of subject teachers. (Ibid.: para. 8.2)

Prime Minister Tony Blair summarised the intentions in these terms: 'Deregulation will give all successful schools greater freedom and less central control. New freedoms over governance, the provision of community facilities, and engagement with external partners, will enable them to meet the needs of pupils and parents more effectively' (Blair, 2001: 44).

It is evident that the Blair government is not creating autonomous schools. The outcome will be a higher degree of autonomy within a system of self-managing schools. A centrally determined framework remains but there is a degree of deregulation for schools deemed to be successful. There is an expectation that greater autonomy will improve outcomes for students.

Tracks for change

Caldwell and Spinks (1998) reviewed the major directions of education reform in a number of countries and identified three tracks for change. Track 1 was the building of systems of self-managing schools. Track 2 was an unrelenting focus on learning outcomes. Track 3 was the creation of schools for the knowledge society. The concept of 'tracks' was employed rather than 'stages' because schools, systems and nations were moving on all three at the same time, but differed in respect to the distance they had moved.

Developments in Britain in the second term of the Blair government constitute further movement down Track 1 ('building systems of self-managing schools') with a commitment to continue down Track 2 ('an unrelenting focus on learning outcomes'). Recognition of the importance of education to the well being of the nation and the energising role of information and communications technology characterised movement on Track 3 ('creating schools for the knowledge society').

There are similar developments in Victoria, Australia, selected for particular mention because its system of self-managing schools has evolved over 25 years to the point where it is now the largest system of public education, with more than 1,600 schools, to have decentralised as much as 94 per cent of the state's school education budget to the school level. It is especially noteworthy because the major thrust that occurred under the Kennett government from 1992 to 1999 (often compared with that of the Thatcher government) was continued by the Bracks Labor government. An interesting parallel is that a small number of self-governing schools were created in the final year of the Kennett government, and the Bracks government, in similar style and for much the same reasons that the Blair government abolished grant-maintained schools, immediately abandoned them. The Bracks government lived up to its commitment to enhance self-management for all schools by increasing the proportion of state funds that were decentralized to the school level (Connors, 2000).

Much attention has been paid over the last decade to trends in self-management in Australia, Britain, some systems in Canada, New Zealand, and some districts in the United States. There is growing momentum in many other nations, indeed, one is hard pressed to find any nation engaged in education reform that has not implemented some measure of self-management. There have been significant developments in nations as diverse as Israel, where the concept of autonomous schools has been employed (see Gibton et al., 2000; Volansky, 2001); Japan (Yoshida, 2001); and Thailand (National Education Act of B.E. 2542, 1999).

Three generations of studies on the impact of self-management

After several decades of reform, it is fair to ask about the extent to which there has been an impact on outcomes for students. It is sobering to note the consistent finding in early research that there appeared to be few if any direct links between local management, self-management or school-based management and learning outcomes (Malen et al., 1990; Summers and Johnson, 1996). Some researchers have noted that such gains are unlikely to be achieved in the absence of purposeful links between capacities associated with school reform, in this instance, self-management, and what occurs in the classroom, in learning and teaching and the support of learning and teaching (see Bullock and Thomas, 1997; Cheng, 1996; Hanushek, 1997; Levačić, 1995; OECD, 1994; Smith et al., 1996).

Research of the kind cited above can now be seen as constituting the first generation of studies of self-management, and that second and third generations of studies are now discernible. It is in the third generation that the nature of the linkage between self-management and learning outcomes can be mapped in a manner that can be trustworthy in policy and practice.

The inconclusive nature of the linkage in first- and second-generation studies

Summers and Johnson (1996) provided a meta-analysis of the first generation of research. They located 70 studies that purported to be evaluations of school-based management, but only 20 of these employed a systematic approach and just seven included a measure of student outcomes. They concluded that 'there is little evidence to support the notion that school-based management is effective in increasing student performance. There are very few quantitative studies, the studies are not statistically rigorous, and the evidence of positive results is either weak or non-existent' (ibid.: 80). Apart from the 'overwhelming obstacles' in the way of assessing impact, Summers and Johnson drew attention to the fact that few initiatives 'identify student achievement as a major objective. The focus is on organisational processes, with virtually no attention to how process changes may affect student performance' (ibid.: 1996: 92–3).

In a report on the effects of school resources on student achievement, Hanushek (1997: 156) drew attention to the finding 'that simply decentralising decision-making is unlikely to work effectively unless there exist clear objectives and unless there is direct accountability'. It is the absence of this framework that characterises the context for what are described here as first-generation studies.

The second generation of studies accompanied the more far-reaching reforms in self-management, with most of the available budget in a school system decentralised to the local level within a comprehensive and centrally determined curriculum, standards and accountability framework. In general, the findings were as inconclusive as those from the first generation.

In Britain, for example, there was no research that mapped a cause-and-effect relationship between local management and discretionary use of resources, on the one hand, and improved learning outcomes for students on the other, building on the findings of studies that yielded strong opinion-based evidence that gains had been made (for example, Bullock and Thomas, 1994). Drawing predominantly on evidence from Britain, but referring also to outcomes elsewhere, Bullock and Thomas concluded that:

> It may be that the most convincing evidence of the impact of local management is on the opportunities which it has provided for managing the environment and resources for learning, both factors that can act to support the quality of learning in schools. What remains elusive, however, is clear-cut evidence of these leading through to direct benefits on learning, an essential component if we are to conclude that it is contributing to higher levels of efficiency. (Bullock and Thomas, 1997: 217)

Bullock and Thomas then went to the heart of the issue:

If learning is at the heart of education, it must be central to our final discussion of decentralisation. It means asking whether, in their variety of guises, the changes characterised by decentralisation have washed over and around children in classrooms, leaving their day-to-day experiences largely untouched. In asking this question, we must begin by recognising that structural changes in governance, management and finance may leave largely untouched the daily interaction of pupils and teachers. (Ibid.: 219)

Illuminating the links in third-generation studies

A third generation of studies emerged in the late 1990s. The policy context was the same as for the second generation, namely, for local management in Britain and self-management in Victoria, with the emergence of more comprehensive and coherent systemic reform in the United States, as in Chicago. There are, however, three important differences to mark this generation of study. First, by the late 1990s, a substantial set of data on student achievement had been established as a result of system-wide tests that enabled change at the local level to be tracked over several years. Schools were also able to draw on an increasingly deep pool of other indicators. Second, the policy framework had become more explicit with respect to expectations for schools to make the link between elements in the school reform programme and learning outcomes for students. This reflected change on Track 2 ('an unrelenting focus on learning outcomes') in the classification of Caldwell and Spinks (1998). Third, researchers were utilising an increasingly sophisticated array of techniques for analysis of data, including structural equation modeling, along with more focused approaches to case study.

Macro-analysis of TIMSS data on student achievement   The Third International Mathematics and Science Study (TIMSS) was the largest international comparative study of student achievement ever undertaken. Information was gathered on a range of factors as part of the project, including student and family characteristics, resources and teacher characteristics, and institutional settings including the extent of centralisation in examinations, distribution of responsibilities between centre and schools, teachers' and parents' influence in decision-making, extent of competition with independent private schools and incentives for students. Analysis of the performance of more than 260,000 students from 39 countries was undertaken at Kiel University in Germany and reported by Woessmann (2001). Regression analysis yielded interesting findings that are certain to create much discussion and debate.

They show that institutions strongly matter for cross-country differences in students' educational performance, while increased resource inputs do not contribute to increased performance. Controlling for indicators of parents' education levels and resource inputs, three indicators of institutional features of the education system have strong and statistically significant effects on country-level student performance. Increased school autonomy in supply choice and increased scrutiny of performance assessment lead to superior performance levels, and a larger influence of teacher unions in the education process leads to inferior performance levels. Together, the variables explain three quarters of the cross-country variation in mathematics test scores and 60 per cent of the variation in science test scores, whereas previous studies which focused on family and resource effects explained only up to one quarter of the cross-country variation in student performance tests. (Woessmann, 2001: 6)

Woessmann (2001: 79) concludes 'the only policy that promises positive effects is to create an institutional system where all the people involved have an incentive to improve student performance'. He suggests that nine features are favourable to student performance:

- central examinations
- centralised control mechanisms in curricular and budgetary affairs
- school autonomy in process and personnel decisions
- an intermediate level of administration performing administrative tasks and educational funding
- competition from private educational institutions
- individual teachers having both incentives and powers to select appropriate teaching methods
- limited influence of teacher unions
- scrutiny of students' educational performance
- encouragement of parents to take an interest in teaching matters.

There are some important observations to make about the list. First, 'centralised control mechanisms in curricular and budgetary affairs' refers to centrally determined frameworks not to the manner of implementation at the school level. In the case of budget, this refers to the existence of a funding mechanism that specifies how funds shall be allocated to schools; schools then determine how these funds are deployed at the local level. Second, Woessmann is cautious about the findings on the influence of teacher unions. It is important to record his caution because the matter is contentious (see Steelman et al., 2000, for findings that suggest unions have a positive impact on educational performance). He notes that the indicator of influence in the study might serve as a 'proxy for the effect of a standard salary scale as opposed to merit differentials in teacher pay' (Woessmann, 2001: 81).

This international study provides evidence on an international comparative scale of the efficacy of approaches such as school-based management, local management or self-management that are set in a centrally determined framework.

Comprehensive reform in Chicago   An increasing number of school districts in the United States are establishing local management on the scale now evident in England and Wales, but these are still a small minority among the 15,000 jurisdictions in that nation. The public school district in Chicago is one such system with a comprehensive and relatively coherent set of reforms dating from 1988. The stated goal of the Chicago School Reform Act was to raise the level of student achievement to match national norms. According to Hess (1999: 67) the chief mechanism to achieve this goal is a system of school-based decision-making, with school councils and local responsibility for school improvement planning, budget allocation and selection of staff within a framework of system-wide standards and tests.

The most powerful evidence of linkage between self-management and learning outcomes in Chicago, arguably in any jurisdiction, has emerged in the longitudinal studies of the Consortium on Chicago School Research (Bryk, 1998; Bryk et al., 1998). Value-added measures of student achievement over a number of years were included in the design of an innovative productivity index. A model of direct and indirect effects, including a capacity for self-management, was derived. The observations of Hess (1999) on experience in Chicago is striking:

> budget analyses . . . and interview comments from [headteachers] show that discretionary funds were important to schools in their efforts to change. [Headteachers] said over and over that these funds were the engine that allowed them to make changes in their schools. We found, however, that their efforts were compromised to the extent that they were forced to siphon off resources to maintain programs cut by the board of education to balance the budget each year. Further, we have seen that some schools spent a lot of new discretionary money without much to show for those expenditures in terms of effective use of funds to foster improved student learning. More money was crucial to improvement in the schools where improvement was taking place. But more money did not automatically translate into better student outcomes. How the money was used does appear to matter. (Hess, 1999: 81)

Research in Victoria helps explain how money may be used in efforts to achieve improvements in learning outcomes for students.

Self-managing schools in Victoria   The objectives and purposes of the reforms in Victoria in the 1990s in the Schools of the Future (SOF) programme range over educational ('to enhance student learning outcomes', 'actively foster the attributes of good schools'); professional ('recognise teachers as true professionals', 'allow [headteachers] to be true leaders'); community ('to determine the destiny of the school, its character and ethos') and accountability ('for the progress of the school and the achievement of its students').

Successive surveys in the Cooperative Research Project (1994; 1995a; 1995b; 1996; 1997; 1998) consistently found that headteachers believed there had been moderate to high level of realisation of the expected benefit in respect to improved learning outcomes for students. In the final survey in 1997, 84 per cent gave a rating of 3 or more on the 5-point scale (1 is 'low' and 5 is 'high').

Figure 3.1 contains a model showing the effects of six sets of benefits on curriculum and learning benefits, which are the object of interest in this section of the chapter, based on ratings in the final survey in 1997. (All effects are statistically significant. The analysis involved structural equation modeling using LISREL 8 [Jöreskog and Sörbom, 1993]. See Cooperative Research Project [1998] or Caldwell and Spinks [1998] for detailed explanations.)

The model shows that three factors have a direct effect on curriculum and learning benefits, which includes improved learning outcomes for students. These are personnel and professional benefits (which reflects ratings for realisation of the expected benefits of better personnel management, enhanced professional development, shared decision-making, improved staff performance, more effective organisation following restructure, increased staff satisfaction and an enhanced capacity to attract staff); curriculum improvement due to CSF (which reflects ratings for improvement of capacity for planning the curriculum, establishing levels and standards for students, moving to a curriculum based on learning outcomes and meeting the needs of students); and confidence in attainment of SOF objectives.

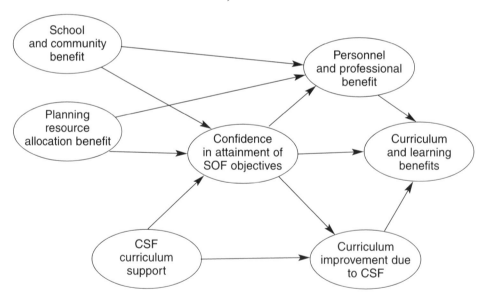

Note: SOF = Schools of the Future (the reform initiative that included a higher level of self-management)
CSF = Curriculum and Standards Framework

Figure 3.1   Model of effects of six sets of benefits of self-management on perceptions of curriculum and learning benefits
Source: Cooperative Research Project (1998)

Noteworthy are the pathways of indirect effects, illustrated for planning and resource allocation benefits, which is mediated in respect to its effect on curriculum and learning benefits through personnel and professional benefits and confidence in attainment of SOF objectives. Expressed another way, realising the expected benefits of better resource management, clearer sense of direction, increased accountability and responsibility, greater financial and administrative flexibility, and improved long-term planning, will have no direct effect on curriculum and learning benefits but will have an indirect effect to the extent they impact on personnel and professional benefits which in turn have a direct effect on curriculum and learning benefits.

Also noteworthy are factors that have a direct impact on confidence in attainment of SOF objectives. High ratings of confidence were associated with high ratings for the achievement of planning and resource allocation benefits, school and community benefits and CSF curriculum support. The likely explanation is that unless headteachers experience benefits in these last three domains, they are unlikely to have confidence in the reform.

The findings in these surveys are limited to the extent that they are based on the perceptions of headteachers rather than measures of student achievement. This has been a concern in most efforts to determine the impact of reform in recent years. In the case of the Cooperative Research Project, there was no system-wide baseline data on student achievement when the reform was implemented.

Two sets of case studies in Victoria (Hillier, 1999; Wee, 1999) help illuminate the links illustrated in Figure 3.1 under conditions where headteachers report improved learning outcomes. Are the linkages evident in the model confirmed in deep on-site investigations in particular schools where improvement is claimed? The research design in both studies thus started with schools where headteachers made such a claim. The first task was to test the validity of these claims, drawing on evidence in the particular schools selected for study. The second task was to seek explanations for how such improvement occurred and then to match it against the linkages or pathways that are shown in the model in Figure 3.1.

The studies differed in one important respect. Hillier's was conducted in two stages, with one round of data collected in 1996, soon after each element of the reform was in place and the pool of indicators was in the early stages of implementation. The second stage occurred in 1998, when Hillier returned to the three schools to assess progress since 1996.

Wee's study in four schools was conducted in late 1997, when the pool of indicators was well developed and a substantial body of evidence was available to test claims of improved learning outcomes. Findings revealed that schools could cite evidence that their efforts had led to improved outcomes for students. They drew on many sources of data in recognising improved student learning in their schools. This illustrated the capacity being developed in the system to gather information about the performance of schools.

Maps of direct and indirect links were prepared by Wee for each school using the rigorous approach to data collection, data display and data reduction for qualitative research proposed by Miles and Huberman (1994). These maps show how school capacity associated with being a School of the Future had led to improved outcomes for students. Actions at the school level that had a direct impact on student learning are in the domains of professional development, implementation of the curriculum and standards framework, and monitoring. The impact of resource allocation is indirect, mediated through curriculum, professional development, monitoring and staffing.

Self-managing schools in developing nations

The worldwide trend to self-management is further illustrated by initiatives in developing nations, supported by international aid agencies, including the World Bank, UNESCO and UNICEF. UNESCO hosted a forum in Paris in February 2001 that provided an opportunity for the sharing of experiences in recent years.

It is likely that some of the best evidence of the impact of self-management on learning outcomes may come from these settings. An explanation lies in the manner in which self-management has been linked to learning. This writer was invited to serve as international evaluator of a project in Indonesia supported by UNESCO and UNICEF under the title 'Creating Learning Communities for Children'. Four initiatives were combined in a pilot project conducted in 79 schools in three provinces (Central Java, East Java and South Sulawesi), including the introduction of a limited form of self-management, with a small budget for each school; professional development for teachers; encouragement of parents and other members of the community to support their schools; and, most important, changes to learning and teaching under the theme 'active joyful effective learning'. Improvement on key indicators such as student attendance and learning outcomes was documented for most schools.

Implications for policy-makers and practitioners

The research suggests that structural rearrangements are but a precondition if there is to be an impact on learning outcomes. Whether there is impact depends on making links across several levels to reach the classroom and the student, so that 'the changes characterised by decentralisation have washed over and around children in classrooms' (Bullock and Thomas, 1997: 219).

The implications for policy-makers and practitioners are relatively clear. These may be expressed in the form of strategic intentions, along the lines proposed by Caldwell and Spinks (1998), who derived a set of 100 from their review of developments on the three tracks for change around the world. The following reflect the findings reported in this paper. An action statement for the system or school may preface each. For 1, this may be 'In Metropolitan Education Authority, it is recognised that the primary purpose of self-management is . . .' or 'In Local College, it is recognised that the primary purpose of self-management is . . .', with appropriate amendment in the subsequent text. Each such intention can form the basis of more detailed planning or the design and delivery of professional development programmes.

1 The primary purpose of self-management is to make a contribution to learning, so schools that aspire to success in this domain will make an unrelenting effort to utilise all of the capacities that accrue with self-management to achieve that end.
2 There will be clear, explicit and planned links, either direct or indirect, between each of the capacities that come with self-management and activities in the school that relate to learning and teaching and the support of learning and teaching.
3 There is a strong association between the mix and capacities of staff and success in addressing needs and priorities in learning, so schools will develop a capacity to optimally select staff, taking account of these needs and priorities.
4 There is a strong association between the knowledge and skills of staff and learning outcomes for students, so schools will employ their capacity for self-management to design, select, implement or utilise professional development programmes to help ensure these outcomes.
5 A feature of staff selection and professional development will be the building of high-performing teams whose work is needs based and data driven, underpinned by a culture that values quality, effectiveness, equity and efficiency.
6 Schools will have a capacity for 'backward mapping' in the design and implementation of programmes for learning, starting from goals, objectives, needs and desired outcomes, and working backwards to determine courses of action that will achieve success, utilising where possible and appropriate the capacities that accrue with self-management.
7 A key task for headteachers and other school leaders is to help make effective the links between capacities for self-management and learning outcomes, and to ensure that support is available when these links break down or prove ineffective.

While there is much that is still uncertain about the nature and impact of school reform, it is evident that the means are at hand to create a system of public schools that will provide a high quality of education for all students and that will be professionally rewarding for teachers and other professionals. The challenge is how to put the pieces together. Making effective the linkage between self-management and learning outcomes is a promising start. We are very close to a theory of learning in the self-managing school.

Further reading

Beare, H. (2000) *Creating the Future School*, London: Routledge/Falmer.

Caldwell, B. J. and Spinks, J. M. (1998) *Beyond the Self-Managing School*, London: Falmer.

Woessmann, L. (2001) 'School resources, educational institutions, and student performance: the international evidence', Kiel Institute of World Economics, University of Kiel (available at
http://www.unikiel.de/ifw/pub/kap/2000/kap983.htm). This paper was presented at the annual conference of the Royal Economic Society, Durham, 9–11 April 2001.

References

Blair, T. (2001) 'A second term to put secondary schools first', *The Times*, 5 September.

Bryk, A. S. (1998) 'Chicago school reform: linkages between local control, educational supports and student achievement', presentations with colleagues in the Consortium on Chicago School Research in a Symposium at the Annual Meeting of the American Educational Research Association, San Diego, April.

Bryk, A. S., Sebring, P. B., Kerbow, D., Rollow, S. and Easton, J. Q. (1998) *Charting Chicago School Reform: Democratic Localism as a Lever for Change*, Boulder, CO: Westview Press.

Bullock, A. and Thomas, H. (1994) *The Impact of Local Management in Schools: Final Report*, Birmingham: University of Birmingham and National Association of Head Teachers.

Bullock, A. and Thomas, H. (1997) *Schools at the Center: A Study of Decentralization*, London: Routledge.

Caldwell, B. J. and Spinks, J. M. (1988) *The Self-Managing School*, London: Falmer Press.

Caldwell, B. J. and Spinks, J. M. (1992) *Leading the Self-Managing School*, London: Falmer Press.

Caldwell, B. J. and Spinks, J. M. (1998) *Beyond the Self-Managing School*, London: Falmer Press.

Cheng, Y. C. (1996) *School Effectiveness and School-Based Management: A Mechanism for Development*, London: Falmer Press.

Connors, L. (2000) *Public Education: The Next Generation*, Report of the Ministerial Working Party (Lyndsay Connors, Chair), Melbourne: Department of Education, Employment and Training.

Cooperative Research Project (1994), *Base-Line Survey*, Report of the Cooperative Research Project on 'Leading Victoria's Schools of the Future', Directorate of

School Education, Victorian Association of State Secondary Principals, Victorian Primary Principals Association, The University of Melbourne (Fay Thomas, Chair) (available from Department of Education, Employment and Training).

Cooperative Research Project (1995a) *One Year Later,* Report of the Cooperative Research Project on 'Leading Victoria's Schools of the Future', Directorate of School Education, Victorian Association of State Secondary Principals, Victorian Primary Principals Association, The University of Melbourne (Fay Thomas, Chair) (available from Department of Education, Employment and Training).

Cooperative Research Project (1995b) *Taking Stock*, Report of the Cooperative Research Project on 'Leading Victoria's Schools of the Future', Directorate of School Education, Victorian Association of State Secondary Principals, Victorian Primary Principals Association, The University of Melbourne (Fay Thomas, Chair) (available from Department of Education, Employment and Training).

Cooperative Research Project (1996) *Three Year Report Card*, Report of the Cooperative Research Project on 'Leading Victoria's Schools of the Future', Directorate of School Education, Victorian Association of State Secondary Principals, Victorian Primary Principals Association, The University of Melbourne (Fay Thomas, Chair) (available from Department of Education, Employment and Training).

Cooperative Research Project (1997) *Still More Work to be Done But . . . No Turning Back*, Report of the Cooperative Research Project on 'Leading Victoria's Schools of the Future', Department of School Education, Victorian Association of State Secondary Principals, Victorian Primary Principals Association, The University of Melbourne (Fay Thomas, Chair) (available from Department of Education, Employment and Training).

Cooperative Research Project (1998) *Assessing the Outcomes*, Report of the Cooperative Research Project on 'Leading Victoria's Schools of the Future', Department of Education, Victorian Association of State Secondary Principals, Victorian Primary Principals Association, The University of Melbourne (Fay Thomas, Chair) (available from Department of Education, Employment and Training).

Department for Education and Skills (2001) *Schools Achieving Success*, White Paper, London: DfES.

Gibton, D., Sabar, N. and Goldring, E. B. (2000) 'How principals of autonomous schools in Israel view implementation of decentralization and restructuring policy: risks, rights and wrongs', *Educational Evaluation and Policy Analysis*, 22 (2): 193–210.

Hanushek, E. A. (1997) 'Assessing the effects of school resources on student performance: An update', *Educational Evaluation and Policy Analysis*, 19 (2): 141–64.

Hess, G. A. (1999) 'Understanding achievement (and other) changes under Chicago school reform', *Educational Evaluation and Policy Analysis*, 21 (1): 67–83.

Hillier, N. (1999) 'Educational reform and school improvement in Victorian primary schools 1993–1999', unpublished thesis for the degree of Doctor of Education, University of Melbourne.

Jöreskog, K. G. and Sörbom, D. (1993) *LISREL 8: User's Reference Guide*, Chicago: Scientific Software, Inc.

Levačić, R. (1995) *Local Management of Schools: Analysis and Practice*, Buckingham: Open University Press.

Malen, B., Ogawa, R. T. and Kranz, J. (1990) 'What do we know about site-based management: a case study of the literature – a call for research', in W. Clune and J. Witte (eds), *Choice and Control in American Education Volume 2: The Practice of Choice, Decentralization and School Restructuring*, London: Falmer Press.

Miles, M. B. and Huberman, A. M. (1994) *Qualitative Data Analysis: An Expanded Sourcebook*, 2nd edn, Thousand Oaks, CA: Sage.

National Education Act of B.E. 2542 (1999) Office of the National Education Commission, Office of the Prime Minister, Thailand.

OECD, Directorate of Education, Employment, Labor and Social Affairs, Education Committee (1994) *Effectiveness of Schooling and of Educational Resource Management: Synthesis of Country Studies*, Points 22 and 23, Paris: OECD.

Smith, M. S., Scoll, B.W. and Link, J. (1996) 'Research-based school reform: the Clinton Administration's agenda', in E. A. Hanushek, and D. W. Jorgenson (eds), *Improving America's Schools: The Role of Incentives*, Washington, DC: National Academy Press, Paper 2.

Steelman, L. C., Powell, B. and Carini, R. M. (2000) 'Do teacher unions hinder educational performance: lessons learned from state SAT and ACT scores?', *Harvard Educational Review*, 70 (4): 437–66.

Summers, A. A. and Johnson, A. W. (1996) 'The effects of school-based management plans', in E. A. Hanushek and D. W. Jorgenson (eds), *Improving America's Schools: The Role of Incentives*, Washington, DC: National Academy Press, Paper 5.

Volansky, A. (2001) 'From experiment to educational policy: the transition in Israel schools to school-based management', paper presented at the First National Conference in Israel on School-Based Management, organised by the Ministry of Education, Kfar Maccabiah, Israel, 2–3 April.

Wee, J. (1999) 'Improved student learning and leadership in self-managed schools', unpublished thesis for the degree of Doctor of Education, The University of Melbourne.

Woessmann, L. (2001) 'School resources, educational institutions, and student performance: the international evidence', Kiel Institute of World Economics, University of Kiel (available at http://www.uni-kiel.de/ifw/pub/kap/2000/kap983.htm). This paper was presented at the annual conference of the Royal Economic Society, Durham, 9–11 April 2001.

Yoshida, K. (2001) 'Japanese educational reform after World War II', invited presentation at The First International Forum on Education Reform: Experience of Selected Countries, organised by the Office of the National Education Commission (ONEC) in Thailand, Bangkok, 30 July–2 August.

Section II
Leadership and Strategic Management

4
Leadership and Strategy
Yin Cheong Cheng

Introduction

In facing up to the challenges of rapidly changing local and global environments in the new century, there have been numerous education reforms and school restructuring movements in different parts of the world since the 1990s and even earlier (Cheng and Townsend, 2000). In these great efforts for education change and effectiveness, the role of leadership at both the system and site levels is often found to be crucial to their success. Responding to the need for understanding and development of leadership and strategy in such a changing educational environment, this chapter aims to give an overview of the traditional and alternative concepts of leadership, introduce some general models of adopting leadership styles and strategies, and highlight the roles of leadership in strategic management, action learning and paradigm shift in education for the new century.

Concepts of leadership

Different scholars interpret the concept of leadership differently (Yukl, 1998). Some typical examples can be listed as follows: leadership is the process of influencing the activities of an organised group toward goal-setting and goal achievement (Stogdill, 1974); leadership is the initiation of a new structure or procedure for accomplishing an organisation's goals and objectives or for changing an organisation's goals and objectives (Lipham, 1964); and leadership is a force that can initiate action among people, guide activities in a given direction, maintain such activities and unify efforts toward common goals (Kenzevich, 1975). It is really difficult to achieve only one definition that is acceptable to all (Bass, 1985). Cheng (1996a) found two general elements of leadership in the numerous definitions: first, leadership is related to the process of influencing others' behaviour; and, second, it is related to goal development and achievement. For the first element, there are many methods to influence followers or other people to work. Based on different perspectives, different approaches may be developed to lead, to manage, to influence and even to control people and their activities in the educational institution.

51

For the second element, how to set goals, create meanings, direct actions, eliminate uncertainty or ambiguity and achieve goals is also a core part of leadership activities in education.

Traditional concepts

Leadership, as studied through traditional theories such as the Ohio State University studies (Halpin, 1966), the managerial grid model (Blake and Mouton, 1985), and the contingency theories (Fiedler, 1978; Kerr and Jermier, 1978) is often assumed to occur between a leader and a follower group in a steady situation where a task is given to complete in a relatively short time period (Hampton et al., 1987). Explicitly or implicitly, the traditional theories often focus on the transactional process in which a leader gives something to followers in exchange for their satisfactory effort and performance in the task. The educational leader tends to survey followers' needs, clarify with them how their needs can be fulfilled in exchange for the performance of tasks, and set achievable goals for them to work towards (Bass, 1985).

The traditional leadership theories concentrate on leaders' management techniques and interpersonal skills and encourage leaders to adapt their behaviour to the situation. There seems to be no need for educational leaders to question the goals of their organisations, expect their followers to perform beyond the ordinary limits, and transform the situation and their followers' beliefs, values, attitudes and behaviours. In Zaleznik's (1977) term, a transactional leader is a manager but not a leader.

Contingency theories assume that the relationship between leadership style and organisational outcomes is moderated by situational factors, and therefore the outcomes cannot be predicted by leadership style unless the situational variables are known. They suggest that leaders have to adapt their behaviour to the situation but not change the situation. From a research perspective, Hackman (1985) pointed out that the contingency models are sometimes generated out of a researcher's desperation because variation in findings across studies and samples may be explained successfully only by individual differences and situational attributes. Furthermore, it is also very difficult to use complex contingency theories as behavioural guides.

Transformational perspective

Responding to the limitations of the traditional theories, an alternative perspective that emphasises transformational leadership has emerged since the late 1970s (e.g. Bass, 1985; Bennis, 1984; Leithwood et al., 1996; Zaleznik, 1977). From this perspective, a leader in an educational institution is one who not only adapts his/her behaviour to the situation but also transforms it. A transformational leader is proactive about the organisational vision and mission, shaping members' beliefs, values, and attitudes and developing options for the future, while a manager or a transactional leader is reactive about the organisational goals, using a transactional approach to motivate followers. Therefore, it is important for a leader to shape organisational culture and define the vision and mission of the organisation (Cheng, 1996a; Firestone and Louis, 1999; Schein, 1992). Particularly when there is a paradigm shift in education in a new era of globalisation, information technology and a knowledge-based economy, educational leaders inevitably need to play a key role as transformational leaders to facilitate paradigm shifts in learning, teaching and curriculum, transform various contextual constraints and create opportunities for new development for their institutions, students and staff (Cheng, 2000b; 2001a; 2001b). Numerous ongoing education reforms in many countries in the Asia-Pacific region, Europe and America are requiring transformational leadership at both system and institutional levels and from kindergarten to vocational and higher education (Cheng and Townsend, 2000).

From Cheng's (1996a) two elements of leadership, the process of influencing members and others and goal development and achievement, we can see that the traditional theories, assuming that organisational goals are static and given to be achieved, focus mainly on the process of influencing members to achieve these given goals. But, the transformational perspective conceptualises these two elements of leadership in a dynamic way. It is assumed that the organisational goals and tasks are often ambiguous, outdated and not well defined, particularly in a changing environment. Therefore, both development of goals and the process of influencing members are necessary in educational institutions when facing challenges from rapidly changing local and global environments. According to Bass (1985), a transformational leader in an educational institution is one who motivates people to do more than they are originally expected to do in any one of the following ways:

- Raising their level of awareness and consciousness about the importance and value of designated outcomes, and ways of reaching them. For example, a senior leader in a tertiary institution helps faculty members to understand current trends of educational reform, the importance of paradigm shifts in tertiary learning and the related impacts of these changes on their tertiary institution;
- Getting them to transcend their own self-interest for the sake of the team, organisation, or large polity. For example, a leader in a vocational training institute facilitates staff members to appreciate the vision and mission of the institute, understand the significance of their job to the larger society and become committed and synergic to achieve the institute's vision and goals; and
- Altering their need level on Maslow's (1943) hierarchy or expanding their portfolio of needs and wants from low level (e.g. physiological or safety

needs) to high level (e.g. esteem or self-actualisation needs). For example, it is quite common in educational institutions, particularly in higher education in the USA, UK or Hong Kong, that leaders create opportunities for members to enrich their working experiences and empower themselves to pursue more challenging and meaningful tasks and goals.

From this perspective, leadership is not only a process to influence the behaviours of members or constituencies but also their attitudes, values and beliefs; not only individual members but also the whole organisation; not only the goal achievement but also goal development and organisational culture building.

Layer perspective

Responding to the complexity and multiplicity in current contexts of educational management, Cheng (1996a; 2001c) proposed a layer perspective of leadership. Leadership can be conceptualised as a layer including three levels of leaders and three domains of leadership influence. Constituencies of educational institutions are multiple and very diverse.

Levels of leaders   In current educational reforms, shared decision-making or participative management is recommended and implemented in educational institutions, and many faculty members or teachers take up the leader role in some management activities and at the same time they are also members in other management activities. As suggested by Barth (1988), there should be a community of leaders in an educational institution like a school or higher education institute. The leader may be a single individual. Leadership may be provided by the institutional head/individual staff, or a group of staff members, or all members in the educational institution. In other words, there are three levels of leaders, namely individual leaders, group leaders and whole-institution leaders.

Domains of leadership influence   The leaders exercise their leadership through their affective, behavioural and cognitive performance. The affective performance often refers to the personal commitment, attraction or charisma at the individual level and to the team spirit, social attitudinal norms and social intimacy at the group level and the institutional level. The behavioural performance refers to the general leadership behaviour (for example, consideration, initiating structure, etc.) or management skill practice (for example, planning, supervision, etc.) at the three levels. The cognitive performance refers to the understanding, purposing, meaning, development, clarification of uncertainty and ambiguity, and building values and beliefs about education and management. Affective and cognitive performance is often expressed in popular terms such as human, cultural, symbolic or charismatic leadership

(Bolman and Deal, 1997; Conger et al., 1988; Shamir et al., 1993). Behavioural performance is often named as technical or structural leadership (Bolman and Deal, 1997; Sergiovanni, 1984), overt behaviours (see the Leader Behavior Description Questionnaire (LBDQ) of the Ohio State University Studies, Halpin, 1966; Blake and Mouton, 1985), or even managerial behaviours (Cheng, 2000c; Yukl, 1998).

Multiple and diverse constituencies   In ongoing international trends of educational development, parental participation, community involvement, partnership with other sectors like business, and accountability to the public are a necessity in educational management and leadership. There are potentially many types of constituencies or stakeholders involved in the educational management and leadership process, externally and internally, explicitly and implicitly, locally and even globally in the new millennium (Cheng, 2001b). They include those inside the educational institution such as staff and students and those outside such as parents, members of the management board, officers of the education authority, people from social service organisations, people from business and industrial organisations, and the public. Also the involvement of constituencies may be not only at the individual, site and community levels, but also at the society and international levels. Particularly we are making efforts to globalise our classrooms and institutions through different types of worldwide networking and information technology to allow our students and teachers to achieve world-class learning and teaching in the new millennium (Cheng, 2000b). The involvement of international constituencies for collaboration and partnership inevitably becomes a necessity. For example, currently there are more and more international exchange programmes and immersion programmes organised at the tertiary and secondary education levels in Australia, Hong Kong, Japan, the USA and European countries. This direction of leadership extending influence on external constituencies has been repeatedly reflected in terms of environmental leadership or strategic leadership in some recent literature (Cheng, 2000a; Goldring and Rallis, 1993; Goldring and Sullivan, 1996).

Influence process   In this layer conception, the leadership process is an influencing process from the whole leader layer (including the affective, behavioural and cognitive performance of different leaders at the individual, group and institutional level) to the various constituencies or stakeholders. For example, in a higher education institution, not only individual leaders take a leadership role. Group and institution members can lead different aspects of the institutional functions and tasks; and these leaders can influence internal members and external constituencies through their managerial behaviours and their own charisma, vision and inspiration. This is a holistic way to perform leadership. From the layer perspective, the domains of constituencies to be led or influenced include not only the behavioural aspects but also the affective and cognitive aspects; also not only individual constituencies but also groups in and beyond the educational institution.

From the above discussion, we can see that the layer concept can provide a more comprehensive approach to understanding the complex nature of leadership process and leadership effect. The transformational perspective can highlight the significant role of leadership to pursue excellence and relevance to the future in an era of transformation in education.

Leadership and strategy

The above concepts and perspectives provide an important base for understanding the nature of leadership in education. But the application and practice of these leadership concepts in different aspects of an educational organisation to serve different functions may result in different types of leadership styles and also different strategies in educational management and development. In traditional theories, the duality of leadership in terms of the concern for people and the concern for task is often emphasised and applied in educational management (Blake and Mouton, 1985; Halpin, 1966; Stogdill, 1974). This conceptualisation of leadership ignores important aspects such as the cultural and political aspects of the organisational process and life in educational institutions (Bolman and Deal, 1997; Yukl, 1998).

Five-dimensions of leadership

Based on the four frames of understanding organisations, Bolman and Deal (1997) suggest that there are four leadership functions to serve four fundamental aspects of organisations: structural leadership, human resource leadership, political leadership and symbolic leadership. For educational organisations, Sergiovanni (1984) proposes a five-leadership forces model to explain how the principal's leadership is related to excellent school performance. The five leadership forces that contribute to different aspects of performance of an educational institution include technical leadership, human leadership, educational leadership, symbolic leadership and cultural leadership. Cheng (1994) integrated the above two models and proposed that leadership in educational institutions should be composed of five dimensions: structural leadership, human leadership, political leadership, cultural leadership and educational leadership. Specifically, they are further explained as follows:

- *Human leadership* refers to the leadership that develops positive social relationships, facilitates social interactions and participation, and enhances staff commitment and satisfaction in the educational institution.

- *Structural leadership* refers to the leadership that develops clear goals and policies, establishes appropriate organisational structure for different roles, holds staff accountable for results, and provides suitable technical support to plan, organise, co-ordinate and implement policies in the institution.
- *Political leadership* refers to the leadership that builds alliances and coalitions, encourages participation and collaboration in decision-making, and resolves conflicts among constituencies.
- *Cultural leadership* refers to the leadership that inspires and stimulates members to pursue institutional vision and excellent performance, builds up new institutional culture, and transforms the existing values and norms of staff in the institution.
- *Educational leadership* refers to the leadership that provides direction and expert advice on developments of learning, teaching, and curriculum, emphasises relevance to education in management, diagnoses educational problems and encourages professional development and teaching improvement.

The empirical findings based on this model in a number of studies have provided strong evidence to support the validity and comprehensiveness of this model in describing multiple aspects of leadership in educational institution (Cheng, 1994; 1996b; Shum and Cheng, 1997). For example, Cheng (1994) studied the relationship between principal leadership and school performance at the student level, the teacher level and the organisational level in a sample of 190 primary schools, involving 190 heads, 678 classes of mainly Grade 6 students, 21,622 students and 3,872 teachers. The structural, human, political, cultural and educational dimensions of principal leadership were found to be strongly related to the school's perceived organisational effectiveness, principal–teacher relationship, strength of organisational culture, the authority hierarchy (negatively) and teacher participation in decision-making. These dimensions were also found to be strongly related to measures of teachers' group performance such as teachers' esprit, disengagement (negatively) hindrance (negatively) and professionalism, and to nearly all measures of individual teacher performance such as intrinsic satisfaction, extrinsic satisfaction, influence satisfaction, job commitment, feeling of fair role loading and job meaning. There was a moderate correlation between principal leadership and some of the measures of student performance such as student attitudes towards their school, teachers and learning. All these findings confirm that the five-dimension model of leadership is comprehensive and valid to predict the different aspects of performance of an educational institution.

With different leadership, the strategies employed in management may be completely different. If taking the affective, behavioural and cognitive domains of leadership performance into consideration, some key strategies of each of the five dimensions of leadership can be summarised as shown in Table 4.1 (Cheng, 2001c).

Table 4.1   *Strategies based on three domains and five dimensions of leadership*

	Structural leadership and strategies	Human leadership and strategies	Political leadership and strategies	Cultural leadership and strategies	Educational leadership and strategies
Affective domains	• Encourage members to express and communicate their feelings through channels and accept the need of structures • Help members psychologically prepared to implement technological changes	• Enjoy good social relationship between members • Committed to develop an open climate in the institution • Unfreeze the existing social barriers among constituencies through charisma	• Encourage an open climate to deal with diversities and mutual conflicts among constituencies • Unfreeze the psychological biases • Help members affectively prepared to discuss their diversities and confrontations	• Use personal charisma to attract constituencies' attention to the institutional vision and meanings • Help members psychologically prepared to cultural changes • Motivate constituencies to pursue a culture of excellence	• Show strong professional commitment to education and staff development • Motivate members to love students and education and have a strong passion to pursue excellence in teaching and learning
Behavioural domains	• Provide appropriate facilities and resources • Establish the structures and procedures to facilitate effective work and make technological changes	• Facilitate social interactions at different levels • Organise activities for creating friendship and collegiality among internal and external constituencies	• Build up alliance to implement institutional plan • Invite wide participation in decision-making • Use different power bases and tactics to implement plans and changes	• Set a behavioural model to show what is most important to the school and create a unique institutional culture • Arrange opportunities to reflect on the existing behavioural norms and make cultural changes	• Facilitate effective practices for learning and teaching and initiate educational innovations • Bring in frontier ideas for curriculum design and pedagogy • Facilitate technological changes in using IT in education
Cognitive domains	• Value the use of clear policy and coordination to achieve the goals • Help members understand the functions and importance of structures and technological changes	• Emphasise human values and human contacts • Highlight the meaning and values of social relations in education and institutional life	• Interpret the conflicts in a constructive way and value the importance of win-win solution • Emphasise the democratic values in decision-making • Facilitate members to understand the meaning of participation	• Inspire members to pursue intrinsic values in their work and perform beyond expectation • Highlight what is most significant to the future of the institution and education • Help constituencies to internalise the unique set of institutional values	• Signal what is most important to education and stimulate members' professionalism • Facilitate constituencies to appreciate and develop values, beliefs, visions and goals of education in a new era of globalisation and high technology

As for the affective side of *structural leadership*, the leaders may encourage constituencies to express and communicate their feelings through different channels and accept the need of establishing structures and regulations for the educational institution. They help members to be psychologically prepared to implement technological changes in the institution. For the behavioural side, they can provide appropriate facilities and resources, and establish procedures for members to facilitate effective work and make technological changes. For the cognitive aspect of structural leadership, they may value the use of clear policy and co-ordination to achieve the institutional goals and help members to understand the functions and purposes of the structural arrangements and technological changes in their work.

To perform the affective side of *human leadership*, the leaders enjoy good social relationships with members and are committed to developing an open climate in the institution. They unfreeze the existing social barriers among constituencies through their own charisma. For the behavioural side, they facilitate social interactions at different levels and organise activities for creating friendship and collegiality among internal and external constituencies. For the cognitive side of human leadership, they emphasise human values and human contact and highlight the meaning and values of social relations in education and daily institutional life.

For performing the affective aspect of *political leadership*, the leaders encourage an open climate to deal with the diversity in interests and the mutual conflicts among external and internal constituencies. They unfreeze the existing psychological biases and help members affectively prepared to discuss their diversities, confrontations and problems. For the behavioural side, they build up alliances among internal and external constituencies to implement institutional plans and invite wide participation in decision-making. They exercise different power bases (French and Raven, 1968; Yukl and Falbe, 1991) and tactics (Dunham and Pierce, 1989; Pfeffer, 1981; Yukl, 1998) to implement institutional actions and changes. For the cognitive side of political leadership, they interpret the conflicts in a constructive way and value the importance of win-win solutions. They emphasise the importance of democratic values in decision-making and facilitate members' understanding of the meaning of participation in management.

To perform the affective side of *cultural leadership*, the leaders may use their own personal charisma to attract constituencies' attention to the institutional vision and the meanings behind activities. They help members to psychologically prepare for cultural changes due to the challenges of a changing educational environment. They also motivate constituencies to pursue a culture of excellence in education. The strong affective side of cultural leadership, particularly at the individual level, is often perceived as 'charismatic leadership' (Conger et al., 1988; Shamir et al., 1993). For the behavioural side, they set a behavioural model to show what is most important to the institution and create a unique institutional culture. They arrange opportunities for members to reflect on the strengths and weaknesses of existing behavioural norms and values in the institution, and involve them in making cultural changes. For the cognitive side of cultural leadership, they inspire members to pursue intrinsic values in their work and perform beyond expectation. They highlight what is most significant for the future of the institution and education and help internal and external constituencies to internalise the unique set of values behind all the activities of the institution. The leadership that articulates the significance of ethical and moral values in education and management becomes more and more important. Sometimes, the cultural leadership in this moral aspect can be perceived as 'moral leadership' (Sergiovanni, 1992) or 'ethical leadership'.

For the affective side of *educational leadership*, the leaders may show strong professional commitment to education and to staff development. They motivate members to love students and education, and have a strong passion to pursue excellence in teaching and learning. To perform the behavioural side, they facilitate effective practices for learning and teaching and initiate educational innovations. They bring in exciting frontier ideas for curriculum design and pedagogy. Particularly they help members to prepare for using information technology in learning and teaching. For the cognitive side of educational leadership, they can signal what is most important to education and stimulate members' professionalism. They facilitate constituencies to appreciate and develop the values, beliefs, vision and goals of education, particularly in a new era of globalisation and high technology.

Conceptually, the strategies of leadership in education can be a combination of all these five dimensions as well as a combination of the three domains. To maximise the influence of leadership, all the dimensions and domains should be performed in a coherent way (Cheng, 1996a; 2001c).

Leadership for multiple models of educational quality

In ongoing worldwide education reforms, how to improve educational practice for the pursuit of educational quality is one of the key concerns. Educational quality is often a complicated and controversial concept in the current policy debate. According to the literature of management and organisational effectiveness, there are seven models that can be used to conceptualise, manage and pursue education quality (Cheng and Tam, 1997). The required role and strategies of leadership to put these models in to practice are different (Cheng, 2002). From these models, the roles and strategies of leadership can be summarised as in Table 4.2.

Goal developer   According to the goal and specification model, an educational institution's education quality is high if it can accomplish its stated goals

Table 4.2   *Leadership and strategies for education quality*

	Leadership roles	Strategies for achievement of education quality
Goal and specification model	• Goal developer • Goal leader • Planning facilitator	• Develop appropriate institutional mission and goals and establish programmes, plans and standards • Lead members to achieve goals, implement plans and programmes, and meet standards
Resource-input model	• Resource developer • Resource distributor	• Procure needed resources and inputs • Allocate resources to support effective teaching, learning and functioning
Process model	• Process engineer • Process facilitator	• Engineer and facilitate smooth and healthy internal process including learning and teaching • Encourage participation and promote social interactions and positive classroom and institutional climate
Satisfaction model	• Social leader • Social satisfier	• Create opportunities to satisfy the diverse expectations of all powerful constituencies • Lead members to satisfy the needs of key stakeholders in teaching and all other activities
Legitimacy model	• Public relations manager • Environmental leader • Accountability builder	• Establish good public relationship with the community • Market the institution's strengths and image • Build up the institutional accountability
Absence of problem model	• Supervisor • Dysfunction detector • Problem shooter	• Lead members to avoid and solve conflicts and problems successfully • Identify and prevent structural and organisational defects in the institution
Organisational learning model	• Environmental analyser • Learning promoter • Organisational developer	• Lead members to have a full awareness and analysis of environmental changes and internal barriers • Promote organisational learning • Establish a strategic plan for institutional development

and conform to the given specifications. Since the educational environment is changing, goals of an educational institution are not static and often need to be clarified, developed and established. Therefore, leaders should play the role of goal developer, goal leader and school planning facilitator. They need to facilitate institutional and programme planning, and ensure that the priorities of goals and standards for managing, teaching and learning are set appropriately; the expected institutional outcomes are clear and the effectiveness criteria are available and accepted by all strategic constituencies, at least in a given time period.

Resource developer   The resource-input model assumes that more scarce and valued resource input is needed for educational institutions to provide quality education. Therefore, leaders should play the role of resource developer and resource distributor. They clarify the connections between inputs and outputs, and determine what resources are critical to the institution's survival and development. They develop and utilise scarce resources from outside and allocate these resources to support effective internal functioning. They also help internal members to broaden the concepts of human and physical resources, and enhance their professional competence to use and manage scarce resources in teaching and learning for quality outcomes. To reduce the internal political conflicts and struggles for resources but generate more synergy among members is also an important area for leadership.

Process engineer   The quality of internal institutional process often determines the nature of output and the achievement of institutional goals and mission. Therefore, leaders should play the role of process engineer and facilitator. They have to clarify how the internal process is closely related to institutional outputs and educational outcomes. They facilitate participation and involvement of members in decision-making and planning, multiple channels of communication, co-ordination between different units, social interactions among members, classroom and organisational climate, and all learning and teaching activities. If it is necessary, they re-engineer institutional processes and the activities of managing, teaching and learning to meet the new institutional goals and challenges from the changing educational environment so that teachers and students can maximise their effectiveness and potential in the processes of teaching and learning.

Social leader and satisfier   Education quality can be promised when all strategic constituencies of the educational institution are at least minimally satisfied with the services the institution provides. Therefore, leaders should play the role of social leader and social satisfier. They help the internal and external constituencies to communicate their expectations, understand the strengths and weaknesses of the institution and set appropriate targets for the institution to satisfy their needs and expectations. They need to make the effort to ensure that the demands of key stakeholders are comparable so that the institution can satisfy these demands more easily at the same time. If there is serious conflict between the demands of different strategic constituencies, leaders help them to resolve the problem and sustain good social relationships.

Environmental leader The legitimacy model assumes that successful legitimate or marketing activities are very important to the institution's survival and quality reputation. Therefore, leaders play the role of public relations manager, environmental leader and accountability builder. They have to assess the external competitions and challenges of the educational environment that will threaten the survival and quality reputation of their institutions and communicate these threats and opportunities to their members. They lead members to manage the external environment, build up good relations with all strategic external constituencies, market the institution's strengths and contributions to the community, establish the school's public image and ensure the school's accountability to the public, particularly on the quality of education services they provide.

Supervisor According to the absence of problems model, the education quality of an educational institution depends on whether there is an absence of characteristics of ineffectiveness in the institution. The role of leaders should be supervisor, dysfunction detector and problem-solver. They have to supervise institutional activities, identify weaknesses, conflicts, dysfunctions, difficulties and defects in teaching and learning, and help members to eliminate and solve the problems. They lead members to set up the necessary procedures or systems that can monitor and evaluate the performance, troubles and problems in the process and outcome of learning, teaching and managing. Particularly among members, they can reduce defensive mechanisms and develop an open culture to encourage the use of feedback or findings from monitoring and evaluation to improve educational and management practice.

Organisational developer The organisational learning model assumes that the impact of environmental changes and the existence of internal barriers to institutional functioning and education quality are inevitable. An educational institution's education quality can be enhanced and ensured if it can learn how to make improvements to its internal and external environments. Leaders play their role as environmental analyser, learning promoter and organisational developer. They help members to be sensitive to environmental changes and internal barriers, analyse them, reflect on findings, draw implications, establish strategies, plan actions and develop the organisation (Yuen and Cheng, 2000). They use strategic management or development planning to promote organisational learning and continuous improvement and development among members (Cheng, 2000a).

According to the concepts of total quality management (Tenner and Detoro, 1992), quality in education can be totally ensured if an educational institution can involve and empower all its members in functioning, conduct continuous improvement in different aspects of internal process, and satisfy the requirements, needs and expectations of its external and internal powerful constituencies even in a changing environment. To a great extent, the total quality management concept is an integration of the above seven models, particularly the organisational learning model, the satisfaction model and the process model. From this total quality concept, leaders need to play the role as a *total quality leader*. In other words, they assume nearly all the leadership roles, derived from the seven models, such as goal developer, resource developer, process engineer, social leader and satisfier, environmental leader, supervisor, learning promoter and organisational developer. They can employ a wide spectrum of strategies related to each of these leadership roles in pursuing total education quality in a complicated and changing educational environment.

Conclusion: leadership in the new millennium

The above concepts and perspectives of leadership can provide a basic understanding of leadership in educational management. Particularly the five-dimensional model of leadership can give a comprehensive framework for developing leadership strategies and actions to lead and manage five fundamental aspects of educational organisations including the human, structural, political, cultural and educational. In the pursuit of education quality in current education reforms, the multiple roles and strategies of leadership derived from the multiple models of education quality should also be important. In addition to these concepts and models, the following trends in leadership and strategy development should receive serious attention.

Leadership for strategic management

As strategic management is strongly emphasised in a rapidly changing educational environment in the new millennium, leadership for such strategic management in educational institutions inevitably becomes a necessity. Currently, the discussion of strategic leadership is still meagre and the domain of studying strategic leadership is relatively diffuse and uncharted. According to Cheng (1996a), the strategic management process includes the stages such as environmental analysis, planning and structuring, staffing and directing, implementing, monitoring and evaluating. This process can keep the institution as a whole appropriately matched to its environment, improve performance, achieve objectives and develop itself continuously. Then, *strategic leadership* in an educational institution can be considered as leadership for initiating, developing and maintaining the strategic management process. Cheng

(2000a) has shown how the five dimensions of leadership – structural leadership, human leadership, political leadership, cultural leadership and educational leadership – can be applied to leading each stage of the strategic management process.

Leadership for action learning

In contemporary educational management, there is a strong emphasis on organisational learning to meet the challenges of a changing educational environment (Rait, 1995; Senge, 1990). Staff members' continuous reflection on their actions and learning to improve and enhance their teaching and daily practice becomes a necessity (Schön, 1987; Watkins and Shindell, 1994). How leadership can facilitate teacher action learning is a crucial but relatively unexplored area for research and leadership development. Yuen and Cheng (2000) have proposed a preliminary framework to show how leadership can facilitate staff members' action learning. The framework comprises three dimensions and eight components. The *inspiring dimension* is composed of three components: building and institutionalising shared vision, providing individualised job design and modeling. The *social supporting dimension* encompasses three components such as reducing defensive routines, fostering learning culture and mobilising social support. The *enabling dimension* comprises two components: enhancing theoretical knowledge and repertoires of skills and providing intellectual stimulation. The framework provides an important theoretical base for understanding what staff members' cognitive and behavioural characteristics are in each stage of the action learning cycle and how the three dimensions and eight components of leadership can facilitate each stage of learning, finally single-loop learning and double-loop learning can occur to enhance teacher competence and performance in their professional practice (Argyris and Schön, 1974).

Leadership for paradigm shifts in education

In the new millennium, there are numerous transformations at both system and school-site levels. Paradigm shifts in education are evident, particularly from the traditional site-bounded paradigm to the triplisation paradigm including globalisation, localisation and individualisation in learning, teaching and schooling, with the support of information technology and various types of networking (Cheng, 2000b; 2001a). Education leaders inevitably find themselves facing many challenges, uncertainties and ambiguities in their educational practice and management. All these demand a paradigm shift for leaders to lead their educational institutions and members more effectively to prepare both external and internal transformations and pursue institutional effectiveness and educational quality in such a rapidly changing environment

(Macbeath et al., 1996). It seems that leaders should have a new set of leadership beliefs and competences that can transform the old and traditional constraints, facilitate educational changes and develop an appropriate school environment for staff members and students to work, learn and develop effectively. Inevitably, there is an urgent need for a new paradigm of leadership to direct the practice and development of leaders in educational institutions (Berg and Sleegers, 1996; Fullan, 1996; Smylie and Hart, 1999). Particularly, a crucial issue in leadership research and development, is how leadership can be developed for facilitating the paradigm shifts in education towards globalisation, localisation and individualisation that can provide unlimited opportunities for students and teachers to learn and develop in such a challenging new millennium.

It is hoped that the overview of leadership and strategy in educational management discussed in this chapter can benefit all the efforts of research, development and practice of leadership in different parts of the world in the new millennium.

Further reading

Cheng, Y. C. (1996) *School Effectiveness and School-Based Management: A Mechanism for Development*, London: Falmer Press.

Cheng, Y. C. (in press). 'The changing context of school leadership: Implications for paradigm shift', in K. Leithwood, J. Chapman, D. Corson, P. Hallinger and A. Hart. (eds), *International Handbook of Educational Leadership and Administration*, 2nd edn, Dordrecht: Kluwer Academic.

Macbeath, J., Moss, L. and Riley, K. (1996) 'Leadership in a changing world', in K. Leithwood, J. Chapman, D. Corson, P. Hallinger and A. Hart (eds), *International Handbook of Educational Leadership and Administration*, Dordrecht: Kluwer Academic.

References

Argyris, C. and Schön, D. A. (1974) *Theory in Practice: Increasing Professional Effectiveness*, San Francisco: Jossey-Bass.

Barth, R. S. (1988) 'School: A community of leaders', in A. Lieberman (ed.), *Building a Professional Culture in Schools*, New York: Teachers College Press.

Bass, B. M. (1985) *Leadership and Performance beyond Expectations*, New York: Free Press.

Bennis, W. (1984) 'Transformative power and leadership', in T. J. Sergiovanni and J. E. Corbally (eds), *Leadership and Organizational Culture*, Urbana, IL: University of Illinois Press.

Berg, R. V. D. and Sleegers, P. (1996) 'Building innovative capacity and leadership', in K. Leithwood, J. Chapman, D. Corson, P. Hallinger and A. Hart (eds), *International*

Handbook of Educational Leadership and Administration, Dordrecht: Kluwer Academic.

Blake, R. G. and Mouton, J. S. (1985) *The New Managerial Grid III*, Houston: Gulf.

Bolman, L. G. and Deal, T. E. (1997) *Reframing Organizations: Artistry, Choice, and Leadership*, 2nd edn, San Francisco: Jossey-Bass.

Cheng, Y. C. (1994) 'Principal's leadership as a critical indicator of school performance: Evidence from multi-levels of primary schools', *School Effectiveness and School Improvement: An International Journal of Research, Policy, and Practice*, 5 (3): 299–317.

Cheng, Y. C. (1996a) *School Effectiveness and School-Based Management: A Mechanism for Development*, London: Falmer Press.

Cheng, Y. C. (1996b) 'Monitoring education quality in schools: framework and technology', ERIC, (Educational Resources Information Center) Microfiche (no.ED381891-EA026683), 41pp., February 1996, Eugene, OR: ERIC Clearinghouse on Educational Management.

Cheng, Y. C. (2000a) 'Strategic leadership for educational transformation in the new millennium', *Chulalongkorn Education Reviews*, 6 (2): 15–32.

Cheng, Y. C. (2000b) 'A CMI-triplization paradigm for reforming education in the new millennium', *International Journal of Educational Management*, 14 (4): 156–74.

Cheng, Y. C. (2000c) 'The characteristics of Hong Kong school principals' leadership: the influence of societal culture', *Asia-Pacific Journal of Education*, 20 (2): 68–86.

Cheng, Y. C. (2001a) 'Educational relevance, quality and effectiveness: paradigm shifts', invited keynote speech presented at the International Congress for School Effectiveness and School Improvement held 5–9 January, Toronto, Canada, with the theme 'Equity, Globalization, and Change: Education for the 21st Century'.

Cheng, Y. C. (2001b) 'The changing context of school leadership: trends and implications for paradigm shift in leadership', paper presented at the Symposium on 'The Changing World of Leadership: Drawing Together Perspectives on Leadership from Australia, Canada, Denmark, Hong Kong, Scotland, England, & USA', of the International Congress for School Effectiveness and School Improvement, 5–9 January, Toronto, Canada.

Cheng, Y. C. (2001c) 'A paradigm shift in school leadership: the layer theory for transformational and strategic leadership', paper presented at the International Congress for School Effectiveness and School Improvement, 5–9 January, in Toronto, Canada.

Cheng, Y. C. (2002) 'Multi-models of education quality and principal leadership', in K. H. Mok and D. Chan (eds), *Globalisation and Education: The Quest for Quality Education in Hong Kong*, (pp. 69–88), Hong Kong: Hong Kong University Press.

Cheng, Y.C. and Tam, W.M. (1997) 'Multi-models of quality in education', *Quality Assurance in Education*, 5 (1): 22–31.

Cheng, Y. C. and Townsend, T. (2000) 'Educational change and development in the Asia-Pacific region: trends and issues', in T. Townsend and Y. C. Cheng (eds), *Educational Change and Development in the Asia-Pacific Region: Challenges for the Future*, Rotterdam: Swets and Zeitlinger.

Conger, J. A. and Kanungo, R. N. (1988) *Charismatic Leadership*, San Francisco: Jossey-Bass.

Dunham, R. B. and Pierce, J. L. (1989) *Management*, Glenview, IL: Scott, Foresman.

Fiedler, F. E. (1978) 'The contingency model and the dynamics of the leadership process', in L. Berkowitz (ed.), *Advances in Experimental Social Psychology*, New York: Academic Press.

Firestone, W. A. and Louis, K. S. (1999) 'Schools as cultures', in J. Murphy and K. S. Louis (eds), *Handbook of Research on Educational Administration*, San Francisco: Jossey-Bass.

French, J. R. P. and Raven, B. (1968) 'The bases of social power', in D. Cartwright and A. Zander (eds), *Group Dynamics*, 3rd edn, New York: Harper and Row.

Fullan, M. (1996) 'Leadership for change', in K. Leithwood, J. Chapman, D. Corson, P. Hallinger and A. Hart (eds), *International Handbook of Educational Leadership and Administration*, Dordrecht: Kluwer Academic.

Goldring, E. B. and Rallis, S. F. (1993) 'Principals as environmental leaders: the external link for facilitating change', paper presented at the annual meeting of the American Educational Research, Atlanta, USA.

Goldring, E. B. and Sullivan, A. V. (1996) 'Beyond the boundaries: principals, parents, and communities shaping the school environment', in K. Leithwood, J. Chapman, D. Corson, P. Hallinger and A. Hart (eds), *International Handbook of Educational Leadership and Administration*, Dordrecht: Kluwer Academic.

Hackman, J. R. (1985) 'Doing research that makes a difference', in E. E. Lawler III, A. M. Mohrman, Jr., S. A. Mohrman, G. E. Ledford Jr. and T. G. Cummings (eds), *Doing Research that Is Useful for Theory and Practice*, San Francisco: Jossey-Bass.

Halpin, A. W. (1966) *Theory and Research in Administration*, New York: Macmillan.

Hampton, D. R., Summer, C. E. and Webber, R. A. (1987) *Organizational Behavior and the Practice of Management*, 5th edn, Glenview, IL: Scott, Foresman.

Kenzevich, S. (1975) *Administration of Public Education*, 3rd edn, New York: Harper and Row.

Kerr, S. and Jermier, J. M. (1978) 'Substitutes for leadership: their meaning and measurement', *Organizational Behavior and Human Performance*, 22: 375–403.

Leithwood, K., Tomlinson, D. and Gene, M. (1996) 'Transformational school leadership', in K. Leithwood, J. Chapman, D. Corson, P. Hallinger and A. Hart (eds), *International Handbook of Educational Leadership and Administration*, Dordrecht: Kluwer Academic.

Lipham, J. A. (1964) 'Leadership and administration', in D. Griffiths (ed.), *Behavioral Science and Educational Administration* (sixty-third yearbook of the National Society for the Study of Education), Chicago: University of Chicago Press.

Macbeath, J., Moos, L. and Riley, K. (1996) 'Leadership in a changing world', in K. Leithwood, J. Chapman, D. Corson, P. Hallinger and A. Hart (eds), *International Handbook of Educational Leadership and Administration*, Dordrecht: Kluwer Academic.

Maslow, A. H. (1943) 'A theory of human motivation', *Psychological Review*, 50: 370–96.

Pfeffer, J. (1981) *Power in Organizations*, Marshfield, MA: Pittman.

Rait, E. (1995) 'Against the current: organizational learning in schools', in S. B. Bacharach and B. Mundell (eds), *Images of Schools: Structures, Roles, and Organizational Behavior*, Thousand Oaks, CA: Corwin Press.

Schein, E. H. (1992) *Organizational Culture and Leadership*, 2nd edn, San Francisco: Jossey-Bass.

Schön, D. A. (1987) *Education and the Reflective Practitioner: Toward a New Design for Teaching and Learning in the Professions*, San Francisco: Jossey-Bass.

Senge, P. M. (1990) *The Fifth Discipline: The Art and Practice of the Learning Organization*, London: Century Business.

Sergiovanni, T. J. (1984) 'Leadership and excellence in schooling'. *Educational leadership*, 41 (5), 4–13.

Sergiovanni, T. J. (1992) *Moral Leadership*, San Francisco: Jossey-Bass.

Shamir, B., House, R. J. and Arthur, M. B. (1993) 'The motivational effects of charismatic leadership: a self-concept based theory' *Organization Science*, 4, 1–17.

Shum, L. C. and Cheng, Y. C. (1997) 'Perceptions of woman principal's leadership and teacher's work attitudes', *Journal of Educational Administration* 35 (2): 168–88.

Smylie, M. A. and Hart, A. W. (1999) 'School leadership for teacher learning and change: a human and social capital development perspective', in J. Murphy and K. S. Louis (eds), *Handbook of Research on Educational Administration*, San Francisco: Jossey-Bass.

Stogdill, R. M. (1974) *Handbook of Leadership*, New York: Free Press.

Tenner, A. R. and Detoro, I. J. (1992) *Total Quality Management*, Reading, MA: Addison-Wesley.

Watkins, K. E. and Shindell, T. J. (1994) 'Learning and transforming through action science', *New Direction for Adult and Continuing Education*, 63, 43–55.

Yuen, B. Y. and Cheng, Y. C. (2000) 'Leadership for teachers' action learning', *International Journal of Educational Management*, 14 (5), 198–209.

Yukl, G. (1998). *Leadership in Organizations*, 4th edn, Upper Saddle River, NJ: Prentice-Hall.

Yukl, G. and Falbe, C. M. (1991) 'The importance of different power sources in downward and lateral relations', *Journal of Applied Psychology*, 75, 132–40.

Zaleznik, A. (1977) 'Managers and leaders: are they different?', *Harvard Business Review*, 55 (5), 67–80.

5

School Leadership in Context – Societal and Organisational Cultures

Clive Dimmock and Allan Walker

A burgeoning literature on educational leadership has developed over the last decade. A significant part of this has looked at the relationship between leadership and organisational culture. Most of these studies have targeted English-speaking Western school settings, but without formally recognising the influence of the national or societal culture. Meanwhile, the influence of societal culture on educational leadership – even in Anglo-American societies – has rarely been studied. With few notable exceptions (for example, Bush, et al., 1998; Bush and Qiang, 2000; Hallinger and Kantamara, 2000; Morris and Lo, 2000; Walker and Dimmock, 1999; 2000a), an important void in our understanding of school leadership exists, especially in regard to non-English-speaking Western and non-Western school settings. The body of knowledge on educational leadership and culture is thus heavily skewed towards Anglo-American studies of organisational culture. The systematic study of school leadership on a comparative and international basis – using societal and cross-cultural analysis – has yet to develop (Dimmock 1998, Dimmock and Walker, 1998a; 1998b). In short, surprisingly little is known about the relationship between societal culture and educational leadership.

   This chapter has four sections. The first briefly discusses the meaning of culture and the differences between societal and organisational culture. The second presents two sets of dimensions as a framework for studying the relationship between leadership and societal – and organisational – cultures. The third illustrates a societal and cross-cultural perspective of educational leadership through application of the dimensions. The fourth identifies challenges to the future development of the field of societal and cross-cultural comparative educational leadership.

The meaning of culture

Culture forms the context in which school leadership is exercised. It thus exerts a considerable influence on how and why school leaders think and act as they do. Studies of leadership that ignore or minimise the cultural context risk constructing only partial understandings of how leadership in different settings is played out. As discussed elsewhere (see for example, Dimmock and Walker, 1998a; Walker and Dimmock, in press) culture is an amorphous and contested concept. For the purposes of this chapter, however, 'culture' is defined as the enduring sets of beliefs, values, ideologies and behaviours that distinguish one group of people from another (Hofstede, 1991). Moreover, the group of people in question can be conceptualised at a number of interrelated levels, from the micro-school or organisational level, through local and regional levels to the macro-national or societal level.

At the outset, we do not claim that 'culture' provides a comprehensive explanation to account for educational leadership and its different characteristics around the globe. Clearly, other factors, such as politics, economics, religion and demography may play a crucial part. The boundary lines between culture and these other factors are, however, quite blurred. Hofstede (1991), for example, argues that all the 'other' factors are reducible to, or at least strongly influenced by, culture in the end. Whatever one's view on this issue, there is no denying that the influence of societal culture on educational leadership has been a neglected area of research.

Differences between societal and organisational cultures

There are fundamental qualitative differences between societal and organisational culture. Societal cultures differ mostly at the level of basic values, while organisational cultures differ mostly at the level of more superficial practices, as reflected in the recognition of particular symbols, heroes, and rituals (Hofstede, 1991). This allows organisational cultures to be deliberately managed and changed, whereas societal or national cultures are more enduring and change only gradually over longer time periods. School leaders influence, and in turn are influenced by, the organisational culture. Societal culture, on the other hand, is a given, being outside the sphere of influence of an individual school leader.

It is logical to expect that the underpinning structures, processes and practices found in schools reflect culture at both societal (including regional and local) level and organisational level. However, little or nothing is known of the ways in which the different types and levels of culture interact at school level. Corresponding research in the corporate world suggests that organisational culture – even in multinational companies – fails to erase or even diminish societal culture (Adler, 1997). Indeed, Laurent (1983) found that far from organisational culture diminishing the effect of societal cultural in multinational companies, the differences among employees were more pronounced than those among employees working for organisations in their native lands. That is, when working for multinational companies, Chinese became more

Chinese, Japanese more Japanese, British more British, and so on. In the absence of causal explanation, one can only speculate as to why this should be so. No equivalent study has been conducted in education and, of course, it is invariably dangerous to assume the same conditions apply to education as to the corporate world.

If we aim to study the interaction of different levels of culture, then we should first differentiate between them. A promising way of so doing is to identify a set of dimensions for each, as outlined in the following sections.

Educational leadership and dimensions of societal culture

Scholars in the field are beginning to seek ways of making authentic comparisons between educational leadership in different societies. Hitherto, comparative study of school leaders has been largely confined to descriptive country-by-country studies, with minimal analysis and only meagre attempt to draw rigorous, systematic comparison based on culture and cultural difference.

Over the past few years the present authors have focused on developing a systematic framework and methodology for a robust comparison of educational leadership based on cross-cultural analysis (see Dimmock, 2000; Dimmock and Walker, 1998a; 1998b; 2000a; 2000b; Walker and Dimmock, 1999). In this section, we provide an outline of the cultural dimensions part of the methodology, while encouraging readers to pursue the references provided if they are interested in the full model.

An authentic approach to the systematic cross-cultural comparative study of educational leadership is predicated on agreement as to what constitutes first, educational leadership, and second, societal culture. Elsewhere, we have provided a full exposition of both, recognising eight components of educational leadership and six (recently revised to seven) dimensions of societal culture (Walker and Dimmock, 1999). Cross-cultural comparison of school leaders in different societies is achieved by applying each of the dimensions of societal culture to educational leadership. Below, we outline the components of leadership followed by the dimensions of societal culture.

Educational leadership

Eight interrelated elements of leadership are recognised. Although other elements might have been included, the eight provide a convenient and manageable way of encapsulating school leadership. Close and complex interrelationships exist between all eight and between these and other school functions such as curriculum, educational structures and teaching and learning. The eight are:

- *collaboration and participation*: the ability to empower others, to collaborate and share power is a necessary part of contemporary leadership (Pounder, 1998)
- *motivation*: inspiring effort and commitment among followers through motivation is a core leadership function (Sergiovanni, 1995)
- *planning*: visioning and strategic planning are central leadership roles (Quong et al., 1998)
- *decision-making*: decision-making is a set of skills and techniques often exercised politically
- *interpersonal communication*: communication as a key leadership practice is vital in enabling understanding and sharing of knowledge and information (Goldring and Rallis, 1993)
- *conflict management*: leadership involves the management of conflicts within the school community (Maurer, 1991)
- *evaluation and appraisal*: staff appraisal and evaluation is a key leadership responsibility (Cardno and Piggot-Irvine, 1997)
- *staff- and professional-development*: leadership involves developing staff professionalism in line with school needs (Darling-Hammond, 1997).

We do not claim that the eight elements present a complete picture or that they address all the complexities of real-life leadership situations. Rather, our contention is that for purposes of analysis, it is useful to recognise them as key operational areas of leadership. In studying the influence of societal culture on educational leadership, the eight elements described above need to be combined with key cultural dimensions. In the following section, we outline these dimensions.

Dimensions of societal culture

The identification of cultural dimensions, defined as core axes around which significant sets of values, beliefs and practices cluster, not only facilitates their description and measurement in terms of societal culture, but promotes comparison between cultures. Dimensions provide a common baseline against which cultural characteristics at the societal level can be described, gauged and compared (Dimmock and Walker, 1998b). Despite their usefulness, however, we agree with Hofstede's (1994) cautionary remarks about dimensions, when he claims that the same limitations apply to them as to culture itself: 'They are also constructs that should not be reified. They do not "exist"; they are tools for analysis which may or may not clarify a situation' (ibid.: 40). The dimensions we describe, therefore, should not be regarded as uni-dimensional. They do not aim to polarise cultural influence on educational leadership, but rather to provide a basis for comparison. For example, we would argue that it is possible for school leaders within a given culture to be both aggressive and considerate at different times in different situations. Therefore, although the dimensions are presented as pairs of alternatives, to view them as polarities along a uni-dimensional scale is too simplistic and could lead to serious misconceptions (Dimmock and Walker, 1998b).

The following dimensions of societal culture – each of which is a continuum – represent a synthesis of research findings, reworking of previous studies and relabelling of concepts (Walker and Dimmock, 1999):

1 *Power-distributed/power-concentrated*: power is either distributed more equally among the various levels of a culture or is more concentrated. Hofstede (1991) calls this 'power distance'. In societies where power is widely distributed through decentralisation and institutionalised democracy, inequity is treated as undesirable and effort is made to reduce it where possible. In societies where power is commonly concentrated in the hands of the few, inequities are often accepted and legitimised. Some societies, such as Asian, tend towards power concentration, while others, such as Anglo-American, favour power distribution.

2 *Group-oriented/self-oriented*: people within a given culture tend to focus on *self* or on their place within a *group*. This dimension describes the degree to which individuals are integrated into groups and the closeness of relationships between persons. In *self-oriented* cultures, relations are fairly loose and relational ties tend to be based on self-interest. People in such societies primarily regard themselves as individuals first, and members of a group, second. People in *self-oriented* cultures perceive themselves to be more independent and self-reliant. In *group-oriented* cultures, ties between people are tight, relationships are firmly structured and individual needs are subservient to the collective needs. Important collectivist values include harmony, face-saving, filial piety and equality of reward distribution among peers. In *group-oriented* cultures, status is traditionally defined by factors such as age, sex, kinship, educational standing, or formal organisational position. In *self-oriented* cultures, people are judged and status ascribed in line with individual performance or what has been accomplished individually.

3 *Consideration/aggression*: in so-called *aggression* cultures, achievement is stressed, competition dominates and conflicts are resolved through the exercise of power and assertiveness. School norms are set by the best students, the system rewards academic achievement while failure at school is seen as serious. In an organisational context, assertiveness is taken as a virtue; selling oneself, decisiveness and emphasis on career are all valued. In contrast, *consideration* societies emphasise relationship, solidarity and resolution of conflicts by compromise and negotiation. At school, norms tend to be set by the average students, while system rewards reflect students' social adaptation and failure is not seen as disastrous. In the work-

place, assertiveness is not appreciated, people are expected to undersell themselves, and emphasis is placed on quality of life and intuition.

4 *Proactivism/fatalism*: this dimension reflects the proactive or 'we can change things around here' attitude in some cultures, and the willingness to accept things as they are in others – a fatalistic perspective. The dimension addresses how different societies and cultures react to and manage uncertainty and change in social situations. In proactive societies, people tend to believe that they have at least some control over situations and over change. They are tolerant of different opinions and are not excessively threatened by unpredictability. In fatalistic cultures, on the other hand, people believe 'what is meant to be, will be'. Uncertainty is often viewed as psychologically uncomfortable and disruptive, and people seek to reduce uncertainty and to limit risks by hanging on to the way things have always been done. This often involves the inflexible retention of rules and dogmas that breed orthodoxy. People hold that these principles are fixed and that they have little or no control over them.

5 *Generative/replicative*: some cultures appear more predisposed towards innovation, or the generation of new ideas and methods, whereas other cultures appear more inclined to replicate or to adopt ideas and approaches from elsewhere. In *generative* cultures people tend to value the generation of knowledge, new ideas and ways of working. They are more likely to seek creative solutions to problems, to develop policies and ways of operating which are original and unique – which stretch and challenge knowledge in various directions. In such cultures, new inventions and approaches often appear. In *replicative* cultures, people are more likely to adopt innovations, ideas and inventions developed elsewhere. While these are either adopted *in toto* or undergo partial adaptation, there is little consideration of alignment to the indigenous cultural context.

6 *Limited relationship/holistic relationship*: this dimension reflects the importance of connections and relationships in cultures. In some cultures, interpersonal relationships are limited by the fixed rules applied to given situations, whereas in other cultures, relationships are more holistic, or underpinned by association and personal considerations. In *limited relationship* cultures, interactions and relationships tend to be determined by explicit rules which are applied equally to everyone. For example, when a leader needs to make a decision on a promotion, objective criteria are applied regardless of who are the candidates. Relationships matter less than rules. In *holistic* cultures on the other hand, greater attention is given to relationship obligations (for example, kinship, patronage and friendship) than to impartially applied rules (see Walker and Dimmock, 1999). Dealings in formal and structured situations in *holistic* cultures are driven more by complex, personal considerations than by the specific situation or by formal rules and regulations.

7 *Male influence/female influence*: this dimension has been added to capture the degrees of influence in society exerted by men and women. In some societies, the male domination of decision-making in political, economic and professional life is perpetuated. In others, women have come to play a significant role. Moreover, the respective roles played by men and women may be undergoing considerable change in some societies, while remaining relatively static in others.

The seven dimensions of culture outlined above represent salient characteristic values underpinning societies. They are generic in the sense that they are present in every culture, but to different degrees – hence their expression in terms of a range or continuum. In the following section, we illustrate the application of societal cultural dimensions to educational leadership.

Illustrating societal and cross-cultural analysis of educational leadership

One of the main distinctions between the US and Japanese societies is the Japanese group orientation versus American individualism (McAdams, 1993). Cheng (1998) agrees, holding that Chinese societies, such as Hong Kong and the People's Republic of China (PRC), are more collectivist than individualist. Both these observations are supported by Hofstede's (1991) empirical findings. In terms of the framework presented in this chapter, Japanese and Chinese principals are more group- than self-oriented. A repercussion of this in schools, and on principals' beliefs and actions, is that in many English-speaking and non-English-speaking Western societies principals are more inclined to consider the individual needs of both teachers and students in the operation of schools. As Cheng (1998) states: 'In European nations such as Germany, France and The Netherlands, schools cater to students with different aptitudes and interests' (ibid.: 16). In East Asian societies, such as China, Thailand and Japan, on the other hand, education is seen as a means by which students adapt to the expectations of the community. In such group-oriented societies, the role of the school and the principal may focus on developing and ensuring harmony among staff and enforcing common, standard approaches to governance, organisation, curriculum and instruction.

Group-oriented cultures, such as China, Japan, Singapore and Hong Kong, and South American countries, including Venezuela and Columbia, are collectivist (also see Cheng, 1998) and tend to place the preservation of relationships above pursuit of tasks. In contrast, self-oriented societies, including the USA, Australia, France and Germany (Hofstede, 1991; McAdams, 1993) generally focus on task achievement rather than the maintenance of relationships. Principals in such societies have a tendency to put task achievement before relationships, and to judge staff on the basis of performance. Such principals may be classified according to our framework as engaging in *limited relationships*. In contrast, promotion in the *holistic relationship* societies is often made on the basis of a combination of contacts, relationships and performance.

Status, respect and power are variously attributed according to different cultural norms (Hofstede, 1991; Trompenaars and Hampden-Turner, 1997). For example, in Chinese societies, respect may be attributed to position, age or family background, whereas in New Zealand, it is attributed more to personal or on-the-job competence (Trompenaars and Hampden-Turner, 1997). In societies where power is linked to extrinsic factors, leadership tends to be from the 'top' and exercised in an authoritarian or autocratic manner. School principals in many Asian countries illustrate well the *power-concentrated* nature of their society. In contrast, principals in other societies are located towards the *power-distributed* end of the spectrum. For example, McAdams (1993) found that German principals, because of their relationships with staff and their route to the principalship, were collaborative and collegial, even more so 'than is typically the case in the United States' (ibid.: 118). A further aspect of power concentration in society is the likelihood that devolving power through school-based management is harder to achieve, or that it assumes a different form from its manifestation in power-distributed societies (Dimmock and Walker, 2000a).

Culture influences how people deal with conflict and participation. According to Bond (1991), the disturbance of interpersonal relations and group harmony through conflict can cause lasting animosity in Chinese cultures. As a result, the Chinese tend to avoid open confrontation and assertiveness. In the school or group context, this is manifested by teachers and principals tending to avoid open disagreement, with the leader's view apparently being accepted (Walker et al., 1996). Principals in such cultures tend to avoid situations which risk conflict and to rely instead on authoritarian decision-making modes. A possible side effect of conflict avoidance and a requirement for harmonic relationships is that decisions and policies are seldom challenged, or approached creatively, by the group. In such cultures, classified by us as *replicative*, system administrators, principals and schools may readily accept policies and edicts and tend towards preserving the status quo.

Hofstede (1991) and Trompenaars and Hampden-Turner (1997) suggest that cultures differ in their approach to change. Some societies tend to be more creative and innovative (termed *generative* in our model), while others seem to be more *replicative*. These differences find expression in the curriculum and schooling of different countries. In Australia there tends to be a reasonably high tolerance for change and people in schools take a proactive stance to engineer the effect of change on their work lives. Policy and operational changes are challenged, questioned and negotiated at the school level and outside. In other societies, change and uncertainty is accepted almost as a *coup de grâce*, as the way things are and are meant to be. For example, principals in countries such as Thailand and China which tend toward this fatalistic view, tend to rely on established philosophies, responsibilities and power relationships to provide staff with security, while accepting and implementing change, whether they agree with it or not (Hallinger et al., 1999).

Finally, in an insightful analysis of China, Bush and Qiang (2000) reveal how the Chinese culture has periodically undergone four phases of reform, each of which has left its mark on contemporary school leadership. First, the traditional culture, elements of which continue with respect for authority, collectivism and harmony in relationships. Second, the introduction of socialism after the Second World War which reaffirmed traditional values while at the same time politicising schools and the principal's role. A third – more recent phase – has seen an entrepreneurial spirit introduced as principals seek innovative ways to generate non-government sources of school income. Finally, as reported by Coleman et al. (1998), schools continue to reflect society at large in their unmistakable patriarchal nature.

Insights such as those presented above are illustrative of cultural influences on leadership practices. It is prudent, however, to resist making value judgements as part of any comparison, since cultures place different emphases on what they regard as effective practices.

While the application of the dimensions for cross-cultural comparison is capable of exposing interesting and worthwhile insights, it is only a starting point. Many issues remain outstanding in the construction of a cross-cultural comparative approach to leadership, some of which are briefly addressed towards the end of this chapter.

Educational leadership and the dimensions of organisational culture

Leaders are responsible for building and maintaining the organisational culture. In turn, the organisational culture is expressed through customs, traditions, ceremonies, rituals, norms, heroes and heroines that come to characterise each school. It is visible in words and actions as people go about their daily activities. Culture is a constructed reality, and as such, demands considerable thought, skill, integrity and consistency on the part of the leader to build and maintain in a way that connects (Dimmock, 2000) all members of the school community.

Clarifying the leader's role in building and maintaining organisational culture is but one aspect to be considered. Another equally important issue concerns the characteristics of the particular organisational culture to be cultivated. How can leaders and others identify the organisational culture they have, want or need? And is there a useful classification or taxonomy that presents the range or types of cultures to facilitate comparison? We address both of these questions below.

Research studies on the organisational cultures of companies have found large differences in their practices (symbols, heroes, rituals), but only minor differences in their values (Hofstede, 1995). Most of the variation in practices can be accounted for by six dimensions, although further validation of these is required. These six provide a useful baseline for organisational culture in our framework. We have, however, adapted the six, in line with our own research (Dimmock and Wildy, 1995). The six dimensions are as follows:

1 *Process- and/or outcomes-oriented*: leaders, along with their school communities, are instrumental in shaping the relative emphasis placed on process and outcome. Some cultures are predisposed towards technical and bureaucratic routines and processes, while others emphasise outcomes. Evidence suggests that in outcomes-oriented cultures people perceive greater homogeneity in practices, whereas people in process-oriented cultures perceive greater differences in their practices. Some schools are process-orientated, emphasising the processes and the skills of decision-making, and teaching and learning, while others are results-oriented, stressing learning achievements, such as examination results. Many schools and school systems are currently reforming their curricula to reflect specific student learning targets or outcomes expressed in terms of knowledge, skills and attitudes, indicating a trend towards designing curricula on the basis of, and measuring student and school performance by, a learning outcomes approach. Strong cultures tend to be more homogeneous and therefore results- or outcomes-oriented. It is easier to target outcomes than define effective processes.

2 *Task- and/or person-oriented*: leaders are influential in determining the blend of task and person emphasis in schools. In task-oriented organisational cultures, emphasis is placed on job performance and maximising productivity, while human considerations, such as staff welfare, take second place and may even be neglected. Conversely, person-oriented cultures accentuate the care, consideration and welfare of employees. Blake and Mouton (1964) recognised these leadership orientations in the 1960s. Applied to schools, a task-oriented culture exacts maximum work effort and performance out of its teachers in a relatively uncaring work environment. A person-oriented culture on the other hand, values, promotes and shows consideration for the welfare of its teachers. It is conceivable that some schools might score highly (or lowly) on both task and person orientations.

3 *Professional and/or parochial*: in professional cultures, qualified personnel identify primarily with their profession, whose standards are usually

defined at national or international level. In parochial cultures, members identify most readily with the organisation for which they work. Sociologists, such as Gouldner (1957) have long recognised this phenomenon in their distinction between locals and cosmopolitans. In regard to schools, some leaders and teachers, especially those with an external frame of reference, are primarily committed to the wider system context and to the teaching profession as a whole, while others with a strong internal frame of reference are more committed to the particular school in which they work.

4 *Open and/or closed*: this dimension refers to the ease with which resources, such as, people, money and ideas, are exchanged between the organisation and its environment. The greater the transfer and exchange of resources between the environment and the organisation, the more open the culture. Schools and their leaders vary between those which champion outside involvement in their affairs and maximum interchange with their environment, and those which eschew such interaction and communication, preferring a more closed, exclusive approach. Trends in education over the last decade have favoured the opening of school cultures, particularly to parental influence and involvement.

5 *Control and linkage*: an important part of organisational culture concerns the way in which authority and control are exerted and communicated between leaders and other members. This dimension has three sub-dimensions:

(a) *Formal–informal.* Organisations vary in the extent to which their practices are guided by rules, regulations and 'correct procedures' on the one hand, and the extent to which they reflect a more relaxed, spontaneous and intuitive approach on the other. Highly formalised organisations conform to the classic bureaucracies; they emphasise definition of rules and roles, they tend towards inflexibility and are often characterised by austere interpersonal relationships. By contrast, informal organisations have fewer rules dictating procedures, roles are often ill-defined, they display flexibility in their modes of work and interpersonal relationships tend to be more relaxed.

(b) *Tight–loose.* This gauges the degree to which members feel there is strong commitment to the shared beliefs, values and practices of an organisation. Such strong commitment might come through hierarchical supervision and control, or through members' own self-motivation. An organisation which has strong homogeneity and commitment in respect of its members' values and practices is tightly controlled (whether control is externally imposed by superordinates or self-imposed by employees). Conversely, a loosely controlled culture is one with only weak commitment to, or acceptance of, shared beliefs, values and practices, and little or no control is exerted to achieve homogeneity either by superordinates or by members themselves.

(c) *Direct–indirect.* This aspect captures the linkages and patterns of communication through which power, authority and decisions are communicated. In some organisations, managers assume direct personal responsibility to perform certain tasks and to communicate directly with their staff, often circumventing intermediate levels in the vertical hierarchy or chain of command. In other organisations, managers exert control indirectly by delegating to staff the tasks they would otherwise do themselves.

6 *Pragmatic and/or normative*: this dimension defines the way an organisation serves its clients, customers or patrons. Some display a flexible, pragmatic policy aimed at meeting the diversity of customer needs. Others exhibit more rigid or normative approaches in responding bureaucratically, failing to meet individual needs. This dimension measures the degree of client orientation. In the educational context, some schools consciously try to meet individual student needs by offering a more diversified curriculum with flexible timetables and alternative teaching strategies. They mould their educational services to meet student needs. Others may be less student focused, expecting them to fit into the agenda determined for them by the school. A school's mission and strategy as well as its leadership shapes its degree of pragmatism.

Challenges in conducting cross-cultural study of educational leadership

In pioneering new approaches there are bound to be imperfections, unresolved issues and many challenges (for a full discussion of these, see Walker and Dimmock, in press). The concept of culture itself, for example, has generated multiple definitions and ambiguities. Alone, it does not have the explanatory power to account for all the differences between schools in different societies or regions. As previously acknowledged, economic, political, religious and demographic factors, for example, may also play a key role, and their relationship to culture is equivocal.

A further challenge is the dynamic nature of many societal cultures as they become truly multicultural. Such cultural 'hybridity' increases the heterogeneity of cultures and creates as much divergence within them as between. A related issue concerns the tension between 'traditionalist' notions of culture (only those aspects which are enduring and historic are to count) and 'modernity' notions that are inclusive of recent changes.

A key challenge to researchers is the development of methodology and instrumentation to advance empirical study in the field of cross-cultural educational leadership. There is need for both quantitative and qualitative methods. Having developed a mixed-method approach, relying on survey, interview and vignette data collection, our own work is now at the stage of publishing the first empirical results comparing school leadership in Hong Kong, Singapore and Perth, Australia. Through further empirical studies, we hope to refine our instrumentation and methodology and thus the theory that we build. In conducting cross-cultural studies of leadership, there is a strong argument for the formation of cross-cultural research teams, which combine 'insider' and 'outsider' perspectives.

An important purpose of this chapter has been to signal the possibilities and prospects of future research in the field of cross-cultural research in educational leadership. The following questions are illustrative of promising directions for future research:

- To what extent is it appropriate to transpose policies and practices of school improvement from one society to another without consideration of cultural context?
- How do sets of dominant values and practices associated with cultures and sub-cultures affect the meanings attributed to the implementation of change in schools and school systems? What meanings do key concepts such as 'collaboration', 'micropolitics', 'school-based management' and 'accountability' have in different cultural settings?
- In what ways do societal cultures and sub-cultures influence the practice of school leadership? For example, what influence is culture on the relationships between the school and its environment, including parents, and processes within the school, such as appraisal, teamwork and shared leadership?
- How can the development of cross-cultural research and understanding in educational leadership and management inform the issues associated with multicultural schools within societies? For example, in what ways might an improved knowledge base on cross-cultural education have application to how multicultural schools can better understand and serve their diverse communities?
- To what extent can the development of cross-cultural research contribute to a better understanding of globalisation and its relationship to policy formation, adoption, implementation and evaluation?

Conclusion

The potential benefits of a cross-cultural comparative approach to educational leadership – for scholars and practitioners alike – are attractive and enticing. The justification for studying leadership from a societal and cross-cultural perspective is not solely based on improving our knowledge of the similarities and differences regarding school leadership and administration in other countries and systems. Rather, through adopting a cultural and cross-cultural 'lens', we can come to know more about our own systems of schooling, leadership and management.

Further reading

Dimmock, C. (2000) *Designing the Learning-Centred School: A Cross-Cultural Perspective*, London: Falmer Press.

Dimmock, C. and Walker. A. (guest eds) (2000) *School Leadership and Management*, 20 (2).

Walker, A. and Dimmock, C. (guest eds) (2000) *Asia Pacific Journal of Education*, 20 (2).

References

Adler, N. (1997) *International Dimensions of Organizational Behavior*, 3rd edn, Cincinnati, OH: South-Western College.

Blake, R. R. and Mouton, J. S. (1964) *The Managerial Grid*, Houston, TX: Gulf.

Bond, K. (1991) 'Cultural influences on modes of impression management: implications for the culturally diverse organisation', in R. Giacalone and P. Rosenfield (eds), *Applied Impression Management: How Image-Making Affects Managerial Decisions*, Newbury Park, CA: Sage.

Bush, T. and Qiang, H. (2000) 'Leadership and culture in Chinese education', *Asia Pacific Journal of Education*, 20 (2): 58–67.

Bush, T., Coleman, M. and Si, X. (1998) 'Managing secondary schools in China', *Compare*, 28 (2): 183–96.

Cardno, C. and Piggot-Irvine, E. (1997) *Effective Performance Appraisal: Integrating Accountability and Development in Staff Appraisal*, Auckland: Longman.

Cheng, K. M. (1998) 'Can educational values be borrowed? Looking into cultural differences', *Peabody Journal of Education*, 73 (2): 11–30.

Coleman, M., Qiang, H. and Li, Y. (1998) 'Women in educational management in China: Experience in Shaanxi province', *Compare*, 28 (2): 141–54.

Darling-Hammond, L. (1997) *The Right to Learn: A Blueprint for Creating Schools that Work*, San Francisco: Jossey-Bass.

Dimmock, C. (1998). 'Restructuring Hong Kong's schools: the applicability of Western theories, policies and practices to an Asian culture', *Educational Management and Administration*, 26 (4): 363–77.

Dimmock, C. (2000). *Designing the Learning-Centred School: A Cross-Cultural Perspective*, London: Falmer Press.

Dimmock, C. and Walker, A. (1998a) 'Towards comparative educational administration: the case for a cross-cultural, school-based approach', *Journal of Educational Administration*, 36 (4): 379–401.

Dimmock, C. and Walker, A. (1998b) 'Comparative educational administration: developing a cross-cultural conceptual framework', *Educational Administration Quarterly*, 34 (4): 558–95.

Dimmock, C. and Walker, A. (2000a) 'Developing comparative and international educational leadership and management: a cross-cultural model', *School Leadership and Management*, 20 (2): 143–60.

Dimmock, C. and Walker, A. (2000b) 'Globalisation and societal culture: re-defining school leadership in the twenty-first century', *Compare*, 30 (3): 303–12.

Dimmock, C. and Wildy, H. (1995) 'Conceptualising curriculum management in an effective secondary school', *The Curriculum Journal*, 6 (3): 297–323.

Goldring, E. and Rallis, S. (1993) *Principals of Dynamic Schools: Taking Charge of change*, Newbury Park, CA: Corwin Press.

Gouldner, A. (1957) 'Cosmopolitans and locals: toward an analysis of latent social roles – 1', *Administrative Science Quarterly*, 2: 291–306.

Hallinger, P. and Kantamara, P. (2000) 'Educational change in Thailand: Opening a window onto leadership as a cultural process', *School Leadership and Management*, 20 (2): 189–206.

Hallinger, P. Chantarapanya, P., Sriboonma, U. and Kantamara, P. (1999) 'The challenge of educational reform in Thailand: Jing Jai, Jing Jung, Nae Norn', in T. Townsend and Y. C. Cheng (eds), *Educational Change and Development in the Asia Pacific Region: Challenges for the Future*, Rotterdam: Swets and Zeitlinger.

Hofstede, G. H. (1991) *Cultures and Organisations: Software of the Mind*, London: McGraw-Hill.

Hofstede, G.H. (1994) 'Cultural constraints in management theories', *International Review of Strategic Management*, 5: 27–48.

Hofstede, G. H. (1995) 'Managerial values: the business of international business is culture', in T. Jackson (ed.), *Cross-Cultural Management*, Oxford: Butterworth-Heinemann.

Laurent, A. (1983) 'The cultural diversity of western conceptions of management', *International Studies of Management and Organization*, 13 (1–2): 75–96.

Maurer, R. (1991) *Managing Conflict: Tactics for School Administrators*, Boston: Allyn and Bacon.

McAdams, R. (1993) *Lessons from Abroad: How Other Countries Educate their Children*, Lancaster, PA: Technomic.

Morris, P. and Lo, M. L. (2000) 'Shaping the curriculum: contexts and cultures'. *School Leadership and Management*, 20 (2): 175–88.

Pounder, D. (ed.) (1998) *Restructuring Schools for Collaboration*, Albany, NY: University of New York Press.

Quong, T., Walker, A. and Stott, K. (1998) *Values-Based Strategic Planning: A Dynamic Approach for Schools*, Singapore: Prentice-Hall.

Trompenaars, F. and Hampden-Turner, C. (1997) *Riding the Waves of Culture*, 2nd edn, London: Nicholas Brealey.

Walker, A. and Dimmock, C. (1999) 'A cross-cultural approach to the study of educational leadership: an emerging framework', *Journal of School Leadership*, 9 (4): 321–48.

Walker, A. and Dimmock, C. (2000a) ' School principals' dilemmas in Hong Kong: sources, perceptions and outcomes', *Australian Journal of Education*, 44 (1): 5–25.

Walker, A. and Dimmock, C. (2000b) 'One size fits all? Teacher appraisal in a Chinese culture', *Journal of Personnel Evaluation in Education*, 14 (2): 155–78.

Walker, A. and Dimmock, C. (in press) 'Moving school leadership beyond its narrow boundaries: developing a cross-cultural approach', in K. Leithwood and P. Hallinger (eds), *Second International Handbook of Educational Leadership and Administration*, Dordrecht: Kluwer Academic.

Walker, A., Bridges, E. and Chan, B. (1996) 'Wisdom gained, wisdom given: instituting PBL in a Chinese culture', *Journal of Educational Administration*, 34 (5): 12–31.

6

Vision and Strategic Planning

Jacky Lumby

The compulsion to plan

Planning is a requirement in schools and colleges in many countries, including Hong Kong, Singapore and Australia (Quong et al., 1998). In the UK, even though not enshrined in legislation, the inclusion of development planning in Ofsted inspection and the linking of funding with planning in the learning and skills sector effectively compels schools and colleges to plan. Even where there is no formal requirement to produce a plan, current orthodoxy demands educational organisations demonstrate their managerial competence by production of long-term plans based on vision and/or mission. This partly follows from the greater degree of autonomy in educational institutions in many parts of the world which has led to a perceived need for each organisation to take responsibility for planning its future.

Literature related to vision and strategic planning in education spans a range of analysis offering contradictory views. The identified purposes of vision and strategic planning are diverse. Models of the process span a range from positing a rational, sequential process (FEDA, 1995) to theories which portray the activity as a much more diffuse cultural and intuitive evolution (Quong et al., 1998). It is suggested that strategic planning is critical for managing education effectively (West-Burnham, 1994), or alternatively, that it may be ineffective and therefore irrelevant or even a distraction from the essential business of improving teaching and learning (Bell, 1998). Planning can embody freedom, allowing institutions to shape the possibilities provided by greater autonomy. It can also be used as a vehicle for external control, where apparently greater 'autonomy' is actually constrained by the need for plans to be agreed or approved. Concepts of vision and strategic planning are apparently both embraced warmly by staff and greeted cynically and resisted. This chapter will address the plethora of diverse views in the literature to:

- consider the nature and place of vision and mission within strategic planning
- define strategic management and strategic planning

86

- explore the process of strategic planning
- relate approaches to strategic planning to educational management theoretical models.

Finally it will conclude on the question which matters most of all, whether strategic planning offers benefits to staff and to learners or not.

Vision and mission

The chapter opened by emphasising that strategic planning has become, in effect, compulsory. The inclusion of vision building is also, as Macbeath (1998: 4) states, '*de rigeur*'. The reason given for this is often that achieving a corporate vision is a practical necessity, in that if the changes mooted by planning are in contradiction to the values of those implementing them, they will not happen (Wideen, 1994).

Agreement on values is therefore an essential first step if planning is not to be merely a rhetorical activity. There are dissenting voices. Holder (1996) argues from a case study that the school in question got on quite effectively without an agreed vision. However, the dominant opinion appears to be that of Quong et al. (1998: 107) 'Planning for school improvement, we argue, must be based on the premise that schools have different values and that these values must be mapped before strategic intent can be determined.' This also appears to be an expectation from both internal and external customers. In a study of schools in England, Scotland and Denmark, teachers, parents and board members expected the principal to achieve vision, though the priority given to this varied amongst the groups and amongst the countries (Moos et al., 1998). The same expectation was strongly felt amongst parents and teachers in Australia (Dempster and Logan, 1998). The inclusion of teachers in the latter survey revealed that there is a professional expectation of vision building. Quong et al. (1998: 32) assert that in their work with principals based in Australasia, when asked what will ensure a successful future for their school, principals say 'you must have a vision'.

The words vision, mission and purposing are all used largely synonymously, even when purporting to differentiate amongst concepts. All three are seen to centre on values which are 'by their very nature, abstract, vague and subjective' (Kenny, 1994: 17), or 'general abstract ideas that guide thinking' (Warnet, 1994: 221). Thus vagueness and generality go with the territory. Vision itself is defined as:

some futuristic ideal, (to) some notion of how things could/should be, and reflect an aspired state of being for either an individual, an organisation, or society at large. (Kenny, 1994: 17)

goal-consensus. (Staessens and Vandenberghe, 1994: 192)

shared understanding, shared decision-making, shared evaluation. (Staessens and Vandenberghe, 1994: 199)

However, mission is very similarly defined, in the case of Jennings and Wattam (1998: 261) as 'the purpose and values of the organisation'. Perhaps the only distinction that can be suggested is that definitions of mission include the word 'direction' more often and therefore imply a greater degree of concreteness than vision. However, the distinction is not clear or consistent. The third term of purposing also appears to be in the same ball park. It is a 'continuous stream of actions by an organisation's formal leadership which has the effect of inducing clarity, consensus and commitment regarding the organisation's basic purposes' (Vaill, 1984, quoted in Warnet, 1994: 233).

Where the ongoing nature of the creation of vision or purpose is stressed, it is difficult to distinguish how the process may differ from that of cultural management, which also is concerned with managing or influencing 'a pattern of shared basic assumptions . . . (seen as) the correct way to perceive, think and feel' (Schein, 1997:12). Whether the process is termed vision-building, purposing or managing culture, the common element is the attempt to achieve some degree of shared principles or guiding assumptions. Senge categorises the degree as ranging from commitment, which is in his view rare, to apathy (Table 6.1).

The most that the majority of principals could hope for is enrolment. Many will have to settle for compliance. Such a typology is helpful in that many writers challenge the realism of achieving commitment, that is a vision shared and agreed by all. The recognition that staff may engage in different ways provides a more tenable description of the process.

Table 6.1 *Possible Attitudes toward a vision*

Commitment: Wants it. Will make it happen. Creates whatever 'laws' (structures) are needed.

Enrolment: Wants it. Will do whatever can be done within the 'spirit of the law'.

Genuine compliance: Sees the benefits of the vision. Does everything expected and more. Follows the 'letter of the law'. 'Good soldiers'.

Formal compliance: On the whole, sees the benefits of the vision. Does what's expected and no more. 'Pretty good soldier'.

Grudging compliance: Does not see the benefits of the vision. But, also, does not want to lose job. Does enough of what's expected because he has to, but also lets it be known that he is not really on board.

Noncompliance: Does not see the benefits of vision and will not do what's expected. 'I won't do it, you can't make me'.

Apathy: Neither for nor against vision. No interest. No energy. 'Is it five o'clock yet?'

Source: Senge (1990: 219–20)

How is shared vision achieved?

The responsibility for building a shared vision is often ascribed to the princi-pal. If vision may be not only a dream of what the institution could be like in the future, but also related to a wider aspiration of what the community or society could be, then the creation of a shared vision may relate to the leader's task to bequeath a legacy. De Pree (1999) distinguishes strategic planning and the concept of a legacy. The latter is longer term, passing on the values under-pinning relationships and a passionate care for the tasks of the organisation, and belongs uniquely to the most senior member of the organisation. However, even though the principal may lead in this process, it is clear that all staff share in the re-creation and adjustment of vision on a daily basis, by actions which embody or symbolise the shared values or assumptions. Staessens and Vandenberghe (1994) provide an illustration of this. They describe the staff of a Belgian primary school who, when asked about their school's vision, not only all identified the same three key ideas, but used the same sort of language to describe them and could be specific about the ways in which they translated the key ideas into actions within teaching and learning. Vision in this case was cre-ated through activity, not through awaydays or strategic planning meetings or consultation on documents. The activity was underpinned by daily informal discussion of what the teachers were doing and why. A principal of a further education college in England isolated the same component of the necessity to talk. Working in an underfunded and undervalued sector of education: 'It is actually about galvanising yourself into some conscious thought about what you are there to do. *You have to say things to yourself and to each other* if you are to be able to act purposefully', (Lumby, 1999: 75, original emphasis).

Rather than a formal process, or conceivably as well as formal processes, vision can be created by an ongoing informal dialogue which nudges under-standing towards greater congruence. In Senge's terms, this daily discussion may move staff from compliance to enrolment and even, sometimes, commit-ment. In this way rather than in Beare et al.'s (1989: 149) assertion that 'shared vision must pervade day-to-day activities', shared vision grows out of day-to-day activities and is constantly renegotiated through them.

In many educational organisations, the process does not accord at all with what has been described above. The vision or mission has been more formally derived through being written by senior management and, sometimes, sent out for consultation. The process is ineffective in influencing people. In the world of business and industry, Collins and Porras (1991: 30) aver 'most corporate statements we've encountered – be they called mission, vision, purpose, phi-losophy, credo or the company way – are of little value. They don't have the intended effect'. Similarly in education Murgatroyd and Morgan (1993) criti-cise the mission statement characterising it as not memorable, unlikely to pro-duce alignment, ambiguous and unlikely to inform daily action. In a review of the effectiveness of mission statements in schools in Singapore, Stott and Walker (1992) found they were vague, self-righteous and undifferentiated. Staff were often unclear about what was in them. The statements had little impact on the school's activities. Finally, they were evidently dishonest in proposing various platitudes as the aim of the institution when in fact the schools aimed above all to achieve the best possible examination results. The vagueness had an advantage in that it made it more difficult for any criticism to be levelled at the institution. If objectives are unclear, then it is difficult to conclude how far they have been achieved or not. Similarly, the espousal of acceptable if vague moral and social objectives served the useful purpose of shielding the professionally less acceptable aim to focus on academic results above all else. Clearly, the purpose of these mission statements was different to the orthodox model of aligning values and direction. The purpose was much more political.

Holder (1996: 9) asks whether shared vision is 'workable strategy' or 'an appealing myth'? The evidence presented in this section suggests that it spans the range. Shared vision-building is certainly expected. Its effects may be various, from a genuine force shaping teaching and learning to a political means of defusing criticism and disguising unpalatable truths. As a component of strategic planning vision building is therefore potentially a multi-purpose tool.

Strategic management and planning

Strategic management can be defined as the overarching process which includes strategic thinking, strategic planning, implementation and review. This chapter focuses on the relationship between vision/mission and planning. There are many definitions of strategy and strategic planning, containing a number of elements, including the purpose of planning, for example to chose a direction, to achieve commitment from staff and other stakeholders, and the process, selecting the means to move in the desired direction, perhaps involving staff, and then translating the choices into specific goals and actions to achieve them. All agree that the activity is one where managers lift their heads from day-to-day operational concerns and look forward in a longer timescale of anything from three to ten years to in some sense plan to secure a successful future for the institution. Thus some definitions emphasise simplicity: 'select a destination, figure out the best way of getting there, then explain how you know you have arrived' (Quong et al., 1998: 10). Others, in their incorporation of numerous elements, place an emphasis on the all-embracing nature of the process which touches every aspect of managing the organisation:

> a continuous process in administration which links goal-setting, policy-making, short-term and long-term planning, budgeting and evaluation in a manner which spans all levels of the organisation, secures appropriate involvement of people according to their responsibility for implementing plans as well as of people with an interest or stake in the outcomes of those plans, and provides a frame-

work for the annual planning, budgeting and evaluation cycle. (Caldwell and Spinks, quoted in Beare et al., 1992: 143)

Some definitions indicate an inward looking orientation, with the values of staff as the foundation for planning (West-Burnham, 1994). For others the process is essentially outward looking, positioning the school or college or university in relation to the external environment, particularly competitors (Jennings and Wattam, 1998). A synthesis of the range of definitions suggests that strategic planning may involve establishing values, analysing information on the external and internal environment, synthesising all of this to make choices about what is important to the organisation's future, translating such choices into the goals and the means to achieve them and finally linking the implications to every aspect of operational management, such as budgeting, staff development, etc. Most of the hortatory or prescriptive literature emanating from government, government agencies or donor bodies tends to be based on this holistic and essentially rational model.

However, there is also a debate about whether educational institutions are in any position to undertake strategic planning so defined. Public sector organisations are clearly in a different position from businesses, from which concepts and practice derive. Unlike a business, a school cannot choose to do something radically different. It has no equivalent of the choice of, for example, Virgin, in moving from the production and sale of music to running a travel operation in aeroplanes and trains. Educational institutions can make small choices, to emphasise this aspect of the curriculum or that, to add additional value through sporting or leisure activity, but these choices are marginal. It is questionable whether they can be genuinely seen as strategic. Their choices are constrained by legislation, by state funding, by the expectations of the community, by custom and practice. Their choice of customer is limited. Schools may be obliged legally and morally to provide for the local community, rather than trawling further afield. Even in non-compulsory vocational and higher education, the emphasis on inclusion and/or participation may compel institutions to enrol a defined range of students. Finally, schools particularly may not be equipped to undertake the environmental scanning exhorted in the literature. Even post-compulsory education, which might be assumed to have more resource and expertise in this area, may be constrained. A survey of technical colleges in South Africa discovered a desire to research the needs of employers and students better but no resource to do so (Lumby, 2000).

There exists, then, a dominant normative view of strategic planning, but its relevance to education and its existence in practice remain subject to doubt. The existing research highlights the wide range of purposes and approaches to planning, which only in part conform to the normative model.

The latter can be challenged on a number of grounds. First, in its emphasis on a rational process, beginning with aligning staff, it ignores the profound influence of micropolitical factors. Johnson (1993) and Ansoff and McDonnell (1990) posit that any plan for change will evoke a range of essentially political reactions from strong support to strong rejection. Strategic management, that is not only planning but achieving what is in the plan, will therefore inevitably involve a micropolitical process if it is to be successful. Second, no educational organisation plans in a static environment. The more turbulent the situation, the more plans laid one, two or more years ago, may lack relevance. Plans may need to change from the moment they are completed. Consequently a number of schools of thought have grown describing the process variously. Quong et al. (1998) list 10 different schools of thought, several of which do not envisage a linear relationship between plans and outcomes. Under one broad umbrella lie 'adaptive' definitions which construe planning and implementation as in some measure interactive with the environment in an ongoing way. Thus Mintzberg and Waters (1985) suggest strategy may be 'emergent' arising from the situation as it evolves rather than as the result of a decision at one point in time. Alternatively, Quinn (1980) uses the term 'logical incrementalism' to describe a process by which change is built not by implementing monumental plans, but by carefully constructing each step on the foundation of that which preceded it.

There is also a range of views on two further important factors, the basis of decision and how far all staff/stakeholders need to be involved. Particularly literature which offers guidance from the state or donor bodies tends to emphasise the rational basis of making choices, by gathering and analysing relevant factual data (FEDA, 1995). Others stress the place of intuition, that true strategic thinking is in short supply and involves the use of a creative process engaging both intuition and emotion as well as rational intellect (Ansoff and McDonnell, 1990; Ohmae, 1982). For some, the involvement of staff is axiomatic for success (FEDA, 1995). For others, the requirement to achieve 'ownership' is unrealistic (Holder, 1996). As Cowham (1992) reports, even within a single senior management team in one institution, the range of views on the most effective approach to strategic planning can span staff who are self-avowedly 'Stalinist' to those who believe it is more appropriate to adopt a collegial stance.

There are then a plethora of models of strategic planning. It may be that the models are strongly contingent and that what works well in an affluent, well-supported primary school in the Home Counties in England may not work at all in an African university torn by student protest and destabilised by deficit caused by student debt.

The nature of strategic planning

In the field of education, management is characterised by 'conceptual pluralism'. No one perspective on strategic planning is likely to aid managers to fully comprehend the activity in their own institution, let alone the range of practice throughout the world. The analysis in this chapter has shown strategic planning to operate on a number of platforms. First, it is clearly a bureaucratic process. Particularly when required by regional or national administration, or when required by those who may donate funds, the primary purpose of the activity will be to satisfy external bodies. It is evident that in many cases, without this compulsion, educational institutions would not engage with strategic planning at all. For example, those African universities most forward with strategic planning are those most heavily reliant on donor aid (Farrant and Afonso, 1997). The planning undertaken may invest much more effort in the operational than the strategic aspect, moving from the general and rather weakly formulated strategic corporate vision/mission and goals to a much more incisive and clear business plan or development plan. Such plans do work. As Mintzberg and Waters (1985: 320) point out 'deliberate strategies are more prevalent than emergent ones'. They warn about moving to a view which sees strategies as generally emergent in a turbulent world. Saying what you are going to do and then doing it is more common than imagined. A principal in a college in England found his college could be surprisingly accurate in estimating what they planned to do, based on their corporate goals (Lumby, 2001).

Strategic planning also operates on a political platform. The mission statements of schools in Singapore are a clear example of an aspect of planning which has little impact on activity in the school. Rather, the mission is used to provide an acceptable rhetoric, reassuring to administration and parents alike, that educational values are at the core. In parts of the world, such as Japan, where it is asserted that 'schools have become fact-grinding and knowledge-based institutions even at elementary level' (Sugimine, 1998: 121), a mission which paints a different picture of an orientation to develop the whole child may serve a characteristic political aim, the disguise or camouflage of reality. Less bleak may be the view of Warnet (1994) that the process of strategic planning provides a vehicle for the negotiation and accommodation of the different priorities and expectations of society, as embodied within the different stakeholder groups. Strategic planning in this sense is political in a positive way, much more than a bureaucratic process of providing an acceptable plan. It is a means of accommodating conflict and contradiction in the community's and wider society's aspirations for learners.

Finally, strategic planning functions on a cultural platform. Culture shifts constantly but the underlying shared assumptions are to some degree controlled by being coalesced within the plan. The latter becomes the means of supporting or blocking actions and requests for resources. If it is not in the plan, then it can be blocked. To some degree, therefore, the assumptions enshrined in the plan may have a greater impact or longevity than they would otherwise. The cultural process also relates to maintaining the emotional well being of the organisation. If the future may be unknowable and plans quickly inadequate, the mere fact of having thought about the future and tried to bring some control to its course may reassure, resulting in what Quong et al. (1998: 36) call 'a useful palliative'.

Linking vision and strategic planning

The debate on whether vision-building is an essential first step in strategic planning or is more properly seen as an ongoing simultaneous process is unnecessary. Values are dynamic and, therefore, will never reach a point of stasis. Consequently, even if there were an agreed set of values preceding planning, they would not remain stable. They will continue to be renegotiated and reconfirmed as part of the warp and weft of the organisation's shifting culture. A more pertinent point is how far it is possible to use the value base, as embodied in the vision, to shape concrete targets and goals. Sometimes the values may be such that it is relatively easy to make the link. For example, if a school is driven by a value of passing on a tradition of skills and culture to be an international centre of excellence in one field, for example the Royal Ballet School, the implications for the selection and education of pupils may be more easy to discern. However, values may often be more general and more difficult to link to particular paths of action. If an underpinning value is to respect all individuals, this provides only the most general of guidance and offers no basis for prioritising amongst what may be a host of possibilities. Does it imply developing individual tutorial systems, or focusing on equal opportunities initiatives, or focusing on interpersonal relations with anti-bullying policies etc.? Resources are unlikely to allow the institution to do all it wishes. How does the agreed value in this case guide planning? The answer may be that it does not to any great extent, being too vague, but may act as a weak filtering force. For example, a suggested target to increase the proportion of able students entering the institution would seem to be in contradiction to the value. In this sense the common sort of values agreed may exert a weak negative force rather than a strong positive one.

Attempts to link vision and strategy happen both at the inception of a plan, in trying to relate the targets and goals to the vision, and on an ongoing basis by asking staff to justify requests for resources or other operational activity by relating them to the strategic plan. In both cases, the result is often rather tenuous. In a study of the strategic plans of further education colleges in England, it was clear that plans attempted to follow the expected form of a statement of vision/mission followed by a sequential statement of plans, each level supplying more exact details than the last and relating to what has been stated previously (Lumby, 1999). The plans did not achieve this. It was difficult to discern how some of the more detailed actions specified in the final stages of the plan related to the vision or even to the corporate goals which were the next level down. The plan which is a paper representation of intended actions prefigured the same process in reality, with staff in departments unaware of and unaffected by the vision or corporate goals. Similarly, the attempt to link actions to vision and goals was problematic. In one study, staff had been asked to link their development needs to the strategic plan but found it difficult to do so consistently (Lumby, 1997a; 1997b). For example, managers felt the need to become more efficient at managing but they could not link this explicitly to the vision, which related to targeting particular markets and to aspects of teaching and learning.

In order to attract general agreement and support, the vision and its underpinning values need to be general. The more specific they become, the more they are likely to be in contradiction to the range of views of staff. Values are in any case, by definition 'abstract, vague and subjective' (Kenny, 1994). The potential for vision to provide guidance on choices and priorities is therefore limited. It may be that vision in action in many institutions may relate far more strongly to achieving a general sense of corporateness, a belief, justified or otherwise, in a degree of common aim. Vision building and maintaining provides a background wash which colours but does not shape strategic plans.

The impact on teaching and learning

Weick (1976) argues that educational organisations are loosely coupled. The degree of autonomy given to staff, the complexity of both the technology of teaching and learning and of the environment renders problematic any simple translation of intention or instruction into the planned outcome. This being the case, it is particularly hard to relate specific management activity to improvements in teaching and learning. Strategic planning is no exception. When the multiple purposes of the process, bearing in mind the different perspectives outlined in this chapter, are also taken into account, concluding whether strategic planning brings benefits for learners and educators is complex. There is evidence that the mere fact of undertaking the process makes staff *feel* more effective. In a survey of college principals in England, all the principals agreed that the process of strategic planning had resulted in:

- a greater sense of purpose
- an increased feeling of independence
- a benchmark against which decisions could be measured
- better systems and efficiency
- better communication as there was something important to communicate (Lumby, 1999: 81).

There are other examples where the process of planning had led staff in schools to feel similarly purposeful and committed (Staessens and Vandenberghe, 1994; Warnet, 1994). Equally, there are examples where strategic planning is undertaken which has little or no impact (Quong et al., 1998; Thomas, 1998). The impact of planning is obviously contingent on a wide range of factors. First, what should be the primary source of support, the state, is often the most acutely felt barrier. The frequent changes in government policy are clearly seriously impeding planning in the UK and other parts of the world (Lumby, 2000; 2001; Wallace, 1992). Staff capacity and resource vary, particularly the resource of time. Lieberman and Miller detail the many frustrations of principals in American schools:

- They ought to show concern for individual problems and individual growth; but because they were in charge of the whole school, they had to sacrifice personal vision for a more pragmatic view.
- They ought to do long-range thinking but frequently they had to make short-range, even instantaneous, decisions to keep small brush fires from becoming conflagrations.
- They ought to be colleagues; but often they were bosses.
- They ought to be innovators; but they were maintaining the status quo.
- They ought to be champions of ideas: in reality they were masters of the concrete, paying attention to detail before worrying about abstractions (Lieberman and Miller, 1999: 40).

Many thousands of miles away in South Africa the same conditions prevail. As Van der Westhuizen and Legotlo (1996: 74) state, 'Most of the black schools have their mission statements buried beneath a pile of problems'. The question is therefore not only has strategic planning provided benefits for learners and staff but also what is its potential? If governments could be persuaded to cease the rain of changing policies, for example, would the potential benefit increase? At the moment the process appears to be bringing a range of possible benefits contingent on the environment. These include:

- securing staff engagement with the purpose of the institution
- reassuring staff in an uncertain world
- acting as a symbol of managerial competence
- directing choices
- delineating actions
- providing a vehicle to negotiate and accommodate conflict or contradictions in the wishes and expectations of different groups
- providing political camouflage.

Jennings and Wattam (1998) provide a table (Table 6.2) of the differences between current practice/assumptions in strategic planning and a proposed future approach.

Rather than seeing this dichotomy as the past and the future, the evidence reviewed suggests that the two columns in Table 6.2 may represent parallel

Table 6.2 *Chaos: a new framework for strategic management*

Today's frame of reference	A new frame of reference
Long-term future is predictable to some extent.	Long-term future is unknowable.
Visions and plans are central to strategic management.	Dynamic agendas of strategic issues are central to effective strategic management.
Vision: a single shared organisation-wide intention, a picture of a future state.	Challenge: multiple aspirations, stretching and ambiguous. Arising out of current ill-structured and conflicting issues with long-term consequences.
Strongly shared cultures.	Contradictory countercultures.
Cohesive teams of managers operating in a state of consensus	Learning groups of managers, surfacing conflict, engaging in dialogue, publicly testing assertions.
Decision-making as a purely logical, analytical process.	Decision-making as exploratory, experimental process based on intuition and reasoning by analogy.
Long-term control and development as the monitoring of progress against planned milestones.	Control and development in open-ended situations as a political process.
Constraints provided by rules, systems and rational argument.	Constraints provided by need to build and sustain support. Control as self-policing and learning.
Strategy as the realisation of prior intent.	Strategy as spontaneously emerging from the chaos of challenge and contradiction, through a process of real-time learning and politics.
Top management drives and controls strategic direction.	Top management creates favourable conditions for complex learning and politics.
General mental models and prescriptions for many specific situations.	New mental models required for each new strategic situation.
Adaptive equilibrium with the environment.	Non-equilibrium, creative interaction with the environment.

Source: Jennings and Wattam (1998: 323)

processes currently in operation and likely to continue as such. As far back as 1987, Garrat framed the process of successful change as dealing with questions of who knows, who cares and who can. The process of strategic planning will continue to deal with gathering relevant information, but also with the need to establish 'care' to achieve commitment. It will also add details of who can, who is responsible, what are their resources and timescales and targets. As such the process will remain both rational and political, preplanned and emergent. A metaphor which perhaps captures strategic planning in the twenty-first century is the flight of a rocket into space. It is guided by the best knowledge and technology that can be provided and its course is carefully charted. At the same time it is a leap of faith into what is essentially unknown. The goal may be to increase our knowledge of the universe, but equally to increase the prestige of the country which launched it. It may get to the target planet, star or universe, or not. Just as humans cannot envisage ceasing to attempt such flight, educational managers, whatever the problems and weakness in the process of strategic planning, cannot abandon the attempt. No change is no option. Nor is there any option but to attempt to impose order on change, through agreeing a vision of the future and strategically planning to reach the desired destination.

Further reading

Fidler, B. (1996) *Strategic Planning for School Improvement*, London, Pitman.
Smith, C., Gidney, M., Barclay, N. and Rosenfeld, R. (2002) 'Dominant logics of strategy in FE colleges', *Research in Post-Compulsory Education*, 7 (1).
Staessens, K. and Vandenberghe, R. (1994) 'Vision as a core component in school culture', *Journal of Curriculum Studies*, 26: 187–200.

References

Ansoff, H. I. and McDonnell, E. J. (1990) *Implanting Strategic Management*, 2nd edn, Englewood Cliffs, NJ: Prentice-Hall.
Beare, H., Caldwell, B. and Millikan, R. (1989) *Creating an Excellent School*, London: Routledge.
Beare, H., Caldwell, B. and Millikan, R. (1992) 'A model for managing an excellent school', in N. Bennett, M. Crawford and C. Riches (eds), *Managing Change in Education*, London: Paul Chapman Publishing.
Bell, L. (1998) 'From symphony to jazz: the concept of strategy in education', *School Leadership and Management*, 18 (4): 449–60.
Collins, C. and Porras J. I. (1991) 'Organizational vision and visionary organizations', *California Management Review*, Fall: 30–52.
Cowham, T. (1992) 'Strategic planning in the changing external context', in N. Bennett, M. Crawford and C. Riches (eds), *Managing Change in Education*, London: Paul Chapman Publishing.
De Pree, M. (1999) 'The leader's legacy', in F. Hesselbein and P. Cohen (eds), *Leader to Leader*, San Francisco: Jossey-Bass.
Dempster, N. and Logan, L. (1998) 'Expectations of school leaders: an Australian picture', in J. MacBeath (ed.), *Effective School Leadership: Responding to Change*, London: Paul Chapman Publishing.
Farrant, J. and Afonso, L. (1997) 'Strategic planning in African universities', *Higher Education Policy*, 10 (1): 23–30.

FEDA (1995) *Implementing College Strategic Plans*, London: FEDA.

Garrat, B. (1987) *The Learning Organization and the Need for Directors Who Think*, London: Fontana.

Holder, B. (1996) 'Is blurred vision healthier?', *Management in Education*, 10 (3): 8–9.

Jennings, D. and Wattam, S. (1998) *Decision Making: An Integrated Approach*, 2nd edn, London: Pitman.

Johnson, G. (1993) 'Processes of managing strategic change', in C. Mabey and B. Mayon-White (eds), *Managing Change*, 2nd edn, London: Paul Chapman Publishing.

Kenny, T. (1994) 'From vision to reality through values', *Management Development Review*, 7 (3): 17–20.

Lieberman. A. and Miller, L. (1999) *Teachers Transforming their World and their Work*, New York: Teachers College Press.

Lumby, J. (1997a) 'Developing managers in further education. Part 1: the extent of the task', *Journal of Further and Higher Education*, 21 (3): 357–66.

Lumby, J. (1997b) 'Developing managers in further education. Part 2: the process of development', *Journal of Further and Higher Education*, 21 (3): 367–75.

Lumby, J. (1999) 'Strategic planning in further education: the business of values', *Educational Management and Administration*, 27 (1): 71–83.

Lumby, J. (2000) 'Technical colleges in South Africa: planning for the future', *Journal of Vocational Education and Training*, 52 (1): 101–18.

Lumby, J. (2001) *Managing Further Education: Learning Enterprise*, London: Paul Chapman Publishing.

MacBeath, J. (1998) 'Seven selected heresies of leadership', in J. MacBeath, (ed.), *Effective School Leadership: Responding to Change*, London: Paul Chapman Publishing.

Mintzberg, H. and Waters, J.A. (1985) 'Of strategies deliberate and emergent', *Strategic Management Journal*, 6: 257–72.

Moos, L., Mahoney, P. and Reeves, J. (1998) 'What teachers, parents, governors and pupils want from their heads', in J. MacBeath (ed.), *Effective School Leadership: Responding to Change*, London: Paul Chapman Publishing.

Murgatroyd, S. and Morgan, C. (1993) *Total Quality Management and the School*, Buckingham: Open University Press.

Ohmae, K. (1982) *The Mind of the Strategist*, London: McGraw-Hill.

Quinn, J. B. (1980) *Strategies for Change: Logical Incrementalism*, Homewood, IL: Irwin.

Quong, T., Walker, A. and Stott, K. (1998) *Values-Based Strategic Planning*, Singapore: Simon and Schuster.

Schein, E. H. (1997) *Organizational Culture and Leadership*, 2nd edn, San Francisco: Jossey-Bass.

Senge, P. (1990) *The Fifth Discipline: The Art and Practice of the Learning Organization*, London: Century Business.

Staessens, K. and Vandenberghe, R. (1994) 'Vision as a core component in school culture', *Journal of Curriculum Studies*, 26 (2): 187–200.

Stott, K. and Walker, A. (1992) 'The nature and use of mission statements in Singaporean schools', *Educational Management and Administration*, 20 (1): 49–57.

Sugimine, H. (1998) 'Primary schooling in Japan', in J. Moyles and L. Hargreaves (eds), *The Primary Curriculum: Learning from International Perspectives*, London: Routledge.

Thomas, H. (1998) 'Developing a strategic plan: a case study from the National University of Lesotho', *Higher Education Policy*, 11: 235–43.

Van der Westhuizen, P. and Legotlo, M. (1996) 'Perceptions of skills for beginning school principals', *South African Journal of Education*, 16 (2): 69–74.

Wallace, M. (1992) 'Flexible planning: a key to the management of multiple innovations', in N. Bennett, M. Crawford and C. Riches (eds), *Managing Change in Education*, London: Paul Chapman Publishing.

Warnet, M. (1994) 'Towards clarification in determining school strategy', *School Organisation*, 14 (2): 219–33.

Weick, K. (1976) 'Educational organisations as loosely coupled systems', *Administrative Science Quarterly*, 21 (1): 1–19.

West-Burnham, J. (1994) 'Strategy, policy and planning', in T. Bush and J. West-Burnham (eds), *The Principles of Educational Management*, Harlow: Longman.

Wideen, M. F. (1994) *The Struggle for Change: The Story of One School*, London: Falmer Press.

Section III
Human Resource Management

7
Professional Development and Professionalism
Ray Bolam

Introduction

Professional development is widely accepted as fundamental to the improvement of organisational performance and, therefore, as a core task of management and leadership. That this is also true for school management is evident from the importance attached to teachers' professional development over several decades by the member countries of the Organisation for Economic Cooperation and Development (e.g. OECD, 1982; 1998; 2001). In addition, one distinctive, though by no means unique, feature of teacher development is its focus on an occupational group whose professional status and conditions of service vary between countries and, indeed, over time in any one country. The problematic and changing nature of their work and professionalism is, therefore, an important underlying consideration for all those concerned with managing the development of teachers.

The aim of this chapter is to consider the implications for school leadership and management of selected recent developments in theory, research, policy and practice in teachers' professional development and professionalism. Although they raise many related issues, studies on induction (e.g. Tickle, 2000) and leadership development (e.g. Leithwood and Hallinger, 2002) are not dealt with, largely because they are now so extensive. Although some reference is made to selected international studies, the chapter focuses on experience in England and Wales. This is largely because many key issues relevant to the concerns of this book – autonomy, accountability, teaching and learning, strategy and partnerships – are well exemplified in that experience.

The working definition of professional development adopted in this chapter is that it is:

- an ongoing process of education, training, learning and support activities
- taking place in either external or work-based settings
- proactively engaged in by qualified, professional teachers, headteachers and other school leaders
- aimed primarily at promoting learning and development of their professional knowledge, skills and values

- to help them to decide on and implement valued changes in their teaching and leadership behaviour
- so that they can educate their students more effectively
- thus achieving an agreed balance between individual, school and national needs.

However, as we shall see, this definition is far from being unproblematic.

External changes

Perhaps the most powerful recent influences on the management of professional development and professionalism have been those generated by the extensive national reforms introduced in many countries during the 1990s. School leaders increasingly work in a political context in which external, 'restructuring' changes, initiated by national, state or local authorities to raise standards of achievement, exert priority over their own vision of desirable improvements. Their dilemma is, therefore, how to manage the implementation of an onerous external change agenda while simultaneously trying to promote school-initiated improvement and the associated professional development.

The nature and extent of this dilemma necessarily varies according to the situation in each school and with the content and scope of the national reforms. For example, while many countries decentralised school management tasks to the local or school levels, in England and Wales the redistribution of power was more complex. Schools gained some powers but local authorities lost many powers which were centralised to national level (Karstanje, 1999). Some countries, like Hungary (Balazs, 1999) and England and Wales (Whitty, 1997), introduced forms of neo-liberal deregulation, notably the promotion of increased competition between schools, in the belief that quasi-market mechanisms would promote quality improvement; others, like Norway and Spain (Bolam et al., 2000), did not. Nevertheless, many countries adopted the same broad 'steering' strategies, often based on dedicated or categorical funding, to couple professional development tightly to the implementation of their reform policies. Indeed, this approach has probably become the dominant paradigm for systemic change in OECD member countries (Halasz, 2000).

Compared to most other OECD countries, the approach in England and Wales was noteworthy for the sheer scale and scope of the post-1986 reform programme, which covered all 25,000 schools in the country. In summary, the main features of the reforms relevant to the theme of this chapter were as follows: local management of schools (LMS) (i.e. site-based management) with school level control over delegated budgets, pupil recruitment, strategic policy and planning, the hiring and firing of staff, staff development and buildings; the introduction of a quasi-market or regulated market in which parents as customers/consumers exercise choice and schools as providers compete for custom (i.e. pupil numbers); substantial increases in the powers of central government and reductions in the powers of local education authorities (LEAs); the introduction of: a national curriculum and national testing; regular external inspections by a 'privatised' inspectorate; strengthened accountability mechanisms; government-imposed, national salary scales, conditions of service, career-ladders and appraisal, for all teachers and head teachers; an extended role for schools in initial teacher training which requires all training institutions to pay for training places and mentor support in their 'partner' schools; and the funding of selected schools to run school-based initial teacher training schemes themselves, buying in help from universities as necessary. Since May 1997, the Labour government has continued with much of the reform thrust of its predecessors but its policy emphasis has shifted away from marketisation to focus on the control of inputs, processes and outputs. Its main initiatives include the imposition of so-called 'tough targets' and the introduction, in primary schools, of literacy and numeracy schemes in which teaching time, content and pedagogy are specified.

These reforms resulted in extensive and radical changes in the roles and responsibilities of headteachers, other senior staff and teachers in general in what was, in effect, a cultural shift in schools and the teaching profession. Weindling (1999) reported that 90 per cent of a cohort of British secondary headteachers said their role had changed significantly over the previous five years while a European study found that Welsh heads were much more likely than their counterparts in The Netherlands, Norway and Spain to see government reforms as causing them substantial problems (Bolam et al., 2000). The reforms also resulted in the creation of new managerial posts associated with the national curriculum and assessment. The roles of existing heads of subject departments were also extended. For example, a head of mathematics in a secondary school may now be responsible for managing a devolved budget, including a component for professional development. They play a major role in the inspection process, are often responsible for staff appraisal and development and, latterly, for the new performance management and pay scheme. Their accountability for the performance of their department is also much more explicit and they are now held accountable for students' standard achievement tests (SATs) targets and examination results.

Changes in teachers' workloads and motivation are also evident. Campbell and Neill (1994) reported that their sample of 384 secondary school teachers, on average, worked 54.5 hours each week during term time, seven and a half hours per week more than for their 1978 sample, an increase which they concluded was largely due to the impact of the reforms. Comparing their findings with those for other countries and occupations, they concluded that their sample of teachers: 'actually work significantly longer hours than most other non-manual and manual workers in Great Britain and Europe' (ibid.: 68).

Although there are considerable financial incentives for teachers to apply for senior management positions – headteachers can earn up to five times the salary of a beginning teacher – teachers are less motivated to apply for promotion to deputy headships and headships and other posts carrying extra responsibilities. The number of such vacancies is increasing, mainly due to early retirements caused by stress, ill health and workload pressure, all of which are also having a negative impact on teachers' motivation and morale (School Teachers' Review Body, 1996: 15; Travers and Cooper, 1996). Teacher retention has also been negatively affected: up to 40 per cent of teachers with three years' experience now leave the profession. According to the Chief Inspector of Schools, if this situation is to be remedied, 'A careful look at the bureaucratic demands on teachers and a reduction in those at all levels was essential' (Smithers, 2001).

This experience is not unique to Britain. In New Zealand, teachers also reported high levels of stress and a decline in morale (Whitty, 1997: 305). In a similar vein, a comparative study of teachers' experience in Australia, New Zealand, the UK and the USA refers to the 'erosion of the profession', key features of which include decreased status, external interference, excessive change and increased workload (Scott et al., 2000).

Professional development

The centrality of teachers' work and professional development to the management tasks of headteachers is evident from international research and experience. For example, approximately 700 new, primary and secondary headteachers in five European countries were asked about the extent to which certain tasks or issues were a problem for them. The following were rated as a 'serious or very serious problem': 'ineffective teachers' by 40 per cent of respondents; 'getting teachers to accept new ideas' by 33 per cent; 'promoting professional development' by 25 per cent; and 'regular formal appraisal of teachers' by 20 per cent (Bolam et al., 2000: 28). The links between professional development and changing notions of professionalism and accountability were also apparent. Thus, in The Netherlands, 'promoting professional development' posed particular problems, apparently because of:

> the tradition of teachers' professional freedom in determining whether or not they take part in such activities. With the introduction of greater autonomy for schools and school level control of funding for professional development, there has been a greater need for consistent school policies in this area. Teachers' traditional autonomy has posed problems for Dutch headteachers wishing to introduce a policy on professional development. (Karstanje, 2000: 30)

More generally, professional development is also accepted as being 'central to the way principals manage schools, in at least two respects: first, as instructional leaders, principals may be expected to coordinate professional progression of their staff; second, they need to manage the learning community as a whole, using development as part of school change' (OECD, 2001: 27).

Approaches to professional development have varied considerably between countries over the past 20 years and continue to do so (OECD, 1982; 1998). The dominant paradigm in England and Wales, from the 1960s through to the early 1980s, gave primacy to the needs of individual professionals. Developments in national policy and in the financing of professional development in the mid-1980s changed this situation dramatically (Bolam, 1993). The most important changes included the introduction of five compulsory training days for all teachers; the creation of a regulated-market in which schools received annual funding to provide and buy training and consultancy services; a framework of national priority topic areas linked to the national reforms; a substantial reduction in the capacity of local authorities to deliver training; a substantial increase in the number of professional associations and unions, private trainers and consultants, and other commercial agencies offering training; more flexible, market-driven, university-based, Master's-level provision (e.g. modularisation, credit transfer and accumulation, accreditation of prior learning and experience, professional development profiles, distance and open learning programmes); and a substantial increase in the number of taught doctorates, especially the education doctorate.

The intended model of professional development consequential on these changes can be characterised roughly as follows. Self-developing, reflective teachers, in self-managing schools with devolved funding and five training days, design, implement and evaluate professional development programmes aimed at meeting an appropriate balance of individual teacher, school and national needs and priorities. However, research evidence from England and Wales indicates that the actual impact on professional development and professionalism was somewhat different from the intended model.

McMahon (1999) reported on a study based on a sample of teachers in 66 secondary schools in four English LEAs. She found that the operation of the in-service training market was substantially influenced by two major sets of factors – geographical location and the size of individual continuing professional development (CPD) budgets. Rural schools had poorer access to provision than their urban counterparts and some schools had three times as much money as others. The five training days were most often used for administrative purposes (e.g. departmental planning) and in any case were based on needs derived from the schools' development plan; only 28 per cent of schools allocated any of these days for individual professional development needs. The aims and content of all training activities were primarily driven by the national reform agenda with most activities taking the form of short training courses which, as research has demonstrated over the years (GTC Trust, 1993), are weak at promoting sustained change. McMahon concluded that this tendency for the training agenda to be centrally determined was increased by two factors: first, the government's emphasis on training teachers to meet the numeracy and literacy targets; second, the policy of linking the funding for university courses to national priorities, as a result of which several lost their funding. These findings, which are broadly consistent with earlier research, indicate that the notion of site-based management of professional development within a regulated market did not operate widely in practice. Rather, the professional development agenda was determined largely by the needs of centrally imposed reforms and by the needs of the schools and departments to implement them. This left little scope, given their limited resources and access to provision, for schools to meet the professional development needs of individual teachers, with obvious implications for teacher professionalism.

Emerging policies have acknowledged the importance of these issues by increasing investment in professional development for individual teachers (DfEE, 2000). Two examples are worth highlighting. First, professional bursaries are being paid directly to teachers to help them achieve their individual career goals, for example by studying for a Master's degree. Second, £3million is being allocated for individual Research Scholarships, again to be paid directly to teachers, to carry out research in partnership with a university and other schools.

Some contemporary trends

Certain key trends are currently affecting both professional development and teacher professionalism in many countries. They often take the form of a 'modernisation' or 're-structuring' strategy and can be far-reaching in their effects. Thus, in Norway a 'New Employment Agreement' was introduced in the mid-1990s. Although a new pay structure was at its heart, its main aim was to facilitate the introduction of new school policies by promoting teamwork, flexibility and the development of teaching competencies (Jordet, 2000: 85). In this section, four important developments are highlighted.

First, a number of countries have introduced national *standards of professional practice* for teachers and headteachers. One of the first examples was in the USA where the National Board of Professional Teacher Standards (NBPTS) developed standards and assessment procedures for 30 subject areas based on five principles:

- Teachers are committed to students and their learning.
- Teachers know the subject they teach and how to teach those subjects to students.
- Teachers are responsible for managing and monitoring students' learning.
- Teachers think systematically about their practice and learn from experience.
- Teachers are members of learning communities (NBPTS, 1993).

According to Fullan (2001: 257), there is some evidence that this is producing positive outcomes.

In England and Wales, the Teacher Training Agency (TTA) introduced a comprehensive 'national curriculum' framework for initial and in-service teacher education, including head teacher training, which was tightly coupled to the strategies of successive governments for raising standards and school improvement. The framework for professional development was based on four sets of national standards for newly qualified teachers, special needs teachers, subject leaders and headteachers. The Standards for Qualified Teacher Status are presented in four sections:

1 Knowledge and understanding (i.e. of subject matter).
2 Planning teaching and class management.
3 Monitoring, assessment, recording, reporting and accountability.
4 Other professional requirements (TTA, 1998a).

The equivalent set for subject leaders is in five parts:

1 Core purposes of the subject leader.
2 Key outcomes of subject leadership.
3 Professional knowledge and understanding.
4 Skills and attributes.
5 Key areas of subject leadership (TTA, 1998b).

At present there is little research evidence about the usage or impact of these standards. Those for newly qualified teachers are used in initial training but their use in schools beyond that is unclear. Those for headteachers are used in the assessment for the National Professional Qualification for Headteachers but their use for headteacher appointments or in-service training is unclear. The extent to which those for subject leaders are used is also unclear.

A second emerging feature of the 'modernisation' strategy in several countries is *performance management and performance-related pay*. In the USA, various types of schemes are being tried (Pecori, 2000). The scheme in England and Wales requires those wishing to go beyond a pay threshold to engage in a rigorous assessment process which itself is rooted in a new annual appraisal system for all teachers. The scheme is currently being implemented following considerable, but by no means united, opposition from teachers' associations, some of whom argued that teacher accountability for student outcomes dominates the system. To the surprise of many, the take-up by teachers of the opportunity to cross the 'threshold' has been high. However, experience and research on the management of change tell us that such complex and controversial innovations are often jeopardised in the medium to longer-term process of implementation. Specifically, problems are likely to arise in two areas. First, the scheme is labour intensive, logistically complex and expensive to operate. Second, the costs of the threshold payments are initially being funded centrally. How far schools will be able to sustain the system when they have to pay for it from their own budgets remains to be seen: the early signs are that it is likely to be too expensive. Third, and more fundamentally, it runs the serious risk of being counterproductive and non-cost-effective in terms of achieving its strategic objectives if, as many have predicted, performance-related pay proves to be professionally divisive. The government proposes that each school should become a learning organisation, which it defines as: 'an organisation in which learning is a continuing, strategically used process, integrated with and running parallel to core activities and where interactions with other organisations and communities are perceived to be further opportunities for learning' (DfEE, 2000, para. 9).

Research and experience both indicate that a collaborative professional culture is a *sine qua non* for a learning organisation engaged in ongoing improvement. For example, Gray et al. (1999) concluded that improving schools, 'had found ways of facilitating more discussion among colleagues about classroom issues than hitherto' (ibid.: 144). The contradictions between these findings and the potentially divisive consequences of performance-related pay are clear. In a North American context, Fullan (2001) endorses the conclusion that effective schools have established professionally collaborative cultures. He points out, 'Certainly individual merit pay, career ladders and similar schemes have failed miserably' (ibid.: 258).

Third, in England, and elsewhere, there is an increasing focus on *evidence-informed practice* as a means of promoting school improvement, professional development and for teacher professionality (Hoyle and John, 1995). A major part of its rationale is the belief that teaching ought to emulate medicine and aim to be a research-informed profession (Hargreaves, 1996). Three broad, interconnected approaches are open to school leaders who wish to promote evidence-informed practice. They can:

- promote systematic research and evaluation in the school, in departments and by individual classroom teachers
- adopt a more systematic approach to the collection, analysis and use of 'routine' data, for example, in relation to students' examination results, value-added data and external school inspection reports
- search for and use externally generated research.

The first mode is well established in action research but the second is becoming more common. George (1998) reported an evaluation of a project in which 42 small schools used value-added data to plan specific follow-up action. Myers (1996) reported on a school improvement project in eight secondary schools, which involved teachers as action researchers. Joyce et al. (1999) proposed a model of improvement based on the school as a centre of inquiry 'which involves the collection and analysis of data and reflection on it' (ibid.: 12) and explored their model in a series of rigorous case studies. Southworth and Conner (1999) presented a rationale for evidence-based management together with practical guidelines and case studies. Financial support for teachers wishing to engage in these two modes is now available from government (TTA, 1999). The rationale for the third mode is the belief that practitioners should have access to high quality research and should use it to inform their decisions and actions. A government-funded research unit is promoting the use of systematic reviews of research as its central methodology for building up robust knowledge to inform practice (EPPI, 2000). It is committed to the involvement of users and practitioners from the design to dissemination stages of systematic reviews

None of these modes is unproblematic. For example, Dudley (1999) highlighted the difficulties faced by teachers when they try to use data to improve their teaching. Similarly, Chapman (1995), in a headteacher's perspective, reported on two pieces of action research, both of high quality, conducted at a secondary school. The first, by a head of department, was well received and acted upon. The second, by a trainer, was not. He concluded that a collaborative approach is likely to be most effective and that it is the head teacher's job to create the conditions for this to take place. There is evidence (e.g. Joyce et al., 1999; Sebba, 1997) to suggest that the strategy may work and that it deserves further exploration as a means of promoting professional development, the school as a learning organisation and school improvement.

This links directly with the fourth trend – the emerging importance of the idea of schools as *professional learning communities*. The concept of a professional learning community is informed by literature about what it is to be a professional, adult learning and the meaning of community. A new form of professionalism is emerging in which teachers work more closely and collaboratively with colleagues, students and parents, linking teacher and school development (Hargreaves, 1994; Stoll et al., in press). Thus, King and Newmann (2001), argue that teacher learning is most likely to occur when teachers:

- can concentrate on instruction and student outcomes in the specific contexts in which they teach
- have sustained opportunities to study, to experiment with and to receive helpful feedback on specific innovations
- have opportunities to collaborate with professional peers, both within and outside their schools, along with access to the expertise of researchers.

Similarly, in the USA, Smylie (1995) drew upon a range of adult learning theories to identify conditions of effective workplace learning, including opportunities for teachers to learn from peer colleagues in collaborative group work settings, with open communication, experimentation and feedback. The community focus emphasises mutually supportive relationships and the development of shared norms and values whereas the focus in the literature about professionals and professionalism is towards the acquisition of knowledge and skills, orientation to clients and professional autonomy (Louis et al., 1995).

To some extent these developments are rooted in earlier ideas on school-focused in-service training as a mechanism for promoting school improvement (Fullan, 2001: 255; OECD, 1982: 20). The attractiveness of these ideas is explained by recognising the power of teachers' practicality ethic. Moreover, they find support from more specific theories like experiential learning (Kolb, 1975), reflective practice, (Schön, 1987), process knowledge (Eraut, 1994), cognitive and problem-based professional learning (Grady et al., 1995; Leithwood et al., 1995) and professional socialisation.

Discussion and conclusion

The implications of these developments and issues for autonomy, accountability, teaching and learning, strategy and partnerships are manifold and interconnected. The following are among the most important. First, there is a continuing need for better evaluations focused on outcomes and impact measures and directed as closely as possible at student learning. It is salutary to note how few published evaluation studies about continuing professional development make any reference to impact on teacher behaviour or student learning outcomes. The simple explanation is that researchers in universities and elsewhere have simply not carried out enough robust studies. However, the underlying reason is that such evaluations have been acknowledged as problematic for some time (GTC Trust, 1993) for, as Guskey points out: 'Because of the powerful and dynamic influence of context, it is impossible to make precise statements about the elements of an effective professional development programme' (Guskey, 1995: 117–18). Yet such evaluations are certainly possible, as Joyce et al. (1999) for example, have demonstrated.

Second, some issues are new, or at least have taken on a new significance in the changing political climate. In particular, it is worth noting that many analysts have located them within a broader theoretical framework – that of managerialism or new public management (NPM). This concept was adapted from the private sector (Ferlie et al., 1996; Levačić, 1999) and applied across the public sector in health, social services and housing. In education, its main features include increased centralisation of decision-making to the national level, reduced collegial involvement in national policy-making, an increased emphasis on line management and managerial control of teachers' work in the interests of efficiency, the weakening of teacher autonomy, the creation of new managerial roles, skills and responsibilities and the emergence of a more distinct managerial layer in schools. In addition, it is linked closely with various forms of market-oriented mechanisms together with an increased emphasis on target-setting, 'rational' management and accountability. Moreover, the phenomenon is by no means unique to Britain. Similar approaches have been adopted by other countries in Europe and North America and by Australia and New Zealand (Moos and Dempster, 1998). The relevance of this perspective to the issues discussed above will be apparent. Moreover, it seems likely that, because NPM is supported by governments of all parties and in international agencies like the OECD, its techniques and the overall strategy are likely to continue to exercise a considerable influence on education and, more specifically, on professional development and professionalism.

Third, although there is general agreement that various forms of partnership can make a useful contribution to the provision of professional development (Graham et al., 1999), NPM techniques in universities have rendered this problematic. Thus, although university schools of education have traditionally played a key role in the provision of professional development opportunities, their contribution is now much reduced. The reasons are largely because they now operate in a quasi-market and are simultaneously subject to the pressures of NPM (Bolam, 2000). In turn, this makes it difficult for them to collaborate and compete with other, often commercial, providers in a partnership or to become professional schools, alongside law, medicine and engineering. Such professional schools could be the main source of professional education and development, providing independent settings for sustained periods of professional study, aimed at improving teaching and learning in classrooms and schools, as well as for reflection on professional values. Moreover, this would also strengthen their contributions to research and evidence-informed practice (Furlong, 2000).

Fourth, the implied question – what is the most appropriate institutional location for professional education? – raises related issues about the distinctive characteristics of *professional* development and *professionalism* and, accordingly, about the values and principles which should inform them. A recent policy paper in England adopted an instrumentalist position: 'Professional development is all about making sure that teachers have the finest and most up-to-date tools for their job' (DfEE, 2000: 1). Unexceptionable as this is, as far as it goes, it does not address issues like what it means to be a professional educator, what kind of development professional educators need, or the many ethical and values issues thrown up by professional development policy and practice.

The position adopted here is that:

professional development is the process by which teachers and headteachers learn, enhance and use appropriate knowledge, skills and values. The notion of appropriateness must itself be based on shared and public value judgements about the needs and best interests of their clients. Thus, although this perspective certainly includes staff, management and human resource development directed at raising standards and the improvement of teaching and learning, it recognises that, because these are essentially employer- and organisation-oriented concepts, they should be seen as only a part of professional development, albeit a fundamentally important part. The essence of professional development for educators must surely involve the learning of an independent, evidence-informed and constructively critical approach to practice within a public framework of professional values and accountability, which are also open to critical scrutiny. (Bolam, 2000: 272)

These issues need to be addressed at the level of practice as well as policy. For example, it is notable that the Scottish version of the NPQH takes professional values as its starting point. The first Standard is called 'Professional Values' and requires head teachers: 'to hold, articulate and argue for professionally defensible educational values . . . based on the professional obligations of headteachers to serve the interests of children and young people in schools' (The SQH Development Unit, 1998: 4). There is nothing comparable in the National Standards for Headship nor, indeed, in any of the other national standards for England and Wales.

Fifth, these issues raise broader theoretical questions about the nature of a profession. Thus, Hoyle and John (1995) distinguish between professionalism, professionality and professionalisation in stressing the importance of considering: 'questions about the *nature* of teachers' autonomy, knowledge and responsibility, as these relate to effective practice, (ibid.: 16). In a similar vein, Whitty (2000) uses the terms 'new professionalism' and 'democratic professionalism' in exploring related issues in a broader discussion about the future of the teaching profession. From the perspective of policy and practice in England and Wales, it is encouraging to note that these issues are firmly on the agenda of the newly-established General Teaching Council for England (GTC, 2001).

Finally, it is important to raise the question: what do these developments and issues mean for headteachers and other school leaders with teacher management responsibilities? From a practical perspective, tools for implementing these and related ideas are widely available. They include professional development profiles (GTC Trust, 1993), action research (McMahon, 1999), action learning (Wallace, 1991), coaching (Joyce and Showers, 1988) mentoring and peer-assisted learning (Bolam et al., 1995) and the overall management of continuing professional development (e.g. Craft, 1996). From a theoretical perspective, there is no simple, straightforward answer to satisfy all school leaders. A response based loosely on contingency, situational and pluralist theories of leadership (see Bush, 1995: 154) must suffice. Essentially these argue that there is no single or 'correct' way either to lead or structure an organisation since the 'leaders', the 'led' and the organisation itself each have distinctive, even unique, characteristics, as do the tasks of leadership and management, in what is invariably a changing, turbulent environment. Given the unavoidably contingent and unpredictable nature of their work, effective leaders and managers should adopt strategies and methods appropriate to their particular organisations, tasks, staff and contexts – local and national. It follows that they should learn and use a repertoire of styles and techniques and exercise informed professional judgement to operate effectively within the constraints and opportunities of their unique situation. This chapter has reviewed a range of contextual factors, developments and issues, including changing notions of professionalism, bearing on the task of managing professional development. The intention has been to offer insights to inform professional judgements and actions, which must, perforce, be made by individual professionals in their particular settings.

Further reading

Craft, A. (1996) *Continuing Professional Development: A Practical Guide for Teachers and Schools*, London: Routledge and the Open University Press.

Joyce, B., Calhoun, E. and Hopkins, D. (1999) *The New Structure of School Improvement: Inquiring Schools and Achieving Students*, Buckingham: Open University Press.

Organisation for Economic Co-operation and Development (1998) *Staying Ahead: In-service Training and Teacher Professional Development*, Paris: OECD.

References

Balazs, E. (1999) 'Institution-level educational management in Hungarian public education', in R. Bolam and F. van Wieringen (eds), *Research on Educational Management in Europe*, Munster/New York: Waxmann.

Bolam, R. (1993) 'Recent developments and emerging issues' in GTC Trust (ed.), *The Continuing Professional Development of Teachers*, London: GTC Trust.

Bolam, R. (2000) 'Emerging policy trends: some implications for continuing professional development', *Journal of In-service Education*, 26 (2): 267–79.

Bolam, R., Dunning, G. and Karstanje, P. (eds) (2000) *New Heads in the New Europe*, Munster/New York: Waxmann.

Bolam, R., McMahon, A., Pocklington, K. and Weindling, R. (1995) 'Mentoring for new headteachers: the British experience', *Journal of Educational Administration*, 33 (5): 29–44.

Bush, T. (1995) *Theories of Educational Management*, London: Paul Chapman Publishing.

Campbell, R. J. and Neill, S. R. St J. (1994) *Secondary Teachers at Work*, London: Routledge.

Chapman, N. (1995) 'Developing a sense of mission at Whitefields School: the tension between action research and school management', *Educational Management and Administration*, 23 (3): 206–11.

Craft, A. (1996) *Continuing Professional Development: A Practical Guide for Teachers and Schools*, London: Routledge and the Open University Press.

Department for Education and Employment (DfEE) (2000) *Professional Development: Support for Teaching and Learning*, London: DfEE.

Dudley, P. (1999) 'How do teachers respond to data?', in C. Conner (ed.), *Assessment in Action in Primary Schools*, London: Falmer Press.

EPPI (2000) *Evidence for Policy and Practice* (pamphlet), London: EPPI Centre, Institute of Education.

Eraut, M. (1994) *Developing Professional Knowledge and Competence*, London: Falmer Press.

Ferlie, E., Ashburner, L. and Pettigrew, A. (1996) *The New Public Management in Action*, Oxford: Oxford University Press.

Fullan, M. (2001) *The New Meaning of Educational Change*, 3rd edn, London: Routledge/Falmer.

Furlong, J. (2000) *Higher Education and the New Professionalism for Teachers: Realising the Potential of Partnership*, London: Committee of Vice-Chancellors and Principals of the Universities of the United Kingdom.

General Teaching Council (GTC) (2001) *Professional Learning Framework: A Draft for Discussion and Development*, London: GTC.

General Teaching Council Trust (GTC) (1993) *The Continuing Professional Development of Teachers*, London: General Teaching Council Trust.

George, M. (1998) 'The Lincolnshire Small Schools Project', in J. West-Burnham and F. O'Sullivan (eds), *Leadership and Professional Development in Schools*, London, Financial Times/Pitman.

Grady, N., Macpherson, M. and Mulford, B. (1995) 'Problem-based learning in educational administration through block delivery modes', *International Studies in Educational Administration*, 23 (1): 58–64.

Graham, J., Gough, B. and Beardsworth, R. (1999) *Partnerships in Continuing Professional Development: Interim Project Findings*, London: Standing Conference for the Education and Training of Teachers.

Gray, J., Hopkins, D., Reynolds, D., Wilcox, B., Farrell, S. and Jesson, D. (1999) *Improving Schools: Performance and Potential*, Buckingham: Open University Press.

Guskey, T. R. (1995) 'Professional development in education: in search of the optimal mix', in T. R. Guskey and M. Huberman (eds), *Professional Development in Education: New Paradigms and Practices*, New York: Teachers College Press.

Halasz, G. (2000) 'System regulation changes in education and their implications for management development', unpublished keynote paper for the Annual Conference of the European Network for the Improvement of Research and Development in Educational Management (ENIRDEM), 23 September, Tilburg University, Netherlands.

Hargreaves, A. (1994) *Changing Teachers, Changing Times: Teachers' Work and Culture in the Post-modern Age*, London: Cassell.

Hargreaves, D. H. (1996) *Teaching as a Research-Based Profession: Possibilities and Prospects*, The Teacher Training Agency Annual Lecture 1996, London: TTA.

Hoyle, E. and John, P. D. (1995) *Professional Knowledge and Professional Practice*, London: Cassell.

Jordet, C. (2000) 'New heads in Norway', in R. Bolam, G. Dunning and P. Karstanje (eds), *New Heads in the New Europe*, Munster/New York: Waxmann.

Joyce, B. and Showers, B. (1988) *Student Achievement through Staff Development*, London: Longman.

Joyce, B., Calhoun, E. and Hopkins, D. (1999) *The New Structure of School Improvement: Inquiring Schools and Achieving Students*, Buckingham: Open University Press.

Karstanje, P. (1999) 'Developments in school management from a European perspective', in R. Bolam and F. van Wieringen (eds), *Research on Educational Management in Europe*, Munster/New York: Waxmann.

Karstanje, P. (2000) 'New heads in five countries', in R. Bolam, G. Dunning and P. Karstanje (eds), *New Heads in the New Europe*, Munster/New York: Waxmann.

King, M. B. and Newmann, F. M. (2001) 'Building school capacity through professional development: conceptual and empirical considerations', *International Journal of Educational Management*, 15 (2): 86–93.

Kolb, D. A. (1975) *Experiential Learning*, Englewood Cliffs, NJ: Prentice-Hall.

Leithwood, K. and Hallinger, P. (eds) (2002) *Second International Handbook of Educational Leadership and Administration*, Norwell, MA: Kluwer Academic.

Leithwood, K., Jantzi, D. and Steinbach, R. (1995) 'An organisational learning perspective on school responses to central policy initiatives', *School Organisation*, 15 (3): 2–20.

Levačić, R. (1999) 'Managing resources for school effectiveness in England and Wales: institutionalising a rational approach', in R. Bolam and F. van Wieringen (eds), *Research on Educational Management in Europe*, Munster/New York: Waxmann.

Louis, K. S., and Kruse, S. D. (1995) *Professionalism and Community: Perspectives on Reforming Urban Schools*, Thousand Oaks, CA: Corwin Press Inc.

McMahon, A. (1999) 'Promoting continuing professional development for teachers: an achievable target for school leaders?', in T. Bush, L. Bell, R. Bolam, R. Glatter and P. Ribbins (eds), *Re-defining Educational Management*, London: Paul Chapman Publishing.

Moos, L. and Dempster, N. (1998) 'Some comparative learnings from the study', in J. MacBeath (ed.), *Effective School Leadership: Responding to Change*, London: Paul Chapman Publishing.

Myers, K. (1996) *School improvement in practice: The Schools Make a Difference Project*, London: Falmer Press.

National Board for Professional Teaching Standards (NBPTS) (1993) *What Should Teachers Know and Be Able to Do?*, Detroit: NBPTE.

Organisation for Economic Co-operation and Development (OECD) (1982) *In-service Education and Training for Teachers: A Condition for Educational Change*, Paris: OECD.

Organisation for Economic Co-operation and Development (OECD) (1998) *Staying Ahead: In-service Training and Teacher Professional Development*, Paris: OECD.

Organisation for Economic Co-operation and Development (OECD) (2001) *New School Management Approaches*, Paris: OECD.

Pecori, J. (2000) 'State innovations: pay-for-performance teacher compensation plans', *The State Education Standard*, Winter: 44.

School Teachers' Review Body (1996) *Fifth Report*, London: HMSO.

Schön, D. A. (1987) *The reflective practitioner: How professionals think in action*, New York: Basic Books.

Scott, C., Stone, B. and Dinham, S. (2000) 'International patterns of teacher discontent', paper for the AERA Annual Conference.

Sebba, J. (1997) 'Educational research: developing and implementing the government's action plan', *Research Intelligence*, 67: 19–20.

Smithers, R. (2001) 'Teacher shortage: staff praise Ofsted chief', *Guardian* 29 August: 4.

Smylie, M. A. (1995) 'Teacher learning in the workplace: implications for school reform', in T. R. Guskey and M. Huberman (eds), *Professional Development in Education: New Paradigms and Practices*, New York: Teachers College Press.

Southworth, G. and Conner, C. (1999) *Managing Improving Primary Schools: Using Evidence-Based Management and Leadership*, London: Falmer Press.

Stoll, L., Bolam, R. and Collarbone, P. (in press) 'Leadership for and of change: building capacity for learning', in K. Leithwood and P. Hallinger (eds), *Second International Handbook of Educational Leadership and Administration*, Dordrecht: Kluwer Academic.

Teacher Training Agency (TTA) (1998a) *National Standards for Qualified Teacher Status*, London: TTA.

Teacher Training Agency (TTA) (1998b) *National Standards for Subject Leaders*, London: TTA.

Teacher Training Agency (TTA) (1999) *Improving Standards: Research and Evidence-Based Practice*, London: TTA.

The SQH Development Unit (1998) *The Standard for Headship in Scotland*, Stirling: University of Stirling, Institute of Education.

Tickle, L. (2000) *Teacher Induction: The Way Ahead*, Buckingham: Open University Press.

Travers, C. J. and Cooper, C. L. (1996) *Teachers under Pressure: Stress in the Teaching Profession*, London: Routledge.

Wallace, M. (1991) *School-Centred Management Training*, London: Paul Chapman Publishing.

Weindling, D. (1999) 'Stages of headship', in T. Bush, L. Bell, R. Bolam, R. Glatter and P. Ribbins (eds), *Educational Management: Redefining Theory, Policy and Practice*, London: Paul Chapman Publishing.

Whitty, G. (1997) 'Marketisation and the teaching profession', in A. H. Halsey, H. Lauder, P. Brown and A. Stuart Wells (eds), *Education: Culture, Economy and Society*, Oxford: Oxford University Press.

Whitty, G. (2000) 'Teacher professionalism in new times', *Journal of In-service Education*, 26 (2): 281–96.

8

Appraisal and Performance Management

David Middlewood

Introduction

This chapter refers to the importance in the current world context which is given to assessing the performance of teachers and of leaders of schools and colleges. The two key elements of managing systems for this assessment, accountability and professional development, are explored. The tension and/or balance between these two are considered in the context of various factors which affect the effectiveness of the management of performance. Emphases upon different elements of performance appraisal management are shown to differ according to perceptions and requirements in different contexts, both at national and at institutional level. The chapter concludes by drawing out key principles for effectiveness on which institutional managers might base their practice in this field, with the need being stressed for adaptability to reflect changes occurring now and in the future.

The significance of performance and appraisal in education

In the global context of competitiveness and comparison between industrialised nations, the necessity for a well-educated workforce in achieving economic prosperity has become increasingly recognised by their governments.

> In the United States, the growth of economic competition has led to a widespread appreciation that knowledge is now the key to wealth creation. The American saying 'Wise up or fall out' captures a growing perception that a highly trained, highly skilled workforce is the basis of future economic power. (Lofthouse et al., 1995: 15)

Since the quality of learning and teaching in educational organisations is the main factor in the provision of such a workforce, it is hardly surprising that there is considerable pressure to identify the means to assess accurately the performance of those responsible, i.e. teachers and headteachers or principals. In noting this link, it is interesting that several governments have borrowed the language of business and industry to apply in this field, such as 'performance management', 'performance-related pay', etc. (O'Neill, 1997a: i). This criticism of educational management as a discipline – that it borrows too readily from business and industry – is made by Bush (1999: 15) when he argues that this practice fails to recognise the uniqueness of leadership and management in education in specific areas. The specific area referred to is that of learning and teaching, and is therefore relevant to any process of assessing the performance of teachers. Because of the pressure from governments to try to ensure effective performance in education, it is clear that one of the most obvious and overt reasons for appraising teacher and headteacher perform-ance is for the purpose of *accountability*. This may be defined here as ensur-ing that teachers are fulfilling their role of providing effective teaching for quality learning for their students. Those who argue that teacher appraisal schemes have been proposed primarily for purposes of government control of individual accountability (e.g., O'Neill, 1997b) might point to the irony of the situation in the UK in the 1990s, where teacher appraisal was introduced as a statutory requirement in the early part of the decade *before* any clear ideas about performance (i.e. what was to be appraised) emerged in 1999–2000. If the original purpose was to ensure a check upon teachers, it was ill conceived as a concept and hardly surprising that the original proposals foundered because of the 'so what?' principle. (Middlewood, 2001a). A further irony was that, in seeking to introduce an appraisal model at any cost, the UK govern-ment produced one which was essentially driven not by accountability but by professional development needs. Only later was the issue of performance linked clearly with its appraisal.

What the UK government did was acknowledge that, as the original appraisal scheme was 'discredited' (the actual word used by the Secretary of State), the appraisal of teachers needed to be set in a context of performance management. This involved directly linking 'rewards' with how well teachers had performed in, for example, improving their students' achievements as measured in tests and examinations. Initially, this was linked to a national exercise in 2000 requiring teachers who had taught for at least nine years to produce evidence that they had raised student achievement, so that they could cross a 'threshold' and gain a pay rise. The rather simplistic format that is cur-rently in place requires teachers to set agreed annual goals for performance in their schools and be 'appraised' according to these goals being attained. The issues concerning the effectiveness or otherwise of such a scheme are exam-ined in this chapter.

As this 'performance management' process, of which appraisal was a key part, has developed in countries such as New Zealand and the UK, it has become closely linked with the issue of career progression. In countries such as Israel, Japan, Singapore and the USA, the notion of being assessed for per-formance before progressing to the next stage of a career in teaching is well established, although national schemes differed considerably in their details.

This link means that for educational leaders and managers appraising performance is also related to the management of the *recruitment* of teachers – both in the profession itself and, in some countries, in individual schools and colleges. A further strand is that of the *retention and motivation* of teachers. In other words, any scheme of managing performance and its appraisal may have to ensure that it answers the question: 'How can effective teachers be encouraged to remain (a) in the profession (b) in the classroom, through being confident that they will have opportunities to progress, to gain greater rewards and that this will be done by their being assessed fairly?'

The recent history of performance and appraisal management in education therefore suggests that not only is it of great importance, both at national and institutional level, but that it needs to be considered in terms of its purposes and its relationship to other important aspects of human resource management.

Accountability and professional development

If accountability is a key purpose of appraisal of performance, then equally the need to recognise the opportunity for the performer to develop is crucial. Without that opportunity, performance may remain static. However good that performance might be, the emphasis in performance management is on *improvement*. In the case of professional employees such as teachers or school leaders, it may be particularly important to ensure that personal professional development is central to any scheme of managing their performance, since the ultimate motivation to improve must come from themselves. In fact, I know of no performance appraisal scheme which does not recognise the need for some form of training or development to be acknowledged as part of that scheme. However, given the overwhelming acceptance of the need for accountability to be a key reason for having appraisal, the balance between accountability and professional development lies at the heart of how effectively performance appraisal is managed. If seen as a continuum, the two extremes may be polarised, as in Figure 8.1

Appraisal solely
for accountability

Appraisal solely
for professional development

Figure 8.1   Continuum of performance appraisal emphases

South Africa provides a striking example of the two extremes of approach, based as they are on teacher appraisal in the apartheid and post-apartheid periods. Under apartheid, the appraisal of teachers was seen by many, e.g.

Christie (1999), as discriminating against black teachers and was essentially used for control (Beardall, 1995). The scheme introduced post-apartheid, in the New Republic of South Africa, as described in detail by Thurlow (2001), has all the features of a scheme which is now at the opposite end of the continuum.

The appraisal of principals in Singapore (Chew, 2001) focuses on the principal's accountability for school improvement and any training for the principal is related strictly to the needs of the school as seen by the external assessor. The England and Wales scheme, on the other hand, as originally introduced in 1993, focused almost exclusively on the professional needs of teachers (Middlewood, 2001a).

This tension between accountability and professional development has implications for such matters as:

- the kind of data needed and used for the appraisal
- the ethos and context within which it takes place
- the areas of education upon which it focuses
- the identification of future aims or targets.

These two elements of performance appraisal are shown in Figure 8.2.

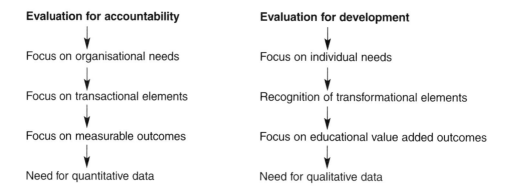

Evaluation for accountability	Evaluation for development
Focus on organisational needs	Focus on individual needs
Focus on transactional elements	Recognition of transformational elements
Focus on measurable outcomes	Focus on educational value added outcomes
Need for quantitative data	Need for qualitative data

Figure 8.2   The two elements of performance appraisal

The two elements often lead to systems being 'muddied' (Hall, 1997: 152) in their purposes and Beer summarises the tension as it may affect the individual who:

> desires to confirm a positive self-image *and* to obtain organisational rewards of promotion or pay. The organisation wants individuals to be open to negative information about themselves so that they can improve their performance. As

long as individuals see the appraisal process as having an important influence on their rewards (pay, recognition), their career (promotions and reputations), and their self-image they will be reluctant to engage in the kind of open dialogue required for valid evaluation and personal development. (Beer, 1986: 289)

Each of the elements described here has problems associated with it, if the emphasis taken in the management of performance and review tends too much towards *either* accountability *or* professional development. The problems arising from too much management emphasis on evaluation for accountability may be:

- alienation of staff, as they perceive themselves as assessed from above with little ownership for themselves in the scheme
- weak and even hostile relationships between staff appraised and their appraisers
- frank discussion about weaknesses is unlikely to occur
- encouragement of a concept of education which is narrow and focused on what is measurable.

On the other hand, problems arising from the management emphasis being too much on individual professional development may be:

- weaker teachers are insufficiently challenged
- training and development needs are not guaranteed to be available
- links with improvement in student achievement are difficult to ascertain
- teachers who are 'comfortably competent' may not improve, or may decline, in their performance.

Factors affecting performance appraisal

Clearly therefore some balance between these two elements is necessary for an effective scheme to be operated. However, in examining the extent to which this applies in some existing schemes, it is helpful to consider some of the complexities which affect the management of appraisal of performance in educational institutions.

Teacher autonomy

Ultimately the model of teaching which is still the predominant one in schools and colleges depends upon the teacher working in relative isolation from other staff. As Whitaker points out: 'school teachers are unusual in starting their careers in charge of quite large organisations – a learning company of thirty or so individuals. In terms of the responsibilities and challenges this presents, they compare favourably with chief executives of medium-sized companies' (Whitaker 1997:78).

Unlike chief executives, classroom teachers manage their business on their own most of the time. This isolation and the autonomy that necessarily accompanies it in the authority and ability to handle the class in the way deemed most suitable by the teacher is not only highly prized by teachers as part of 'professionalism' (see Bolam: Chapter 7, this volume) but makes comparisons difficult, and therefore also any set of standards on which assessment is based.

Furthermore, the middle managers (e.g. heads of departments) in schools and colleges who are responsible for teachers' performance and its assessment are themselves teaching for most of the time. Unlike some organisations, these managers do not operate in a purely supervisory capacity and, therefore, any observations of performance have to be 'snapshots' and run the risk of being artificial.

Similarly for headteachers and principals, the uniqueness of each school, with its own needs and stage in its development, means that a common form of assessment of performance is problematic.

Variety of models of effective teaching

As Kyriacou (1986) asks whether teaching is best seen as an art, a craft or a science, so there are inevitably a number of different ways in which effective teaching may be offered. Any model of appraising teacher or headteacher performance therefore needs to be flexible enough to take account of this. The temptation (Middlewood and Cardno, 2001) is to assume that there is one model only by which all teaching or all leadership will be assessed. Formal inspection systems (such as Ofsted in the UK) tend to use one model, because they are required to look at all schools in a similar way, in the interests of raising national standards. Such models inevitably rely on a competences approach, but run the risk of condemning effective teachers who do not fit the mould. One head of a secondary school in England illustrates this:

> Frank taught Mathematics his way. One day, he damaged the passenger door of his car. The next day, he arrived at school with an old fridge door welded in its place. I had to appraise Frank. His style and approach certainly didn't match any known specification of quality teaching. This was a great shame because he was undoubtedly highly effective in certain situations. He was a star with what we might term 'the more challenging' but not in a conventional way. He was clearly disappointed with my lesson observation feedback and requested a second opinion! He also informed me of the powerful influence of his background and that Wigan folk did things differently to the rest of the world anyway. (Marson, 1999: 7)

Similarly with regard to assessing school leaders, MacBeath and Myers (1999: 2) describe the risk of 'precluding the X factor – the surprise, the chemistry, the shift in perspective that may be brought by a candidate who does not fit the arithmetic but may, nonetheless, bring a magical quality to the leadership task.'

Context

If even in a single school a teacher's performance may vary according to the individual students that make up any one class, then the differences between schools and their contexts is even more marked. Thrupp (1999: 157) believes 'contextual differences related to student composition will have to be carefully considered if we are at all serious about assessing teachers fairly'.

Thrupp's own research indicated that effectiveness in teaching differed sharply in an advantaged school from that in one in a more working class context. In the latter, effective teachers took on highly structured roles in controlled classroom environments whereas those in the advantaged schools took comparatively low-key roles, providing stimulus for discussion or action for students' independent learning. Both were effective in their specific contexts.

A further political reality emerges in discussion of the issue of context. Some schools, indeed some areas or even whole countries, struggle to find sufficient teachers of even modest quality and many developing countries operate with large numbers of unqualified teachers. An assessment scheme which applies a single model in all circumstances will simply exacerbate the problem for those already struggling to find staff. As Thrupp bluntly expresses it: 'Senior staff . . . were aware that some staff were ineffectual but consoled themselves that such teachers were valuable to the school in other ways' (Thrupp, 1999: 114–15).

Context may be similarly crucial in developing criteria for appraising school leaders. Leithwood (2001) points out that in a competitive environment experienced by most self-governing schools, not only the attitudes of school leaders towards this competition would differ, but that the wishes of the communities their schools served would differ also. Although marketing and entrepreneurial skills would be needed, and therefore any assessment of the leaders' work should seek evidence of these, the community contexts may differ. They could range from that where success at the expense of others would at the very least not be criticised, to:

> Communities in which equity is a strongly valued goal will want to add criteria to their school leader evaluation policies which reflect the effort of leaders to market their schools in ways that make access possible even for those children and families from diverse and economically disadvantaged backgrounds. (Leithwood, 2001: 48)

125

A new emphasis on learning

Whilst it is easy to gain agreement that the ultimate purpose of appraising teacher or headteacher performance is to gain improvement in the quality of student learning, and therefore the focus should be on learning outcomes, it is complicated by new understandings of learning in terms of what constitutes effective learning and how it can be recognised. Law and Glover (2000: 164), in adapting Ferguson's (1982) model, suggest a new learning paradigm, which essentially focuses on 'learning how to learn'. Among various features of this paradigm, four may be selected to illustrate the point:

> Learning is a process, a journey . . .
> Teacher learns too – from pupils . . .
> Education is a lifelong process, moves beyond schooling
> Self-image as a generator of performance is a priority. (Law and Glover, 2000: 164)

Each of these features has two important elements – first, the recognition that the learning is unique to each individual and secondly that learning during schooling is only part of a process that continues through life. It follows that the point reached by a group of individuals at any one stage, supported by teacher performance, cannot realistically be assessed by common standards (usually testing) except at the most minimum levels of competence.

However, in the world of competition already referred to, the focus for comparisons between countries, and between schools and colleges within countries, is inevitably upon measurable learning outcomes, such as 'proficiency in literacy and numeracy, examination results, test scores, numbers of students continuing beyond statutory schooling' (Middlewood and Cardno, 2001: 1). In fact, as Preedy (2001: 94) points out, 'Many of the most valuable outcomes of education are multi-dimensional, complex and long-term . . .', and she explains how models that focus upon product evaluation ignore unplanned outcomes and also fail to explore the value and worth of the prescribed objectives. Leithwood goes further and suggests that making judgements about schools, teachers or leaders based on these measurable results can have:

> disastrous unintended consequences . . . for example, minimising individual differences among students, narrowing the implemented curriculum, consuming enormous amounts of valuable instructional time, negatively influencing schools' willingness to accept students with weak academic records, and providing incentives for cheating. (Leithwood, 2001: 53)

Dolton (2000: 8) gives the example in the UK that where schools needed to boost their results in grades A–C at GCSE (16-plus examinations), they implemented strategies of coaching, mentoring and giving extra tuition to 'borderline' students, so that these would improve from grade D to C. He argues that incentives for teachers through performance related pay would inevitably compel or at least encourage staff to increase this practice, not only fostering a considerable narrowing of educational aims but also conveying a false message to students about what is important in learning.

Similarly, in appraising school leaders, a focus upon measurable outcomes is attractively simplistic, but as West-Burnham (2001: 26) points out, new understanding of leadership at institutional level involves 'challenging authority, risk-taking' as well as 'courage, creativity, emotional intelligence, trust, honour and resilience'. How should these be assessed in terms of outcomes, especially if the authority to be challenged may be responsible for the appraisal process!

The issue of rewards

The linking of an appraisal of performance with some form of reward is clearly very important as an incentive for improving that performance. Fidler and Cooper (1992: xi) suggest that earlier writing on appraisal tended to focus on it either as operating 'in a rather independent way' or solely concerned with developing staff. The former refers to appraisal as a separate process in which, at certain times, an assessment is made of a person's performance and rewards (or not) would follow this accordingly.

In several countries, this appraisal is intended to be built into a career at specific stages, so that the reward for a successful appraisal is advancement to the next stage. Examples of this occur in Israel (Yariv, 2001), New Zealand (Fitzgerald, 2001) and the UK (DfEE, 1999). The doubts about the effectiveness of this lie in the fact that first, the process is a 'one model fits all' (as discussed above) and, second, inherent in it is the acceptance that the vast majority of staff will automatically be successful. Criticism of this approach includes that of Dolton (2000) who argues that it is a negative concept because teachers have to prove they are not incompetent and Ingvarson who describes such schemes in Australia and the U.K. as having a: 'pass rate (which) will be around 90%. The consequence? The assessment gains no respect, there is no recognition and the salary progression quickly becomes automatic, which was what the teacher unions aimed for anyway' (Ingvarson, 2001: 170).

Management of performance appraisal at institutional level

The key question here is similar to that in several areas of management, i.e. how are national requirements to be managed at individual school or college level, so that statutory requirements are met and at the same time the special features of the individual institution and the people who work there are recognised? In countries where self-management of schools and colleges is well developed (see Chapter 3 of this book), and therefore the majority of resources are managed at site level, there is clearly scope for this recognition. For example, early in 2001, the Chancellor of the Exchequer in England and Wales decreed that much of the new money for education would go directly to headteachers and principals for them to spend on recruitment and retention of staff as they saw fit. Headteachers could therefore use these funds, for example, for paying higher salaries to attract staff where the supply was limited, or reward high performing staff to retain them.

In countries with more centralised control, although individual schools will inevitably differ to some extent, managers will necessarily experience tensions arising from any national scheme. This may result in the scheme falling into disrepute and/or disuse such as in some regions of Greece (Middlewood, 2001b). Another possibility is the scheme remains vague and therefore difficult to implement, as in Slovenia (Erculj, 2001), or in Israel (Yariv, 2001).

The overriding consideration for managers at institutional level appears to be that managing performance and its appraisal needs to be managed firmly within the context of the integrated management of staff as a whole. Managing performance and its appraisal cannot be separated from all the other processes and aspects involved in managing people – such as recruitment and selection, induction, mentoring, motivation, equal opportunities, delegation, teamwork, stress and time. All of these impact on the performance of individuals, of teams and of the whole organisation, and any attempts to manage performance appraisal as a separate process, introduced occasionally or regularly, without it being viewed by those involved as relevant to themselves, their jobs *and the current time*, will ensure that it eventually falls down the list of priorities.

Managing the process

In any scheme of performance appraisal, certain components are common, although the relative importance of individual components will vary according to perceived needs at institutional level. These components are:

- some form of self-evaluation
- collection of data about the appraisee
- observation
- a dialogue between appraiser(s) and appraisee
- targets or goals being set.

Practice varies in the importance given to these according to such factors as:

- national scheme requirements
- the principles of the management approach in the organisation

- the ethos affecting relationships in the organisation
- resources available (including time).

For example, the extent to which self-evaluation is a genuinely full part of the process will have a large influence on the extent of ownership of it by the appraisee, something seen as crucial by a number of writers (Cardno and Piggott-Irvine, 1997; Middlewood, 1997). Classroom observation may be a key feature of many schemes (New Zealand, the UK, South Africa), but how the other aspects of a teacher's contribution to the school's effectiveness (e.g. leadership and management at any level, extra-curricular work, community liaison) are to be effectively appraised and recognised remains an issue for managers of individual institutions.

Underpinning many of the factors determining the extent to which managing performance and its appraisal is perceived to be effective within schools and colleges is the question as to who should appraise whom. In some national schemes, this is the responsibility of the headteacher or principal, although in larger institutions it may and will be delegated. At middle management level, a line management model is most common but in South Africa, for example, a panel must be used (Thurlow, 2001), particularly to ensure objectivity and fairness in the process. There are those who question whether it is possible for a school leader to be sufficiently expert or objective to assess their own staff: 'it is unwise to put principals in this role of making evaluations about the quality of teaching of their own staff when they have to live with the consequences' (Ingvarson, 2001: 170).

The contrary argument is of course that it is precisely because they have to 'live with the consequences' that makes school leaders the people best placed to do this, in a self-managing school. The proviso must be that any potential prejudice needs to be recognised and managed. The UK scheme for a team of external assessors to monitor the processes of assessment for threshold payments in schools seems a barely adequate check on the quality of the assessments, intended though it apparently was to add some objectivity.

The appraisal of school leaders themselves is, perhaps inevitably, mostly done by those external to the school but with a knowledge of it. For example, principals in Singapore are appraised by the area inspector (Chew, 2001), in the UK by a nominated external assessor, and in South Africa by a panel, as mentioned above. Goals for school leaders will also often involve these being set by governors or school councils (as in Canada).

Assessment of the quality of teaching, according to some writers (e.g., Ingvarson, 2001; O'Neill, 1997b) can only be effectively and fairly done by other teachers because they understand the professional standards required and the professional context within which they operate. Ingvarson (2001) describes the scheme of professional certification of teachers being developed in the USA, with its success, it is argued, owing to the fact that it is provided by an independent professional body (the National Board for Professional Teaching Standards) and that the teachers are fully engaged in the process. Members of the board's committees 'cannot assess teachers personally known to them' (Ingvarson, 2001: 173). As teachers reach the standards for certification, forms of recognition may be given to them by their employers, including salary increases. Whilst the independence of the external body does strengthen the validity of the process, it also appears to run the risk of excessive bureaucracy, for example, 'Each entry takes about 20–30 hours to prepare and is about 12 pages long' (ibid.: 170). The use of panels (South Africa) or committees (the USA) seems unlikely to meet the needs of school managers concerned with ever-increasing demands to raise standards and coping with the pace of change in the twenty-first century, because of the huge demands it places upon managers' time.

O'Neill's (1997b) argument is that any system of appraising the performance of teachers which is occasional and detached from its real context is invalid and he believes that:

> professional knowledge and skills, the essential craft element of teaching, are better developed, analysed and *evaluated* within:
>
> - the normal currency of teaching talk in staffroom, classroom and corridor;
> - the routines of syndicate or departmental collaboration; and
> - the process of translating intangible school and community values into concrete learning opportunities within the classroom.
> (O'Neill, 1997b: 118)

While research widely supports the notion of collaboration between teachers as being one of the biggest factors in teaching and learning effectiveness, the accountability aspect discussed earlier is so important that the role of somebody outside the teachers' network seems an inevitable requirement for a scheme to have credibility.

This whole issue, therefore, of considering who should be responsible for appraising whom does suggest that managers would be well advised to consider possibilities such as team appraisal for teachers and 360-degree feedback for leaders. The two provisos are that, first, such possibilities are legitimate within any statutory requirements and, second, the time and context is judged to be appropriate – other stages may well have to be worked through first.

As far as team appraisal is concerned, O'Neill (1997b: 118), without specifying how, argues that appraisal 'needs to focus at the level of group practices and meanings'. Draper (2000) describes a team appraisal approach within which individuals have their own goals and develop professional career portfolios. Research into the perceived impact of individual appraisal on team unity in secondary school subject departments (Middlewood, 2001a) showed that teachers overwhelmingly believed it could be damaging and divisive to collaborative working, widely seen as effective in schools. When rewards for individual performance were added to this, these were perceived as likely to cause even more damage.

The increasing need for leaders to be linked effectively with an increasing number of stakeholders, both internal and external to the organisation, makes the process of '360-degree feedback' (which involves collecting qualitative data from a range of sources) a potential 'power for genuinely evaluating individual performance and supporting development' (Tomlinson, 2000: 94). It has the added advantage of the leader being in touch with and accountable to a variety of people, including a number who are technically lower in the organisational hierarchy.

Conclusion: effectiveness in managing performance and appraisal

It is likely that, in industrialised countries in the twenty-first century, models of learning will develop which may drastically alter the role of the teacher. However, the teacher's role is certain to remain pivotal in educational institutions and thus methods of effectively managing and evaluating teachers' performance will continue to be sought after and debated. Effective managers will always be aware of the changing environment within which their institutions exist and, therefore, be conscious that any performance appraisal approach will need to be flexible accordingly, for example, as concepts of rewards, desired outcomes, etc. change. Evidence from experience to date, however, suggests that there are some key principles that will remain relevant to effectiveness in this area.

Whichever scheme is operated, evidence suggests that it should:

- operate within a climate of trust. Trust is always the basis of sound manager/subordinate relationships and moral and ethical issues are always present in the assessment of one person by another. Having a 'procedurally sound system alone will not necessarily produce effective, accurate, ethical performance ratings' (Longenecker and Ludwig, 1995: 68)
- be an integral part of the whole process of managing people within the institution, so that the way people are recruited and inducted, for example, is perceived as similar to the way they are appraised
- balance accountability and personal professional development. As has been argued, any scheme that is too near to either extreme will have major drawbacks
- balance the needs of the organisation and the individual. This can be done, for example, by ensuring that targets or goals set demonstrate recognition of the individual's right to development as well as his/her responsibility to the employer

- recognise that the quality of the students' learning experiences remain central to the ultimate purpose of staff performance, whether teacher, principal or technician
- be constantly reviewed and where necessary adjusted in the light of changed circumstances
- recognise that some of the intended benefits of managing performance and appraising it may inevitably be longer term than others, owing to the complexity of the educational experience and the difficulty of measuring its outcomes in a tangible manner.

Further reading

Cardno, C. and Piggott-Irvine, E. (1997) *Effective Performance Appraisal*, Auckland: Addison Wesley Longman.

Holloway, J., Lewis, J. and Mallory, G. (eds) (1995) *Performance Measurement and Evaluation*, London: Sage.

Middlewood, D. and Cardno, C. (eds) (2001) *Managing Teacher Performance and Appraisal: A Comparative Approach*, London: Routledge/Falmer.

References

Beardall, J. (1995) 'Teacher appraisal and professional accountability in South Africa', *Perspectives in Education*, 16 (2): 365–72.

Beer, M. (1986) 'Performance appraisal', in J. Lorch (ed.), *Handbook of Organisational Behaviour*, Englewood Cliffs, NJ: Prentice-Hall.

Bush, T. (1999) 'Headship training' *Headship Matters*, 1 (1): 14–15.

Cardno, C. and Piggott-Irvine, E. (1997) *Effective Performance Appraisal*, Auckland: Addison Wesley Longman.

Chew, J. (2001) 'Principal performance appraisal in Singapore', in D. Middlewood, and C. Cardno (eds), *Managing Teacher Appraisal and Performance: A Comparative Approach*, London: Routledge/Falmer.

Christie, P. (1999) 'Inclusive education in South Africa: achieving equity and majority rights', in H. Daniels and P. Garner (eds), *Inclusive Education: World Year Book of Education 1999*, London: Kogan Page.

Department for Education and Employment (DfEE) (1999) *Teachers: Meeting the Challenge of Change*, London: DfEE.

Dolton, P. (2000) 'Why it's an obstructed threshold', *Times Educational Supplement*, 29 September: 4.

Draper, I. (2000) 'From appraisal to performance management', *Professional Development Today*, 3 (2): 11–21.

Erculj, J. (2001) 'Appraisal in Slovenia – the headteachers' burden?', in D. Middlewood and C. Cardno (eds), *Managing Teacher Appraisal and Performance: A Comparative Approach*, London: Routledge/Falmer.

Ferguson, M. (1982) *The Aquaian Conspiracy*, London: Granada.

Fidler, B. and Cooper, R. (1992) *Staff Appraisal and Staff Management in Schools and Colleges*, Harlow: Longman.

Fitzgerald, T. (2001) 'Evolving issues in teacher appraisal in New Zealand', in D. Middlewood and C. Cardno (eds), *Managing Teacher Appraisal and Performance: A Comparative Approach*, London: Routledge/Falmer.

Hall, V. (1997) 'Managing staff', in B. Fidler, S. Russell and T. Simkins (eds), *Choices for Self-Managing Schools*, London: Paul Chapman Publishing.

Ingvarson, L. (2001) 'Developing standards and assessments for accomplished teaching: a responsibility of the profession', in D. Middlewood and C. Cardno (eds), *Managing Teacher Appraisal and Performance: A Comparative Approach*, London: Routledge/Falmer.

Kyriacou, C. (1986) *Effective Teaching in Schools*, Oxford: Basil Blackwell.

Law, S. and Glover, D. (2000) *Educational Leadership and Learning*, Buckingham: Open University Press.

Leithwood, K. (2001) 'Appraising school leaders: the accountability context issue', in D. Middlewood and C. Cardno (eds), *Managing Teacher Appraisal and Performance: A Comparative Approach*, London: Routledge/Falmer.

Lofthouse, M., Bush, T., Coleman, M., O'Neill, J., West-Burnham, J. and Glover, D. (1995) *Managing the Curriculum*, London: Pitman/Longman.

Longenecker, G. and Ludwig, D. (1995) 'Ethical dilemmas in performance appraisal revisited', in J. Holloway, J. Lewis and G. Mallory (eds), *Performance Measurement and Evaluation*, London: Sage.

MacBeath, J. and Myers, K. (1999) *Effective School Leaders*, London: FT/Prentice-Hall.

Marson, S. (1999) 'Advanced skills teachers', *Headship Matters*, 1 (1): 6–7.

Middlewood, D. (1997) 'Managing appraisal', in T. Bush and D. Middlewood (eds), *Managing People in Education*, London: Paul Chapman Publishing.

Middlewood, D. (2001a) 'Managing teacher appraisal and performance in the United Kingdom: Pendulum Swings', in D. Middlewood and C. Cardno (eds), *Managing Teacher Appraisal and Performance: A Comparative Approach*, London: Routledge/Falmer.

Middlewood, D. (2001b) 'The future of managing teacher performance and appraisal', in D. Middlewood and C. Cardno (eds), *Managing Teacher Appraisal and Performance: A Comparative Approach*, London: Routledge/Falmer.

Middlewood, D and Cardno, C. (2001) 'The significance of teacher performance and its appraisal', in D. Middlewood and C. Cardno (eds), *Managing Teacher Appraisal and Performance: A Comparative Approach*, London: Routledge/Falmer.

O'Neill, J. (1997a) 'Preface', in J. O'Neill (ed.), *Teacher Appraisal in New Zealand*, Palmerston North: ERDC Press.

O'Neill, J. (1997b) 'Teach, learn, appraise: the impossible triangle', in J. O'Neill (ed.), *Teacher Appraisal in New Zealand*, Palmerston North: ERDC Press.

Preedy, M. (2001) 'Curriculum evaluation: measuring what we value', in D. Middlewood and N. Burton (eds), *Managing the Curriculum*, London: Paul Chapman Publishing.

Thrupp, M. (1999) *Schools Making a Difference: Let's Be Realistic!* Buckingham: Open University Press.

Thurlow, M. (2001) 'Transforming educator appraisal in South Africa', in D. Middlewood and C. Cardno (eds), *Managing Teacher Appraisal and Performance: A Comparative Approach*, London: Routledge/Falmer.

Tomlinson, H. (2000) '360 degree feedback – how does it work?', *Professional Development Today*, 3 (2): 93–8.

West-Burnham, J. (2001) 'Appraising headteachers or developing leaders? Headteacher appraisal in the UK', in D. Middlewood and C. Cardno (eds), *Managing Teacher Appraisal and Performance: A Comparative Approach*, London: Routledge/Falmer.

Whitaker, P. (1997) *Primary Schools and the Future*, Buckingham: Open University Press.

Yariv, E. (2001) 'Teachers' effectiveness and its appraisal', unpublished doctoral dissertation, University of Leicester.

9
Managing for Equal Opportunities
Marianne Coleman

Introduction

Equality of opportunities is an ideal for students and teachers, and it is the responsibility of educational managers to ensure that the ideal is put into practice. In the UK, the Human Rights Act (1998) has brought the rights of the individual under European legislation within the bounds of domestic law. The inclusion of Citizenship as part of the compulsory core curriculum for older secondary age pupils in England and Wales has endorsed the importance attached to issues of rights and equal opportunities. The same concern for equality of opportunity can be seen in the declared aim for the development of the South African education system to: 'ensure that the human resources and potential in our society are developed to the full' (ANC, 1995: 3). In Israel, education is to be based, amongst other values, on 'foundations of freedom, equality, tolerance, mutual assistance, and love of mankind' (Ministry of Education and Culture (Israel), 1998: 7).

Before considering the management of equal opportunities in education, it is useful to itemise the characteristics that are usually the cause of inequality, and also to look more closely at the definition of equality of opportunity.

Facing inequality of opportunity

The most obvious characteristics linked with discrimination and the resulting limitations on opportunity are: gender; nationality; ethnicity and religion. In addition, sexuality, disability and special needs can be characteristics that differentiate groups and individuals and that might lead to the denial of equality of opportunity. Areas that tend to be mentioned less often and are less overtly considered in the management of equal opportunities are class and age. In a special collection of articles on equal opportunities, the 'resounding silence on class' as an issue for researchers was noted by Siraj-Blatchford and Troyna (1993: 225). The current difficulties with the concept of class are associated by Hickey (2000: 162) with a postmodern analysis which differentiates sub-units of population only: 'on the basis of the unstable characteristics of "lifestyle choices" ' rather than on an economic basis. However, Mortimore and Whitty (1997: 12) refer to 'long-established patterns of disadvantage' linked with a widening gap between the educational achievements of the advantaged and disadvantaged. In the UK it is notable that the majority of children who are excluded from schools can be identified as working class (Plummer, 2000).

Discrimination on the grounds of age remains legal in the UK and, for managers in schools and colleges there may be an issue of age in relation to staff development opportunities. At a time when an increasing proportion of the teaching force in the UK and elsewhere is over 50 and training for older men and women might be questioned: 'it cannot be assumed that in-service training (with its related expenses) is inappropriate for those near retirement' (Thompson, 1992: 263). In relation to age, women may face double discrimination if they are seen to be too old for promotion having taken time out to raise a family.

Equal opportunities defined

The concept of equality of opportunity within existing societies should be differentiated from the more radical concept of equality, which implies a transformed society with more equal access for all to wealth and to power. However:

> Work on the development of equal opportunities policies in the UK suggests that it is not possible to draw a clear-cut line between liberal and radical strategies . . . Nonetheless, some policies are clearly associated with a wider political project of economic redistribution, some with recognition of group identity, while others are concerned at a very minimal level with formal legal compliance. (Riddell and Salisbury, 2000: 7)

The idea of equal opportunities may be interpreted in different ways and raises questions: 'Does managing for equality of opportunity mean all staff are treated the same, or according to their individual need? Does the latter imply treating some more favourably than others to overcome previous and/or current disadvantage?' (Middlewood and Lumby, 1998: 34).

Leicester (1996) implicitly recognises these questions and differentiates gradations of meaning of the phrase 'equal opportunities', the most radical of which addresses the issue of treating some more favourably than others, implying use of social engineering, including positive discrimination. The other meanings of equal opportunities would imply treating all staff and pupils the same and would therefore aim to improve the status quo rather than attempt more radical change. Treating people as the same, includes:

● equal opportunities as removing unfair barriers such as direct discrimination or ensuring physical access in the case of disabled

- promoting equal opportunities by increasing ability and motivation, e.g. though the provision of access courses to higher education, the provision of more nursery places in deprived areas or the recent provision of Education Maintenance Grants for students in financial need who are over 16 and in full time education
- promoting equal opportunities through the development of respect for all including those groups who may experience discrimination. In schools, this promotion of equal opportunities is likely to imply at least some curriculum development.

The concept of equal opportunities has legal, social and moral implications and there are implications for action at the national, organisational and individual levels. This chapter focuses on the management of equal opportunities at organisational level. However, the national level provides the background against which institutional managers work, and individuals inside schools and colleges are responsible for implementing the policies on a day-to-day basis.

The context for the management of equal opportunities

Managers in education may work in a national context where problems of equality of opportunity are beyond their influence. For example, drop out and poor rates of participation particularly for girls is a fact of life in developing countries (Harber and Davies, 1997: 11). Commenting on the Asian experience, Jayaweera (1997: 246) states that: 'gender and class operate as determinants of participation at each level'.

In some instances managers may operate in a culture in which responsibility has been taken at a national level in favour of positive or affirmative action. However, this is now less likely to be the case. Positive discrimination has been used in the USA where it is now being perceived as: 'dysfunctional, outmoded, and most recently, unconstitutional' (Glazer, 1997: 71). In Australia recent legislation has led to the policy being 'watered down' (Blackmore, 1999: 102) and there is talk of a 'backlash' (ibid.: 138).

The most basic requirement of a manager is to take account of statutory provision in relation to equal opportunities. In addition to the Human Rights legislation originating in Europe, UK institutions are subject to the legal requirements of the Sex Discrimination Act (1975), the Race Relations Act (1976) and the Equal Pay Act (1970). Schools are subject to the Education Act (1981), which established the duty to ensure special educational provision for those who need it, and are also subject to the infamous Clause 28 of the Local Government Act (1988) forbidding 'the promotion of homosexuality'.

In respect of the law as it operates in England and Wales, it is important to differentiate direct and indirect discrimination, both of which are illegal, and are therefore the concern of managers. Direct discrimination on grounds of race or sex occurs when someone is treated less favourably than others, i.e. not being employed simply on grounds of their sex or race. Indirect discrimination may occur for example, when a non-essential requirement for a job has the effect of excluding one sex or race rather than another. Another example might be where recruitment is by word of mouth which may discriminate against ethnic minority networks (Leicester, 1991).

In implementing and managing equal opportunities, managers in schools and colleges must obviously take note of any statutory requirements, but will also be aware of the responsibility to lead on moral issues as they relate to both students and staff through the values transmitted via management and leadership decisions. Management and leadership will impact on equal opportunities in a number of ways:

- through nurturing a culture of equal opportunities
- through planning and development of a specific policy on equal opportunities
- through human resource management policies and their implementation
- through the management of the curriculum, including the hidden curriculum.

Promoting an equal opportunities culture

The establishment of a culture of equal opportunities within a school or college may be part of a wider change in culture. For example, the concept of a more democratic management style in schools, moving away from an authoritarian culture, is being advocated in South Africa where: 'Above all educators should realise the important role they are going to play in cultivating democratic values and norms in the education sphere and, particularly, in the wider South African community' (Bray, 1996: 150).

Within the educational environment the development of an ethos of equal opportunities is crucial. The importance of high expectations in creating success is well documented in the school improvement and school effectiveness literature (Sammons et al., 1995). In particular, the type of school ethos which will ensure equality of opportunity for disadvantaged children, is seen as: 'a non-authoritarian, child-centred school [which] will discourage bullying, and by developing security and self-esteem, encourage each pupil to realise their learning potential' (Leicester, 1991: 21). It may be that this type of ethos is recognised and well integrated into the views, or at least aspirations, of senior managers in schools. For both male and female headteachers in England and Wales (Coleman, in press) the concept of 'respect' for all, including pupils, rated equally with that of 'achievement' as the main values that they wished to promote in their school.

Whether the importance of equal opportunities is being promoted as part of a national change in culture or whether it is part of the educational *zeitgeist*, there are implications for every aspect of the management of an educational establishment and these implications extend to all members of the educational community, staff, students, parents and governors, who will be reliant on the leadership that is offered. Writing about further education colleges, Warwick states that the key to success of the implementation of equal opportunities depends on:

- commitment by the senior management to a value system which sees human resource development as vital to the continuation of the organisation
- clear leadership in the implementation of this value system
- firm and public support for equal opportunities within this value system
- real and adequate resources for the implementation of equal opportunities (Warwick, 1990: 7).

Planning for equal opportunities

The moral imperative associated with equality of opportunity implies that managers may need to see it 'as a central organisational goal, requiring management techniques – planning, resource allocation (costing) time scales for delivery, monitoring and performance indicators, etc., for its achievement'. (Reeves, 1993: 262).

One of the implications of such a model, and of planning the integration of equal opportunities into the culture, may be the development of an institutional policy on equal opportunities. Since such a policy impinges on the values of the organisation, it will require consideration in light of the vision and mission of the institution in the sense that a vision implies commitment from the members of an institution (Beare et al., 1993). The development of a policy may involve stakeholders, particularly staff and governors, who then may require a training programme to be instituted. Once the policy is implemented it will require monitoring and evaluation. It seems that this part of the process of incorporating equal opportunities is problematic. One of the main findings of an Ofsted report on raising the attainment of ethnic minority pupils was that: 'Although most schools have equal opportunities policies, few have clear procedures for monitoring their implementation and their impact on practice is limited' (Ofsted, 1999: 7).

Three surveys of university departments in respect of their equal opportunities practice in relation to gender, race and disability did find evidence of good practice but it was particularly limited in the area of staff development and the monitoring of equal opportunities 'was extremely rare' (Leicester and Lovell, 1994: 19). Although at institutional level most of the universities employed equal opportunities officers, good practice was

139

described as 'patchy' at departmental level. Although equal opportunities is an ideal, in practice full implementation appears to present difficulties for managers.

In many areas of the world there has been a move towards institutional autonomy and the resulting devolution of power has meant that leaders of schools and colleges may be more accountable than previously for the development and implementation of equal opportunities. For example, the employment of staff in schools and colleges in England and Wales is no longer the remit of the local education authority, therefore governors and managers in schools and colleges who are responsible for appointment must be particularly vigilant in regard to their statutory duties. However, the additional freedom that this gives may actually allow the development of support for equal opportunities. Reeves (1993) quotes the example of a principal of a college who now has the authority to set up a child-care facility, whereas previously he or she would have been hampered by having to seek the permission of three LEA committees: education; personnel and finance.

Human resource management and equal opportunities

Human resource management policies relating to the appointment, mentoring, appraisal, performance management, professional development and promotion of staff are particularly relevant to the management of equal opportunities in educational institutions. They impact on equal opportunities in a variety of ways. The appointment and promotion of staff acts as a vivid illustration of whether or not equal opportunities is actually practised. The inclusion or exclusion of women and members of ethnic minorities in a senior management team sends out messages that substantially affect the hidden curriculum. In addition, mentoring, appraisal and professional development can be used to help promote change within an institution both by actively supporting the development of equal opportunities for individuals and by supporting changes in attitudes and perceptions of all staff.

Recruitment

There are difficulties associated with equal opportunities at the level of recruitment. In relation to initial teacher training and job opportunities in teaching in the UK, age may be a discriminant. Howson (1996) comments that fewer of the mature students end up in teaching than the younger students and that also a relatively small proportion of students from ethnic minorities are offered places to train. In addition, gender is emerging as a major recruitment issue especially for primary teaching. This phase of education has always been identified with women, and in England and Wales this is now even more the case, with a well-documented shortage of male entrants to train in this sector

(Thornton, 1999). 'Young, white and female: this is the picture of the average new entrant to the profession' (Howson, 1996: 40).

In relation to potential applicants for recruitment and promotion, research by Leicester and Lovell (1994: 47) indicates that when compared with racism and sexism, there is little awareness of discrimination in regard to disability and that in higher education there is 'significantly less action taken to increase the proportion of staff and students with disabilities than to increase black and female representation'.

Promotion

Issues of equal opportunities in educational management are perhaps at their most noticeable in relation to appointment to promoted posts. The relative absence of women and members of ethnic minorities from such posts is well documented. Although the career of teaching tends to be dominated numerically by women, they generally constitute a minority in management positions in education, with the exception of those schools which cater for very young children, which are more often managed by women. For women teachers in junior, middle and secondary schools and in colleges and universities the likelihood is that they are less likely to achieve management positions than their male peers (Coleman, 2001). Where women have made substantial progress in terms of becoming school principals as in Israel (Goldring and Chen, 1994), the more powerful administrators outside the schools are almost exclusively male.

In relation to career planning for promotion, evidence from a national survey of headteachers in England and Wales (Coleman, in press) shows that about 40 per cent of the women and about 35 per cent of the men do take some action to ensure that women teachers receive some form of career development that is tailored to their specific needs. This could be women only courses, mentoring or some form of encouragement such as individual consultation.

With regard to racial inequality, UK evidence indicates that: 'black teachers were more likely to be recruited into the lowest scales, into low-paid part-time posts, and into the support services and to remain in disproportionate numbers in these positions' (Blair, 1994: 284). When in post they tend to be pigeon-holed as the providers of the multicultural curriculum. Similarly, Thompson (1992) reports that teachers from ethnic minorities tend to be stereotyped as dealing with students from racial minorities and are less likely to be considered for promotion. Osler's (1997) analysis allows that black teachers may accept the school's designation of duties but also identifies a further range of strategies that may be adopted by black educators in response to racism in schools. These include leaving teaching, feeling that there is 'no problem', acting as an advocate of black students and teachers, challenging narrow designations and working to transform structures and power relations.

Where there is the double difficulty of race and gender to surmount, the experience is particularly difficult. Referring to her work in higher education in a South African university, one woman comments:

> I never quite feel I'm one of them . . . I sometimes wonder which one it is, is it because I'm Black or is it because I'm a woman, that no one takes me seriously . . . Maybe if I was a White female it would be easier to know, or if I was a Black male. But being both Black and female I'm not sure why they see me as so different. (Walker, 1998: 349)

What emerges from much of the relevant empirical data is the prevalence of stereotypes in relation to women and minorities. Whilst the legislation prevents both direct and indirect discrimination, negative and unhelpful attitudes may be firmly entrenched in the minds of the 'gatekeepers' who are typically white, male and middle class.

Illustrations of this inherent tendency to stereotype are quoted below from responses to the survey of women secondary headteachers in England and Wales (Coleman, 2000; 2001), where over 60 per cent of the respondents reported experiencing sexism, both in respect of appointment and in terms of treatment by peers. Active discrimination was remembered by older headteachers who had experience of being told that they would not be considered for a particular post simply because they were women. However, a more subtle form of discrimination was widely reported as still prevalent, and this was related to seeing women in terms of the domestic stereotype and thus as inferior. It is exemplified by an identification of women with certain roles particularly at deputy head stage. One woman, appointed as deputy, recalled being met by 'Expectations that I would be pastoral care – look after the girls/-flowers/coffee/tampon machines'.

This form of discrimination was sometimes overtly identified with the attitude of governors. The headteachers felt that their applications were trivialised simply because of stereotypes that were identified with them as women: 'governing body members suggested the job was too much for someone with children' (headship interview); 'I was once asked by governors at interview how a little thing like you would discipline a great big boy, would you say "hey, is it cold up there?" '. The difficulties were not only experienced with governors, the female headteachers (in this case one who was also aware of racial discrimination) had to work hard to establish credibility with staff and other colleagues: 'On my third day of headship I had to cope with a very irate member of staff who took great pains to inform me that I had only got my job because I was an Asian female.'

The instances of discrimination cited here are illustrations of the difficulties in managing an equal opportunities policy in areas as obvious as recruitment and promotion, with implications for training for staff and governors. Some of the other ways in which human resource management may be helpful in mitigating the effects of subtle and not so subtle discrimination are through fostering mentoring programmes, ensuring that there are appropriate role models and through the sympathetic and informed use of appraisal within the school or college.

Mentoring and the provision of role models

Mentoring is recognised as being of great importance in the development of career and also as a strategy to motivate under-achieving students (Coleman, 1999). Research findings such as those of Davidson and Cooper (1992) identify the importance of both formal and informal mentoring for women staff but report that informal mentoring, which is seen to enhance career progress, is generally much more likely to be experienced by men. This points to the importance of senior management establishing a formal programme of mentoring to ensure that women and minorities do obtain the benefit of mentoring (Cullen and Luna, 1993). The female headteachers surveyed by Coleman (2000; 2001), were generally advocates for mentoring, although half of them reported having been mentored by a man. Such cross-gender mentoring may be inevitable whilst there is a relative lack of senior women. However, research by Kram (1983) identified limitations in cross-gender mentoring including: young female managers lacking an adequate role model in a male mentor; male mentors maintaining stereotypical behaviour to encourage 'feelings of dependency and incompetence' (Kram, 1983: 623) and concerns about the intimacy of the relationship and the way in which it was viewed.

Same-gender mentoring avoids the problems that can be encountered in cross-gender mentoring and does provide valuable role model benefits. Although men may act as role models for women, there is evidence of the importance of female role models in encouraging the development of female managers. Davidson and Cooper, (1992: 87) make the point that female role models can change the attitudes of both women and men, acting positively on males who, without the evidence, tend to doubt the ability of women to successfully hold a senior position.

The importance of providing a role model for black women is evident. Elaine Foster comments on being a role model: 'Many black colleagues contact me to ask for advice on their futures. As a black woman, I became tired of people implying that black people could not become heads. Being a role model in areas like Handsworth is also very important' (Hustler et al., 1995: 39). Women headteachers give examples of encouraging women by modelling good practice, showing that they could manage both children and career and appointing women to stereotypically male roles, such as head of physics (Coleman, 2000; 2001).

Provision of mentoring and of appropriate role models is relatively easy, but there is a wealth of subtleties that may be involved in the management of a specific case. Coldron and Boulton (1998) carried out an in-depth investigation of the appointment of a deputy headteacher in a secondary school. In this case, the appointment of a male, previously head of the sixth form, meant that the entire senior management team was now male. In the face of the concern of the whole school, three women were elected to be part of the senior management team although they were not paid and did not take on any additional tasks. Although there was general agreement to this, over a period of time a wide range of reactions were recorded by the researchers of which a selection follows:

- the men in the team felt that they wanted to respect the women's view and promote justice for women whilst at the same time they felt excluded from understanding just by virtue of being a man
- the women were unaware of these feelings on the part of the men
- some of the men resented what they saw as 'positive action' to promote women
- the women incorporated into the senior management team felt that they were in an ambiguous position and this created tensions
- the action signalled to the staff the importance of recognising the contributions of women and that the women were taken seriously
- it allowed the headteacher to retain control, whilst the women actually still held traditional female roles that were not rewarded by pay or formal status.

However, overall the initiative was felt to be 'radical and worthwhile' (Coldron and Boulton, 1998: 330). Nevertheless the intricate and contradictory nature of the reactions to this positive scheme does act as an illustration of the difficulties faced by managers trying to promote equal opportunities.

Appraisal and training for appraisal

Both appraisal and associated professional development can be used to combat discrimination. Training for appraisal, just as for membership of an appointment panel should include at least an awareness of equal opportunities issues and an understanding of direct and indirect discrimination. In relation to the appraisal of teachers who are older, who may come from ethnic minorities or who are women, it is felt that the potentially intimate and reflective nature of appraisal raises particular issues in relation to skills and training: 'School management must become aware of how it may be involving these teachers unreasonably. Fair and equal treatment means varying and sensitive treatment. It requires understanding, confidence and maturity in the appraiser.' (Thompson, 1992: 263). These demands call for training that gives due emphasis to these more subtle issues and skills in addition to the practical knowledge of systems and law.

Earlier in the chapter it was mentioned that putting equal opportunities into practice through human resource management had an impact on the hidden curriculum. Issues of equality of opportunity actually impact directly on every area of the management of the curriculum and some examples follow.

Managing the curriculum and equal opportunities

In a chapter where the focus is on the broad area of the management of equal opportunities, it is not possible to explore in depth the range of issues that arise in relation to the management of equal opportunities within the curriculum. However, the equal opportunities values that have been articulated in the vision for the school or college will be tested through the ways that the curriculum is managed. Messages about the importance that is actually given to equal opportunities will feed through every aspect of the wider curriculum including the attitude of staff to students and the responsibilities that students are given.

Inclusion

The most obvious area for the implementation of equal opportunities is in offering access to all, which has implications for the content and delivery of the curriculum. Hatcher claims that education will only be made inclusive by 'bringing the experiences and concerns of the child or young person into the curriculum and reconstructing the curriculum on a basis which combines high intellectual quality with the perspectives of the socially deprived and oppressed rather than those of the privileged and powerful' (Hatcher, 2000: 195). This implies a complete reassessment of the values that are being transmitted through the curriculum, the nature of knowledge and pedagogy. Inclusion implies making the whole curriculum accessible to all students irrespective of gender, race and ability.

The question of how best to educate children with special educational needs is common to all countries who may deal with the issue in different ways. In China, there is simply no provision for a minority with severe problems (Merry and Zhao, 1998), while in the Western world the most common practice is to provide specialist schools alongside a range of types of integration:

- periodic integration, e.g. an 'integration event'
- geographical integration, where a unit might be on a school campus
- social integration, where disabled children share meals and playtimes
- functional integration where disabled and non-disabled children are taught in the same class (adapted from Rieser, 2000: 150–1).

Even functional integration stops short of inclusion which requires a fundamental rethink of the whole school, and challenges the traditional approach to education: 'Building a school community that accepts and values difference' (Rieser, 2000: 151).

Personal and social education

Within the existing curriculum, personal and social education and the role of pastoral care is of particular relevance to equal opportunities. The importance that is given to these areas will be indicated to students and other stakeholders by fairly unsubtle messages related to the amount of time that is spent on personal, social and moral education, by the expertise of teachers involved in teaching it and by the resources that are put into it. Where academic qualifications are particularly valued, as in Hong Kong, a subject that is not examinable may not be considered of any real worth. This view appears to inhibit the development of personal and social education in the Special Administrative Region (Tsang, 2001).

Gender issues and achievement

Decisions also have to be considered in relation to the relative achievement of male and female students and the issue of single-sex teaching. An analysis of the gender bias against girls in Chinese schools, includes the advice to teachers to 'guide girls to attribute their academic success to their efforts in order to reduce their feeling that girls are naturally inferior to boys' (Qiang, 2000: 154). However, in the UK and in a number of other countries (Epstein et al., 1998) the debate has turned from concerns about equality of opportunity for girls, to one where the focus is on the relative underachievement of boys. The context for this is complex, and relative changes should not lead to simplistic conclusions. Just one factor that might be taken into account is that in the UK, historically, girls consistently outperformed boys at the eleven-plus examination when results were deliberately skewed to the disadvantage of the girls to ensure that the numbers of girls who passed were roughly equal to the number of boys (Epstein et al., 1998).

The educational environment

Other areas where equal opportunities have a particular impact are those of student grouping, types of assessment and styles of teaching, all of which have been shown to have differential effects on male and female students. It is important that monitoring on the basis of ethnicity, class and gender takes place to ensure that equal opportunities policies are both fully informed and implemented. The physical environment including displays of art should be monitored to ensure that there are no unintentional messages being given, and provision made for parents should take into account the possibility of cultural differences and second language difficulties. Inappropriate educational materials are still found in schools, despite the fact that there is general awareness of gender and racial stereotyping in books, and that equal opportunities policies are common (Ofsted, 1999).

Conclusion

It can be seen that the management of equal opportunities lies at the heart of the management of any educational institution. Concluding on the evidence gathered from a life history approach focusing on race and gender, Burton (1993: 286) states that 'only a whole institutional focus can make a difference to the promotion and retention of women and minorities'. She goes on to list the strategies which are thought to be linked to changing the representation of ethnic minorities and female staff:

1 Ensure that equal opportunities is on the agenda, talked about and discussed.
2 A woman in a senior role is providing a role model.
3 Provide career opportunities which draw on non-conventional sources or provide differently constructed openings.
4 Monitor and use the results of the monitoring exercise to make changes.
5 Ensure that interview panels are representative.
6 Peruse all institutional documentation from an equal opportunities perspective looking at language, metaphors, images.
7 Create close links with the community and listen to what they are saying about the institutional obstacles that are experienced (Burton, 1993: 287).

A stance on equal opportunities is implicitly and explicitly linked with the strategic management of the school or college through the articulation of values. The care with which these values are then put into place will be evident through the operation of human resource management applications of recruitment, appointment, induction, mentoring and appraisal, and professional development. Equally, decisions made about the management of the curriculum, particularly attitudes to inclusion and expectations of pupils, will tend to mirror the importance placed on the development of equal opportunities. Each management team is likely to have some leeway in taking decisions about possible positive action within the school or college. However, the decisions that are made by managers will be affected and constrained by the national and social context in which they are working.

Further reading

Cole, M. (ed.) (2000) *Education, Equality and Human Rights*, London: Routledge/Falmer.

Gaine, C. and George, R. (1999) *Gender, 'Race' and Inclusive Schooling*, London: Falmer Press.

Riley, K. (1994) *Quality and Equality: Promoting Opportunities in Schools*, London: Cassell.

References

African National Congress, (ANC) (1995) *The Reconstruction and Development Programme: A Policy Framework*, Johannesburg: Umanyano.

Beare, H., Caldwell, B. and Millikan, R. (1993) 'Leadership', in M. Preedy (ed.), *Managing the Effective School*, London: Paul Chapman Publishing.

Blackmore, J. (1999) *Troubling Women: Feminism, Leadership and Educational Change*, Buckingham: Open University Press.

Blair, M. (1994) 'Black teachers, black students and education markets', *Cambridge Journal of Education*, 24 (2): 277–91.

Bray, E. (1996) 'The South African bill of rights and its impact on education', *Suid-Afrikaanse Tydskeif Opovoedkk.*, 16 (3): 150–8.

Burton, L. (1993) 'Management, 'race' and gender: an unlikely alliance?', *British Educational Research Journal*, 19 (3): 275–90.

Coldron, J. and Boulton, P. (1998) 'The success and failure of positive action to mitigate the effects of an all-male senior management team in a secondary school', *British Educational Research Journal*, 24(3): 317–31.

Coleman, M. (1999) 'Working with employers and business', in J. Lumby and N. Foskett (eds), *Managing External Relations in School and Colleges*, London: Paul Chapman Publishing.

Coleman, M. (2000) 'The female secondary headteacher in England and Wales: leadership and management styles', *Educational Research*, 42 (1): 13–27.

Coleman, M. (2001) 'Achievement against the odds: the female secondary headteachers in England and Wales', *School Leadership and Management*, 21 (1): 75–100.

Coleman, M. (in press) *Women as Headteachers: Striking the Balance*, Stoke-on-Trent: Trentham Books.

Cullen, D. and Luna, G. (1993) 'Women mentoring in academe: addressing the gender gap in higher education', *Gender and Education*, 5 (2): 125–7.

Davidson, M. J. and Cooper, C. L. (1992) *Shattering the Glass Ceiling: The Woman Manager*, London: Paul Chapman Publishing.

Epstein, D., Elwood, J., Hey, V. and Maw, J. (1998) *Failing Boys?* Buckingham: Open University Press.

Glazer, J. S. (1997) 'Affirmative action and the status of women in the academy', in C. Marshall (ed.), *Feminist Critical Policy Analysis: A perspective from Post-Secondary Education*, London: Falmer Press.

Goldring, E. and Chen, M. (1994) 'The feminization of the principalship in Israel: the trade-off between political power and cooperative leadership', in C. Marshall (ed.), *The New Politics of Race and Gender*, London: Falmer Press.

Harber, C. and Davies, L. (1997) *School Management and Effectiveness in Developing Countries: The Post-Bureaucratic School*, London: Cassell.

Hatcher, R. (2000) 'Social class and school: relationship to knowledge', in M. Cole (ed.), *Education, Equality and Human Rights*, London: Routledge/Falmer.

Hickey, T. (2000) 'Class and class analysis for the twenty-first century', in M. Cole (ed.), *Education, Equality and Human Rights*, London: Routledge/Falmer.

Howson, J. (1996) 'Equal opportunities and Initial Teacher Training', *Education Review*, 10 (1): 36–40.

Hustler, D., Brighouse, T. and Rudduck J. (eds) (1995) *Heeding Heads: Secondary Heads and Educational Commentators in Dialogue*, London: David Fulton.

Jayaweera, S. (1997) 'Higher education and the economic and social empowerment of women – the Asian experience', *Compare*, 27 (3): 245–61.

Kram, K. (1983) 'Phases of the mentor relationship', *Academy of Management Journal*, 26 (4): 608–25.

Leicester, M. (1991) *Equal Opportunities in School: Social Class, Sexuality, Race, Gender and Special Needs*, Harlow: Longman.

Leicester, M. (1996) 'Equal opportunities in education: a coherent, rational and moral concern', *Journal of Philosophy of Education*, 30 (2): 277–87.

Leicester, M. and Lovell, T. (1994) 'Equal opportunities and university practice; race, gender and disability: a comparative perspective', *Journal of Further and Higher Education*, 18 (2): 43–51.

Merry, R. and Zhao, W. (1998) 'Managing special needs provision in China: a qualitative comparison of special needs provision in the Shaanxi region of China and England', *Compare*, 28 (2): 207–18.

Middlewood, D. and Lumby, J. (1998) *Human Resource Management in Schools and Colleges*, London: Paul Chapman Publishing.

Ministry of Education and Culture (Israel) (1998) Circular from General Director.

Mortimore, P. and Whitty, G. (1997) *Can School Improvement Overcome the Effects of Disadvantage?*, London: Institute of Education.

Office for Standards in Education (Ofsted) (1999) *Raising the Attainment of Minority Ethnic Pupils*, London: Ofsted.

Osler, A. (1997) *The Education and Careers of Black Teachers: Changing Identities, Changing Lives*, Buckingham: Open University Press.

Plummer, G. (2000) *Failing Working Class Girls*, Stoke-on-Trent: Trentham Books.

Qiang, H. (2000) 'Gender difference in schooling and its challenges to teacher education in China', *Asia-Pacific Journal of Teacher Education and Development*, 3 (1): 143–62.

Reeves, F. (1993) 'Effects of the 1988 Education Reform Act on racial equality of opportunity in further education colleges', *British Educational Research Journal*, 19 (3): 259–73.

Riddell, S. and Salisbury, J. (2000) 'Introduction: educational reforms and equal opportunities programmes', in J. Salisbury and S. Riddell (eds), *Gender, Policy and Educational Change*, London: Routledge.

Rieser, R. (2000) 'Special educational needs, or inclusive education: the challenge of disability discrimination in schooling', in M. Cole (ed.), *Education, Equality and Human Rights*, London: Routledge/Falmer.

Sammons, P., Hillman, J. and Mortimore, P. (1995) 'Key characteristics of effective schools: a review of school effectiveness research', a report by the Institute of Education for the Office for Standards in Education.

Siraj-Blatchford, I. and Troyna, B. (1993) 'Equal opportunities, research and educational reform: some introductory notes', *British Educational Research Journal*, 19 (3): 223–5.

Thompson, M. (1992) 'Appraisal and equal opportunities', in N. Bennett, M. Crawford and C. Riches (eds), *Managing Change in Education: Individual and Organizational Perspectives*, London: Paul Chapman Publishing.

Thornton, M. (1999) 'Men into primary teaching', *Education 3–13*, 27 (2): 50–6.

Tsang, W. H. (2001) 'Quality management of extracurricular activities in Hong Kong secondary schools', unpublished Ed. D. thesis, University of Leicester.

Walker, M. (1998) 'Academic identities: women on a south African landscape', *British Journal of Sociology of Education*, 19 (3): 335–55.

Warwick, J. (1990) *Planning Human Resource Development through Equal Opportunities (Gender)*, London: FEU.

Section IV
Managing Learning and Teaching

10
Managing the Curriculum for Student Learning
Margaret Preedy

Introduction

This chapter looks first at a number of key questions that curriculum managers need to address.[1] It then goes on to examine the curriculum management process, involving four main stages. The following sections explore external control of the curriculum and accountability issues, and the tensions between these and the school's own ethos and values in curriculum decision-making. It is then argued that we need to give more attention to the students' experience of the curriculum, and what they bring to the learning process.[2] In conclusion, it is suggested that schools need to look beyond the somewhat narrow and technicist approaches to curriculum management suggested by government agendas and guidance, to develop an approach that is informed by a more holistic view of pupils' current and future needs in the information age.

Curriculum management is a complex task, and this chapter explores some of the main internal and external factors that contribute to this complexity, and the issues that arise for curriculum leaders. Curriculum management is concerned with addressing four key questions:

- Who?   Students and teachers.
- What?   The curriculum.
- Why?   The school's values and aims.
- Where? The school as a learning environment.

Much discussion of curriculum management in the past has tended to focus on the 'what?' question, particularly in terms of the formal, planned curriculum, divided into subject areas as shown on the school timetable. It is argued here that curriculum leadership's essential role is an integrative one, linking the what with the who, why and where. In the light of the pressures on curriculum managers discussed later, this integrative function may not receive the attention it deserves. Given limitations of space, this chapter looks particularly at the what, why and who questions – the school as a learning environment is discussed elsewhere in this volume.

We can identify three main dimensions or stages of the curriculum:

- the *intended* curriculum – what is planned
- the *offered* curriculum – what teachers teach
- the *received* curriculum – what students actually experience in the classroom.

It is a major curriculum leadership task to ensure that these three dimensions are in harmony – an integrative role again, and one that requires particular attention to the who question – how teachers and pupils interpret, enact and give their own meaning to what is planned. The focus in this chapter is on the pupil, rather than the teacher, aspect of this question.

Curriculum management processes

A useful way of conceptualising curriculum management is as a cyclical process, which includes four main stages or tasks: planning, implementing, monitoring and evaluating, and reviewing or auditing (see Figure 10.1). While it is useful to distinguish these stages for the purpose of analysis, in practice they are closely interrelated and overlapping. As the arrows in Figure 10.1 suggest, the curriculum management cycle is a dynamic, or developmental process involving ongoing change directed at improving student learning.

Planning

Planning the curriculum takes place within the framework of the school's values and aims, and the priorities identified in the school improvement/strategic

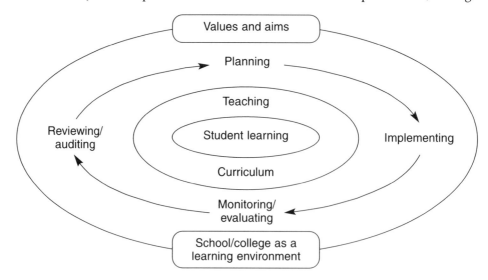

Figure 10.1   Managing the curriculum for student learning
Source: Preedy and Faulkner (1998:8)

plan, set within the context of local district expectations and national statutory requirements and guidelines. A key curriculum leadership task is to provide a clear overview and sense of direction, in ensuring that curriculum planning is related to the school's values and ensuring that there is coherence in the received curriculum as it is experienced by pupils. To enable this to take place a number of strategic issues need to be addressed:

- *breadth* – i.e. coverage of all areas of learning
- *balance* – that each area of learning is given appropriate attention
- *progression and continuity* – pupils' learning experiences should form a coherent and continuous process, within and between years, as they progress through the school, and also at school transfer stages
- *coherence* – within and between the various subjects and components of the curriculum provided
- *relevance* – meeting pupils' current and future needs
- *differentiation* – addressing the individual needs, interests and capabilities of each pupil.

These strategic issues raise a broad and complex agenda that needs to be addressed not only at whole-school level, but also within departments/sub-units and in the classroom. There may well be differences of view about how one operationalises these factors, and the appropriate emphases and priorities between them. There may be dilemmas, for example, between meeting the needs of individual students and those of the year group as a whole. There are also, of course, tensions between the various strategic issues identified above. Thus, for example, it might be difficult, particularly in the upper years of secondary schooling, to reconcile concerns about breadth and balance, while at the same time allowing students a degree of choice in selecting curricular options that they perceive as relevant to their needs.

Continuity and progression between phases of schooling – e.g. nursery, primary, middle and secondary in the UK – raise considerable management issues, since they require co-ordination with other schools. These issues are not made easier by competition between schools and a degree of parental choice – secondary schools, for example, especially in urban areas, may receive pupils from a very large number of primary or middle schools.

Strategic, long-term plans need to be linked to and supported by medium-term plans – and short-term ones i.e. weekly and daily plans – in collaboration with sub-unit leaders and classroom teachers, to ensure that whole-school intentions are translated into a detailed and coherent sequence of learning experiences. Plans represent what ought to happen. It is important for plans to provide clear means for turning 'ought' into 'is', by identifying the results of planning as 'what we want to witness in the classroom' (West, 1997).

A generic, whole-school agreed teaching and learning policy provides a useful means of developing clear links between whole-school policies and what happens in the classroom. Such policies should be linked to the school's overall aims and strategic plan, and include agreed guidance on appropriate teaching methods and strategies to promote various kinds of learning. This helps to promote consistency among teachers' approaches to the offered curriculum, which school improvement studies (see, for example, Hopkins et al., 1994) have shown to be beneficial to pupil learning.

Implementation

Rational planning models suggest that curriculum plans proceed in a logical and systematic way from policy to putting plans into action. However, effective planning only reduces the problems of translating the intended curriculum into practice. There is often a large implementation gap between the intentions of planners at national, local and whole-school levels, and the offered and received curriculum in the classroom. Much work on the management of curriculum change has shown that intended innovation often fails at the implementation stage, largely because we tend to focus on technical, rather than people-related aspects (Fullan, 1993; 2001; Louis and Miles, 1990). Because people have different interpretations and meanings of what a particular change entails for them, implementation should be seen as a gradual and evolutionary learning process, where shared meanings are developed among staff. Fullan (2001) argues that sustained change involves, in ascending order of difficulty, changes in materials, practices and beliefs. Thus for example it might be reasonably easy to persuade a teacher to use a new textbook, but changes in her/his teaching methods to complement the text, and convincing her/him that the text is valuable in meeting the learning needs of pupils, are much harder to achieve.

Some of the main issues in curriculum implementation can be summarised as follows:

- Innovations, externally and internally generated, do not come singly – implementation often involves juggling a range of competing change initiatives
- Planned changes are often unclear and ambiguous – thus for example deciding to move to a new exam board syllabus provides no guarantee that it will meet the needs of students better than the last one
- Top-down, externally initiated change may well be not understood or resisted by staff. Schools are 'loosely coupled' organisations with considerable scope for misunderstanding, adapting or simply ignoring planned changes at the various levels of decision making within the school. Particular difficulties may occur when teachers are critical of curricular changes introduced by national or state governments. An international

comparative study of schooling (Alexander, 2000) found that teachers in the USA and England were more inclined to contest externally initiated change than their counterparts in France, India and Russia, who accepted the externally prescribed curriculum as given and focused on how to implement it.

- Schools, unlike many industrial companies, do not have the time or resources to trial changes and iron out problems before they are put into practice. Changes, for example in the prescribed curriculum, have to be put into effect at the same time as teachers maintain existing areas of work, without disrupting continuity for pupils.

- External curriculum and assessment requirements are subject to frequent, ongoing adjustments, leading to 'moving goalposts' problems for schools in putting these changes into practice.

- A further issue is that unexpected and unplanned events are virtually inevitable – e.g. staff leaving. One study found that 'the vast majority of implementation problems are, in large measure, difficult to anticipate or avoid through advance planning' (Louis and Miles, 1990: 90).

Given these issues, it is important for curriculum managers to develop coping strategies for implementation, including regular discussion and review, expecting problems to occur and dealing with them as they arise, and developing support for implementation by means of staff project groups, co-ordinators for the implementation process, and advice from outside consultants – e.g. other schools with experience of the change(s) involved.

Monitoring and evaluation

Monitoring is concerned with ensuring that plans are being put into practice. It is an ongoing and routine activity that requires systems for collecting and analysing information about the enactment of overall curriculum policy in sub-units and classrooms. Monitoring is sometimes seen somewhat negatively by teachers as checking for problems. It is important for curriculum leaders to establish routine monitoring as a shared and collaborative activity contributing to staff and school development, rather than something that is externally imposed on teachers.

Evaluation is concerned with making judgements about the value, worth or quality of curriculum provision or processes. Since evaluation involves judgements, which depend on values and beliefs about the purposes of education, which may differ among various stakeholders, it is likely to involve contention. It is therefore important for curriculum managers to discuss and agree the purpose and focus of any evaluation activity, and the criteria to be used for making judgements.

We can distinguish between two broad purposes for evaluation:

- evaluation for accountability and justification purposes – internal or external, – proving the quality of the school's work
- evaluation for improvement purposes – improving the quality of the school's activities.

While evaluation activities may include elements of both purposes, the two are likely to be in tension, especially if a strict 'rendering account' approach to accountability is involved. So, for example, if members of a departmental team are reviewing the teaching styles they use, with a view to developing teachers' repertoires of styles, members are likely to acknowledge areas of weakness and seek colleagues' advice on how they might improve and extend their range of styles. If, on the other hand, departmental members are explaining their teaching methods to an external inspector, they are likely to focus on providing a rationale and justification for their existing approaches, rather than acknowledging areas for development

Evaluation criteria are often expressed in the form of performance indicators (PIs). A PI is a statement or piece of information against which achievement in an activity can be assessed, and is only an indicator or signpost, rather than a direct measure. Quantitative PIs, for example pupil examination and test results and attendance figures, are relatively easy to collect and analyse, and may therefore be given undue attention, particularly in the light of external accountability demands discussed below. Qualitative indicators of school performance are equally, if not more important, but are much more difficult to agree, collect and interpret since they involve subjective values and judgements, and hence risk being neglected in favour of quantitative indicators. Qualitative factors include the quality of pupil–staff relationships, pupils' levels of satisfaction with their schooling (Gray, 1993), and areas of pupil achievement not readily measured by examination and tests, particularly their personal, social, moral and cultural development.

Review and audit

This phase of the curriculum management cycle involves a systematic process of review to clarify current policy and practice, involving information gathering and explanation, identifying strengths to build on and weaknesses to address, in order to identify priorities for the next phase of the cycle – planning, discussed earlier in this chapter. Review is closely linked to monitoring and evaluation, and is likely to draw on evidence and judgements from monitoring and evaluation activities. As with earlier stages of the curriculum management cycle, these are important issues for curriculum managers to address in the form of the purposes and focus of the review, methods and criteria to be used in identifying priorities and collecting information, stakeholder involvement, and the timescale and resources to be allocated. As with the evaluation stage, there may be a risk of tending to focus on more easily gathered quantitative data and to neglect qualitative evidence.

A wide range of methods can be used for review or auditing – many local education authorities provide frameworks and guidelines, and there are various published review schemes and schedules (e.g. Drakeford, 1997). One useful approach is to conduct a SWOT or TOWS analysis, focusing on a particular area of provision – say a subject area. This provides a structured way of assessing the external threats and opportunities facing the subject area as a basis for considering how to maximise internal strengths and reduce weaknesses. External factors might include: recent research findings, evidence from other schools, national, local and community initiatives, funding, training and other sources of support, or lack of them, for the specific subject area.

It is also important for curriculum leaders to take account of and draw on published inspection criteria in planning and conducting reviews, in order to ensure that the school and its curriculum policies and practices are able to meet external inspection requirements. This raises issues of external control and accountability which are explored in the next section.

Control and accountability

An important consideration in school curriculum decision-making is the framework of control and accountability within which these decisions take place. In the UK context, five main levels can be identified: national, local education authorities (i.e. district level), whole-school, departmental and classroom levels. For most of the twentieth century, schools had a relatively high degree of autonomy over the content of the curriculum. The introduction of a national curriculum towards the end of the twentieth century considerably constrained the scope for schools to determine the content of the curriculum and also to some extent teaching approaches, and meant that curriculum managers were faced with the implementation issues discussed earlier in putting into place major externally initiated change.

The UK government also introduced a more rigorous school inspection regime against published criteria. This was coupled with a requirement for schools and LEAs to set regular targets for year-on-year improvements in pupil performance, and the publication of annual comparative data on test and examination results for schools and LEAs. Similar changes, introducing national curricula and more systematic quality control arrangements, took place in various other countries including Hong Kong and South Africa (Lumby, 2001).

Many countries, such as France, have had a centrally prescribed curriculum for a considerable period of time. The later years of the twentieth century saw a trend towards greater central control not just in the UK, but in other countries which had hitherto had relatively decentralised education systems, such as Australia and New Zealand. It has been accompanied by the development of national inspection agencies and databases in order to monitor and provide national evidence on standards of school performance. This trend has also been evident in the USA, at state level, (though to a less marked extent than in the UK), with many state education departments producing curriculum statements or guidelines. The trend for governments to secure greater curricular uniformity and systematic ways of monitoring pupil performance has been driven by national concerns about educational standards in the light of economic needs for more highly educated workforces, to enable national economies to compete and hence survive in an increasingly globalised marketplace. Changes in curriculum control in the UK have been both more rapid and more profound than in many other countries. A comparative study of education in France, England, the USA, India and Russia noted that: 'England for long bracketed with the USA as an emblem of decentralisation and professional autonomy, became within the space of a decade the most centralised and ruthlessly policed of all our five systems' (Alexander, 2000: 532).

The externally prescribed curriculum and associated inspection arrangements give rise to a number of dilemmas for curriculum leaders, in balancing competing priorities – particularly between: external requirements and the school's own curriculum purposes and values; products in the form of test and examination results, and processes; quantitative and qualitative measures of performance and attainment; national curriculum subjects and broader aspects of the curriculum.

Given the expectation for schools in England and Wales to demonstrate year-on-year improvements in test and examination performance, there may also be tensions between meeting the needs of different groups of pupils, e.g. seeking to boost the examination/test performance of borderline students at the expense of attention given to higher and lower attaining pupils, raising equity issues. Moreover, schools and teachers may be 'colonised' (Jeffrey and Woods, 1998) by the discourse, approach and ideology of Ofsted[3] inspections, target-setting, and associated aspects of the UK governments' agenda to drive up standards of pupil performance. The system of inspection, analysis and publication of results, feeding into national policy-making exerts a powerful control over schools, determining not only the agenda for what schools are to do, but how it is conceptualised and debated.

It is, of course, important for schools to render account for their work, both to educational agencies responsible for monitoring their work – i.e. inspectors and, more broadly, to the public at large as taxpayers and parents. However, the hard-edged, managerial forms of accountability (Kogan, 1986) backed by sanctions, to which English schools are subject, focus on narrow areas of pupils' and schools' work, and tend to prioritise evaluation for justification rather than improvement purposes.

Aims, values and cultures

Given these external accountability pressures, it is important for curriculum leaders to maintain a clear focus on the school's own core values and priorities – the why question identified earlier. Unless these core school values are understood and agreed by its members, then its learning aims are unlikely to be achieved successfully. Individuals – teachers and other stakeholders – have deep-seated underlying values and assumptions about the nature and purposes of education, based on their experiences and professional socialisation. These assumptions may often be unacknowledged.

Most people would agree that a fundamental purpose for schools is to prepare students for life, but priorities and emphases will vary, based on differing values about meeting the needs of individual learners and the group, between social expectations and individual needs, and between the various forms of learning experience provided in schools. Thus, for example, in looking at the school's values for the individual student there are competing priorities – concern with the student's academic, social, moral and cultural development, preparation for adult life, the workplace, leisure, responsibilities as a parent and citizen, and decisions about the appropriate balance between each of these purposes. Different individuals and different stakeholder groups – teachers, students, parents, governors – are likely to balance these priorities in differing ways.

Thus, schools have multiple and often competing values and purposes for student learning. It is important to review these regularly as part of professional dialogue, so that tensions between competing priorities do not build up. It is also necessary to track school aims into practice, by ensuring that policies, schemes of work and practice in the classroom actually reflect these overall aims.

Peoples' underlying sets of values exert a fundamental influence on curriculum management processes. These sets of values or ideologies affect what are perceived as curriculum management issues and how they are tackled and resolved. We can identify four main curriculum ideologies (Ross, 2000; Skilbeck, 1976). Each of these suggests a particular approach to the structure and content of the curriculum.

1 *Classical humanism* – focuses on cultural heritage and the understanding and appreciation of the highest achievements in the arts, sciences and other areas of endeavour – based around the organisation of knowledge into subject areas, and content driven.
2 *Progressivism* – a developmental approach, which starts from the child's interests and needs, stressing the importance of giving children scope to explore their individual interests and talents – process driven.
3 *Reconstructionism* – conceives of education as a means of improving society, a force for planned social change, and the development of a more democratic and just society; social needs led and objectives driven.

161

4 *Instrumentalism* – education perceived as a means to an end (rather than an end in itself as in 1 above) – preparing children for adulthood – working life, citizenship, parenthood, in some forms stresses vocational relevance; objectives driven.

Any school's list of aims is likely to reflect parts of several of these ideal type ideologies, reflecting the demands of a pluralist society. Similarly national curricula will embrace elements of various ideologies – the English prescribed curriculum, for example, incorporates ideas from 1 and 4 above in particular.

While different curricular ideologies suggest various ways of conceptualising the curriculum, curriculum management processes are also influenced by organisational cultures and, more broadly, societal cultures. The planned, offered and received curricula reflect not just the norms and values of the school or college but also those of the broader society. The role of culture in educational leadership has been somewhat neglected (Cheng, 1995) but has begun to receive increasing attention (Dimmock and Walker, 2000). Clarke (1996) identifies three broad cultural approaches to the curriculum and teaching. In the European model, the curriculum is accepted as given, but teaching methods are negotiable, the teacher is seen as the controller of learning, and both group and individual teaching methods are used. In the North American model, the curriculum is seen as negotiable, the teacher acts as 'carer' rather than controller, and individual learning is of central importance. By contrast, in the non-Western cultural approach the curriculum is accepted as given, the teacher is an authority figure, and the group, rather than the individual, is important, with whole-class teaching methods predominating.

Students – the 'who?' question

In the light of the demands of the prescribed curriculum, it is important for curriculum leaders to maintain a clear focus on the 'who?' question – the student as learner – identified at the beginning of this chapter, and shown as the central circle in Figure 10.1. The requirements of a national curriculum, and associated testing, may tend to lead to a relative neglect of broader aspects of learners' needs at the expense of attention given to products in the form of measurable performance in prescribed subjects.

In maintaining a focus on the who question, I would argue that five main concerns need to be addressed. Each of these is outlined below.

Students as active participants

The student as an active participant in the learning process not a passive recipient. Learning is a creative process, in which the learner constructs her/his own understandings and meanings, making sense of new knowledge and experience by relating them to prior experience and context. The English national curriculum tends to promote a transmission approach to learning, with the pupil as an empty vessel which the teacher, as 'expert', fills with appropriate knowledge, skills, etc. This is hardly conducive to helping students to become self-organising independent learners. Recognising pupils as active participants in learning, if this is to be taken seriously, would suggest the need to include pupil perspectives much more closely than is often the case in curriculum decision-making.

As various studies have shown (e.g. MacBeath, 1999; Rudduck et al., 1996), pupils can provide a valuable input to school decisions about learning and teaching. There are important ethical as well as practical reasons (Preedy, 2001) for involving pupils in the management and evaluation of their own learning. It is argued by Fielding (1997) that we need a 'transformative' approach to student participation, where their involvement is a routine and normal part of school life and they are seen as partners in the dialogue which informs the development of the school as a community. Equally, the more students are involved in the management cycle shown in Figure 10.1 with respect to their own learning, the more able they will be to take responsibility for their learning.

Broader capabilities and needs

The second concern is recognising the broader capabilities and needs of pupils, which extend far beyond the largely cognitive and knowledge-based areas that are covered in the prescribed curriculum. Gardner's (1993) concept of multiple intelligences suggests the importance of transcending our rather narrow and restrictive view of pupils abilities and attainments. Drawing on Gardner's work, Handy (1997) suggests a range of intelligences or talents. The first three – factual, analytic and numerate – receive considerable attention in tests and examinations, and in schooling generally. Some of the others receive less attention – linguistic, spatial, athletic, intuitive, emotional, practical, interpersonal and musical. This range of intelligences indicates a need to broaden the curriculum beyond the subjects that form the focus of the English prescribed curriculum. It is interesting in this context to look at the Norwegian government's curricular aims below, which suggest a broader range of educational aspirations, addressing some of the areas of development identified by Handy:

- a person searching for meaning
- a creative person
- a working person
- an enlightened person
- a co-operating person
- an environmentally sensitive person (cited by Dalin and Rust, 1996: 156).

The capabilities identified by Handy are important life skills that people increasingly need for adult life. Employers no longer provide a job for life, and employees need to be flexible, adaptable, prepared to continually update their skills, and to manage their own career paths, what Handy calls 'portfolio' people. Given this context, development of interpersonal and social skills becomes an important priority. Technological developments also serve to highlight the importance of these broader skills and capabilities. In our information age, new knowledge is continually being created, and hence all our knowledge has a provisional status; it is subject to uncertainty and reformulation. Students can access an enormous range of ever-changing knowledge and information via the Internet. In this situation, they arguably need not a body of received knowledge, but skills in finding, analysing and evaluating information, so that they can construct their own knowledge. The evaluative dimension is important in helping students to take a critical stance towards the seemingly limitless information that they now have access to electronically, and the ability to be selective and discriminating in constructing their own frameworks for making sense of the world. This involves what Brookfield (1987) calls 'critical thinking', coming 'to our judgements, choices and decisions for ourselves, instead of letting others do this on our behalf' (ibid.: x).

Affective factors

The third area for attention by curriculum leaders is what students bring to the learning process in terms of what might be broadly called affective factors. Three main aspects of the affective dimension of pupil learning are outlined below: preferred learning styles, attitudes and motivation.

1 Young people, like adults have different *learning styles* – usually one or two dominant styles with which they are most comfortable. It is important for curriculum managers and staff to review pupil learning styles and to consider the implications for how pupils are grouped, and how far teaching methods and pupil activities address the range of preferred learning styles. This raises the issue of the extent to which teachers are responsive to pupil learning styles and the ways in which they seek to develop pupils' facilities in using different approaches for various learning activities.

2 *Students' attitudes* towards school have a major influence on their own attainment and that of other pupils. It is an important curriculum management task to ensure that the school seeks to foster positive student attitudes, to try and ensure that as many students as possible feel themselves to be valued members of the school community.

There is considerable evidence from the UK, USA and elsewhere (see, for example, Elliott, 1998; Keys and Fernandes, 1993) that many pupils, especially in secondary schools, are disaffected and disengaged from schooling, leading to truancy and disruptive behaviour. It is therefore important for curriculum managers to develop strategies to engage pupils and to plan and offer learning experiences that pupils perceive as relevant to their own needs. Such strategies include:

(a) taking account of student motivation issues in planning the curriculum
(b) promoting high expectations about work and behaviour, with regular feedback, and praise both for good work and effort
(c) helping students to develop high self-esteem through opportunities to experience success in the classroom and in extra-curricular activities
(d) encouraging pupils to take responsibility for their work and progress
(e) clear communications with students about expectations and responsibilities for work and student conduct.

3 *Student motivation* is an important and complex component in effective learning. Curriculum managers need to explore how to help pupils to become more highly motivated and engaged in their work. A distinction is often made between two sources of motivation. *Intrinsic* motivation arises from interest in the activity itself. *Extrinsic* motivation arises where factors external to the activity are important to the learner. Three main areas of extrinsic motivation are:

(a) *instrumental* – where motivation is engendered by rewards and sanctions external to the task
(b) *social motivation* – where the activity is valued in the context of pleasing other people, e.g. peer group, teachers
(c) *achievement motivation* – where students wish to perform well to achieve success in tests or examinations or to compete with others.

Reinforcement of extrinsic motivational factors – e.g. by means of encouragement, praise, achievement awards – can help to boost intrinsic motivation.

A useful way of taking account of motivational issues is to gather evidence from students and use the findings in the planned and offered curriculum. One such study (Williams, 1997), asked pupils about what made them want to learn and what factors in the school generally and in lessons helped and hindered their learning. The study found that some pupils perceived that staff–pupil communication was poor. A major demotivating factor for pupils was that interactions with teachers focused largely on negative aspects of pupil work and behaviour, e.g. lateness, missing homework, rather than positive aspects. The school then instituted strategies to improve staff–pupil communications and to encourage teachers to adopt a more positive focus in their interactions with pupils.

Social dimensions of learning

The fourth main pupil related concern for curriculum leaders to take into account relates to the *social dimensions* of learning. The prescribed curriculum and associated testing arrangements give prominence to individual learning and attainment. However, from a social constructivist perspective, learning is a form of social participation, and emerges from social interaction. Knowledge is dynamic; we construct and reconstruct our knowledge and understanding by discussing and negotiating insights and ideas with other members of a social culture to build shared new meanings. As Bruner suggests 'most learning in most settings is a communal activity . . . It is not just that the child must make his knowledge his [her] own, but that [s]he must make it his [her] own in a community of those who share his [her] sense of belonging to a culture' (Bruner, 1986: 127). Moreover, much that pupils will do in adult life, both in the workplace and elsewhere, will be done in collaboration with other people.

Recognising that much learning is situated in social interaction, and acknowledging pupils' social as well as individual needs, would suggest that it is important for schools to foster the interpersonal and social capabilities discussed earlier – abilities to work collaboratively and constructively as members of a team, to plan, implement and achieve tasks with others, to negotiate and debate, to be flexible and open minded, to handle conflict, and so on.

Holistic view of learning

The fifth and final pupil-related concern for curriculum leaders, embracing those discussed above, is taking a *holistic view of learning*, what Young (1998) calls 'connectivity'. Much of the prescribed curriculum, and the organisation of schooling generally, is segmented into separate components – discrete knowledge areas and subjects, key stages for assessment, different education sectors – primary, middle, secondary, further/higher education, school learning and lifelong learning – with wide disjunctures between these components. This inevitably leads to a lack of cohesion in the received curriculum as experienced by pupils, and fails to provide them with a clear framework to help them make sense of the world, where things are connected, rather than separate.

In developing a curriculum that is appropriate for current and future individual and societal needs, Young (1998) argues that we need to think beyond the confines of a subject-based prescribed curriculum to debate our educational purposes and the sort of society we wish to see in the future. There will be multiple and competing perspectives, both about purposes and concepts of a future society. In terms of the curriculum ideologies discussed earlier, Young is arguing for greater weight to be given to ideas from the reconstructionist and progressive traditions. He suggests that a curriculum for the future needs to emphasise the links or connections, between the currently segmented components of school, non-school and lifelong learning, giving pupils an integrated and holistic view of learning and life. From this point of view, a connective curriculum strategy involves identifying the educational purposes of the school, recognising learning as a social process, and linking the purposes and activities of both learners and teachers with how they relate to developments in the wider society. Such an approach not only shapes learners' purposes in the light of the societal context, but is also shaped by and responsive to learners' perceived needs and purposes.

Conclusion

This chapter has looked at a number of fundamental questions that curriculum leaders need to address, and the issues involved in the curriculum management process. Later sections explored the tensions between external curricular controls and requirements and the school's own purposes and values. It has been argued that, notwithstanding the demands of the prescribed curriculum, it is essential for schools to maintain and develop their own clear curricular agendas, based on addressing the why and who questions discussed earlier. This entails, first, identifying our educational purposes and striving to ensure that these are reflected in the planned, offered and received curricula. Second, it entails not being preoccupied with external demands for measurable outputs, but instead, maintaining a holistic focus on pupils' current and future needs and involving them in progressively taking responsibility for their own learning, and helping them to go beyond the ability to ingest facts and received knowledge, to develop the broader capabilities that are necessary for survival in our postmodern information age.

Notes

1 This chapter uses the terms 'curriculum leaders' and 'curriculum managers' interchangeably, to avoid the more lengthy 'curriculum leaders and managers', to denote those with responsibility for curriculum decision-making at whole school/college level. It is argued that their roles integrate both leadership, i.e. a strategic overview, and management tasks.
2 The terms 'pupils' and 'students' are used interchangeably, again in the interests of brevity, and 'schools' rather than 'schools and colleges'. The discussion here includes both these groups of learners and types of educational organisation.
3 Ofsted – the Office for Standards in Education – inspects and reports on educational standards in English state-maintained schools and provision for 16–19 year olds in colleges.

Further reading

Middlewood, D. and Burton, N. (eds) 2001) *Managing the Curriculum*, London: Paul Chapman Publishing.
Ross, A. (2000) *Curriculum: Construction and Critique*, London: Falmer Press.
Young, M. F. D. (1998) *The Curriculum of the Future*, London: Falmer Press.

References

Alexander, R. (2000) *Culture and Pedagogy*, Oxford: Blackwell.

Brookfield, S. (1987) *Developing Critical Thinkers*, San Francisco: Jossey-Bass.

Bruner, J. (1986) *Actual Minds, Possible Worlds*, Cambridge, MA: Harvard University Press.

Cheng, K. (1995) 'The neglected dimension: cultural comparison in educational administration', in K. Wong and K. Cheng (eds), *Educational Leadership and Change: An International Perspective*, Hong Kong: Hong Kong University Press.

Clarke, P. (1996) 'Cultural models of teacher thinking and teaching', unpublished paper, Cambridge, MA: University of Harvard, cited in Alexander, R. (2000) *Culture and Pedagogy*, Oxford: Blackwell.

Dalin, P. and Rust, V. (1996) *Towards Schooling for the Twenty-first Century*, London: Cassell.

Dimmock, C. and Walker, A. (2000) 'Developing comparative and international educational leadership: a cross cultural model', *School Leadership and Management*, 20 (2): 140–63.

Drakeford, B. (1997) *The Whole-School Audit*, London: David Fulton.

Elliott, J. (1998) *The Curriculum Experiment*, Buckingham: Open University Press.

Fielding, M. (1997) 'Beyond school effectiveness and school improvement: lighting the slow fuse of possibility', *Curriculum Journal*, 8 (1): 7–27.

Fullan, M. (1993) *Change Forces*, London: Falmer Press.

Fullan, M. (2001) *The New Meaning of Educational Change*, 3rd edn, New York: Teachers College Press.

Gardner, H. (1993) *Multiple Intelligences: The Theory in Practice*, New York: Basic Books.

Gray, J. (1993) 'The quality of schooling; frameworks for judgement', in M. Preedy (ed.), *Managing the Effective School*, London: Paul Chapman Publishing.

Handy, C. (1997) *The Hungry Spirit*, London: Hutchinson.

Hopkins, D., Ainscow, M. and West, M. (1994) *School Improvement in an Era of Change*, London: Cassell.

Jeffrey, B. and Woods, P. (1998) *Testing Teachers*, London: Falmer Press.

Keys, W. and Fernandes, C. (1993) *What Do Students Think about School?*, Slough: NFER.

Kogan, M. (1986) *Education Accountability*, London: Hutchinson.

Louis, K. and Miles, M. (1990) *Improving the Urban High School: What Works and Why*, New York: Teachers College Press.

Lumby, J. (2001) 'Framing teaching and learning in the twenty first century', in D. Middlewood, and N. Burton (eds), *Managing the Curriculum*, London: Paul Chapman Publishing.

MacBeath, J. (1999) *Schools Must Speak for Themselves*, London: Routledge/Falmer.

Preedy, M. (2001) 'Curriculum evaluation: measuring what we value', in D. Middlewood, and N. Burton, (eds), *Managing the Curriculum*, London: Paul Chapman Publishing.

Preedy, M. and Faulkner, S. (1998) *Teaching and Learning*, Professional Experience Guide, NPQH Supported Open Learning Programme, Buckingham: Open University Press.

Ross, A. (2000) *Curriculum: Construction and Critique*, London: Falmer Press.

Rudduck, J., Chaplain, R. and Wallace, G. (1996) *School Improvement: What Can Pupils Tell Us?* London: David Fulton.

Skilbeck, M. (1976) E203, *Curriculum Design and Development*, Unit 3, Buckingham: Open University Press.

West, N. (1997) 'A framework for curriculum development, policy implementation and monitoring quality', in M. Preedy, R. Glatter and R. Levačić (eds), *Educational Management: Strategy, Quality and Resources*, Buckingham: Open University Press.

Williams, C. (1997) 'Managing motivation', *Managing Schools Today*, 6 (9): 28–9.

Young, M. F. D. (1998) *The Curriculum of the Future*, London: Falmer Press.

11

Monitoring and Evaluating Learning

Ann R. J. Briggs

Introduction

The primary purpose of a college or a school is to enable learning. Whether what is learned is prescribed by the state or the institution, or negotiated with individuals or with groups of learners, a learning process is designed to take place, which may be social, cultural, vocational or intellectual in its nature, but which in some way serves the individual and collective needs of society. Colleges and schools are accountable for the nature and quality of the learning which takes place within them, and learning may be formally and informally evaluated within that framework of accountability. Based on Scott's (1989) analysis, the college or school's accountability can be:

- political: in a system which is supported by public funds, the institution is accountable for the best use of those funds
- market: it is accountable to its customers, partners and stakeholders
- professional: colleges and schools are accountable for maintaining the highest possible standards of teaching and training; this includes an accountability to fellow professionals
- cultural: education can be seen as fostering new insights, knowledge and understanding; it can be a force for change in society.

However, as Le Metais points out:

> In terms of measuring outcomes, whilst the achievement of some aims, such as functional literacy, may be assessed at specific points during compulsory education, success in others, such as achieving individual potential, developing positive attitudes to lifelong learning and flexibility to deal with change, may not emerge until much later and the specific contribution of formal education, as distinct from other influences, may not be identifiable at all. (Le Metais, 1999: 96)

Given the framework of accountability within which colleges and schools are placed, some of their political, market, professional and cultural relationships will include systems of monitoring and evaluating learning. As colleges and schools strive for better outcomes for their learners, they will need ways of evaluating for themselves how good those outcomes are, and how they are to be maintained and improved. However, the nature of learning itself, especially its subjective nature and often long-term qualitative outcomes, will mean that it often evades the necessarily blunt instrument which seeks to define and measure it.

How do we learn?

> We must move towards creating an appropriate learning environment; concentrate on understanding better how people learn so that they can be better helped to learn . . . redesigning the very process of learning, assessment and organisation so as to fit the objectives and learning styles of the students. (Tomlinson, 1996: 4)

Advances in understanding the processes of the mind and the impact of social and cultural factors upon learning have led to an increasing interest over the past two decades in assessing the conditions under which learning is taking place. Recent research and discourse about how people learn are starting to influence models of teaching, and may also influence ways in which teaching and learning are evaluated.

One of the most influential researchers in this field is Gardner (1983), in his work on multiple intelligences. He defines eight 'intelligences', possessed by each person in different proportions, and argues that in order to enable learners best to use their blend of intelligences, attention should be paid to five entry points which lead to understanding:

- the narrational or storytelling approach
- the logical-quantitative approach
- the foundational or philosophical approach
- the aesthetic approach
- the experiential approach.

This analysis would influence those evaluating learning processes to look for a range of settings to be available to the learner. These might include whole-class teaching using a narrational approach, learning environments rich in aesthetic stimuli supporting an aesthetic approach or a 'hands-on' learning experience providing an experiential approach.

Other analyses of the learning process similarly point to the proposition that groups of learners need to experience a range of stimuli and strategies for learning. For example, the sensory analysis of learning styles, following work by Reinert (1976), is based on the theory that information is processed through visual, auditory and kinaesthetic channels. Individuals are considered to have predominant channels for processing information, which lead to individual strategies for learning which are based on their visual, auditory or kinaesthetic preferences. Research by Wood and Bennett (1999) and Katz (1999) into the needs of children in the early years of education indicates that they benefit from a highly interactive, varied learning environment, with the chance to express themselves through painting, drawing and building things as well as verbally and through writing. As learners mature, they can assess their own preferred sensory learning style, or blend of styles, by means of self-assessment questionnaires, and identify strategies for learning which are appropriate to their dominant style. If their tutor also has access to the analysis, both teaching and learning styles can be adapted to suit the predominant needs of the group, and to have regard for the needs of individuals.

Dimmock (2000) points out cross-cultural differences in approaches to learning, observing that approaches which are predominant in one culture may be undervalued in another. An interesting example here is the place of rote learning. Dimmock, drawing also on the work of Watkins and Biggs (1996) and Marton et al. (1996), notes that Chinese and Asian students have a tendency to rote learn, with repetition and memorisation being used as strategies to deepen understanding. On the other hand, Western educationalists regard rote learning as superficial, and as unlikely to contribute to deep learning. Cultural norms and preferences may thus affect the efficiency with which an individual can learn through a particular strategy.

A further perspective on learning has been provided through research by Goleman (1996) into emotional intelligence. This was based on work by Salovey and Mayer (1990), who identify five major domains of emotional intelligence:

- knowing one's emotions
- managing emotions
- motivating oneself
- recognising emotions in others
- handling relationships.

These domains are balanced differently in different people, and an individual's personal strengths and strategies, and their interactions with others, will be governed by that balance. Goleman (1996) considers that emotional intelligence is a crucial factor in determining a person's life chances, and that it can be fostered and developed. Emotional 'illiteracy', according to Goleman, is costly to the individual and to society, and is preventable. Whilst the main development of emotional competence takes place within the family, colleges and schools have also a role to play here: 'Developing emotional literacy is obviously a crucial part of preparing young people to survive and succeed in adult life, and Goleman's work provides powerful evidence that schools can play an important part, though not an exclusive one, in supporting it' (Bentley, 1998: 26).

The perspectives on learning offered above are only a small sample from a body of research which has profound implications for the management and evaluation of learning.

> If schools confront the all-important question – how do students best learn? – they may have to modify other elements as well, in order to promote learning. These include organisational structures, such as the timetable and student and teacher grouping, as well as school culture and patterns of resource allocation. (Dimmock, 2000: 109)

They may also include a reassessment of how learning, and the progress of individual learners, is to be monitored and evaluated.

The learning-centred organisation

Where colleges and schools are learning-centred, learning is not confined to the student and pupil. Where staff, whatever their role, also learn – about their subject, their support or management function, about student learning, about leadership and strategic direction – and in a symbiotic and organised fashion, the whole organisation collectively and continuously learns how to become more effective as an institution, then the college or school can be deemed to be learning-centred. (See, for example, Lumby, 1997; Stoll and Fink, 1996; Lundy and Cowling, 1996) Evaluation of the learning capability of an organisation would be an enlightening, but daunting, task and not one to be attempted in any detail here. Some measure could be taken by using one of the many checklists of school effectiveness (see, for example, Sammons et al., 1996). However, a brief glance at the first three of Sammons's 11 most salient factors associated with effectiveness – professional leadership; shared vision and goals; a learning environment – shows that each of the features listed would need a detailed further analysis of how the organisation was 'learning its way forward' in that particular case. A simpler answer might be that the true 'learning organisation' would learn how to evaluate itself.

Morgan (1986: 89) notes that 'many organisations have become proficient at single loop learning, developing an ability to scan the environment, to set objectives, and to monitor the general performance of the system in relation to its objectives . . . However, the ability to achieve proficiency at double loop learning has often proved more elusive'. Double-loop learning involves reviewing and challenging norms, policies and procedures in relation to the changing environment of the organisation – in other words, it regularly questions the objectives themselves. Even within the variously bounded systems of autonomy experienced by educational organisations across the world, there may be scope to challenge the 'norms, policies and procedures' of the college or school –

through the individual and collective learning of its staff – so that the organisation can learn how to respond most appropriately to its changing environment.

Moving from organisational learning to its ultimate objective – student learning – analysing the process of evaluation may seem easier. Most colleges and schools have systems of monitoring the learning which takes place, both for the purposes of internal assessment and improvement and for external evaluation. However, if the debate also moves from the 'learning-centred organisation' to the 'learner-centred organisation', other issues intervene.

To be learner-centred assumes a knowledge of what learners need. Fazey observes: 'Being learner-centred . . . means acknowledging that each learner has individual needs and aspirations – that their reasons for study are as different as their personal resources, affective responses, knowledge of the environment and experiences' (Fazey, 1996: 31). Does the evaluation of learning involve taking into account the wishes and aspirations of the learner? Lumby (2001: 5) is pessimistic about the extent to which learners are consulted: 'The predominance of a discourse on learn*ing* rather than the learn*er* reflects the relative powerlessness of learners in discussions about learning and teaching.' In her view, students are rarely consulted about their satisfaction with the learning process and environment until they reach post-compulsory education, where they are more likely to be regarded as 'clients' whose custom can be won and lost. Ruddock et al. (1996), in a survey of UK secondary school pupils, underline the importance of asking individual students about their needs. Research at Mount Edgecumbe High School in Sitka, Alaska (Cotton, 1994), emphasises the success of involving the students in curriculum developments. Being learner-centred, and having the capacity to monitor and evaluate the organisation's effectiveness in supporting students' learning needs, can involve regular consultation of the students and pupils themselves, whatever their age may be.

However, the needs of the individual learner may not always be the main focus of the education system. In Denmark, 'Jante's Law', which celebrates collective, rather than individual, achievement is well respected in education. 'If a pupil is more capable at doing maths than another it is her responsibility to help other pupils to reach the same level' (White, 1997: 41). White presents the memorable analogy of tulips in a bulb field – where for one individual to stand up above the others is a feature 'not universally admired' (ibid.: 41). Similarly, in post-Pinochet Chile, educational reforms have focused upon 'the basic cultural skills necessary for the child's personal, social and intellectual development', and the 'equitable distribution of those learning outcomes within the population' (Aedo-Richmond and Richmond, 1999: 198).

Cultural differences in approaches to learning are also noted by Lumby:

> For some, helping each learner to fulfil his/her individual potential is key. In
> other societies, helping learners to become productive members of society with
> less stress on individuality (Satow and Wang, 1994) or obtaining high examina-

tion marks to gain a job with the highest possible salary (Chan and Watkins, 1994) is the aim. (Lumby, 2001:4)

The effects of cultural difference on the contexts in which effective learning may take place are illustrated by research in secondary schools in the Shaanxi province of China by Bush et al. (1998). Here, class sizes of up to 75 pupils were observed – although 50 was more typical – where: 'whole class teaching predominates, using the traditional modes of learning, recitation and review'. However, the researchers concluded that in the Chinese schools 'large classes and formal approaches do not appear to be inimical to high standards' (ibid.: 189)

Dimmock (2000: 125–6) comments that: 'Chinese students are highly motivated to do well at school, as this is seen to be the route to social and economic advancement as well as improvement in the person', and Bush et al. (1998) report that the Shaanxi teachers had a larger proportion of non-contact time than their UK counterparts. This time was spent in preparing lessons, marking work, giving extra support to children and working together in the 'jaioyanzu' – curriculum groups – to make decisions about curriculum and instruction and to observe and comment on each other's work. Viewed from this perspective, the schools observed might be judged as 'learning-centred', even though the emphasis was not on the individual learner.

Cultures change, however, and learning preferences may change with them. Chan and Watkins report from a study of student preferences in Hong Kong secondary schools that:

> Clearly many of the students would prefer their science classroom to be a friendlier place where both students and teachers enjoyed working together planning a variety of interesting but challenging activities. Such an environment would encourage both the deeper level and more achievement-oriented learning strategies that students would prefer. (Chan and Watkins, 1994: 245)

At present, there is little evidence that this change has taken place.

Evaluating learning will thus be individual to each culture, and probably to each institution. It will depend on the learning capacity of the staff of the college or school, and will be based upon the cultural norms of the system, the individual and collective needs of the learners, and the specific learning aims of the institution. It will be driven by an evaluation of both the current learning environment and the success and satisfaction of the students, and, given the changing nature of societies and education systems today, will often involve challenging the 'status quo'.

Monitoring the management of learning

Colleges must lead and support staff in their new roles as managers of learning, at a time when morale may be low and sub-cultures may be in conflict with the emerging corporate culture. Raising staff awareness, overcoming cynicism, dealing with role-change problems, involving part-time staff more, and gaining the acceptance of non-teaching staff are on every college's agenda. (FEU, 1993: 58)

The above quotation, written at a time when English further education colleges were going through a painful process of change, reminds us that even such a fundamental task as managing the curriculum – sustaining a role as a manager of learning – is not straightforward, and will be influenced by external and internal political factors.

How well the curriculum is managed – and therefore how well the learning process is progressing – may, according to West-Burnham (1994) be judged by one of a number of processes, which include: assessment, assurance, inspection, evaluation and monitoring.

1 '*Assessment is a summative process, providing measurements against objective criteria*' (ibid.: 158). In its simplest terms, where curriculum management is concerned, the teacher, the institution, or the local or national government may set targets as to what percentage of students of a certain age will pass a test at a specified grade. The success of the teacher, the department or the school will be judged by whether this is achieved or not. More complex systems of institutional self-assessment exist, where an annual review of the whole college or school is carried out, using measurements against a number of performance indicators. This may in turn be combined with the next process: inspection.

2 '*Inspection is an external, summative process, judging the extent to which an organisation meets externally imposed criteria*' (ibid.: 158). As well as considering student achievements – as in the simple example above – the process of teaching and learning will usually be observed and judged against the inspectors' criteria, as well as the systems of management operating in the college or school. If a system of self-assessment is in operation, the inspection report may also judge how well the institution has assessed itself.

3 '*Assurance is a process designed to remove the need for external, summative inspection by designing a process to guarantee conformity*' (ibid.: 158). This process is more often applied to college and school systems of administration than to the management of learning. However, the government-prescribed format for the teaching of literacy and numeracy in UK schools could be described as an attempt at assurance: the aspiration is that if the format is adhered to, attainment levels will rise. In this case, as in many examples of quality assurance, the process of external inspection is still retained.

4 '*Evaluation is an internal or external formative process designed to give feedback on the total impact or value of a project or activity*' (ibid.: 158). It will usually be combined with monitoring: 'the collection of data and evi-

dence to inform other review activities' (ibid.: 158) The key word in the
definition is 'formative'. An evaluation system is set up in order to enable
those involved in managing the work of a department, a developmental
project or a teaching activity to understand how well it is progressing, so
that adjustments and changes to process or even to aims and overall direction can be made. As such it is a system which can facilitate the 'double-
loop learning' referred to in this chapter on p. 173.

A cycle for monitoring and evaluating aspects of curriculum management in a
college or school can be represented as in Figure 11.1. One striking feature of
this cycle is the distance between 'identify need' and 'carry out activity'. If the
curriculum activity is to be properly monitored and evaluated, then its design
and purpose must be clear, and all involved must know both what its targets
and outcomes are, and how they are to be measured, within what time frame.
The 'necessary resources' may include time and staffing for the monitoring
activities to take place, access to administrative support for data analysis, and
time for staff to meet and evaluate the activity. If double-loop learning is to
take place, then the evaluation process will not only assess the activity against
the original targets and outcomes, but also consider whether policies and practice now need to be changed and new objectives set.

Representations of this type can give the discouraging impression of a treadmill where a predetermined cycle is endlessly repeated. What the diagram cannot easily show is the progress made. The circle is not static: it is like a wheel
moving along a road, often moving forward at some speed as those involved

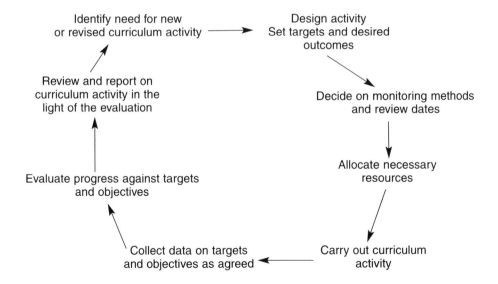

Figure 11.1   Curriculum monitoring and evaluation cycle

177

learn more about the process in which they are involved, and if it is not moving forward at all, or is moving in directions which are not appropriate, then the whole process needs to be re-examined.

The cycle can be used to evaluate innovations, both in curriculum content – for example, where a new course is to be piloted and evaluated – and in curriculum delivery: evaluating new staffing patterns or teaching and learning methods for an existing course. Where innovations are concerned, it is important to have comparative data to use as benchmarks in order to evaluate success.

The cycle can also be used to support routine planning for a curriculum area, subject or class. Given the existing workload of teachers and managers, monitoring in the form of data collection and analysis will usually be kept simple, using statistical data which are readily available, or the visible achievement of specified outcomes. This does not prevent the monitoring activity from being rigorous and objective. As Hardie (2001: 72) comments: 'Monitoring . . . is finding out what is really happening, not what managers might think is happening or what managers would like to be happening.' Hardie (2001: 70–1) comments that monitoring uses a planned, routine gathering of information, and seeks to answer the question: 'Do we do what we say we do?'

Monitoring student progress

In 1997, Yair reported on a piece of large-scale research which had been carried out in the primary school sector in Jerusalem. The results of over 19,000 children in school grades 2–6 throughout the city for standardised tests in reading and mathematics were analysed for gender, socio-economic status and level of parental education. Unsurprisingly, results were lower for children with low socio-economic status and for those whose parents had low educational achievements; girls were found, on average, to have better reading scores than boys, whilst the reverse was true in mathematics. However, when these known factors were taken into account, there was still a statistically significant difference between the results from different schools. What was more startling, and was treated to extensive statistical analysis by the researchers to ensure the elimination of confounding factors, was the extent of the variation in results of individual classes within schools. In other words – to quote the title of the research paper: 'classrooms matter'. In the case of a primary school system where single teachers teach most of the school curriculum to their particular class: class teachers matter.

This research confirms objectively what most teachers and managers subjectively know: that some classrooms are more successfully managed than others, and that more learning takes place in them. It is not the remit of this chapter to investigate the reasons and remedies for this. The focus of this chapter is on evaluating learning, and it is important that curriculum managers find ways of evaluating what learning is taking place, and under what circumstances, in the classrooms for which they are accountable.

Their evaluation will probably involve the collection of both quantitative and qualitative data. Quantitative data may be in the form of test scores, or the statistical analysis of student or parental satisfaction surveys; the collection of qualitative data may involve systematic observation of teaching, or consultation with students. In these investigations, evaluation can be attempted of some of the more intangible aspects of learning. For example, Mortimore et al. (1988) report in their Junior School study ways in which children's self-image, behaviour and attitudes towards school activities can be measured; MacBeath et al. (1992) have developed 'ethos indicators' for schools in the Scottish system.

Observation of teachers and lecturers at work – evaluation of the learning process at work within the college or school – has traditionally been a key feature of external inspection. Observation as a system of internal monitoring has in some countries encountered operational and professional difficulties. Sometimes there is simply not the opportunity in the college or school day for either line managers or peers to observe and evaluate the work of colleagues in the classroom; sometimes there is a reluctance to judge: to 'get myself into a situation where I appear to be judging the work of a colleague whom I know to be my superior as a superb teacher of her subject', a reticence to intrude: 'sometimes there is a real sense that we are intruding into the realm of another professional' (subject leaders, quoted in Glover et al., 1998: 284).

However, where these difficulties can be overcome, systematic, planned observation of lessons can take its place alongside other monitoring methods. McGilchrist et al. (1997) report on the monitoring methods in place at one London secondary school. The written work of pupils of high, average and low ability is regularly sampled and examined for evidence of pupil achievement, of appropriate work being set and helpfully assessed, and whether the pupils' various needs are being met. The sampled pupils are observed in class, they and their parents are interviewed and positive feedback is given to the pupils and family. Areas of concern for the school are discussed as appropriate with the school managers and class tutors.

The most common focus of monitoring is that of examining data on student progress and achievement. Most institutions where students take public examinations will consider their results year on year as part of their internal evaluation process, and many are publicly judged – or in the case of English further education colleges, funded – according to the examination success of their students. Even when such seemingly unambiguous quantitative data are used for evaluation purposes, adjustments will have to be made if meaningful action is to follow. For example, it may be necessary to take into account the concept of 'value added' – acknowledging that even the youngest student arrives with some learning already accomplished. 'Without a "value added" dimension, the obvious basis for judgment is that "higher" scores represent better practice and "lower" scores worse. This could lead to unwarranted complacency on the part of some schools . . . and, conversely, to despair on the part of others' (Dearing, 1993: 77).

Taking baseline testing on entry, or national examinations taken just prior to entry as a benchmark, the institution calculates how much progress has been made by individual students and by aggregated student groups. The calculation can be further refined by including an element which takes account of the degree of social deprivation of the student. This should not preclude the setting of challenging targets and high expectations for all students, as: 'schools can make a difference and that being in an effective as against a less effective school is a crucial determinant of life chances for many individual young people' (MacBeath and Mortimore, 2001: 2).

But should social deprivation simply be identified as a contributory factor to the student's present level of attainment, or as a factor which must be addressed in order to promote future success? In post-Pinochet Chile, this question has led to a rethinking of the principle of equity:

> Until now, the application of the principle of equality of opportunities has insisted that all children receive a similar education; in future one must look for a differentiated education in order to achieve similar results. This implies flexibility in order to spend more resources on the schools and programmes which are attended by the poorest children, young people and adults in the countryside and the city. (Garcia-Huidobro, 1990: 165, quoted in translation in Aedo-Richmond and Richmond, 1999: 198)

Equity and effectiveness at an institutional level can be addressed by systems of monitoring such as those below. They were written in the UK by the DFE/Ofsted (1995) for schools, but could equally apply to other educational institutions, and other countries.

1 How is our school currently performing?
2 Are some parts of the school more effective than others?
3 Are some groups of pupils doing better than others?
4 How does the school's performance compare with its previous achievement?
5 How does the school's performance compare with that of other schools?

Where issues of equity are concerned, answers to questions 2 and 3 will be crucial. Stoll and Fink offer useful comment here which can be applied to all phases of education:

> Equity is a fundamental tenet of school effectiveness. Some schools are differentially effective: they offer better opportunities to one pupil group than another, for example girls rather than boys, younger rather than older pupils,

pupils of one ethnic or social class background, pupils taking particular subjects or courses, or pupils in different levels or streams. During evaluation, data should be disaggregated to examine differences between such groups. (Stoll and Fink, 1996: 169)

Once it is found, for example, that engineering trainees have had better examination success in recent years than hairdressing trainees, that students on short, part-time courses have tended to drop out before the end, whereas those on longer, full-time courses have not, that the traditionally strong mathematics department has actually had declining success in national tests and examinations over the past five years, that over the past three years pupils working with teacher A have done better than those working with teacher B, that children from a particular ethnic group perform better than children from another, then the college or school is in a position to address the situation.

These examples include the practice of evaluating relative achievement over time – question 4 in the list above. Comparison with other institutions of similar type can also be useful, as indicated in question 5. Data can be obtained, either through partnership with the other institution(s), through examination of data in the public domain, or by providing information for, and 'buying into' the use of, databases of college and school statistics collated by commercial companies.

Examination of monitored data in answer to questions 2–5 can enable managers and staff to answer question 1: 'How is our school [or college] currently performing?' Following the precepts of the learning organisation, if all staff have been involved in collecting and analysing the data, they may be more ready to understand and address issues which are of concern, and to make proposals which will start the process of change.

Conclusions: evaluate what you value

Why have non-educators determined a narrow range of outcomes on which schools are to be judged? It is too easy to point out that 'they' are misguided or perverse. If there is a problem for educators and researchers, we did it to ourselves. We have never demonstrated to ourselves, let alone anyone else, that schools make a difference to pupils' learning, knowledge, skills and attitudes which will enable them to be successful citizens in the twenty-first century. If most educators are not assessment literate how can we expect our publics to understand the issues that relate to assessment? (Stoll and Fink, 1996: 167)

In the course of this chapter, it has been argued that colleges and schools can evaluate:

- the learning needs of individual students, which can inform individual tutorial practice and class teaching styles

- the differential effectiveness of departments, tutors, gender groups and ethnic groups
- the progress and future direction of a curriculum department, curriculum project or a class group
- whole-institution effectiveness – e.g. by examination results adjusted for value added and social factors
- the developmental needs of staff, including their capacity to work in synthesis to promote the learning goals of the organisation.

The focus of the evaluation will depend upon the values and aspirations of the institution, and the process will be undertaken with a sense of purpose. The evaluation may identify issues which need to be addressed, and the monitoring process can pinpoint where remedial or developmental action can take place; there will also be successes to celebrate. Over a period of time performance – and success – will be judged both externally and internally, formally and informally, in formative ways which enable future direction to be determined, and in summative ways which may place a 'snapshot' judgment, fixed in time.

In considering the subject of evaluation, Gray (1990) points to what he calls the 'missing dimension'. He considers that this refers to 'moments of quality', significant learning experiences where the learner makes a leap in understanding. These may not easily be evaluated, but Gray asserts that 'schools and teachers must be encouraged to identify and celebrate their moments of excellence' (ibid.: 30). In this way, the intangible essence of learning may be captured and made memorable.

The value of learning lies in the memories and life experiences of the learners.

Further reading

Hardie, B. (2001) 'Managing monitoring of the curriculum', in D. Middlewood and N. Burton (eds), *Managing the Curriculum*, London: Paul Chapman Publishing.
Sammons, P., Mortimore, P. and Thomas, S. (1996) 'Do schools perform consistently across outcomes and areas?', in J. Gray, D. Reynolds, C. FitzGibbon and D. Jesson (eds), *Merging Traditions: The Future of Research on School Effectiveness and School Improvement*, London: Cassell.
Stoll, L. and Fink, D. (1996) *Changing our Schools*, Buckingham: Open University Press.

References

Aedo-Richmond, R. and Richmond, M. (1999) 'Recent curriculum change in post-Pinochet Chile', in B. Moon and P. Murphy (eds), *Curriculum in Context*, London: Paul Chapman Publishing/Open University.

Bentley, T. (1998) *Learning beyond the Classroom: Education for a Changing World*, London: Routledge.

Bush, T., Coleman, M. and Si, X. (1998) 'Managing secondary schools in China', *Compare*, 28 (2): 183–95.

Chan, Y. and Watkins, D. (1994) 'Classroom environments and approaches to learning: an investigation of the actual and preferred perceptions of Hong Kong secondary school students', *Instructional Science*, 22: 233–46.

Cotton, K. (1994) *Applying Total Quality Management Principles to Secondary Education*, Portland, OR: Northwest Regional Educational Laboratory.

Dearing, R. (1993) *The National Curriculum and its Assessment: An Interim Report*, London: NCC and SEAC.

Department for Education/Office for Standards in Education (DFE/Ofsted) (1995) *Governing bodies and effective schools*, London: Department for Education.

Dimmock, C. (2000) *Designing the Learning-Centred School: A Cross-Cultural Perspective*, London: Falmer Press.

Fazey, D. (1996) 'Guidance for learner autonomy', in S. McNair (ed.), *Putting Learners at the Centre*, Sheffield: DfEE.

Further Education Unit (FEU) (1993) *Challenges for Colleges*, London: Further Education Unit.

Garcia-Huidobro, J. E. (1990) 'Educacion y Democracia', in *PIIE Las reformas educativas en las Transiciones Democracias*, Santiago: PIIE.

Gardner, H. (1983) *Frames of Mind*, Fontana: London.

Glover, D., Gleeson, D., Gough, C. and Johnson, M. (1998) 'The meaning of management: the developmental needs of middle managers in secondary schools', *Educational Management and Administration*, 26 (3): 279–92.

Goleman, D. (1996) *Emotional Intelligence: Why It Can Matter More than IQ*, London: Bloomsbury.

Gray, J. (1990) 'The quality of schooling: frameworks for judgment', *British Journal of Educational Studies*, 38 (3): 204–23.

Hardie, B. (2001) 'Managing monitoring of the curriculum', in D. Middlewood and N. Burton (eds), *Managing the Curriculum*, London: Paul Chapman Publishing.

Katz, L. G. (1999) 'Another look at what young children should be learning', *ERIC/EECE Newsletter*, 11 (2): 1–3.

Le Metais, J. (1999) *Legislating for Change: School Reforms in England and Wales, 1979–1994*, Slough: NFER.

Lumby. J. (1997) 'The learning organisation', in T. Bush and D. Middlewood (eds), *Managing People in Education*, London: Paul Chapman Publishing.

Lumby, J. (2001) 'Framing teaching and learning in the 21st century', in D. Middlewood and N. Burton (eds), *Managing the Curriculum*, London: Paul Chapman Publishing.

Lundy, O. and Cowling, C. (1996) *Strategic Human Resource Management*, London: Routledge.

Macbeath, J. and Mortimore, P. (2001) *Improving School Effectiveness*, Buckingham: Open University Press.

MacBeath, J., Thompson, R., Arrowsmith, J. and Forbes, D. (1992) *Using Ethos Indicators in Secondary School Self-Evaluation: Taking Account of the Views of*

Pupils, Parents and Teachers, Edinburgh: HM Inspectors of Schools, Scottish Office Education Department.

Marton, F., Dall'Alba, G. and Tse, L.K. (1996) 'Memorising and understanding: the keys to the paradox', in D. A. Watkins and J. B. Biggs (eds), *The Chinese Learner: Cultural, Psychological and Contextual Influences*, Hong Kong: Comparative Education Research Centre, University of Hong Kong.

McGilchrist, B., Myers, K. and Reed, J. (1997) *The Intelligent School*, London: Paul Chapman Publishing.

Morgan, G. (1986) *Images of Organization*, London: Sage.

Mortimore, P., Sammons, P., Stoll, L., Lewis, D. and Ecob, R. (1988) *School Matters: The Junior Years*, London: Paul Chapman Publishing.

Reinert, H. (1976) 'One picture is worth a thousand words? Not necessarily!', *Modern Language Journal*, 60: 160–8.

Ruddock, J., Chaplain, R. and Wallace, G. (1996) *School Improvement. What Can Pupils Tell Us?*, London: David Fulton.

Salovey, P. and Mayer, J. D. (1990) 'Emotional intelligence', *Imagination, Cognition and Personality*, 9: 185–211.

Sammons, P., Mortimore, P. and Thomas, S. (1996) 'Do schools perform consistently across outcomes and areas?', in J. Gray, D. Reynolds, C. FitzGibbon and D. Jesson (eds), *Merging Traditions: The Future of Research on School Effectiveness and School Improvement*, London: Cassell.

Satow, T. and Wang, Z. (1994) 'Cultural and organisational factors in human resource management in China and Japan', *Journal of Managerial Psychology*, 9 (4): 2–11.

Scott, P. (1989) 'Accountability, responsiveness and responsibility', in R. Glatter (ed.), *Educational Institutions and their Environments: Managing the Boundaries*, Buckingham: Open University Press.

Stoll, L. and Fink, D. (1996) *Changing our Schools*, Buckingham: Open University Press.

Tomlinson, J. (1996) *Inclusive Learning: The Report of the Learning Difficulties and Disabilities Committee*, Coventry: FEFC.

Watkins, D. A. and Biggs, J. B. (1996) *The Chinese Learner: Cultural, Psychological and Contextual Influences*, Hong Kong: Comparative Education Research Centre, University of Hong Kong.

West-Burnham, J. (1994) 'Inspection, evaluation and quality assurance', in T. Bush and J. West-Burnham (eds), *Principles of Educational Management*, Harlow: Longman.

White, R. C. (1997) *Curriculum Innovation: A Celebration of Classroom Practice*, Buckingham: Open University Press.

Wood, E. and Bennett, N. (1999) 'Progression and continuity in early childhood education: tensions and contradictions', *International Journal of Early Years Education*, 7 (1): 5–16.

Yair, G. (1997) 'When classrooms matter: implications of between-classroom variability for educational policy in Israel', *Assessment in Education*, 4 (2): 225–48.

Section V
Managing Finance and Resources

12

Efficiency, Equity and Autonomy

Rosalind Levačić

Introduction

Over the last 15 years or so, countries in all parts of the world have made efforts to decentralise their education systems and increase the degree of school autonomy. The World Bank (1995) promotes such policies in developing countries. For example Nicaragua and El Salvador have increased state school autonomy (Jiminez and Sawada, 1998; King and Ozler, 1998; King et al., 1999), while projects in Pakistan and Columbia (Kim et al., 1998; King et al., 1998) aim to increase the participation of low-income children in schooling through extending private school provision. Large-scale delegation of management responsibilities to school level has occurred as part of systemic reforms in the UK, Australia, New Zealand, Sweden and The Netherlands. Decentralisation, though not on the scale of the countries just listed, is ongoing in many other countries (e.g. Italy, Israel, Spain). In the USA many states and school districts have introduced various forms of community involvement in the running of schools (e.g. Chicago), greater resource management autonomy (Seattle, Pittsburg, Cincinnati), education vouchers (Milwaukee) and charter schools.

The purpose of this chapter is to examine the development of greater school autonomy as a change in the governance structure of an education system. It examines the arguments for and against decentralisation and school autonomy as ways of improving the efficiency of the school system. It also considers what may be the effects of such developments on equity, that is on the access of different social groups to education. These are controversial issues and remain so despite many empirical studies on the effects of different policies in different settings.

What is school autonomy?

Autonomy

The dictionary definition of autonomy, derived from the Greek, is 'self-governing' and hence 'functioning independently without the control of others'

(West, 1992). West emphasises the autonomy of consumers, 'who must be free to choose a better school and reject an inferior one', as well as to the autonomy of schools. Chubb and Moe (1990) – strong advocates of voucher systems which enable low-income children to attend private sector schools – define autonomous schools as 'free to govern themselves as they want, specify their own goals, programmes and methods'.

As Berka (2000) points out, a school's ability to be self-regulating depends on its power to choose its own actions unconstrained by other organisations or social institutions, which include the economy (market forces) and cultural institutions, such as the churches, as well as the state. In order to have a working definition of autonomy I follow Berka's suggestion that the concept is restricted to the relationship between the educational organisation and the state.[1]

Decentralisation

An increase in institutional autonomy is achieved through decentralisation, which is the process of transferring decision-making authority for particular functions from a higher to a lower level (Hanson, 1998). Powers are devolved to a lower level when this is permanent but are delegated if the central authority can readily reappropriate them (Office for Official Publications of the European Communities, 2001: 180). Deregulation is the process by which the number and extent of regulations (rules and laws) that constrain what a school (or other entity) can do are reduced. Thus extending the scope of decision-making at institutional level is very likely to involve deregulation.

Forms of school autonomy

The degree and nature of school autonomy depends on which domains of decision-making are within the discretion of the school and which are taken at a higher level. The main domains of decision-making are (Karstanje, 1999; Levačić, 1995):

- school organisation: structure, differentiation, decision-making processes, capacity, class size
- curriculum (guidelines, content, hours, textbooks), teaching methods and assessment
- staff: regulations on qualifications, appointment and dismissal, in-service training, appraisal, pay and conditions of service, including methods of performance management
- financial and resource management: spending decisions; size of staffing establishment, premises, information systems, financial assets and liabilities
- external relations: admissions policies, pupil recruitment, relationships with other organisations (e.g. trade unions).

Within each dimension some decisions can be assigned to schools and others to higher levels. What form school autonomy takes and the governance structure of the school system depend on the allocation of the different domains and the extent of delegation to schools within each domain. By classifying the different domains, education systems can be compared for their degree of decentralisation. For example, the Organisation for Economic Co-operation and Development (OECD) publishes indicators of decision making at school level (OECD, 2000). An important distinction, made by Caldwell in Chapter 3, is between self-managing schools and self-governing schools. The former has significant delegation or devolution of decision-making, particularly over resources, but operates within a centrally determined framework of standards and accountability. Self-governing schools do not operate within such a framework, hence private schools in most systems are self-governing.

Self-managing schools

The extent of school autonomy over resources in EU countries is highly variable. Only in the UK[2] and The Netherlands are all state schools allocated a global budget to spend as they choose on the full range of resources including staffing. In Finland and Sweden local authorities have discretion to grant schools full autonomy in resource management. More commonly, in European Union (EU) countries, resource management powers at school level are restricted to operational resources (learning materials, and general supplies and services including administration) (Office for Official Publications of the European Communities, 2001).

In the English system, schools purchase almost all the resources they use out of their delegated budgets. From 2001 delegation was further extended so that all schools have devolved capital budgets to spend on capital projects of their own choosing. Since the implementation of the 1988 Education Reform Act schools have been able to choose their own staffing establishment and select and dismiss staff. However, school performance is highly regulated by central government and its agencies. In 1990 a national curriculum was introduced, as were national key stage tests at ages 7, 11 and 14 and the publication of school key stage test and public examination performance results. In 1993 the Office for Standards in Education (Ofsted) was set up. It oversees the national inspection at regular intervals of all state maintained schools, which are inspected against a published set of criteria. Inspection reports are published and available on the internet. Schools have to produce and implement action plans for the key issues for improvement set out in the inspection report. Schools that fail an Ofsted inspection are 'placed in special measures' and their progress regularly monitored by inspectors who determine whether the school can be removed from special measures. Under the 1998 School Standards and Framework Act, a school in special measures that fails to improve can be closed and reopened as a 'Fresh Start' school. Targets for examination and test results have been set nationally and for local education authorities (LEAs) and schools. Centrally devised literacy and numeracy teaching programmes have been instituted. In 2000 a mandatory system of performance management of headteachers by the governing body of the school and of teachers by the headteacher was introduced. Systems of self-managing can be found elsewhere, as in Australia (Victoria), New Zealand and Edmonton (Canada).

School-based management

However, in other countries the move to greater school autonomy has not occurred or is not occurring within such a strong framework of performance regulation. Often this is because the highest level education authority does not have the power that the British Parliament does to legislate what local government must do, or because teacher trade unions are more powerful. Thus in the USA school autonomy has taken on different forms. There the concept of school-based management has been taken over by the school improvement movement. There is much greater emphasis on school-based management of learning communities by teachers and parents, supported by external capacity-building agents, though the need for a rigorous external accountability framework is also stressed (Fullan and Watson, 2000).

Political decentralization

In other political contexts greater school autonomy is motivated not so much by a press for school improvement, than by the decentralisation of power for its own sake as part of a national democratisation process. Examples cited by Hanson (1998) include Venezuela, Spain, Argentina, Colombia, Chile and Mexico. There has been a similar movement in the ex-communist countries of Central and Eastern Europe (Karstanje, 1999). Greater school autonomy will only result from such decentralisation if it does not cease at local authority level but is extended to schools, as in the Czech Republic.

Self-governing schools and privatisation

In general private schools have greater autonomy, since they are not subject to regulations that state schools have to abide by (e.g. terms and conditions of service for teachers, selection of pupils, choice of curriculum). However, the definition of the private school sector differs across countries, is not always clear cut, and in some countries private schools are extensively state funded and subject to state regulation (Sosale, 2000), so there may be exceptions to the general rule.

Given that private schools have a greater degree of autonomy than state schools, then one way of increasing the overall degree of school autonomy in the system as a whole is to shift provision to the private sector. This is what occurs under voucher schemes, which parents can choose to use for either public or private school places, as in Chile, Colombia, Milwaukee and Sweden, for example. In some developing countries, for example Tanzania, Ghana, Pakistan and Colombia, the shortage of state school places is being tackled by a growth in private schools for which parents pay fees.

This way of increasing the degree of school autonomy in the system as a whole is known as privatisation. This is a general term, which refers to the transfer of responsibility for the production of goods and services from the state to the non-state sector, which includes commercial firms, not-for-profit organisations and households. Apart from vouchers, private sector school sponsorship is another form of extending school autonomy. The state funds or partially funds private sector organisations to provide and manage a school under contract (Hill et al., 1997). The contract stipulates the expected performance of the school, its organisation, admissions policy and other features, as well as payments to the contractor contingent on performance. One example is the increasing number of charter schools being created in the USA. In England there are 15 city technology colleges, set up in 1986 in inner city areas, which are run by private trusts, with private and state funding. The Beaconhouse project in Pakistan, funded in part by World Bank loans, aims to widen access to schooling, particularly for girls, through private sector involvement (Sosale, 2000).

The arguments for and against increased school autonomy

This section examines the arguments for and against increased school autonomy. The basic theory from which the arguments derive applies to both forms of increased school autonomy: self-managed schools and privatisation. More detailed predictions of how increased school autonomy affects the quality of educational provision and the distribution of access to educational opportunities depend on the precise nature of the scheme being proposed or implemented.

Funding and provision

The provision of schooling and the finance of schooling need to be considered separately. Whether the school provider is in the public or private sector depends on whether or not the school's assets (buildings and grounds) are owned and its management employed by a state sector legal entity.[3] Funding can come from either the state or the private sector (parents, charities, churches and business sponsorship). This gives the four possible combinations of private and public provision and funding shown in Figure 12.1.

PROVISION

FUNDING	PUBLIC	PRIVATE
PUBLIC	TRADITIONAL WELFARE STATE: BUREAUCRATIC PROVISION	STATE SUBSIDISED PRIVATE SECTOR PROVISION
PRIVATE	USER CHARGES AND SPONSORSHIP	PURE MARKET PROVISION

Figure 12.1: Combinations of public and private funding and provision of schooling

The traditional welfare state model of school provision consists of state funding together with state provision. At the other extreme is private funding and provision of schooling, where the market alone determines the quantity, quality and distribution of schooling. In between we have different combinations of mixed private/public funding and provision, characteristic of the 'Third Way' now favoured by social democratic politicians who have taken on board many aspects of the policies of previous more right-wing inclined governments (Giddens, 1998). This taxonomy produces four models:

- *model 1*: traditional state bureaucracy with all funding and provision of schooling within the public sector
- *model 2*: state funding and private sector provision (e.g. vouchers)
- *model 3*: private sector funding and state provision
- *model 4*: pure market: private sector funding and provision.

Markets, hierarchies and networks

In order to consider the properties of these models it is useful to distinguish three major types of mechanism which are used by society for co-ordinating decisions about what goods and services to produce, how to produce them and to whom to distribute them (Thompson et al., 1991). The three basic co-ordination mechanisms are:

- market (the price system)
- bureaucracy or hierarchy
- network or mutual adjustment.

The distinguishing feature of the market is that the participants co-ordinate their activities by engaging in exchange of goods and services at a price. Activities that are co-ordinated within an organisation, which can be either in the private or public sector, have different mechanisms of co-ordination. In a bureaucratic organisation co-ordination occurs through a hierarchical chain of authority, by which superiors pass on orders to subordinates and grant subordinates the resources needed to implement the orders.

Another method of co-ordination used in organisations is mutual adjustment or networking, whereby participants engage in informal exchanges of services, including information exchange. Mutual adjustment can occur both within the organisation and between organisations.

The four permutations of school finance and provision are distinguished by their different combinations of hierarchy, market and network. Model 1 relies on hierarchy and model 4 on market co-ordination. All three co-ordination mechanisms affect and are in turn affected by organisational cultures and the values and practices of individuals. Mutual adjustment is particularly dependent for its functioning, which is largely informal, on shared cultures, values and norms.

The development of greater school autonomy marks a decreased reliance on hierarchy or state bureaucracy as a co-ordination mechanism, in favour of markets and networking. Clearly, privatisation means greater use of the market mechanism, but so usually does decentralisation within the state school system. The delegation of budgets for schools to determine how to spend means that schools purchase goods and services from a variety of suppliers and no longer have them bureaucratically allocated by a local education authority or Ministry of Education. Once state schools are allocated budgets, the amount of budget is usually determined by a funding formula. If a high proportion of the funding is allocated on a per pupil basis and if parents can express a choice of state school, rather than be administratively allocated a school place, then the funding of state schools becomes demand led. In this way an internal market in schooling is created, since the provision of education – undertaken by schools – is separated from the purchase of schooling, which is done indirectly by parents, with the funding following the pupil. This system is called a quasi-voucher system, since it functions very similarly to a voucher system in which parents receive actual certificates that they can cash in at a school of their choice which admits their child.

Evaluative criteria: efficiency and equity

The arguments concerning what is the best school governance structure in terms of who provides, who funds and the combinations of hierarchy, market and networking which are used as co-ordination mechanisms are evaluated in relation to the likely impact on the efficiency and equity of the school system. Since there are differing views on what constitutes equity, what is the desirable trade-off between efficiency and equity, and how much should be spent by the state to secure greater equity, the choice of governance structure is necessarily a political one. The role of economic analysis is to predict from theoretical propositions the likely efficiency and equity effects of different governance structures. The purpose of empirical research is to find evidence about the actual relationships in the real world between different governance structures and their impact on the efficiency and equity of the education system.

Efficiency The attraction of the efficiency criterion is that it is concerned with detecting situations in which specific policies or institutional arrangements will produce net benefits for society. So, if a particular way of using a given quantity of resources can produce a higher value of output than another way, then it is more efficient because it produces more value for society. Efficiency is defined as a positive sum game: as long as there are possibilities of exchange between two people, which they would both engage in because it would make them better off, then the economy is not yet in an efficient equilibrium. Hence efficient institutional arrangements encourage all potentially beneficial exchanges between people to take place. When an economy is in an efficient equilibrium it is impossible to make anyone better off without making at least one other person worse off.

Efficiency consists of two elements (Levin, 1990; 1997). The first is *productive efficiency*, which is the relationship between the amount of output produced and the cost of inputs used to produce that output. A cost-efficient method of production produces a given set of outputs at least cost. An equivalent definition of productive efficiency is the maximum possible educational output from a given quantity of resources. If a school is producing less than the maximum feasible educational output then it has a degree of inefficiency, which is the difference between actual output and maximum output.

The productive efficiency of a school is difficult to define and measure in practice because schools produce a variety of outputs, some measurable, like examination results, and others which are intangible, such as socially desirable attitudes and values. Even if we restrict efficiency to measurable outputs, the effect of factors that the school cannot influence directly (except by selecting its pupils), such as pupils' ability, motivation and prior attainment, need to be taken into account statistically. Another problem with productive efficiency is that its value depends on the value attached to the output used in the output/input or output/cost comparisons. A school could be very efficient at producing an educational output (e.g. knowledge of Latin or animal husbandry) to which others in society may attach little value.

Because of this limitation with the definition of productive efficiency, there is a second aspect of efficiency known as *allocative efficiency* which takes into account consumers' valuation of goods and services. A system is said to be allocatively efficient if, with a given amount and distribution of resources, it produces a combination of goods and services which consumers value most. Adapted to schools, allocative efficiency is about giving parents greater diversity in the educational provision (e.g. in school curriculum and ethos) from

194

which they can choose, so that parents can have the type of education for their children that they prefer.

Another way of buttressing productive efficiency is to use the concept of effectiveness. An organisation is effective to the extent that it achieves its objectives. This takes no account of the cost of resources used. Clearly the assessment of effectiveness depends on a prior value judgement about the value of the objectives. Effectiveness is a term widely used in making judgements about schools. A popular definition of effectiveness comes from value-added analysis. A school is effective to the extent that the performance of its students on some measure of educational achievement exceeds that which would be predicted on the basis of the students' prior attainment and other characteristics from analysing the results of a large number of schools (Teddlie et al., 2000).

If an organisation is both effective and efficient it provides value for money. Even though productive and allocative efficiency are difficult to measure and cannot be defined without making value judgements about the social value of the educational outputs, they are widely used – often implicitly – by non-economists. The distinction between them shows up in important differences in emphasis in education policy advocacy. Policies to increase school autonomy that are intended to improve educational standards and are accompanied by strong external accountability systems for schools focus on productive efficiency. Policies that primarily aim to increase school choice are focused on allocative efficiency. A pure market school system would leave consumers to define education standards for themselves and thus would enable diversity in provision to flourish. However, governments often do not trust consumers to have sufficient knowledge, information and incentives to choose wisely on behalf of their children and, thus, to ensure sufficiently high education standards. If a common standard is to be defined, imposed and monitored then a common measure is required which makes it impossible to allow full diversity of provision to flourish. The greater the concern with achieving a common national standard, and with doing this to best effect within the resources provided, the more the government's focus is on productive rather than allocative efficiency. School systems generally display some balance between attending to productive and allocative efficiency.

Equity Equity is the 'fairness' of the distribution of economic welfare amongst individuals. A change in the distribution of income, say to give more to those who have less, is necessarily a zero sum game since some must lose for others to gain. Equity has two dimensions: horizontal and vertical. Horizontal equity refers to the equal treatment of people with similar needs or characteristics. Thus it is horizontally equitable to spend the same amount on educating each child or to ensure equal access to educational opportunities for all children regardless of income or class. Equity may also be measured in terms of outcome. Hence it would be equitable for all children of similar ability to achieve the same educational standards or qualifications, regardless of gender, ethnicity or social class. Vertical equity concerns giving additional resources to those with additional needs. It is more difficult than with horizontal equity to judge whether differences in compensatory amounts are equitable.

Equity is judged separately from efficiency. An efficient system may be judged by some to be inequitable, while an inefficient system might be judged equitable if it produces the same level of educational outcomes for all.

The efficiency and equity properties of greater school autonomy

Economists have long argued that organisations, be they firms or schools, will operate with a degree of inefficiency in the absence of competition from alternative suppliers. This applies equally to private and public sector organisations and will involve both allocative inefficiency (charging prices above the marginal cost of production or not responding to consumer preferences) and productive inefficiency (producing less than the maximum amount of output from a given quantity of resources). This arises from the incentives of managers, workers and shareholders (in the case of the private sector) to pursue their interests in having higher income, less effort in seeking out efficient ways of operating or enjoying job perquisites, rather than pursuing the interests of consumers. Competition from alternative suppliers forces producers to attend more closely to their consumers' interests.

One can usefully distinguish two forms of school autonomy that are intended to improve efficiency:

- self-managing schools
- increased competition.

Self-managing schools   Hierarchical co-ordination is inefficient if the top bureaucrats or managers do not have the information needed to determine the most efficient ways of combining resources and responding to client needs at the operational, i.e. school, level. This is often because they have too much of the wrong information, as when they are making detailed allocation decisions about staffing, textbook use or premises repairs at school level. According to the institutional theory of the firm (Williamson, 1975) it is more efficient for a large multi-product firm (such as an education authority) to delegate operational decisions to the unit (school) managers and to control them by setting them performance targets consistent with the organisation's objectives. Unit managers are given performance incentives and rewarded according to performance, which is monitored. Top managers are then able to concentrate on the information needed for determining organisational strategy and evaluating performance. The system of self-managing schools replicates this management model.

In this analysis, a system of self-managing schools will be more productively efficient than centralised regimes because it provides school managers and teachers with greater incentives to attain high educational standards and provides them with greater managerial flexibility to do so. How much school autonomy is required for this system to work well is a contentious issue. Largely it revolves around how much external assistance and direction schools require for them to adopt better production (i.e. learning) technologies. Fullan and Watson (2000), for example, conclude that school-based management requires external assistance for capacity-building if schools are to improve learning outcomes. The Labour government in Britain from 1997 became highly interventionist in prescribing teaching methods and giving many different forms of specific grant for particular purposes (e.g. national literacy and numeracy strategies, induction of newly qualified teachers, information and communication technology [ICT] investment and many others). Whether school self-management improves productive efficiency depends on incentives and the extent to which these motivate school managers and teachers to higher performance.

Competition as an incentive for efficiency improvements   Those who favour the introduction of greater competition between schools argue that this provides the necessary incentives for managers and teachers to improve productivity. Increased competition can be restricted to giving parents greater choice of state school or be extended to fostering competition between private and state sector schools through vouchers or similar schemes (e.g. charter schools). Whether increased competition improves the efficiency of state schools depends on the degree of organisational slack initially present, on the ability of state schools to improve productivity by adopting more efficient learning technologies, and on the desire and ability of parents to put pressure on inefficient schools by making school choices based on good information about school quality. Alternatively, overall efficiency is improved by shifting more production to the private sector, provided that private schools are more efficient than state schools.

However, competition may fail to improve the productivity of the school system as a whole if it results in 'increased sorting', that is the greater concentration of more able students in some schools and of less able and less motivated students in others. Increased sorting by itself, though often considered socially undesirable because it reduces social cohesion, would not affect the average educational attainment of pupils if the attainment of individual children depended only on their own characteristics and the quality of teaching experienced. However, there is considerable evidence that an individual pupil's educational attainment is also affected by the average level of ability or attainment of the peer group (McEwan, 2000; Sammons et al., 1996). If the less able children are more adversely affected by low-ability peers than the more able children are stimulated by high-ability peers, then increased sorting will reduce average attainment across the school system.

Equity The effect of increased competition on the social composition of schools depends very much on the type of quasi-voucher or voucher scheme introduced. Clearly a non-means-tested voucher, issued to all parents (as in Chile) is less vertically equitable than a means-tested voucher or one limited to low-income parents (e.g. in Milwaukee and Colombia). A means-tested voucher that provides low-income children with access to private schools is advocated by those who believe it will reduce social inequality, since a system of neighbourhood state schools is socially segregated because different social groups are concentrated in different residential districts. How well vouchers achieve more equal access to higher-quality schools depends on whether schools select voucher-paid pupils on grounds of ability and motivation, and on whether all parents make equal use of their vouchers to select the best available school for their child. If schools select pupils and some parents are 'inert' and so fail to exercise choice options, then the least motivated children with least parental interest in learning will become more concentrated in certain schools.

The main equity concern with respect to systems of self-managing schools is that the strong external pressures for school performance, measured in terms of students' academic attainment, makes schools more reluctant to accommodate students who are difficult to teach either through behavioural problems or learning difficulties. In the initial years of local management of schools in England, exclusions from schools increased (Parsons, 1996) but subsequently fell back slightly under government pressure.

Empirical evidence

The empirical literature is vast since it covers evaluations of many different types of education policy involving increased school autonomy, in many countries, and uses a wide range of research methods. It is very difficult to establish valid evidence for causal links between variables in the social world, unless controlled experiments are carried out (Heckman, 2000; Meyer, 1995). Then one can compare the educational outcomes for equivalent groups of children who have experienced a different policy (e.g. greater school autonomy) relative to a control group who have not. Without control groups, correlational analysis is used with quantitative data. However, the existence of a high correlation between two variables does not ensure any causal linkage between them, since the correlation could be due to an unobserved factor. For example, children may make more progress in private schools, not because private schools are more efficient, but because parents who choose private schools take more interest in their child's education. This problem is known as selection bias. Qualitative methods, while they provide insight and understanding of the impact of policy measures, do not establish causality.

I will briefly consider some selected evidence relating to examples of self-managing schools and to increased competition via vouchers.

Self-managing schools

In England studies of the effects of school-based resource management, which were qualitative, concluded that it had improved the efficiency with which schools used resources (Audit Commission, 1993; Bullock and Thomas, 1994; Levačić, 1995; 1998; Maychell, 1994). As indicated by Table 12.1, educational attainment, measured by the key indicators used by the government in evaluating schools' performance, has increased over time, although the real value of expenditure per pupil did not rise over the period as whole, except for primary schools in 1999 and 2000.

Table 12.1 *Educational attainment indicators and government expenditure per pupil: England, 1991–2000*

Year	Key Stage 4: % pupils aged 15+ attaining:		Key Stage 2: % pupils attaining level 4 & above			Key Stage 1: % pupils attaining level 2 & above			Expenditure per pupil (1996/7 prices)	
	5+ A* to C grades	5+ A* to G grades	English	Maths	Science	Reading	Writing	Maths	Primary £	Secondary £
1991	36.8	79.5							1617	2427
1992	39.0	82.0							1673	2446
1993	42.0	84.3							1748	2482
1994	43.3	85.6							1748	2412
1995	43.5	85.7	49	45	70	78	80	79	1748	2412
1996	44.5	86.1	57	54	62	78	79	82	1748	2364
1997	45.1	86.4	63	62	69	80	80	84	1730	2340
1998	46.3	87.5	65	59	69	80	81	85	1695	2293
1999	47.9	88.5	70	69	78	82	83	86	1783	2316
2000	49.2	88.9	75	72	85	84	82	88	1852	2411

Sources: DfEE (1998; 1999; 2000) School Performance Tables (DfEE)

The evidence is consistent[4] with improved productive efficiency, provided that the tests have not become easier. Fullan and Watson (2000: 459), in a review of school-based management in North America conclude that it improves educational attainment, providing that greater school autonomy is combined with local capacity building, rigorous external accountability and access to innovation.

Evidence of inefficiency in resource allocation in centralised schools systems in developing countries has been found in studies of the relationship between the mix of resources used and student outcomes (Fuller and Clarke, 1994;

Hanushek, 1995; Pritchett and Filmer, 1999). Too high a proportion of spending tends to be on teachers and insufficient on textbooks and other learning materials. Investment in the latter has a higher return in terms of gains in student achievement. Hence the World Bank is encouraging greater school autonomy in determining expenditure on resources. For instance in Sri Lanka it is funding a programme to increase the amount of operational resources schools have and enabling schools to purchase these instead of having them allocated bureaucratically by provincial offices (Sri Lanka Ministry of Education and Higher Education, 2000).

Increasing competition: (quasi-) voucher schemes

Research on the effects of competition has investigated the two key questions.

- Is student attainment increased (either average attainment for the whole school system or the 'value-added' attainment of pupils in schools experiencing greater competition)?
- What is the impact on the educational opportunities of socially disadvantaged children? (Do they have access to better quality schools or improve their educational attainment relative to more advantaged children?)

Some examples from particular national settings are summarised below.

Quasi-vouchers in England   Levačić (2001), in a study of over 300 secondary schools from 1991 to 1998, found that a self-reported indicator of the number of competitors a school reported had a statistically significant effect on the percentage of pupils achieving the 'headline' indicator of five or more grades A* to C at GCSE, equivalent to 4–5 percentage points (after controlling for free school meals and school type). There was no impact on the percentage achieving five or more A* to G grades, suggesting that government attention to the headline indicator has affected school policies and performance.

Milwaukee voucher scheme   This scheme has better equity properties than many because it is restricted to low-income families and oversubscribed schools choose students by lottery. Quantitative studies have produced conflicting findings as to whether voucher children attained better results than children who remained in the public school system. Conflicting results occur because of comparing different sets of children (e.g. all those in the public school system or only those who were eligible for vouchers, or including dropouts from private schools or not). Goldhaber's (1999) short review of the research indicates little convincing evidence of private school superiority: at best it is slight. However, private schools are cheaper than public schools in the USA, but even this has been contested (Levin, 1998).

Colombia   In developing countries the more pressing problem is insufficient school places, especially for secondary education. Here vouchers for low-income children are a means to increasing access if the private sector is able to respond more efficiently than the public sector. Colombia introduced vouchers for low-income secondary students in 1991. By 1995, 8 per cent of private school students were funded by vouchers (King et al., 1998). This evaluation found that the scheme was successful in increasing the supply of places by medium-quality and medium-fee not-for-profit private schools, located in major urban areas (about half the private schools) and was successful at targeting low-income children. However, only 25 per cent of municipalities participated, i.e. those which considered that the private sector could expand provision more cheaply than the public sector.

Chile   In 1980 the government decentralised public schools to municipalities and began funding public schools and most private schools according to their monthly enrolments times a fixed per pupil subsidy. Teachers ceased to be civil servants and became employed by municipalities or in private schools where they usually have less job security. In 1980 15 per cent of children attended private schools (30 per cent in urban areas); by 1996 it was 34 per cent (48 per cent in urban areas). McEwan and Carnoy (2000) estimate that 15 years of competition led to modest gains of around 0.16–0.2 percentage points in Spanish and mathematics tests among public schools in Santiago but in other regions (75 per cent of the population) competition had slightly negative effects. Non-elite for-profit private schools spent less per pupil than public or Catholic schools because they paid teachers less. There is also evidence of increased social stratification in urban areas (Carnoy, 2000).

Argentina   Argentina has experienced 'spontaneous privatisation' (Morduchowicz, 2001) over the lasts 50 years with state subsidies for private schools. Twenty five per cent of students, and 50 per cent in Buenos Aires, attend private sector schools, which have higher attainment on average. Enrolment in private schools is strongly related to parental income and education. Only 7 per cent of the lowest fifth of families by income send their children to private schools compared to 64 per cent of the highest fifth of families by income.

England   Research on the equity effects of greater parental choice plus pupil-driven funding in England has focused on two issues: whether the concentration of socially disadvantaged pupils has increased and whether the attainment gap between the lowest achieving pupils and schools and the rest has widened. On balance the evidence suggests both have occurred to some degree. Whether research findings show social segregation has increased depends on the measure and time period used (Fitz and Gorard, 2000; Gorard and Fitz,

1999; 2000; Noden, 2000). Other research suggests that, while the average level of attainment has risen, within the secondary sector there is evidence that the attainment gap widened (Gibson and Asthana, 1999; Levačić and Woods, 2002).

Conclusion

The impact of a policy of increasing school autonomy depends firstly on whether it is primarily in the form of self-managing schools within a central regulatory framework or relies mainly on increased competition, either between state schools or between the public and private sector. If the latter, its effects on the equity of the school system depend on whether vouchers or subsidies are limited to low-income children or are used as a general way of increasing parental choice and the diversity of school provision.

One has to be very careful in assessing the vast amount of research on these questions because it applies to different school systems and uses different methods. It is particularly difficult to establish causal links. With these caveats I would conclude that self-managed schools can raise productive efficiency and that means-tested voucher schemes, if carefully designed, can enhance access to better quality schools for low-income children, though it may not do so for the most deprived. If educational policy-makers are not so concerned with either the productive efficiency of the national school system or with equality of opportunity, then greater school autonomy in a competitive environment promotes allocative efficiency in areas where the private sector has sufficient incentives to respond to market demand.

All the efficiency arguments in favour of school autonomy, in either its regulated or competitive form, depend crucially on the capacity of schools to manage their resources efficiently so as to achieve their educational objectives. This is considered in the following chapter.

Notes

1 In addition the concept of autonomy applies to individuals (e.g. professionals) visà-vis their relationship with the state, other organisations and their own employers and managers. But here I am only considering school autonomy.
2 In Scotland, the local education authority appoints teachers.
3 In some instances a school, which is owned by a state body (such as a local education authority) has its management contracted out to a private sector organisation. In this case, while getting closer to the private sector boundary, the assets and final responsibility for the school, is still with the LEA. The dividing line between state and private also depends on the country's legislation. So, in the UK denominational schools are regarded as state schools because they are 'maintained by the LEA' whereas in The Netherlands they are regarded as in the private sector, because the school board is under full church control, even though the schools are largely funded by the state.

4 This evidence is not proof of a causal link, since there could be other factors than self-managing schools explaining the data which have not been accounted for.

Further reading

Berka, W. (2000) 'The legal and philosophical meaning of autonomy in education', in W. Berka, J. De Groof and H. Penneman (eds), *Autonomy in Education: Yearbook of the European Association for Education Law and Policy Vol. III*, The Hague: Kluwer Law International.

Levačić, R. (2000) 'Linking resources to learning outcomes', in M. Coleman and L. Anderson (eds), *Managing Finance and Resources in Education*, London: Paul Chapman Publishing.

Levin, H. (1998) 'Educational vouchers: effectiveness, choice and costs', *Journal of Policy Analysis and Management*, 17 (3), 373–91.

References

Audit Commission (1993) *Adding up the Sums: Schools' Management of their Finances*, London: HMSO.

Berka, W. (2000) 'The legal and philosophical meaning of autonomy in education', in W. Berka, J. De Groof and H. Penneman (eds), *Autonomy in Education: Yearbook of the European Association for Education Law and Policy Vol. III*, The Hague: Kluwer Law International.

Bullock, A. and Thomas, H. (1994) *The Impact of Local Management on Schools*, Birmingham: National Association of Headteachers and University of Birmingham.

Carnoy, M. (2000) 'School choice? Or is it privatization?', *Educational Research*, 29 (7): 15–20.

Chubb, J. E. and Moe, T. M. (1990) *Politics, Markets and America's Schools*, Washington, DC: Brookings Institution.

DfEE (1998) *Statistics of Education Schools in England*, London: DfEE.

DfEE (1999) *Departmental Report: The Government's Expenditure Plans 1999–00 to 2001–02, Cm 4201*, London: Stationery Office.

DfEE (2000) *Departmental Report: The Government's expenditure plans 2001-02 to 2003-04, Cm 510*, London: Stationery Office.

Fitz, J. and Gorard, S. (2000) 'School choice and SES stratification of schools: new findings from England and Wales', paper presented to American Educational Research Association Annual Meeting, New Orleans.

Fullan, M. and Watson, N. (2000) 'School-based management: reconceptualizing to improve learning outcomes', *School Effectiveness and School Improvement*, 11 (4): 453–73.

Fuller, B. and Clarke, P. (1994) 'Raising school effects while ignoring culture? Local conditions and the influence of classroom tools, rules and pedagogy', *Review of Educational Research*, 64 (1): 119–57.

Gibson, A. and Asthana, S. (1999) 'Schools, markets and equity: access to secondary education in England and Wales', paper presented to American Educational Research Association Annual Meeting, Montreal.

Giddens, A. (1998) *The Third Way: The Renewal of Social Democracy*, Cambridge: Polity Press.

Goldhaber, D. D. (1999) 'School choice: an examination of the empirical evidence on achievement, parental decision making and equity', *Educational Researcher*, 28 (9): 16–25.

Gorard, S. and Fitz, J. (1999) 'Do markets cause segregation? The results of ten years of school choice in England and Wales', mimeo, University of Cardiff.

Gorard, S. and Fitz, J. (2000) 'Investigating the determinants of segregation between schools', *Research Papers in Education*, 15 (2): 115–32.

Hanson, E. M. (1998) 'Strategies of educational decentralisation: key questions and core issues', *Journal of Educational Administration*, 36 (2): 111–28.

Hanushek, E. (1995) 'Interpreting recent research on schooling in developing countries', *World Bank Research Observer*, 10 (2): 227–46.

Heckman, J. J. (2000) 'Causal parameters and policy analysis in economics: a twentieth century retrospective', *Quarterly Journal of Economics*, (February), 45–97.

Hill, P. T., Pierce, L. C. and Guthrie, J. W. (1997) *Reinventing Public Education: How Contracting can Transform America's Schools*, Chicago: University of Chicago Press.

Jiminez, E. and Sawada, Y. (1998) 'Do community-managed schools work? An evaluation of El Salvador's EDUCO Program', *World Bank Working Papers on Impact Evaluation of Education Reforms*, no. 8: 1–37.

Karstanje, P. (1999) 'Decentralisation and deregulation in Europe: towards a conceptual framework', in T. Bush, L. Bell, R. Bolam, R. Glatter and P. Ribbins (eds), *Educational Management: Redefining Theory, Policy and Practice*, London: Paul Chapman Publishing.

Kim, J., Alderman, H. and Orazem, P. (1998) 'Can private schools subsidies increase schooling for the poor? The Quetta urban fellowship program', *Working Paper Series on Impact Education Reforms: Development Research Group*, World Bank Paper, no. 11: 1–46.

King, E. and Ozler, P. (1998) 'What's decentralization got to do with learning? The case of Nicaragua's school autonomy reform', *World Bank Paper Series on Impact Evaluation of Education Reforms*, no. 9: 1–33.

King, E. M., Orazem, P. F. and Wohlgemuth, D. (1998) 'Central mandates and local incentives: the Colombia education voucher program', *World Bank Working Paper Series on Impact Evaluation of Education Reforms*, no. 6: 37.

King, E. M., Ozler, P. and Rawlings, L. B. (1999) 'Nicaragua's school autonomy reform: fact or fiction?', *World Bank Working Paper Series on Impact Evaluation of Education Reforms*, no. 9: 1–33.

Levačić, R. (1995) *Local Management of Schools: Analysis and Practice*, Buckingham: Open University Press.

Levačić, R. (1998) 'Local management of schools: results after six years', *Journal of Education Policy*, 13 (3): 331–50.

Levačić, R. (2001) 'An analysis of competition and its impact on secondary school examination performance in England', *National Centre for the Study of Privatisation in Education Occasional Paper Series*, no. 34: 1–50.

Levačić, R. and Woods, P. (2002) 'Raising school performance in the league tables: disentangling the effects of social disadvantage', *British Educational Research Journal*, 28 (2).

Levin, H. (1990) 'The theory of choice applied to education', in W. H. Clune and J. F. Witte (eds), *Choice and Control in American Education: Volume 1*, New York: Falmer Press.

Levin, H. (1998) 'Educational vouchers: effectiveness, choice and costs', *Journal of Policy Analysis and Management*, 17 (3): 373–91.

Levin, H. M. (1997) 'Raising school productivity: an x-efficiency approach', *Economics of Education Review*, 16 (3): 303–11.

Maychell, K. (1994) *Counting the Cost: The Impact of LMS on Schools' Pattern of Spending*, Slough: NFER.

McEwan, P. (2000) 'The potential impact of large scale voucher programs', *Review of Educational Research*, 70 (2): 103–49.

McEwan, P. and Carnoy, M. (2000) 'The effectiveness and efficiency of private schools in Chile's voucher system', *Educational Evaluation and Policy Analysis*, 22 (3): 213–40.

Meyer, B. D. (1995) 'Natural and quasi-natural experiments in economics', *Journal of Business and Economic Statistics*, 13 (2): 151–61.

Morduchowicz, A. (2001) 'Private education: funding and deregulation in Argentina', *National Centre for the Study of Privatization in Education Occasional Paper*, no. 36: 1–36.

Noden, P. (2000) 'Rediscovering the impact of marketisation: dimensions of social segregation in England's secondary schools, 1994–99', *British Journal of Sociology of Education*, 21 (3): 371–90.

Office for Official Publications of the European Communities (2001) *Key Topics in Education, Volume 2: The Financing and Management of Resources in Compulsory Education in Europe – Trends in National Policies*, Brussels: OOFPEC.

Organisation for Economic Co-operation and Development (OECD) (2000) *Education at a Glance*, Paris: OECD.

Parsons, C. (1996) 'Permanent exclusions from schools in England: trends, causes and responses', *Children in Society*, 10: 177–86.

Pritchett, L. and Filmer, D. (1999) 'What education production functions *really* show: a positive theory of education expenditures', *Economics of Education Review*, 18: 223–39.

Sammons, P., Mortimore, P. and Thomas, S. (1996) 'Do schools perform consistently across outcomes and areas?', in J. Gray, D. Reynolds, C. Fitz-Gibbon and D. Jesson. (eds), *Merging Traditions: the Future of Research on School Effectiveness and School Improvement*, London: Cassell.

Sosale, S. (2000) 'Trends in private sector development in World Bank education projects', *World Bank Policy Research Working Paper 2452*: 49.

Sri Lanka Ministry of Education and Higher Education (2000) *Guidelines for Implementation of Pilot Programme of the Decentralization of Procurement of Quality Inputs at School Level*, Battaramulla: MEHE.

Teddlie, C., Reynolds, D. and Sammons, P. (2000) 'The methodology and scientific principles of school effectiveness research', in C. Teddlie and D. Reynolds (eds), *The International Handbook of School Effectiveness Research*, London: Routledge/Falmer.

Thompson, G., Mitchell, J., Levačić, R. and Frances, J. (eds) (1991) *Markets, Hierarchies and Networks: the Co-ordination of Social Life*, London: Sage.

West, E. (1992) 'Autonomy in school provision: meanings and implications: review essay', *Economics of Education Review*, 11 (4): 417–25.

Williamson, O. (1975) *Markets and Hierarchies: Analysis and Anti-Trust Implications*, New York and London: Free Press/Collier Macmillan.

World Bank (1995) *Priorities and Strategies for Education: A Review*, Washington, DC: World Bank.

13
Resource Acquisition and Allocation
Lesley Anderson

Introduction

This chapter starts from the premise that schools, colleges and educational organisations of all types exist to provide an environment for learning and teaching to take place, and that their purpose is to enable these processes, interpreted in their broadest sense, to provide maximum benefit to pupils and students. It follows from the existence of any such educational organisation that resources have to be acquired or provided and then allocated as a prerequisite to fulfilling this purpose. As elsewhere, resources in education are the means to the end and they are necessarily limited. This is true whatever the nature of the physical manifestation of the educational organisation, for example, conventionally as a school building or from a desktop providing resources for e-learning. On the basis of this fact, the question then arises as to whether the quantity and mix of resources matter in terms of the effectiveness of the educational organisation in achieving its purpose. Levačić (2000: 3) considers this question as the starting point in her discussion on 'linking resources to learning outcomes'. She highlights the problematic nature of the issue in terms of the lack of research evidence to support the popularly held belief that resources, particularly in terms of quantity, do make a difference. Whilst acknowledging this difficulty, this chapter is based on the assumption that to some extent, at least, resources do matter. They matter in terms of having an adequate supply to fulfil the educational function. They matter in terms of the way in which they are allocated internally because, unless they are available in abundance, the principles and assumptions upon which they are managed and deployed are important for the organisation as a whole (Simkins, 1997: 164). They matter in terms of school/college improvement (Thomas and Martin, 1996) and long-term effectiveness (Levine and Lezotte, 1990). Thus, the management of resources is a significant and important management function for any educational organisation.

The chapter, then, is concerned with the ways in which schools and colleges manage the resources available to them. It adopts the traditional view of schools and colleges as places where students go to learn. However, it is suggested that the theory and discussion presented here is generally applicable in educational environments that fall outside this conventional stereotype.

Before moving on to consider the various stages in the management of resources, it is necessary to define what we mean by resources and to consider the way in which organisational theory informs our understanding of the processes of resource management.

Defining resources

In the previous chapter, we saw that inputs – or resources – are key to Levačić's definition of school autonomy. They represent one domain in which decision-making power can be devolved to a school or college to enable more autonomy. So what are these inputs – or resources – whose management can be devolved to the organisational level? The key resource is obviously finance and, as such, financial management is distinctive from that of other resources. It is also evident that books, equipment and consumable items such as paper, art materials and chemicals are required for effective learning and teaching. These have been described as 'real' resources (Simkins, 1997: 163). Simkins lists teaching staff, support staff, materials, services and premises under this heading. In his discussion about changes in the level of resource management delegated to schools and colleges in the UK since 1989, he adds staff and pupil time as another, non-financial, resource. Levačić (2000: 11) takes it further and includes the extent of discretion over setting contracts with teachers, other staff and suppliers, and regulations with respect to space, class size and staffing establishment in her definition of resources.

Resources are significant to Caldwell and Spinks's (1988; 1992; 1998) concept of self-management. The definition they use in their third book on this topic emphasises the centrality of decisions on resources in self-management:

> A self-managing school is a school in a system of education to which there has been decentralised a significant amount of authority and responsibility to make decisions about the allocation of resources within a centrally determined framework of goals, policies, standards and accountabilities. Resources are defined broadly to include knowledge, technology, power, material, people, time, assessment, information and finance. (Caldwell and Spinks, 1998: 4–5)

In their discussions of the range of resource decisions that may have been delegated to school or college level, Bullock and Thomas (1997: 7–8) and Bell (1998) also include admissions and funding, and governance, respectively. Funding in Bullock and Thomas's terms is the setting of fees for the admission of pupils or students and, according to Bell, decisions about the power and composition of governing bodies may also be classified as a resource.

In other situations where schools have limited autonomy, educational managers – or teachers – have little control over the majority of the resources listed. A lack of basic materials and high teacher/pupil ratios may mean that they have to be creative about the way in which they use the limited resources available to them. They would find it difficult to identify resources beyond consumables, basic teaching materials and themselves. For example, in 1999 the headteacher of a 120-pupil primary school in the rural district of Msinga, KwaZula Natal in South Africa, described to the author how she made use of the very limited resources available to her in the mud-hut school building. There were just three teachers, including herself, so she was a teaching head and there was literally no additional accommodation beyond the three small classrooms. As part of a science lesson, she dissolved coloured chalk in water to demonstrate solubility. The pupils then went on to used the coloured water in an art lesson and, finally, they used their paintings to create paper models in a technology lesson (Anderson, 1999).

The point here is that the term 'resources' can be interpreted in a variety of ways depending on context. For the purposes of this chapter, the term 'resources' is taken to include finance, materials, staffing and time. Although what follows is generally applicable to the management of the other categories of resources listed above, it is beyond the scope of this chapter to provide a detailed discussion of each.

Having established the use of the term 'resources' in this chapter, the next section moves on to consider organisational theory in order to provide a context for the various approaches to, and features of, resource management that are identifiable in schools and colleges.

Organisational perspectives and the implications for resource management

In the first section of this book the context of educational management is considered with a view to establishing theoretical and conceptual frameworks as a basis upon which key educational management functions can be explored in the remaining chapters. In Chapter 2, Tony Bush presents a number of models of educational management that draw on organisational theory and serve to explain events, situations and behaviour in educational institutions. This theory and these models, then, provide an appropriate backdrop for discussion of resource management in education.

Four models: rational, collegial, political and ambiguity, feature in the literature on financial management (Bush, 2000: 101). Levačić (2000: 7) also refers to these four models, although she groups the last three together as the human relations approach – or natural system. Additionally, after Scott (1987) and Scheerens (1999), she adds the open systems model to the list and asserts that it is consistent with the other four. From the open systems perspective, the organisation is depicted as a 'complex living organism which interacts with its environment' (Levačić, 1997: 127; see also, Hanna, 1997;

Morgan, 1986). While the organisation is distinct and separate from its external environment, its boundaries are not clearly defined and it interacts with the environment at a variety of levels. The relationship between them is premised on the fact that the inputs used by the organisation are derived from the external environment and the outputs that result from the organisation's activity are released back to it. Thus, the organisation is dependent upon its environment. Moreover, the open systems model also focuses on the way in which inputs and outputs are connected and controlled by the internal processes of the organisation. For example, the technology of the organisation's productive processes and the culture of its human relations affect the internal processes which relate inputs to outputs and the organisation and its external environment. As Levačić (1997: 128) highlights, 'appropriate feedback mechanisms between an organisation and its environment and within the system itself are required for the organisation to be responsive and adaptive'.

These different perspectives on educational management are important because they provide a framework within which resource management in any one organisation may be considered. In other words, the way in which the purpose of managing resources is conceived and how it is, or should be, undertaken can be explained in terms of the organisational perspective that is evident. For example, in schools and colleges where the collegial model dominates there will be an extensive committee system within which decisions about resource allocations are made (Bush, 1995: 55). Of course, in practice, it is likely that the approach used will involve aspects of more than one perspective, although frequently one approach dominates (Bush, 1995; 2000). What it is important to recognise is that the shift to self-management in education in many countries around the world has brought with it greater emphasis on resource management at school/college level. At the same time almost all official (government) pronouncements on resource management are made from a rational perspective (Simkins, 1997: 165) that frequently include value judgements about what 'should be'. Levačić (2000: 9) describes such judgements as 'normative'. She also points out that the rational approach with its tight coupling of inputs and outputs, alongside the lack of clear agreement about the outputs of education, provide some difficulties for schools and colleges. However, in the context of resource management, and after Scheerens (1999), she asserts that the normative issue of which perspective to favour can be resolved by regarding the rational perspective as predominant.

The processes of resource management

Like other aspects of management, it is possible to represent resource management as a set of processes. Levačić (2000: 11) identifies four such processes:

- acquisition
- allocation
- utilisation
- evaluation.

Although sequential, these processes are also interrelated in other ways. For example, to some extent, acquisition and allocation depend on plans for utilisation and should be based on feedback from evaluation. Thus, there are adjustments over time as a result of evaluation data. Simkins (1997: 167) extends the list by replacing evaluation with review and control, the latter being concerned with whether the activities undertaken and resources used correspond to those that have been planned or authorised. However, for the purposes of this chapter, resource management is modelled as a series of sequential processes that together form a cycle as in Figure 13.1.

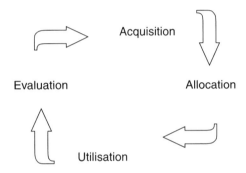

Figure 13.1:   The resource management cycle

As in most organisations, schools and colleges are likely to have a number of annual resource management cycles. These include a financial budgeting cycle (Blandford, 1997) and a staffing/timetabling cycle, but there may be others. It is these operational cycles that frequently dominate the resource management process, mainly because they are inevitable in order to ensure the organisation achieves its core function of learning and teaching (Simkins, 1997: 167). However, schools and colleges are also exhorted to plan strategically. Thus, the operational cycle should be related to, and sit within, the strategic cycle which provides a longer-term policy framework for the management of resources. Issues relating resource management to strategic planning are considered at the end of this chapter. Before that, the four broad operational processes of resource management are considered.

Resource acquisition

In the case of maintained schools and colleges, finance and other resources are acquired, or allocated, from the government and/or sponsors. From the previous chapter we know that there is considerable variation in the level of decision-making devolved to individual schools and colleges around the world. For example, under the system employed in England and Wales, and known as fair funding, funding is devolved to schools according to specific criteria. School governing bodies then have responsibility for a wide range of resource decisions, including determining the number of staff employed at their school and the level of these appointments. However, in China there are significant differences in the sources of funding for schools and in where, and how, resource decisions are made. In the case of staffing, all schools are allocated staff by the local authority although some schools may also employ extra staff, or pay more to existing people, by using income generated at the school (Ryan et al., 1998: 180).

Opportunities and incentives

The extent to which school managers have the freedom or the opportunity to acquire 'additional' resources depends on the nature of the school or college, the context in which it is operating and, to some extent, the personality and style of leadership exhibited. For example, those working in the unregulated private education sector generally have the freedom to set the level of fees charged although it is likely that such a school or college operates within a marketplace and, therefore, seeks to fix a fee level that enables it to survive. Schools and colleges maintained by government and/or other sponsors may be subject to legislation and/or affected by the social context in which they operate in seeking opportunities to generate additional resources to those already allocated to them. For example, in South Africa, maintained schools are required to set an annual fee in consultation with parents. For some schools this income enables them to employ additional teachers over and above those funded through government allocation.

In most countries, maintained or state schools and colleges are subordinate to a local or regional structure with resources channelled from central government through an intermediate tier to them. In situations where resources are allocated according to a transparent formula, school managers have the opportunity to increase their resource allocation by reference to the formula and, with careful management, may secure benefit to the school over and above the straightforward formula funded allocation. For example, English and Welsh schools are funded according to a formula that is significantly weighted towards pupil enrolments. While it is evident that attracting more pupils increases both income and costs, within certain limits, these costs may be absorbed. This is because increasing the number of pupils on roll in any one grouping does not necessarily imply the appointment of an additional member of staff nor the need for more space or materials (except consumables) for learning and teaching. Thus, it may be in the interests of the school or college to increase pupil/student enrolments within certain limits.

In situations where aspects of resource allocation to schools and colleges are not transparent, school or college managers may attempt to acquire additional resources through favour and influence at the local level, for example, by nurturing relationships with individuals deemed influential. Interestingly, this political approach was applied by some headteachers and chairs of governors of grant-maintained (GM) schools at national level in England and Wales during the period of Conservative governments in the early to mid-1990s. Unlike other English and Welsh maintained schools, the funding of GM schools was administered centrally, including an annual allocation for major capital development for which the schools had to bid. Within the sector, it was known that some senior managers and/or governors considered it in the interest of their school to lobby at the highest levels in an attempt to ensure the success of their school's application (Sherratt, 1994: 76).

Some schools and colleges may also be able, or required, to generate income and resources through their own efforts. Such entrepreneurial activities can range from low-level fund-raising through sales and other events in the school or college to the appointment of a business manager whose role it is to generate income, often including his/her own salary. This move towards entrepreneurialism in education is generally associated with the shift to self-management (see Anderson, 2000: 41–58 for a more detailed discussion). In respect of a specific appointment for income generation, Bush (1995: 148) points out that factors of size are relevant. Schools and colleges that have substantial income, probably as a factor of their size in terms of student numbers, may well be in a position to allocate a small proportion of their income to funding a post that is primarily concerned with income generation.

Opportunity costs

In all situations, the decision to commit resources to one line of action brings with it certain 'costs' in terms of the other ways that those resources could have been employed. These are known as opportunity costs. Thus, there are opportunity costs in terms of how else staff could have used their time when it is prioritised for resource acquisition. Indeed, it can be argued that there are opportunity costs in a school or college opting for a particular level of self-management and its associated 'freedoms'. For example, the opportunity costs in gaining freedom to establish their own admissions criteria or aspects of the curriculum can be measured in terms of the related activities that they bring, such as staff and governor time used dealing with admissions appeals and curriculum design. Thus, managers need to balance the benefits gained from deploying staff in various forms of resource acquisition with the other ways in which they could have used their time, for example, on activities more directly related to the core task of teaching.

Resource allocation

The allocation of resources stage of the management cycle involves decisions about how both financial and real resources are deployed within a set time period, usually one year. It is self-evident that, in order to achieve the core purpose of the organisation, financial resources need to be transferred into other forms of resource or into 'real' resources. This process begins with budget-setting. Most of us are familiar with the concept of a budget as an annual estimate of revenue and expenditure of an organisation. The task of setting the budget involves drawing together a range of information about the likely outturns from the present budget period as well as requirements and expectations about the next one. McAleese (2000) describes the various factors that influence and effect setting the annual budget in a secondary school in England. There is a problem in that 'the budget process is a dynamic one with competing forces vying for funds' (Davies, 1994: 329). This, of course, is true for any organisation and a rational approach to resource management requires managers to set a budget that is designed to maximise the organisation's outputs. However, budget-setting in educational establishments often does not include consideration about the way in which specific learning outcomes will be achieved through the deployment of particular resources (Levačić, 2000: 12). In other words, applying a concept developed by Weick (1976), it can be said that decisions at school or college level about financial allocations and those about the real resources obtained with this funding, usually made at departmental level, are not tightly coupled.

The nature of learning and teaching and the way in which it is usually provided means that staff allocation features as the biggest budget heading for educational organisations. In making this allocation, school and college managers and governors may have to make a number of crucial decisions depending on the level of autonomy devolved to them. These include not only the number of qualified teachers and support staff, but also the level at which any post will be offered. The length and utilisation of the working week and the way in which teaching is organised are also relevant. Simkins (1997: 168) describes the timetabling process as 'perhaps the quintessential component of operational resource management in a school'. In the UK, as elsewhere, issues about the length of the school week and class size have been the subject of recent study (Blatchford and Martin, 1998; Goldstein and Blatchford, 1998) and debate but remain controversial. Thus, the lack of tight coupling between staffing allocations and learning outcomes is not a straightforward matter to address.

Similarly, decisions about the deployment of resources to support the curriculum are important but not easy to link precisely to educational outcomes. Various ways to allocate resources within a school or college are described in the literature (see, for example, Blandford, 1997; Knight, 1993;

Simkins, 1986). Generally, the methods employed relate to the organisational perspectives adopted.

Resource utilisation

This stage of the resource management cycle is concerned with putting the budget plan into operation. It involves activities such as staffing, timetabling, ordering supplies, maintenance and development of the premises and so on. The actual activities associated with generating additional income also fall within this stage. Alongside these tasks, the utilisation of resources brings with it the need for managers to monitor the budget regularly throughout the year in order to compare actual income and expenditure under the various budget headings with those intended. If necessary, decisions and adjustments have to be made and better financial controls imposed on internal budget holders in order to curtail or stimulate spending.

It follows that the use or deployment of any resources brings with it associated costs that need to be, or should be, managed within the resource management cycle. This involves addressing a series of questions, such as 'Can we afford it?', 'Which method is better?', 'Is it worth it?', 'How can costs be managed?', 'What should we charge for it?'. Simkins (2000) discusses each of these questions and provides a useful overview of cost analysis. However, he also points out that, despite a number of good reasons why it is important, cost analysis is still relatively underutilised (see Simkins, 2000: 168). He argues that this situation is likely to change over the next few years, and lists three main reasons:

- the ongoing move to delegated responsibility for resource management and increased emphasis on accountability
- the need to identify alternative educational strategies as part of the global drive to improve educational standards
- governments' concerns to address issues of equity.

All these policy initiatives are set within a context of value for money. For example, Thomas and Martin (1996: 36) advocate what they describe as a 'radical audit' as part of its strategy towards improvement. As a result of such an audit the school or college may consider different ways of working as well as more diversity and creativity in the use of resources. Thus, 'the case for assessing their costs and benefits is more obvious . . . This has implications for good information on costs, recognition of forgone alternatives as well as anticipated benefits' (ibid.: 36).

Evaluating the use of resources

The fourth and final process in the management of resources is the evaluation of the past use of resources with a view to informing future decision-making.

At this point, it is important to remind the reader that the concern is for quality of outputs in terms of learning outcomes rather than the maximisation of profit as in the case of most commercial organisations. In considering the evaluation process, it is necessary to understand and take into account a number of resource management concepts.

Efficiency

Efficiency refers to the relationship between the output and the cost of the inputs used to achieve that output. This can be achieved in two ways. An efficient use of resources is one that produces a given quantity of value of output at the least cost (Levačić, 2000: 13) or when the maximum amount of output is produced for a given cost (Wyndham and Chapman, 1990: ch. 7). Levačić (2000: 14) goes on to explain that the most efficient use of resources depends not only on the prices of the various inputs but also on the 'technical' relationship between the combination of inputs and the desired outputs. In the case of education, the latter is usually taken to mean learning outcomes. For example, in order for every child in a group to achieve a certain standard, different combinations of fully qualified teachers, classroom assistants and an integrated learning computer system could be applied. The most efficient method would be the one that produced the greatest progress towards achieving the overall aim for a set sum of money. However, as Levačić (2000: 14) points out, efficiency is a normative concept. Value judgements are made when a school's efficiency is assessed.

Effectiveness

The concept of effectiveness is about matching results with objectives and is usually taken to mean the extent to which intended outcomes are achieved. This interpretation is derived from the rational perspective of organisational theory as discussed above and in Chapter 2. In the context of other organisational perspectives, or a mixture of perspectives, the concept of effectiveness may be different. The important point here is that the evaluation of effectiveness is dependent on the objectives set or, indeed, the evaluator's perception of them.

Equity

This concept is concerned with fairness in terms of allocating resources according to individual needs. Swanson and King (1997: 323) highlight the importance of ensuring equity on a subjective and individual basis in their definition in relation to education. In their view, equity is the distribution of expenditure 'in such a way that each child can access an education appropriate to his/her individual learning potential and needs'.

These three 'e's then, provide the building blocks for the evaluation of the use of resources to produce learning outcomes. However, there are some difficulties with the concept of efficiency in education because of its normative nature and the lack of agreement about desired educational outcomes. Further concepts are, therefore, defined and used alternatively in the literature.

Value for money

Value for money is achieved when the production process is both efficient and effective (Audit Commission, 1984). This requirement is necessary in education because achieving one without the other is unhelpful. It is neither useful to produce educational outcomes that are of little value to society efficiently nor to achieve desirable outcomes effectively if the process is inefficient.

In England and Wales, the requirement of school inspectors to make judgements about value for money gives it some significance as a means of evaluating resource management. However, from their examination of 66 secondary school inspection reports, Levačić and Glover (1994) concluded:

> The concept and criteria for the judgement of value for money appear . . . to be lacking precision and are subject to variable usage. In the main it appears to be a judgement about educational outputs, given the environmental context, relative to unit cost. However, in some cases the inspectors' assessment of efficiency in relation to management processes appears to be the dominant criterion. The lack of sufficiently clear guidance on the application of the value for money criteria leads to inconsistencies in the summative comments and, in these early inspections, to avoidance of making value for money judgements at all. (Ibid.: 25)

Since January 2000, Ofsted has included the inspection of best value in its inspection framework. As well as the requirement to provide economic, efficient and effective education services, best value includes the criterion to work to clear standards. Applied to schools in England and Wales, it has four principles:

- compare – how a school's performance compares with that of other schools
- challenge – whether the school's performance is high enough, and why and how a service is being provided
- complete – how the school secures economic, efficient and effective services
- consult – seeking the views of stakeholders about the services provided (Audit Commission/Ofsted, 2000: 3).

Cost-effectiveness

Another term that is used often in the literature is cost-effectiveness. In the context of schools, Thomas and Martin (1996: 22) describe it as 'among the more abused words from the lexicon of economics'. They point out that, along with efficiency, it is frequently used as a code for 'cheapness' which is, in fact, a contraction to its economic meaning in that cost-effectiveness analysis can provide a means of enhancing quality. For, according to these writers, 'properly applied, cost effectiveness analysis in schools is concerned with the relationship between the learning of children and the human and physical resources which contribute to that learning' (ibid.: 22). It is 'concerned with comparing different ways of achieving the same objective and the most cost-effective choice will be the least costly of the alternatives being compared' (ibid.: 23). They relate it to efficiency but without applying the rigorous economic conditions of efficiency.

The purpose of their research, however, was to identify the general organisational characteristics associated with schools that are effective in their use of resources in relation to their educational purposes. Emphasising that they are in addition to the attributes common to the wealth of literature on school effectiveness, Thomas and Martin summarise these characteristics as follows:

- Periodically undertake a radical audit, particularly in the use of staff.
- Improve information on costs.
- Use the expertise of relevant staff on resource priorities through some internal delegation of decision-making on resources.
- Limit the dangers of complacency about standards and quality by ensuring that the structure of decision making provides for a dialogue of accountability of high quality.
- Reduce the detachment of management by using team meetings, appraisal and surveys to collect information on the quality of teaching and learning from teachers, parents and pupils.
- Develop sources of information which are independent of headteachers and teachers (Thomas and Martin, 1996: 42–3).

Thus, the evaluation of the past use of resources completes the operational stages of this management cycle and provides appropriate data for purposes of accountability. Like all other aspects of management, in practice the stages of this cycle are not enacted discretely. It is likely that managers will be simultaneously concerned with all aspects of the cycle to some extent.

Resource management and strategic planning

The premise of this chapter is that educational organisations are concerned with managing their resources in order to enhance the learning and teaching of their pupils and students, and this is usually approached from a rational perspective. Thus, schools and colleges are not only concerned with annual budgeting that is informed by educational objectives but, to the extent that they are able to plan strategically, the effective manager also has regard to resource use and implications within a longer-term framework of strategic management and organisational development planning. This theme runs through the chapter. It is particularly evident in Thomas and Martin's list of attributes of resource management in the cost-effective school above. The point is also made clearly by the National Audit Office (1997) who argue the importance of strategic planning by all schools and colleges. They point out that 'longer-term decisions will be needed regardless of whether there is a strategic plan, and it is better that these are taken in the context of a plan . . . than in isolation' (ibid.: 95). Among the benefits of strategic planning they include:

- The financial implications of these plans can be identified, options assessed, and resources directed appropriately.
- The resultant plan forms a framework for financial decision-making during the year.
- The plan allocates prioritised tasks across the school and sets clear criteria for the evaluation of achievement at the end of the year (ibid.: 195).

Thus, the strategic plan provides the basis for budgetary decisions that lead to appropriate resources being available at the right time in order to achieve educational purposes. In turn, resource management provides a vital link between strategy and quality (Preedy et al., 1997: 5).

Conclusion

The management of resources at the level of the institution is an integral aspect of the overall management of the organisation. Indeed, with the shift towards school and college autonomy, together with an emphasis on their accountability, the need for educational managers to demonstrate their effectiveness in the management of resources for the purpose of learning and teaching has become much more significant. This is evident in the need to manage resources strategically as well as at an operational level.

Further reading

Coleman, M. and Anderson, L. (eds) (2000) *Managing Finance and Resources in Education*, London: Paul Chapman Publishing.
Simkins, T. (1997) 'Managing resources', in B. Fidler, S. Russell and T. Simkins (eds), *Choices for Self-Managing Schools: Autonomy and Accountability*, London: Paul Chapman Publishing.
Thomas, H. and Martin, J. (1996) *Managing Resources for School Improvement*, London: Routledge.

References

Anderson, L. (1999) 'Field notes made in KwaZula Natal, South Africa during a research visit funded by the British Council', unpublished.

Anderson, L. (2000) 'The move towards entrepreneurialism', in M. Coleman and L. Anderson (eds), *Managing Finance and Resources in Education*, London: Paul Chapman Publishing.

Audit Commission (1984) *Code of Local Government Audit Practice for England and Wales*, London: HMSO.

Audit Commission/Ofsted (2000) *Getting the Best from your Budget*, London: Audit Commission/Ofsted.

Bell, L. (1998) 'Back to the future: the development of site-based management in England with messages, challenges and a vision for Australia', keynote address to the 25th Australian Council for Educational Administration International Conference, Conrad Jupiters, Gold Coast, 27–30 September.

Blandford, S. (1997) *Resource Management in Schools*, London: Pitman.

Blatchford, P. and Martin, C. (1998) 'The effects of class size on classroom processes: it's a bit like a treadmill – working hard and getting nowhere fast!', *British Journal of Educational Studies*, 46 (2): 118–37.

Bullock, A. and Thomas, H. (1997) *Schools at the Centre?*, London: Routledge.

Bush, T. (1995) *Theories of Educational Management*, 2nd edn, London: Paul Chapman Publishing.

Bush, T. (2000) 'Management styles: impact on finance and resources', in M. Coleman and L. Anderson (eds), *Managing Finance and Resources in Education*, London: Paul Chapman Publishing.

Caldwell, B. and Spinks, J. (1988) *The Self-Managing School*, London: Falmer Press.

Caldwell, B. and Spinks, J. (1992) *Leading the Self-Managing School*, London: Falmer Press.

Caldwell, B.and Spinks, J. (1998) *Beyond the Self-Managing School*, London: Falmer Press.

Davies, B. (1994) 'Managing resources', in T. Bush and J. West-Burnham (eds), *The Principles of Educational Management*, Harlow: Longman.

Goldstein, H. and Blatchford, P. (1998) 'Class size and educational achievement: a review of methodology with particular reference to study design', *British Educational Research Journal*, 24 (3): 255–68.

Hanna, D. (1997) 'Open systems', in A. Harris, N. Bennett and M. Preedy (eds), *Organizational Effectiveness and Improvement in Education*, Buckingham: Open University Press.

Knight, B. (1993) *Financial Management for Schools*, London: Heinemann.

Levačić, R. (1997) 'Managing resources in educational institutions: an open systems approach', in M. Preedy, R. Glatter and R. Levačić (eds), *Educational Management: Strategy, Quality and Resources*, Buckingham: Open University Press.

Levačić, R. (2000) 'Linking resources to learning outcomes', in M. Coleman and L. Anderson (eds), *Managing Finance and Resources in Education*, London: Paul Chapman Publishing.

Levačić, R. and Glover, D. (1994) *Ofsted Assessment of Schools' Efficiency: An Analysis of 66 Secondary School Inspection Reports*, Milton Keynes: Open University, CEPAM Report.

Levine, D. U. and Lezotte, L. (1990) *Usually Effective Schools: A Review and Analysis of Research and Practice*, Madison, WI: National Center for Effective Schools Research and Development.

McAleese, K. (2000) 'Budgeting in schools', in M. Coleman and L. Anderson (eds), *Managing Finance and Resources in Education*, London: Paul Chapman Publishing.

Morgan, G. (1986) *Images of Organisation*, London: Sage.

National Audit Office (1997) 'Linking strategic planning with the budgetary process', in M. Preedy, R. Glatter and R. Levačić (eds), *Educational Management: Strategy, Quality and Resources*, Buckingham: Open University Press.

Preedy, M., Glatter, R. and Levačić, R. (1997) 'Introduction: managing quality, resources and strategy' in M. Preedy, R. Glatter, and R. Levačić (eds), *Educational Management: Strategy, Quality and Resources*, Buckingham: Open University Press.

Ryan, P., Duan, C. X. and Merry, R. (1998) 'In search of understanding: a qualitative comparison of primary school management in the Shaanxi region of China and England', *Compare*, 28 (2): 171–82.

Scheerens, J. (1999) 'Concepts and theories of school effectiveness', in A. J. Visscher (ed.), *Managing Schools Towards High Performance*, Lisse: Swets and Zeitlinger.

Scott, W. R. (1987) *Organisations: Rational, Natural and Open Systems*, Englewood Cliffs, NJ: Prentice-Hall.

Sherratt, B. (1994) *Grant-Maintained Status: Considering the Options*, Harlow: Longman.

Simkins, T. (1986) 'Patronage, markets and collegiality: reflections on the allocation of finance in secondary schools', *Educational Management and Administration*, 14 (1): 17–30.

Simkins, T. (1997) 'Managing resources', in B. Fidler, S. Russell and T. Simkins (eds), *Choices for Self-Managing Schools: Autonomy and Accountability*, London: Paul Chapman Publishing.

Simkins, T. (2000) 'Cost analysis in education' in M. Coleman and L. Anderson (eds.) *Managing Finance and Resources in Education*, London: Paul Chapman Publishing.

Swanson, A. D. and King, R. A. (1997) *School Finance: Its Economics and Politics*, 2nd edn, New York: Longman.

Thomas, H. and Martin, J. (1996) *Managing Resources for School Improvement*, London: Routledge.

Weick, K. (1976) 'Educational organisations as loosely coupled systems?', *Administrative Science Quarterly*, 21 (1): 1–21.

Wyndham, D. M. and Chapman, D. W. (1990) *The Evaluation of Educational Efficiency: Constraints, Issues and Politics*, Greenwich, CT: JAI Press.

Section VI
Managing External Relations

14

Governance, Autonomy and Accountability in Education

Ron Glatter

Introduction: a hazardous enterprise

To write about concepts such as those in the title for an international audience is a hazardous enterprise. It is easy to become over-impressed by apparent similarities between 'reforms' in various countries and to neglect continuing deep differences at the level of implementation and practice. For example, Levin (1999; 2000) has conducted research into education reform in national contexts which, in global terms, might seem very similar to one another – Canada, England, New Zealand and the USA. Yet he concludes that even across contexts with such close cultural affinities, reforms such as changes in governance exhibit considerable variation: 'The official commitment to decentralisation and parent involvement is ubiqitous, but within this frame policies and practices are highly variable' (Levin, 1999: 136). This observation is likely to have even greater force where the national contexts being compared are more diverse.

In this connection it is important to distinguish different dimensions of change. Green (1999) conducted an analysis of changing education and training systems in a group of distinctive European and East Asian settings. He found that, as a result of the impact of common global forces, there was clear evidence of convergence around broad policy themes, such as lifelong learning, decentralisation of governance and the growing use of quality control and evaluation measures. 'However this does not appear to have led to any marked convergence in structures and processes' (Green, 1999: 69) nor in the details of policy. Indeed, the different models underlying the operation of the various systems appeared to be as distinctive as they were a decade earlier. Rather than simply concentrating on the discourse of policy, he calls for more attention to be given to structural analysis to enable us to understand better the impact of common trends on particular settings.

As Bottery (2000) indicates, global trends in each nation are strongly mediated by factors such as:

- its central values, for example its orientation towards an individualist or collective ethos
- its long political and social history as embodied in current educational structures
- the particular personalities holding power when reform is being attempted, their beliefs, objectives and political strength.

The combination of such factors may create a highly constrained situation for policy-makers so that often 'reforms focus on what can be done instead of on what might really make a difference' (Levin, 2000: 8).

The lack of attention to culture and context in existing models and theories is criticised by Dimmock and Walker (2000: 159) for being ethnocentric and assuming 'a false universalism'. This assessment leads them to develop a model for cross-cultural comparison in educational leadership and management, covering both system-level and school-level cultural characteristics, 'in order to present holistic and contextualised accounts' (ibid.: 159).

The present chapter seeks to avoid the assumption of a false universalism by presenting a set of models which can be used in different contexts:

- to analyse the governance of school education, as well as degrees of school autonomy and forms of accountability
- to consider the possible impact of proposed changes in this area.

The term 'school' is used throughout this chapter. However, the analysis presented is believed to be widely applicable across different types of educational institution, including those designed for older adolescents and adults, called 'colleges' in some countries. The emphasis may sometimes be different and reference is made to this later.

Governance

Studies of educational management and administration too often neglect the framework of governance within which school leaders operate. The notion of 'governance' itself is contested. Rhodes (1997) has identified six distinct uses of the term. A common contemporary approach is to speak of 'governing without government' to suggest that the task of governing has now outrun the capacity of governments to perform it. Consequently, it is increasingly undertaken by complex external networks of groupings from the private and voluntary sectors, professional 'experts', lay people and others. This leads to difficulties of 'steering' and monitoring and to 'opaque accountability' (Rhodes, 1999: xxiii). A characteristic definition of governance within this approach is as follows: 'a concern with . . . achieving collective action in the realm of public affairs in conditions where it is not possible to rest on recourse to the authority of the state' (Stoker, 2000: 3). Jessop (2000) speaks of the state being forced to share power in order to secure its objectives. Dowling et al. (2000: 109) apply this thinking to local government: 'Governance implies interconnectedness and mutual dependency between a variety of organisations both inside and outside the local authority.'

Such writers adopt the classification of governing structures in terms of markets, networks and hierarchies (Rhodes, 1999; Thompson et al., 1991) but tend to equate 'governance' with networks alone. The related though highly ambiguous concept of 'partnership' attains considerable importance within the perspective (Raab, 2000). However, it is not clear why 'governance' should be conceived in such specific terms, even if, under the so-called New Public Management, government has increasingly adopted the roles of enabler, contractor and regulator (Arnott, 2000). Levin (2000) has drawn attention to the range of 'policy levers' which governments have at their command, including mandates, inducements, capacity-building, system changing and opinion mobilisation (see also Levin, 2001). Increasingly governments in many countries are employing a range of regulatory and monitoring devices such as audits, inspections, target-setting and performance measurement.

These forms of system management are more indirect than the traditional ones based on command and direction, but their overall impact in terms of the distribution of power is an open question, a matter for empirical investigation in each context. Has there been a dispersal of power, as the 'governing without government' approach would suggest, or has there simply been a shift from one form of control to another (Jacobs, 2000)? How successful are governments in 'steering at a distance', or in what Jessop (2000: 23) calls 'metagovernance': 'the process of managing the complexity, plurality and tangled hierarchies characteristic of prevailing modes of co-ordination'? For example, what have been the effects of governments privatising parts of public services and creating arm's length agencies in an attempt to cope with overload by cutting down on direct service provision? Hirst (2000) considers such structural changes have increased not reduced fragmentation and complexity through the requirements they create for enhanced supervision, regulation and co-ordination.

Pending further detailed investigations in different settings, it seems appropriate to adopt more open definitions of governance than Stoker's given above. The *Concise Oxford Dictionary* defines the term simply as 'the act or manner of governing', which would embrace markets, networks and hierarchies and any mixes of them found in particular contexts. Hirst (2000) follows this approach but extends it to include the contemporary concern with results, defining governance as 'the means by which an activity or ensemble of activities is controlled or directed, such that it delivers an acceptable range of outcomes according to some established social standard' (ibid.: 24).

Martin et al. (2000: 121) refer to 'a system of rule which constitutes the form and process of the public sphere' which emphasises the formal rather than the behavioural aspects of governance, though they add that it will 'not be neutral but driven by the values of the dominant institutional or political order'. As Rhodes (1997) argues, altruism between levels of government is rare. Governance must be conceived in political (including micropolitical) and not simply in legal or procedural terms. Also, although the idea of governing *without* government is questionable, the concept of governance clearly encompasses *more than* government.

The changing governance of school systems exhibits a series of tensions which will become evident in the analysis below. These include tensions between:

- integration and fragmentation
- competition and co-operation
- central and local decision-making.

The processes involved are delicate ones, and the balances struck at any point in time (for they will frequently change) will impact significantly on the character of the schooling made available.

Models of governance in school education

The argument presented here is that governance, provided that it is defined in an 'open' manner as suggested above, can be viewed as an overarching concept to establish a framework within which other common concepts relating to structure and process, such as autonomy and accountability, can be located. This should help to promote conceptual coherence and avoid partial and misleading assessments of these other ideas when considered outside their broader context.

Table 14.1 offers a tentative framework (developed from Glatter and Woods, 1995) for understanding and applying models of governance in school education. It is undoubtedly a crude and oversimplified analysis. Four models are distinguished: competitive market (CM), school empowerment (SE), local empowerment (LE) and quality control (QC). These models should be seen as ideal types. They are separated here for analytical purposes. In practice each governance system or jurisdiction is likely to operate on some composite of these models. Sometimes they may complement and reinforce each other as they impact on localities and schools but their interaction is also likely to cause tensions which participants must seek to resolve.

Competitive market

Examples of policies characteristic of each model are shown first, and then specific features of each of them are identified against a number of issues of

Table 14.1 *Models of governance in school education*

Models	Competitive market (CM)	School Empowerment (SE)	Local empowerment (LE)	Quality control (QC)
Indicative policies	Pupil number led funding e.g. by vouchers More open enrolment Published data on school performance Variety of school types	Authority devolved to school on finance, staffing, curriculum, student admissions Substantial powers for school council/governing body	Authority devolved to locality on finance, staffing, curriculum, student admissions Substantial powers for local community council/ governing body	Regular, systematic inspections Detailed performance targets Mandatory curriculum and assessment requirements
Main perspective(s)	Commercial	Political and/or managerial	Political and/or managerial	Bureaucratic
How the individual school is viewed	As a small business	As a participatory community	One of a 'family' of local schools	As a point of delivery/ local outlet
Main focus within the system	The relevant competitive arena	The individual school	The locality as a social and educational unit	Central or other state bodies
Nature of schools' autonomy	Substantial	Devolved	Consultative	Guided
Form of accountability	Contractual; consumerist	Responsive; 'dual'	Responsive; community forum	Contractual; hierarchical
Purpose of performance measurement	Inform consumer choice	Provide management information	Benchmarking across units	Monitor and develop system
Key school leadership role	Entrepreneur	Director and co-ordinator	Networker	Production manager
Function of intermediate authority	Minimal	Supportive, advisory	Strategic co-ordination	Production supervision as agent of controlling body

structure and process. Thus, the major perspective underlying the CM model relates to the analogy with the commercial marketplace. Under this model, the school is viewed as a small or medium-sized business with a high degree of autonomy and few formal links with the governmental structure. The main focus within the system is placed not on the individual school but on the relevant 'competitive arena' (Woods et al., 1998), which will contain a group of (generally) adjacent schools in competition with each other for pupils and funds. The nature of this arena will vary widely from context to context, depending on factors such as the socio-economic character of the area, including access to private transport, and the relative density of the population – where the population is very thinly spread, there may be no arena at all.

School empowerment

The next model is called 'school empowerment' (SE) because policy-makers often claim that they are seeking to empower school-level stakeholders, in particular the headteacher or principal and other staff as well as parents. The delegation of functions to school level has been 'legitimised by a discourse of empowerment' (Arnott, 2000: 70). The perspectives underlying this model might be either or both 'political' (in the broad sense of dispersing power) and managerial. In some national contexts the emphasis has been purely managerial, on the principle that decisions are best taken as close as possible to the point of action, while in others the argument has also been couched in terms of freedom and choice. Although the SE model is often in practice combined with CM, it is analytically distinct and the picture of the school which is implied in the model is different. The focus is more on the institution itself and the way it is run than on its competitive activities 'against' other institutions. It encompasses ideas of participation, identification and partnership – the school conceived of as an extended community and in this respect it seems to provide a contrast with the CM model. The unit within the system which provides its main focus or 'centre of gravity' is the school itself.

Local empowerment

Some countries have been more concerned with devolution to local and municipal authorities than to schools, and it seemed important to represent this model explicitly within the current version of the framework. Although the LE model shares the term 'empowerment' with SE, and there are a number of commonalities, there are also significant differences between them. As with SE, the justification for this form of empowerment can be in either or both political or managerial terms. However, the perception of the individual school is different. The school is here viewed more explicitly as one of a 'family' of schools, as part of a local educational *system* and as a member of a broader community in which there are reciprocal rights and obligations. The contrast with the CM model is particularly evident here. Martin et al. (2000) have developed a framework which 'contrasts a system of local education devolved according to the principles of community governance as against those of the market' (ibid.: 122): they compare 'consumer democracy' with 'local democracy'. Within the LE model, the main focus is on the locality as a social and educational unit and its representative bodies, though numerous difficulties have been found in practice with implementing representative local democracy satisfactorily.

Quality control

Finally, under the pressures of global competition and growing demands on public expenditure, governments are increasingly seeking control over the quality of key school processes and products even in highly devolved and/or market-like systems. The major underlying perspective in the QC model is likely to be bureaucratic, that is involving laid-down rules and requirements and operating through set procedures, controls and monitoring arrangements. The picture of the school implied here is of a kind of 'point of delivery', with many of the 'goods' on offer and the targets established – the 'product mix' and 'product quality' – having been determined at either the central or state level, depending on the constitutional arrangements. Under the QC model, the units within the system which provide the main focus or 'centre of gravity' usually tend to be located within, or closely connected to, central or regional government.

The four models are by no means comprehensive and the framework could well be formulated differently, but it provides a useful instrument through which to examine some key issues of structure and process in the governance of school education.

School autonomy

The framework suggests differences in the nature of schools' autonomy under each of the four models. Before discussing these, some consideration of the idea of school autonomy is needed. The concept is connected with the trend to devolve power to lower levels in many countries. As Green (1999) points out, such devolution can take many different forms: 'Decentralisation has variously meant devolving power to the regions, the regional outposts of central government (deconcentration), the local authorities, the social partners and the institutions themselves' (ibid.: 61). He suggests that there are still clear differences between countries where most power lies at the centre (such as France and Japan), those where regional control is strongest (such as Germany and Switzerland), those where local control now predominates (the Nordic countries) and those where substantial power has been devolved to schools and the marketplace (Netherlands and the UK).

The term 'autonomy' is often used in a rhetorical sense and to guard against this it needs to be examined closely (Maden, 2000). Two key questions are: autonomy for whom and over what? Bullock and Thomas (1997) distinguish between the autonomy of the individual learner, the educator and the institution, arguing that the level of autonomy might be increased for one of these while at the same time being reduced for the others. The fact that autonomy is a relative concept is also seen when we consider the domains in which autonomy might be given to schools. Writing from an Australian perspective, Sharpe (1994) presents a 'self-management continuum' from total external control to total self-management, and attempts to identify movements along four sub-continua in Australia over a 20-year period. These are concerned with *input* variables, such as finance, staff and students, *structure* variables, such as decisions about the patterns of provision, *process* variables, such as the management of curriculum and *environment* variables, to do with reporting and marketing. His conclusion was that increased government control in some

231

areas had modified or even nullified the impact of enhanced self-management in others.

Bullock and Thomas (1997) examined decentralisation in 11 very diverse countries, including China, Poland, Uganda and the USA, along four dimensions: curriculum and assessment, human and physical resources, finance and access (pupil admissions). They found movements towards both more and less autonomy, and concluded that 'Taken as a whole, the impact of decentralisation – and centralisation – on the general principle of autonomy appears uncertain and problematic' (ibid.: 213). They also noted that in some countries, such as England and New Zealand, the 'paradox' of simultaneous centralisation and decentralisation was evident, the centralisation relating particularly to the curriculum and, to some extent, funding regimes, with governments tending to take greater powers to define educational priorities and schools having scope to decide how best to implement them. Simkins (1997) distinguishes between *criteria power*, concerned with determining purposes and frameworks, and *operational power*, concerned with service delivery. Karlsen (2000) also refers to such a distinction in his analysis of educational governance in Norway and British Columbia, Canada: 'We are looking at a decentralisation dynamic in which initiating is a central task, but in which implementation and accountability are local duties' (ibid.: 531).

Despite this paradox of 'decentralised centralism' (Karlsen, 2000: 529), substantial autonomy has been accorded to schools in England in recent years. Indeed, the government has claimed that 'No other education service in the world devolves as much power and responsibility to schools as we do' (DfEE, 2001: 16). It is therefore worth briefly noting some key research findings from this experience. The process has led to a much larger role for head-teachers (principals), particularly in relation to resources. The external pressure for enhanced performance and for the implementation of curricular changes has increased the scope and intensity of the work, and the head's role is now commonly exercised together with a group of senior staff including the deputy head (Levačić, 1998; Wallace and Hall, 1994). The autonomy of other teaching staff has arguably declined as a result of the advent of the National Curriculum and the impact of school-based budgeting on many teachers' employment position (Bullock and Thomas, 1997).

The evidence that devolution has had any impact on pupil learning is extremely thin, but this is due at least in part to the complexity of the processes involved and the inherent difficulty of investigating them. However, there is evidence that devolution has significantly enhanced the quality of schools' internal planning capacities and processes (Levačić, 1998). Enhancing school autonomy in some respects while extending central control in others, in the context of a limited 'market', has had another somewhat paradoxical effect. Schools have not on the whole tended to differentiate themselves in order to focus on a specific *niche*, but rather have sought to appeal to a broad grouping of parents and pupils. Nor have the structural arrangements tended to promote innovation at school level: instead schools have sought to emulate the dominant model of the high-status school (Woods et al., 1998). At the time of writing the government is seeking to introduce measures to deal with these issues (DfEE, 2001).

Key issues in any move towards devolution are the effectiveness of support systems, including development opportunities: 'Unless there is local capacity for management, there is no advantage to making decisions where action takes place. The Principle of Subsidiarity argues not just for moving decisions to the site of action, but also making local decision-makers competent' (McGinn and Welsh, 1999: 66–7).

An OECD study of 14 national school systems (OECD, 1995) sought to distinguish three modes of decision-making: full autonomy; made after consultation with another authority at an adjoining level; made within guidelines set by another authority, generally at the top level. In Table 14.1 we have adapted this (admittedly crude) classification to our ideal-type framework of models of governance. In a 'pure' CM model the autonomy of schools would be very substantial. We have not used the term 'full autonomy' here since this is virtually unimaginable: there are always constraints, not least from the law, even for a highly unorthodox independent school (Sharpe, 1994). A key purpose of the SE model is to maximise schools' autonomy within an overall system, so here we have suggested that 'devolved' is the most appropriate descriptor. The LE model places emphasis on the school as a member of a co-operating family of institutions, so here we use 'consultative' from the OECD study's typology. In the QC model, however, the role of the senior authority at central or state level is more pronounced, so the appropriate form of autonomy here is 'guided', again based on the OECD typology.

Accountability

Writing about school-based management (SBM) in the USA, Wohlstetter and Sebring (2000) comment: 'An underlying premise of SBM is that school-level participants trade increased autonomy for increased accountability' (ibid.: 174). Accountability is a contested concept, not least, as an Australian writer suggests, 'because it is often the engine of policy: what is held to account is what counts' (Cotter, 2000: 12). It is also complex. There is not space here for a full discussion (see, for example, Adams and Kirst, 1999; Feintuck, 1994; Kogan, 1986; Scott, 1989). I will seek to relate different forms of accountability to the four models of governance.

An important distinction is that between *contractual* and *responsive* accountability (Halstead, 1994). Contractual accountability is concerned with the degree to which educators are fulfilling the expectations of particular audiences in terms of standards, outcomes and results. It is based on an explicit or implicit contract with those audiences. It tends to be measurement driven, with the factors to be measured – whether educational, financial or other – selected by those audiences in line with their perceived preferences and requirements. Responsive accountability refers to decision-making by educators after a process of taking into account the interests and wishes of relevant 'stakeholders'. It is more concerned with process than outcomes, and with securing involvement and interaction to obtain decisions which meet a range of needs and preferences.

Such a distinction should not, of course, be drawn too sharply, but it indicates different emphases between conceptions of accountability. Thus in the CM model the provision of schooling is analogous to a commercial service and so the predominant form of accountability is contractual. In the SE model with its focus on the school as a participatory community the dimension of responsiveness is uppermost. In LE the broader local community is the pivotal unit, so responsiveness to stakeholders is even more pronounced here. Finally in the QC model the contractual form will be the significant one, with the 'contract' being specified by governments or their agents rather than by parents or 'consumers' as in CM. The method will tend to be drawn from the

> accounting model of accountability that has pre-specified categories and accounts in terms of discrete scales of measurement ... The accounting dimension is entrenched at government level and is much loved by ministers who want a simple way of demonstrating good news to the electorate. This will often drive the bureaucracy to organise the tests and deliver the numbers. (Cotter, 2000: 4, 12)

Two other aspects of accountability are relevant to the models. First, each of the models implies a different mode of accountability. In the case of CM the mode is consumerist (Halstead, 1994), with power in principle being placed in the hands of consumer-surrogates, in the form of parents or guardians, to decide whether to choose the school for their child or to keep them there. The position is more complex in the case of SE. Many formulations (for example, Halstead, 1994; Kogan, 1986) refer to professional accountability but in school empowerment models such as SBM professionals often have to share authority with school boards or councils which include parents and community members. These are often regarded as relatively weak bodies with unclear roles and the 'agenda' firmly set by the professionals particularly the principal and other senior staff (Levačić, 1995), but the SE model as such incorporates the possibility of a significant element of non-professional as well as professional participation. This may be especially relevant, for example, in 'colleges' for older students where employment interests may be represented on governing boards. Hence we characterise the mode of accountability in this model as 'dual'. Within LE we identify the accountability mode as 'community forum'. This indicates that the ultimate authority within this model will lie at a local level beyond the school, though there are many variations in respect of the size and socio-geographical nature of this unit and the extent to which it operates on collegial or directive principles. The possibility of 'network' or 'partnership' arrangements with their tendency to produce fragmentation and 'opaque accountability' (Rhodes, 1999: xiii), referred to earlier, arises here. The mode in QC will be hierarchical, in that accountability will be owed to the body with power to define and control quality, located generally at national or state level.

A final aspect of accountability to be considered in relation to the models concerns the purpose of performance measurement. Although, as indicated earlier, measuring performance will be more prominent in contractual than responsive versions of accountability, the rise of target-setting, performance management and the 'audit society' (Bottery, 2000; Power, 1997) has been a central feature of public service operations in many countries in recent years. However, the prime purpose of such measurement will vary depending on the model. Thus in CM the chief purpose will be to inform consumer choice. In SE performance measurement and analysis will be conducted in order to provide management information to facilitate organisational improvement. In the LE model a key purpose will be to provide comparative 'benchmarking' information across organisational units to promote local system enhancement. Under QC the main purpose will be to seek to monitor, control and develop the system as a whole.

School leadership

The governance models imply distinct and somewhat contrasting roles for school leadership. In CM, school leaders are expected to provide the kind of education the consumers – and in particular their surrogates, the parents/guardians – want. This means that 'the identification and stimulation of parent demand for the kind of education the organization can produce most efficiently, becomes a primary task of the manager' (McGinn and Welsh, 1999: 47). This requires primarily an entrepreneurial style of leadership. In the SE model the school leader has to draw together the many different educational, managerial and financial threads in the work of the school, as well as to stimulate and if possible inspire the professionals to greater achievement. The evidence suggests that under devolved school management both the roles of chief executive and educational leader attain greater significance (Levačić, 1998). In addition, there is a testing external dimension: 'although headteachers have gained more autonomy, they also have to meet increasingly diverse demands from all sides and are often caught in conflict. Headteachers get headaches' (Hernes, 2000: 2). Thus both a directing and a co-ordinating style are required.

In the LE model, there is a key requirement for school leaders to become effective networkers, both to promote the school's interests within the local system and to collaborate productively in a partnership mode with their peers. Under QC the school leader's role is more akin to that of a production manager, organising the school and its staff to deliver products or outcomes of the requisite quality.

Clearly this analysis is oversimplified. In practice school leaders will interpret and enact their role in a variety of ways depending on their individual personalities, the cultures of their schools and other factors. The analysis is intended to suggest that the governance context is an important and often neglected influence on school leadership. Generalisations are frequently made about the features associated with effective school leadership without taking into account the specific and diverse frameworks of policy and governance within which it is exercised. For example, as Cotter (2000) points out: 'The current exhortations to principals to be transformational do not sit easily beside narrow forms of accountability' (ibid.: 7–8). He argues that such forms, in which principals are expected to accept given categories without reflection, are more consonant with transactional forms of leadership, as in our analogy above with the role of production manager.

However, the position in practice is more complex still. School leaders generally face not a single model of governance but several. So elements of the CM model are combined with others from SE and QC for example. As Leithwood (2001) suggests, in the face of this 'policy eclecticism', school leaders 'can be excused for feeling that they are being pulled in many different directions simultaneously. They *are* being pulled in many different directions simultaneously' (ibid.: 228). From this a series of tensions and dilemmas (Glatter, 1996) arises for school leaders, for example the dilemmas that, within their school 'The principal is required to be both a member of the cast and the star' (Wildy and Louden, 2000: 180) and within the wider system they are expected both to collaborate and to compete. School leaders have the task of successfully managing these tensions and ambiguities – by, for instance, skilful buffering of the staff from external pressures that conflict with the school's goals without insulating them from legitimate influences for improvement (Goldring, 1997; Leithwood, 2001). It is perhaps the most important and difficult task faced by school leaders in many contexts today.

Function of intermediate authority

The key functions and roles of the intermediate authority (where such a level exists) differ significantly between the four models of governance. In a pure CM model its functions are minimal, covering perhaps the provision of information to parents and support for pupils with additional educational needs. In the SE model the intermediate authority's role will be primarily supportive and advisory. Under LE much will depend on whether the geographical scope of its responsibility fits with the 'local system of schooling' concept underlying the model. In some contexts it does: in others 'cluster' arrangements have been developed (for example, the Education Action Zones in England [DfEE, 1999]) based on areas which are smaller and more 'local' than those covered by the relevant intermediate authorities. (By their size intermediate authorities in some countries, for example the municipalities in Sweden and many school districts in the USA, come closer than their counterparts in other countries to a model of 'community governance'.) For simplicity we have disregarded this important distinction in Table 14.1 and suggested that in the LE model the intermediate authority's key function is strategic co-ordination. By contrast, in QC the authority becomes more of a production supervisor as an agent of the central controlling body. The reality of 'policy eclecticism' in many national contexts sets up major tensions and dilemmas for intermediate authorities just as it does for schools and their leaders.

Conclusion

Structures of governance vary widely between different national contexts. Also, as a result of the high level of 'reform' activity in many countries, these structures are often in considerable flux. Practitioners need to analyse their own contemporary settings closely and take this analysis into account in developing their approach to the management of external relations. It is hoped that this chapter will have helped in this challenging process.

Further reading

Arnott, M. A. and Raab, C. D. (2000) *The Governance of Schooling: Comparative Studies of Devolved Management*, London: Routledge/Falmer.
Green, A. (1999) 'Education and globalisation in Europe and East Asia: convergent and divergent trends', *Journal of Educational Policy*, 14 (1): 55–72.
Rhodes, R. A. W. (1997) *Understanding Governance*, Buckingham: Open University Press.

References

Adams, J. E. and Kirst, M. W. (1999) 'New demands and concepts for educational accountability: striving for results in an era of excellence', in J. Murphy and K. S. Louis (eds), *Handbook of Research on Educational Administration, Second Edition*, San Francisco: Jossey-Bass.
Arnott, M. A. (2000) 'Restructuring the governance of schools: the impact of "managerialism" on schools in Scotland and England', in M. A. Arnott and C. D. Raab (eds), *The Governance of Schooling: Comparative Studies of Devolved Management*, London: Routledge/Falmer.
Bottery, M. (2000) *Education, Policy and Ethics*, London: Continuum.
Bullock, A. and Thomas, H. (1997) *Schools at the Centre? A Study of Decentralisation*, London: Routledge.

Cotter, R. (2000) 'Accountability in education and beyond', paper presented at the Annual Conference of the British Educational Management and Administration Society (BEMAS), Bristol, September.

Department for Education and Employment (DfEE) (1999) *Meet the Challenge: Education Action Zones*, London: Department for Education and Employment.

Department for Education and Employment (DfEE) (2001) *Schools Building on Success*, Cm 5050, London: Department for Education and Employment.

Dimmock, C. and Walker, A. (2000) 'Developing comparative and international educational leadership and management: a cross-cultural model', *School Leadership and Management*, 20 (2): 143–60.

Dowling, K., Dunleavy, P., King, D., Margetts, H. and Rydin, Y. (2000) 'Understanding urban governance: the contribution of rational choice', in G. Stoker (ed.), *The New Politics of British Local Governance*, London: Macmillan.

Feintuck, M. (1994) *Accountability and Choice in Schooling*, Buckingham: Open University Press.

Glatter, R. (1996) 'Managing dilemmas in education: the tightrope walk of strategic choice in autonomous institutions', in S. L. Jacobson, E. S. Hickox and R. B. Stevenson (eds), *School Administration: Persistent Dilemmas in Preparation and Practice*, Westport CT: Praeger.

Glatter, R. and Woods, P. A. (1995) 'Parental choice and school decision-making: operating in a market-like environment', in K. C. Wong and K. M. Cheng (eds), *Educational Leadership and Change: An International Perspective*, Hong Kong: Hong Kong University Press.

Goldring, E. B. (1997) 'Educational leadership: schools, environments and boundary spanning', in M. Preedy, R. Glatter and R. Levačić (eds), *Educational Management: Strategy, Quality and Resources*, Buckingham: Open University Press.

Green, A. (1999) 'Education and globalisation in Europe and East Asia: convergent and divergent trends', *Journal of Educational Policy*, 14 (1): 55–72.

Halstead, M. (1994) 'Accountability and values', in D. Scott (ed.), *Accountability and Control in Educational Setting*, London: Cassell.

Hernes, G. (2000) 'Editorial: headway for headteachers', *IIEP Newsletter*, 18 (4), October–December, Paris: International Institute for Educational Planning.

Hirst, P. (2000) 'Democracy and governance', in J. Pierre (ed.), *Debating Governance*, Oxford: Oxford University Press.

Jacobs, K. (2000) 'Devolved management in New Zealand schools', in M. A. Arnott and C. D. Raab (eds), *The Governance of Schooling: Comparative Studies of Devolved Management*, London: Routledge/Falmer.

Jessop, B. (2000) 'Governance failure', in G. Stoker (ed.), *The New Politics of British Local Governance*, London: Macmillan.

Karlsen, G. E. (2000) 'Decentralized centralism; framework for a better understanding of governance in the field of education', *Journal of Educational Policy*, 15 (50): 525–38.

Kogan, M. (1986) *Education Accountability: An Analytic Overview*, London: Hutchinson.

Leithwood, K. (2001) 'School leadership in the context of accountability policies', *International Journal of Leadership in Education*, 4 (3): 217–35.

Levačić, R. (1995) 'School governing bodies: management boards or supporters' clubs?', *Public Money and Management*, April–June: 35–40.

Levačić, R. (1998) 'Local management of schools in England: results after six years', *Journal of Education Policy*, 13 (3): 331–50.

Levin, B. (1999) 'An epidemic of education policy: (what) can we learn from each other?', *Comparative Education*, 34 (2): 131–41.

Levin, B. (2000) 'Conceptualizing the process of education reform from an international perspective', paper presented to the Annual Meeting of the American Educational Research Association, New Orleans, April.

Levin, B. (2001) *Reforming Education: From Origins to Outcomes*, London: Routledge/Falmer.

Maden, M. (2000) *Shifting Gear: Changing Patterns of Educational Governance in Europe*, Stoke-on-Trent: Trentham Books.

Martin, J., McKeown, P., Nixon, J. and Ranson, S. (2000) 'Community-active management and governance of schools in England and Wales', in M. A. Arnott and C. D. Raab (eds), *The Governance of Schooling: Comparative Studies of Devolved Management*, London: Routledge/Falmer.

McGinn, N. and Welsh, T. (1999) *Decentralisation in Education: Why, When, What and How?*, Paris: UNESCO International Institute for Educational Planning.

Organisation for Economic Co-operation and Development (OECD) (1995) *Decision-Making in 14 OECD Education Systems*, Paris: Centre for Educational Research and Innovation, Organisation for Economic Co-operation and Development.

Power, M. (1997) *The Audit Society: Rituals of Verification*, Oxford: Oxford University Press.

Raab, C. D. (2000) 'The devolved management of schools and its implications for governance', in M. A. Arnott and C. D. Raab (eds), *The Governance of Schooling: Comparative Studies of Devolved Management*, London: Routledge/Falmer.

Rhodes, R. A. W. (1997) *Understanding Governance*, Buckingham: Open University Press.

Rhodes, R. A. W. (1999) 'Foreword: governance and networks', in G. Stoker (ed.), *The New Management of British Local Governance*, London: Macmillan.

Scott, P. (1989) 'Accountability, responsiveness and responsibility', in R. Glatter (ed.), *Educational Institutions and their Environments: Managing the Boundaries*, Buckingham: Open University Press.

Sharpe, F. (1994) 'Devolution: towards a research framework', *Educational Management and Administration*, 22 (2): 85–95.

Simkins, T. (1997) 'Autonomy and accountability', in B. Fidler, S. Russell and T. Simkins (eds), *Choices for Self-Managing Schools*, London: Paul Chapman Publishing.

Stoker, G. (2000) 'Introduction', in G. Stoker (ed.), *The New Politics of British Local Governance*, London: Macmillan.

Thompson, G., Frances, J., Levačić, R. and Mitchell, J. (eds), (1991) *Markets, Hierarchies and Networks: The Co-ordination of Social Life*, London: Sage, in association with the Open University.

Wallace, M. and Hall, V. (1994) *Inside the SMT: Teamwork in Secondary School Management*, London: Paul Chapman Publishing.

Wildy, H. and Louden, W. (2000) 'School restructuring and the dilemma of principals' work', *Educational Management and Administration*, 28 (2): 173–84.

Wohlstetter, P. and Sebring, P. B. (2000) 'School-based management in the United States', in M. A. Arnott and C. D. Raab (eds), *The Governance of Schooling: Comparative Studies of Devolved Management*, London: Routledge/Falmer.

Woods, P. A., Bagley, C. and Glatter, R. (1998) *School Choice and Competition: Markets in the Public Interest?*, London: Routledge.

15

Marketing

Nick Foskett

Decentralisation, accountability and marketisation

One of the most distinctive meta-trends in educational management is the movement of schools and colleges from an inward-focused, protected and closed mode of operation to one which is externally focused, accountable, increasingly competitive and open. This change from a 'domesticated' to a 'wild' operating environment (Carlson, 1975) has seen a shift away from a paternalistic relationship between government (central or local) and institutions, and from a protectionist monastic relationship between schools and their local communities, although the extent and form of its development varies between, and sometimes within, different national settings. With a growing engagement with the world beyond the school/college gates, institutions have had to rise to the challenge of managing their external relations. This has brought them into the world of communication management, public relations and marketing to varying extents, areas that have been *terra incognita* for most teachers and managers in education.

The pressures towards such external engagement are a direct result of the processes of globalisation as the global market economy, communication technologies and the international adoption of many common cultural values have impacted both on governments and educators. Three broad pressures can be identified. First, the desire to prepare young people to engage with the global economy and technology has pushed schools and colleges to engage with that external world. Second, to compete internationally, governments have sought to raise the quality and quantity of the 'output' from education. The pursuit of the three 'E's of efficiency, effectiveness and economy has led some to establish quasi-market systems for components of their education system (Whitty et al., 1998). Third, libertarian views of the rights of individuals in society have promoted stronger links between schools and their environments. The right to choose education and training pathways is enshrined in the UN Universal Declaration of Human Rights, while the growth of consumerism, the rise of vocationalism and its requirement for engagement with the labour market, and the egalitarian and economic pressures towards widening participation in education, all require the positive management of external relations by schools and colleges. Marketisation, therefore, is a global phenomenon, but the pressures to engage in activities that fall under the umbrella term of 'marketing' have arisen not simply from the need for institutions to sell education as a consumer product and to compete with other schools and colleges for the allocation of scarce resources. The momentum is at least as much the result of a developing perspective on the nature, purpose and role of education within society. Market accountability, political accountability and social accountability all serve to push schools and colleges in the direction of external relations management.

Marketisation produces a range of management implications for schools and colleges. Of most immediate impact is decentralisation, the movement to some form of self-management with responsibility to some degree for acquiring resources and making choices about priorities for their use. With this responsibility comes accountability for the impact of those resources, both in terms of financial probity and for the effect on pupil/student learning. The view that freeing schools and colleges to manage their own resources will enable them to respond to local conditions to raise standards more effectively than through centralised controls underpins the drive towards markets (e.g. Chubb and Moe, 1990). However, Lauder and Hughes (1999) and Thrupp (1999), focusing on New Zealand, and Gorard and Fitz (2000) and Gibson and Asthana (2000), considering the UK environment, question how far schools can actually ultimately influence standards when the role of school mix effects and socio-economic segregation is such an important factor in pupil achievement. Thrupp (1999), in particular, warns of the rise of the 'politics of blame' in which: 'schools which "lose" . . . are seen as those whose teachers and principals have not been able to improve enough to boost their reputation and hence the size of their student intakes' (ibid.: 7).

The management implications of this are that schools must focus on external scrutiny of their performance and achievement. As a result, responsiveness to changing educational and social environments, the primacy of teaching quality and quality assurance systems, and the management of communication within and beyond the institution have become key priorities. Importantly, though, with this changing focus comes a shift in the culture of schools and colleges and their management organisation. Clarke and Newman (1992), for example, identified the rise of 'new managerialism' with its emphasis on individual performance, and management based in the culture of the market rather than of education. Gewirtz et al. (1995) describe the shift from 'comprehensive values' to 'market values', and the changing nature of headship with an enhanced emphasis on entrepreneurialism and 'bilingualism' (talking the languages of business and education).

Educational markets and marketing

'Markets' and 'marketing' are miasmic concepts, permeated by value-laden perspectives. Both have multiple meanings, and many of the debates about the acceptability of markets and marketing in education have been built on assumptions about the implicit value positions of those promoting or questioning their introduction. The ethical and operational issues this raises for those researching management in educational markets have been explored by Foskett (2000).

A market exists where choice exists and individuals or organisations can choose between products or services. While some form of 'exchange' normally takes place (e.g. payment for the service), this exchange may be direct between provider and supplier or by some indirect resource allocation mechanism (e.g. government provides funding for each student recruited). In education the choosers (the 'demand side') may be parents, young people, employers, government, public or private sector organisations, 'for-profit' or 'not-for-profit' organisations, or schools and colleges themselves. Depending on the service or product, any of these may also be the 'supply side' of the market. For example, schools and colleges may be the demand side in purchasing services from a local education authority (e.g. advisory services) or a commercial supplier (e.g. cleaning services), or in recruiting staff, but are the supply side in recruiting pupils, bidding for central government funding for new initiatives or designing courses to meet the needs of local employers.

Many writers (e.g. Woods et al., 1998) discuss the importance of recognising that markets are highly varied in form and nature, and the concept of the 'micro-market' is an important one. Foskett and Hemsley-Brown (2001: 17) emphasise that 'markets are dynamic and individual, defined as much by local geography and history as by the over-riding principles of the economics of supply and demand', while Gorard (1997) stresses that markets change over time, their form and structure being dynamic. Reading off market outcomes from one situation to another is, therefore, extremely difficult. This suggests that institutions must recognise that the precise form and shape of the markets *they* operate in will be unique, and that understanding their own market is an essential first step to effective management of any external relations.

From an international perspective there exists a full range of market forms, each generating distinctive 'marketing and external relations' management issues for education managers. Broadly speaking, we can identify a spectrum from highly centralised systems where such management tasks are almost proscribed to strongly marketised systems. In Namibia, for example, substantial secondary school restructuring and reorganisation (Auala, 1998) has retained strong central government control and no notion of marketisation. In Tanzania, a similar organisational model has been in operation, with most elements of the education system traditionally centrally directed and controlled (Babyegyega, 2000). Following guidance from the United Nations Educational, Scientific, and Cultural Organisation (UNESCO), however, a National Task Force on Education (1993) recommended that decentralisation should be implemented, with school districts and schools taking most responsibility for finance, resources and curriculum and seeking to engage the community in the life of the schools. The aim is not to establish a 'market' for pupils in terms of school choice, but to seek to promote increased participation in education across all age ranges in a context of declining pupil enrolment. Central to this task is the enhancement of quality in schools, with a key strategy for schools to: 'guarantee instructional hours through supervision and curriculum reform . . . making school committees and headteachers watchdogs in regulating teachers' behaviour, especially the problem of absenteeism' (Babyegyega, 2000: 5). Similar models are beginning to emerge elsewhere in developing countries (e.g. in Malawi (Nsaliwa and Ratsoy, 1998)), but the notions of competition and market accountability are still in their infancy in many countries.

It is in the countries of the developed world where marketisation has had rather more impact on educational management, although even here it is by no means uniform or universal. In Israel (Goldring, 1991; 1997) a range of market forms exists in relation to secondary schools. In Tel Aviv, parental choice of school is operated, and schools must compete for pupils. In other cities such as Jerusalem a much more prescriptive allocation model of school places is applied. Such partial marketisation is in contrast to the strong commitment to choice, delegated management responsibility, and competition that has been introduced in New Zealand and in England and Wales. In New Zealand (Lauder and Hughes, 1999; Thrupp 1999; Waslander and Thrupp, 1997) parental choice has been placed at the heart of the secondary school system, leading to the establishment of clear 'circuits of schooling' (Ball et al., 1995) and to the polarisation of schools. Lauder and Hughes (1999) have shown how schools have adopted management strategies to engage with the market. Those schools serving areas of higher socio-economic status (ses) have been successful in attracting better motivated pupils, while those from lower ses areas or from distinctive ethnically defined localities have struggled to compete. For schools at the bottom of the league, operating in the market is very difficult for, as Lauder and Hughes (1999: 109) show for one such school 'all the marketing in the world has not helped Kea College'.

In England and Wales the school marketplace has many contradictions in that schools are expected to compete for pupils, but are highly constrained by the imposition of a centrally imposed curriculum, a rigid inspection system and the promotion of tightly defined performance indicators which limit the opportunities for schools to differentiate themselves. Furthermore, the existence of a strong independent school sector and the release of some schools from standard pupil selection mechanisms means that the nature of the market place is highly varied at the micro-level (Foskett and Hemsley-Brown, 2001). A strong commitment to school markets in the early 1990s through the introduction of local management of schools (LMS) and parental choice, has been eroded more recently by pressure towards greater collaboration amongst schools and colleges, attempts at rationalisation of provision and a retreat from 'parental choice' to 'parental preference'. Nevertheless, quasi-markets are alive and well in the education system of England and Wales.

Whatever the form or degree of marketisation, though, schools and colleges must engage in the processes of marketing to some extent. The multiple meanings of 'marketing' incorporate some concepts that are 'alien' to traditional views of education and others that are implicit within most education value systems. Marketing may be seen as an operational process, involving, for example, promotional, sales and public relations activities. Alternatively, it may be regarded as an holistic approach to the management of an organisation which encompasses its mission, strategies and operations, and in which the whole ethos and purpose of the organisation is focused on the needs and wants of its clients, partners, stakeholders and customers. Negative conceptions of marketing in education are linked to the idea of 'selling', with a view that parents and young people may be persuaded to take up a particular education or training experience because it is in the interests of the provider that they do so and not necessarily in the interests of the customer or client. However, if marketing is seen as striving to meet the needs of those customers or clients then the true notion of 'service' that is implicit in many educationists' view of their role is clearly present. The idea that marketing involves 'knowing the customer and their needs so well that selling becomes superfluous' (Drucker, 1973: 15) incorporates notions of partnership and relationships which are quite at home in most educational philosophies.

The idea that marketing is simply about 'selling' is challenged by a number of important ideas that relate strongly to educational management – the marketing triad, a recognition that marketing has goals other than recruiting students; the distinction between transactional relationships and other relationships and the importance of partnerships and alliances in education management; and the notion of 'relationship marketing'. These ideas are examined below.

The marketing triad

For many schools and colleges marketing does not have pupil/student recruitment as its only or even its major aim. Where education is compulsory and catchment areas largely fixed, or where a school or college is oversubscribed, little of the effort of external relations management needs to be directed to immediate recruitment. More of the effort will need to be directed to the management of the quality of the educational provision and to the relationships with and responsiveness to partners, stakeholders and the community. The marketing triad model (Foskett, 1995) (Figure 15.1) captures the notion of these multiple aims, and shows how under different circumstances marketing effort may be applied in different directions. Overall, this model is suggesting that marketing is about meeting the organisation's needs (for survival and success), but that those needs in themselves involve meeting the needs and wants of society for high standards of education and training provision. Marketing as 'selling' is a basic survivalist notion and is a relatively unnecessary concept in an effective school or college providing high standards of education and training.

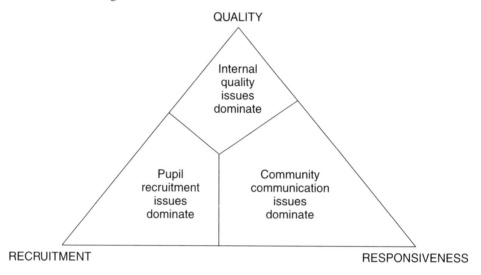

Figure 15.1: The marketing triad model

Transactional relationships, partnerships and alliances

Many of the external relationships which schools and colleges need to manage are not straightforward exchange, transactional relationships. Many involve the development of alliances, allegiances and partnerships in support of shared goals (Foskett 1999; Hall, 1999). Choosing 'partners' may initially be a transactional relationship, for example in persuading a parent to choose the school for their child, or in choosing a business partner for a joint funding bid. More frequently, though, such partners are predetermined, in that a local education authority or district school board may provide advisory services such as psychology or careers support. Once established, though, the relationship is one of working with partners to achieve the identified outcome, and the proactive management of such external relationships is a key continuous task for most educational managers.

Relationship marketing

The concept of relationship marketing has emerged from the commercial business world (Gronroos, 1997) in recognition that for many small businesses in markets of limited spatial extent success is based on the development of a relationship which goes far beyond the sale of the service or product. Goodwill, 'word of mouth' promotion, innovation in 'product or service development', and responsiveness to customer needs with high levels of service are the essence of the relationship. Managing the relationship, with its emphasis on the interpersonal, on responsiveness and on quality assurance, is the essence of relationship marketing, not promotion, advertising and selling. Such activities may be necessary on entering a new market, on seeking expansion, or in re-establishing an organisation whose reputation has declined, but otherwise may be relatively minor areas of effort. Most schools and colleges are clearly small businesses with a defined geographical area to serve, and for them relationship marketing would seem to be a much more appropriate strategy.

'Marketing' is an umbrella term for the management of a wide and dynamic range of external relationships for schools and colleges. The implications of 'selling' within the term, though, mean that a better phrase for this sphere of activity is external relations management, for this can incorporate promotion management, partnership management and relationship management. Even here, though, we must be careful with the conceptualisations, for external relations management has many components which are distinctly internal processes. The establishment of communications systems, internally and externally, the focus on quality assurance within the education and training activities, and the promotion of a client-focused ethos within the school or college (so-called 'internal marketing') are as much a part of external relations management as market research, prospectus publication and seeking out service providers. Internal marketing is linked closely to issues of cultural change in organisations, which are explored later in this chapter.

Strategy, marketing and management

Integrating external relations/marketing into a school or college's strategy and practice is more than a process of 'bolting on' some additional activities. Gray (1991), Hanson and Henry (1992) and Kotler and Fox (1995) all stress how effective external relations management is based on the integration of a market-focused perspective into strategy development. Hanson and Henry, for example, distinguish between 'strategic marketing', where all aspects of an organisation's vision and strategy are linked to 'market analysis', and 'project marketing' which involves undertaking specific activities (often promotional or public relations activities) in response to emerging needs. Gray supports this notion but suggests that both will be present for most organisations. He suggests that strategic planning in schools and colleges should comprise three distinctive elements which link to marketing:

- an institutional plan identifying mission, and medium- and long-term goals, which are based in a clear understanding of the organisation's stakeholders and their needs and wants
- thematic plans linking strategy to operational practice for example, curriculum, estates and buildings, each of which identifies how this activity supports the market-driven aims of the institutional plan
- an operational marketing plan, which draws together the marketing elements of the institutional and thematic plans to ensure a coherent and efficiently operated external relations/marketing activity. One element of this will be the mechanisms in place to identify emerging external relations issues and to be responsive to them. This is the 'project marketing' component of the whole strategic marketing process.

Such a model of planning reinforces the ideas of Johnson and Scholes (1993), who suggest that strategic management comprises three components – strategic analysis, strategic choice and strategic implementation.

Strategic analysis involves scanning and sensing the operational environment within which the institution operates to identify:

- aspects of its operations for future development. The Further Education Funding Council (FEFC, 1997) describe this as anticipatory evidence, indicating the directions that policy and practice in the institution should be going
- how far current provision and operation is meeting external needs and wants. FEFC term this confirmatory evidence.

In the commercial sector these activities would be identified as the processes of 'marketing research', and for most businesses would be the responsibility of a dedicated marketing team. In public sector organisations it is only the largest colleges which use significant resources for these activities. The development of marketing departments in many larger colleges has led to a more substantial formal evidence-base for decision-making. The availability, for example, of labour market information through regional organisations such as the Learning and Skills Councils (LSCs) and the commissioning of bespoke market research are more common than in the past (e.g. Waring, 1999), and sector-specific guidance on such processes is available (e.g. FEFC/NAO, 1998). However, as Foskett suggests:

> Using the data to influence strategy . . . is difficult because of a lack of formal systems to feed data into the planning process, a lack of experience in inter-

preting and analysing such information, and the slow responsiveness of colleges who are locked into timescales of years rather than the shorter timescales of market change. (Foskett, 1998a: 55)

In contrast, most schools rely on the informal information that arises from day-to-day interaction with stakeholders and clients, with few using explicit planned marketing research (Glatter et al., 1997). The reading of policy documents, engagement with the professional arenas of education and the formation of excellent relationships with the local community provide the mechanics of this process. The use of small-scale research to canvas parental or community views on issues provides some strength to the interpretations schools make from other informal sources, but resource constraints mean that active marketing research is not possible. We may argue, too, that it is largely unnecessary, for there is no evidence that schools which do such market research make better strategic decisions than those which do not. This reinforces the belief that relationship marketing is the key to successful external relations management for most schools and colleges.

Strategic choice involves identifying the broad directions and aims that the institution will pursue. Foskett (1999) identifies three elements of strategic choice in relation to the marketing and external relations management activity of a school or college.

1 Target market strategy is the selection of market segments in which the institution will operate. Kotler (1991) has identified three broad market strategies – undifferentiated strategies, in which the school or college seeks to meet the needs of all consumers in all segments; differentiated strategies which involve selecting areas and activities to specialise in; and concentrated strategies in which a single market segment is chosen for focus. Within the school sector in the UK there has been only a limited pursuit of differentiation, for the sense of schools serving their local community is very strong. In post-compulsory education there is more evidence of differentiation, and there is a clear policy direction from government that this is seen as a key way of ensuring high-quality provision for education and training in the sector (DfEE, 2000).
2 Competitive positioning strategy involves identifying the distinctive features of the institution that distinguish it from its competitors in the same market segments. A school may seek to distinguish its faith affiliation, or its single-sex nature. A college may emphasise its distinctive facilities for particular provision (e.g. electronic music laboratories), or its strong pastoral system.
3 Marketing mix strategy is identifying the elements which will be emphasised in the promotional messages of the institution. Traditionally this has been defined in commercial marketing by the 4Ps model (Product, Place,

Price and Promotion), but this has been extended in the service sector to 7Ps by the inclusion of Process, People and Physical Facilities (Kotler and Fox, 1995):

(a) Product – the education/training experience that is being offered.
(b) Place – the location of that provision (e.g. in college, or by distance learning).
(c) Price – the direct, indirect or opportunity costs of the education/training experience.
(d) Promotion – the promotional strategies to be used (e.g. prospectus, advertising, word of mouth).
(e) Process – the manner and style of the education/training experience (e.g. teaching styles, study skills support).
(f) People – the staff at all levels within the school or college.
(g) Physical facilities – the teaching and social facilities and the learning facilities in the school or college.

Strategic implementation is the final element of strategic planning (Johnson and Scholes, 1993), and involves operationalising and then evaluating the strategy. Foskett and Hemsley-Brown (1999) suggest that communication is a key component of implementation, and distinguish between sales communications (e.g. advertising) and relationship communications. Strong within this explicit management of communications with external constituencies has been a concern to demonstrate the key values and aims that the organisation has. Commercial organisations have long had a concern for institutional identity that is reflected in the idea of branding, which is the association of complex but positive images into the name, symbol or logo of an organisation. It is the public representation of product identity, which in the case of most service sector organisations, is almost synonymous with institutional identity.

The importance of branding, image and perception in engaging with the external environment is emphasised in the view that 'purchasing' any good or service, including education, is in fact 'symbolic consumption', or the purchasing of the social values and status that go with that service or product. Values and status are intimately linked to image and perception and Farrell (2001: 173) suggests that 'the marketer has to exploit aspects of the educational institution which have a symbolic significance for the potential clients', which is the principal function of branding and image.

Schools and colleges, while mostly eschewing the idea of 'brand' associated with famous products or commercial organisations, still seek to convey a positive encapsulating image through their publications, their symbols/signs, and their activities (Foskett and Hemsley-Brown, 1999). Olins describes institutional identity in the following way:

In order to be effective every organisation needs a clear sense of purpose that people within it understand. They also need a strong sense of belonging. Purpose and belonging are the two facets of identity. Every organisation is unique, and its identity must spring from the organisation's own roots, its personality, its strengths and weaknesses . . . The identity of the organisation must be so clear that it becomes the yardstick against which its products, behaviour and actions are measured. This means that the identity cannot simply be a slogan, a collection of phrases; it must be visible, tangible and all-embracing. (Olins, 1989: 7)

Institutional identity, therefore, is the image the institution would like to have and to present to its various internal and external audiences. Its development is part and product of the process of developing a strategy for operating in the market(s) the school or college has.

The models of strategic marketing presented here are rarely to be found explicitly in schools, although they can be identified implicitly within school development plans and school promotional materials. Foskett and Hemsley-Brown (1999) show how the marketing mix can be identified in the management processes of Grove Primary School and Greenstreet Community School and also in the explicit mission and development aims of each school. Within the research of Ball et al. (1995) and Maguire et al. (2001) the choice of both target market strategy and competitive positioning strategy is clear in the policies and practices of their case study schools. Most emphasise comprehensive ideals, but still promote the specific specialisms that they have. Similarly, Foskett (1995) shows how Castle School, an 11–16 mixed comprehensive school in central southern England, promotes its distinctiveness in terms of excellence in languages, its strong discipline framework and its strengths in working with more able pupils, while neighbouring Downsview School emphasises its achievements across the ability range, despite its excellence in science and mathematics. In the schools within Lauder and Hughes's study in New Zealand, differentiation by the schools in terms of target markets and competitive positioning can be easily read off, with schools such as Kea College, for example, seeking to raise their attractiveness to a much broader socio-economic range of parents than their 'natural' catchment contains. What all these examples have in common, though, is a very limited explicit commitment to a marketing perspective but a strong implicit recognition of the canons of good marketing in both the strategising and operationalising of external relations management.

In colleges the presence of marketing strategy is much higher profile. Davies (1999) and Foskett (2002) show that colleges have explicitly addressed marketing in their strategic planning and in the establishment of marketing systems and marketing plans. Lowlands College (Foskett and Hemsley-Brown, 1999) has, for example, a section on marketing within its strategic plan, which demonstrates its choice to focus on engineering and to develop its vocational and business-funded training rather than its academic track provision. The limited success of this strategy reflects the product-driven nature of the strategy and the limited use of marketing research or the development of a culture of responsiveness in the college. Foskett (2002) shows that this is a common feature of marketing strategies in further education colleges.

The significant difference between schools and colleges lies not in their use of marketing strategy, therefore, but in their recognition that this is what they are doing, and in the specific marketing systems they establish. This is partly a function of size, for colleges clearly have much greater resources to apply to marketing, but also lies in the more constrained nature of the markets within which most schools operate, both geographically and in terms of diversity.

Marketing, inclusion and widening participation

A key trend in global education has been the increase in participation rates, particularly within the post-compulsory sector of education. Widening participation is in essence a marketing issue for education managers, for the challenge is to raise participation and achievement amongst socio-economic and community groups hitherto under-represented in the sectors. The drive to widen participation is partly driven by the pursuit of increased economic competitiveness, but is also based on a concern for equity and facilitating individual achievement. The second of these is also the main driver behind the inclusion movement in compulsory education, through which there is a drive to integrate into school those who may have been excluded from mainstream education as a result of special educational needs. Both widening participation and inclusion raise important marketing issues.

Widening participation has two distinct components. First, facilitating choice involves the removal of systemic barriers to participation for those who wish to engage in learning but are prevented from doing so. Simplifying admissions procedures, providing alternative modes of programme delivery (e.g. distance or open learning), providing child-care facilities or tailoring pastoral support systems to meet individual needs are some of the 'marketing' approaches that can facilitate choice. Much more challenging is the second component, that of increasing demand for education and training. This requires the changing of perceptions amongst those who are outside education and training about the nature, purpose and, most importantly, value of education and training. It requires the personal benefits of learning to be emphasised. As such it requires the collaboration of the whole education system. As Foskett and Hemsley-Brown suggest:

> breaking through the challenge of increasing demand in post-compulsory education requires a fundamental re-appraisal of how the perceptions, attitudes and beliefs of young people and their parents can be modified by changing the types

of experiences they have and the messages they receive both from within the education/training system and from society as a whole. (Foskett and Hemsley-Brown, 2001: 25)

What is clear is that increasing demand is not simply about selling education. As Woodrow (1998) demonstrates, it requires a wide range of strategies which take education to potential new participants, tailoring programmes and systems to meet *their* needs rather than the needs of institutions. Widening participation requires institutions and their staff to modify their culture and sometimes their values, and provides a good example of marketing acting as a catalyst to cultural change. Foskett (2002) shows how this is still comparatively undeveloped within further education colleges in southern England, where widening participation is seen in terms of being a marketing challenge rather than a project in managing cultural change within the institution.

Inclusion provides a distinctive marketing conundrum for schools and colleges. At the level of the promotion of equity as an important social value it is clear that promoting inclusion is a positive virtue. Schools and colleges are perceived as of high social and moral standing within the community if they are successful with special needs children. However, for most parents there is a moral dilemma between supporting community good and pursuing educational benefit for their own child, and schools which have a record of strong special needs support or inclusion, while attractive to those parents with such children, may find that they decline in popularity with other parents. In defining the distinctive character of the school, therefore, many senior managers must strike a balance between these contradictory pressures, as Gewirtz et al. (1995), and Maguire et al. (2001) have shown in the case of Northwark Park School.

Marketing, responsiveness and cultural change

Central to the development of marketing in education has been the importance of developing responsiveness. Responsiveness is 'the ability of an institution to sense and serve the changing needs of its relevant environment' (Michael et al., 1994: 54), and requires both inputs of knowledge about the wants and needs of all parts of that environment and mechanisms for enabling this information to bring about changes in the way the organisation works. Responsiveness is more than just an operational process, however, for it is a part of the mosaic of culture and ethos. As a bolt-on process it is not capable of providing sensitive, subtle and continuing mutual communication with the world outside the school or college. Achieving responsiveness, therefore, is also about achieving cultural change in institutions, and about embedding in staff at all levels a commitment to adopt the key mores of responsiveness – scanning the external environment for indicators of change; implementing effective quality assurance processes; developing a willingness to change; and developing an outlook which is focused on clients (pupils, parents, commu-nity etc.) rather than subject, school or self. Lumby (1999) suggests that fun-damentally this is about changing the balance of power and authority in relationships between teachers and schools, on the one hand, and parents, pupils, government etc. on the other. Traditional relationships placed the power and authority and the privilege of 'knowing best' and 'being right' with the school and the teacher. Responsiveness, however, requires that authority to be shared, not to an uncritical stance in which only the voice of the client is heard, but to one in which the school/college and the communities it serves are equal partners. Responsiveness is about a move from a culture of profes-sional responsibility to one of market and/or political accountability.

Promoting such cultural change can be a long process. Research during the 1990s in the UK showed little evidence of the strong adoption of responsive-ness either in schools (Foskett, 1998b; Woods et al., 1998) or in further edu-cation (Smith et al., 1995). The initial phases of marketisation appeared to have generated responses in schools that made them less responsive rather than more, retreating into professional experience and knowledge to decide what they could best 'sell' to potential customers, rather than becoming more open and responsive. More recently, however, there is emerging some evi-dence of cultural change towards responsiveness. Ainley and Bailey (1997) see some recognition in the further education sector that teachers and institutions are genuinely more responsive to student needs, although Foskett (2002) shows how that responsiveness still resides largely in the minds of senior man-agers rather than in the actions of most teaching staff and middle managers. Maguire et al. (2001: 48) suggest from their case study of Northwark Park School that there is evidence of cultural adjustment in the school and that 'the language of the market-place [is] . . . being gradually incorporated into the everyday language and practices of the school'. This they see as the outcome of a process of cultural adaptation and change in which 'the conduct of schools, and individual teachers within the market might best be understood as resolutions to the "comprehensive/market" dilemma' (Maguire et al., 2001: 46). This process of change has not been an explicit aim of the school, however, and has developed dynamically in response to the school's operation in the changing external environment and the adoption of language and prac-tice from management activities and professional interaction. It is, rather, the outcome of individual decisions and actions within and outside the school which have led to a significant and quite rapid cultural change.

Conclusion

The rise of marketing in education has challenged educational managers to meet the challenge of reorienting schools and colleges to be focused on the outside world. Despite the global scale of the trend, though, it is clear that there is considerable variability in the market forms emerging, the interpretations of marketing that are being made by managers and hence the pattern of the new education system that is arising. Even in those economies where marketisation has been most strongly planted, schools and colleges have rarely adopted an approach which might be described as strategic marketing. More frequently the development has been in the form of project marketing and a slow migration towards adopting, quite unknowingly, the canons of relationship marketing where quality and community relations and responsiveness are at the heart of the strategy for external relations management.

Further reading

Gewirtz, S., Ball, S. and Bowe, R (1995) *Markets, Choice and Equity in Education*, Buckingham: Open University Press.
Lumby, J. and Foskett, N. H. (eds) (1999) *Managing External Relations in Schools and Colleges*, London: Paul Chapman Publishing.
Thrupp, M. (1999) *Schools Making a Difference – Let's Be Realistic*, Buckingham: Open University Press.

References

Ainley, P. and Bailey, B. (1997) *The Business of Learning*, London: Cassell.
Auala, R. (1998) 'Secondary education reform in Namibia', *International Studies in Educational Administration*, 26 (1): 57–62.
Babyegyega, E. (2000) 'Education reforms in Tanzania: from nationalisation to decentralisation of schools', *International Studies in Educational Administration*, 28 (1): 2–10.
Ball, S., Bowe, R. and Gewirtz, S. (1995) 'Circuits of schooling: a sociological explanation of parental choice of school in social class contexts', *Sociological Review*, 43 (1): 52–78.
Carlson, R. (1975) 'Environmental constraints and organisational consequences: the public school and its clients', in J. Baldridge and T. Deal (eds), *Managing Change in Educational Organisations*, Berkeley, CA: McCutchan.
Chubb, J. and Moe, T. (1990) *Politics, Markets and America's Schools*, Washington, DC: Brookings Institute.
Clarke, J. and Newman, J. (1992) 'Managing to survive: dilemmas of changing organisational forms in the puiblic sector', paper presented at the Social Policy Association, University of Nottingham, July.
Davies, P. (1999) 'Colleges and customers', in J. Lumby and N. H. Foskett (eds), *Managing External Relations in Schools and Colleges*, London: Paul Chapman Publishing.
Department for Education and Employment (DfEE) (2000) *Colleges for Excellence and Innovation*, London: DfEE.
Drucker, P. (1973) *Management Tasks, Responsibilities and Practice*, London: Harper Row.

Farrell, F. (2001) 'Postmodernism and educational marketing', *Educational Management and Administration*, 29 (2): 169–79.

Foskett, N. H. (1995) 'Marketing, management and schools – a study of a developing market culture in secondary schools', unpublished PhD thesis, University of Southampton.

Foskett, N. H. (1998a) 'Linking marketing to strategy', in D. Middlewood and J. Lumby (eds), *Strategic Management in Schools and Colleges*, London: Paul Chapman Publishing.

Foskett, N. H. (1998b) 'Schools and marketization: cultural challenges and responses', *Educational Management and Administration*, 26 (2): 197–210.

Foskett, N. H. (1999) 'Strategy, external relations and marketing', in J. Lumby and N. H. Foskett (eds), *Managing External Relations in Schools and Colleges*, London: Paul Chapman Publishing.

Foskett, N. H. (2000) 'Dancing with the devil – ethics and research in educational markets', in R. Usher and H. Simons (eds), *Situated Ethics in Educational Research*, London: Routledge/Falmer.

Foskett, N. H. (2002) 'Marketing imperative or cultural challenge? Embedding widening participation in the FE sector', *Research in Post-Compulsory Education*, 7 (1): 79–95.

Foskett, N. H. and Hemsley-Brown, J. (1999) 'Communicating the organisation', in J. Lumby and N. H. Foskett (eds), *Managing External Relations in Schools and Colleges*, London: Paul Chapman Publishing.

Foskett, N. H. and Hemsley-Brown, J. (2001) *Choosing Futures: Young People's Decision-Making in Education, Training and Careers Markets*, London: Routledge/Falmer.

Further Education Funding Council (FEFC) (1997) *Identifying and Addressing Needs: A Practical Guide*, Coventry: FEFC.

Further Education Funding Council/National Audit Office (FEFC/NAO) (1998) *Marketing in Further Education: A Good Practice Guide*, Coventry: FEFC/NAO.

Gewirtz, S., Ball, S. and Bowe, R. (1995) *Markets, Choice and Equity in Education*, Buckingham: Open University Press.

Gibson, A. and Asthana, S. (2000) 'What's in a number ? Commentary on Gorard and Fitz's "Investigating the determinants of segregation between schools" ', *Research Papers in Education*, 15 (2): 133–53.

Glatter, R., Woods, P. and Bagley, C. (eds) (1997) *Choice and Diversity in Schooling: Perspectives and Prospects*, London: Routledge.

Goldring, E. B. (1991) 'Parents' motives for choosing a privatised public school system: an Israeli example', *Educational Policy*, 5 (3): 412–26.

Goldring, E. B. (1997) 'Parental involvement and school choice: Israel and the United States', in R. Glatter, P. Woods and C. Bagley (eds), *Choice and Diversity in Schooling: Perspectives and Prospects*, London: Routledge.

Gorard, S. (1997) *School Choice in an Established Market*, Aldershot: Ashgate.

Gorard, S. and Fitz, J. (2000) 'Investigating the determinants of segregation between Schools', *Research Papers in Education*, 15 (2): 115–32.

Gray, L. (1991) *Marketing Education*, Buckingham: Open University Press.

Gronroos, C. (1997) 'From marketing mix to relationship marketing – towards a paradigm shift in marketing', *Management Decision*, 35 (4): 322–9.

Hall, V. (1999) 'Partnerships, alliances and competition: defining the field', in J. Lumby and N. H. Foskett (eds), *Managing External Relations in Schools and Colleges*, London: Paul Chapman Publishing.

Hanson, E.M. and Henry, W. (1992) 'Strategic marketing for educational systems', *School Organisation*, 12 (2): 255–67.

Johnson, G. and Scholes, K. (1993) *Exploring Corporate Strategy*, 3rd edn, Hemel Hempstead: Prentice- Hall.

Kotler, P. (1991) *The Principles of Marketing*, 4th edn, Englewood Cliffs, NJ: Prentice-Hall.

Kotler, P. and Fox, K. (1995) *Strategic Marketing for Educational Institutions*, 2nd edn, New York: Prentice-Hall.

Lauder, H. and Hughes, D. (1999) *Trading in Futures – Why Markets in Education Don't Work*, Buckingham: Open University Press.

Lumby, J. (1999) 'Achieving responsiveness', in J. Lumby and N. H. Foskett (eds), *Managing External Relations in Schools and Colleges*, London: Paul Chapman Publishing.

Maguire, M., Ball, S. and MacRae, S. (2001) ' "In All Our Interests": internal marketing at Northwark Park School', *British Journal of Sociology of Education*, 22 (1): 35–50.

Michael, S., Holdaway, E. and Young, C. (1994) 'Institutional responsiveness: a study of administrators' perceptions', *Educational Management and Administration*, 22 (1): 54–62.

Nsaliwa, C. and Ratsoy, E. (1998) 'Educational decisions in Malawi', *International Studies in Educational Administration*, 26 (2): 63–72.

Olins, W. (1989) *Corporate Identity: Making a Business Strategy Visible through Design*, London: Thames Hudson.

Smith, D., Scott, P. and Lynch, J. (1995) *The Role of Marketing in the University and College Sector*, Leeds: Heist Publications.

Thrupp, M. (1999) *School's Making a Difference? – Let's Be Realisitic*, Buckingham: Open University Press.

Waring, S. (1999) 'Finding your place: sensing the external environment', in J. Lumby and N. H. Foskett (eds), *Managing External Relations in Schools and Colleges*, London: Paul Chapman Publishing.

Waslander, S. and Thrupp, M. (1997) 'Choice, competition and segregation: an empirical analysis of a New Zealand secondary school market', in A. Halsey, H. Lauder, P. Brown and A. Wells (eds), *Education, Culture, Economy and Society*, Oxford: Oxford University Press.

Whitty, G., Power, S. and Halpin, D. (1998) *Devolution and Choice in Education: The School, the State and the Market*, Buckingham: Open University Press.

Woodrow, M. (1998) *From Elitism to Inclusion: A Guide to Good Practice in Widening Access to Higher Education*, London: CVCP.

Woods, P., Bagley, C. and Glatter, R. (1998) *School Choice and Competition: Markets in the Public Interest?*, London: Routledge.

16

New Partnerships for Improvement

Les Bell

Introduction

Partnerships between public and private sector institutions are becoming an increasingly important element of government policy throughout the world (Linder and Rosenau, 2000). This is as true of education policy as it is of other policy spheres (Lissaur and Robinson, 2000). In education, however, the growth of public–private partnerships is often linked to an emphasis on school improvement. Such partnerships are frequently intended to support a series of strategies to enhance the academic performance of children and can be found embodied in many policy statements on education in a large number of countries. Teddlie and Reynolds (2000) argue that there is now a widespread assumption internationally that schools affect children's development, that there are observable regularities in schools and colleges that add value and that the task of educational policies is to improve all schools. They argue that school improvement research seeks to identify how schools and colleges can improve by changing, developing and establishing new forms of educational partnerships with stakeholders both within and outside the accepted boundaries of the school or college. Hopkins notes that school improvement is:

> an approach to educational change that is concerned with process as well as outcomes. School improvement is about raising student achievement through enhancing the teaching–learning process and the conditions that support it. It is about strategies for improving the school's capacity for providing quality education. (Hopkins, 1994: 75)

Sammons et al. (1994) point out that the development of good home–school relations and establishing mechanisms for parental involvement will facilitate school improvement while Davies (1997), in reviewing the school improvement literature relating to schools in both the First and Third Worlds, adds good external relations to aid financial and moral support for the school to her list of such factors. Beare et al. (1989) argue that the parent body of any school has a rich fund of skill and expertise, knowledge and experience that goes beyond the capacities of teachers, and such a resource should be harnessed to support school improvement. Similarly, Stoll and Mortimore (1997) recognise that approaches emanating from business and industry can make an equally valuable contribution. They recognise the value of partnerships that involve parents, community representatives and agencies, local education authorities, business, industry, higher education, government agencies and educational consultants, among others in the school improvement process.

Partnerships within an educational context can take place in a number of different ways and at different organisational levels. Hall (1999) identifies five levels of partnership:

- intrapersonal where individuals vary in their preferences for collaboration
- interpersonal based on forms of relationships between colleagues within institutions
- intra-institutional that focuses on the management of the sections of the school or college
- inter-institutional partnerships between autonomous schools or colleges
- extra-institutional that requires alliances to be formed with public, private or informal groups outside the institution.

In this chapter, two different types of extra-institutional partnerships will be examined. The first is partnerships between educational institutions and their communities, especially parents, and the second is educational partnerships based on links between educational institutions and organisations from the private sector. These partnerships have significantly different characteristics. What they have in common, however, is that their espoused purposes are usually related to the improvement of the educational experience of pupils and students in the schools and colleges to which the partnership agreements relate. They purport to be, as Lareau (1996) points out, a relationship between equals where power and control are evenly distributed.

Partnerships with parents

The development of partnerships between schools and parents as individual family units representing their child or children at a particular school represents a complex and sometimes controversial aspect of state intervention in education. In 1994 a survey of teachers and school principals in Hong Kong conducted by the Education Department indicated a positive belief in the desirability of having effective home–school co-operation. There was far less agreement about the nature of that partnership or about empowering parents. The Hong Kong School Management Initiative, introduced in 1991,

259

encouraged schools to adopt new management practices in order to improve the quality of school education (Cheng, 1999a). These changes included providing greater opportunities for parents to become involved in the planning and management of work in schools and in evaluating that work. On the basis of his research in Hong Kong, Ng (1999) identified a six-level model of involvement in home–school partnerships that is divided into two categories. The lower levels of the partnership are largely focused outside the school and consist, first, of merely communicating with the school; second, providing support for children's learning at home and third, taking part in organised parental activities such as parent–teacher associations. Involvement within the school moves from providing help in classrooms, libraries and with extra-curricular activities, through helping to influence the decision-making process by representing views of parental groups or being part of the consultative process, to the highest level of involvement, full participation in school governance. He noted that the intention of the policy change was for parents to play a much more proactive role in supporting learning and in facilitating the attainment of a much higher level of academic performance by their children. Ng concluded that: 'Both teachers and parents wanted to increase contact at levels one and two . . . Both parties were very keen on improving and increasing communication at the lower levels of the model' (Ng, 1999: 553–6).

Agreement about the nature of partnership was, however, limited to the first two levels of Ng's model. He noted that while parents liked to take part in some school activities in which their children are involved, teachers did not like to be involved in working with parents. He also concluded that most parents were not keen on becoming members of the school management committee but where this was not the case, their involvement was unwelcome. Only a few schools in Hong Kong permitted parents to become partners in the process of determining school policies (Ng, 1999). Nevertheless, the Hong Kong government remains committed to the promotion and strengthening of this form of partnership and links initiatives to involve parents and teachers jointly in school management closely to the improvement of pupil performance and the development of high quality school education (Education Commission, 1997).

The importance of parents in the education of children has long been recognised and, in England, can be traced back to the Plowden Report (DES, 1967) which argued for parent–teacher associations to be established. The extent to which these were partnerships is questionable (Bell, 1999). By the mid-1980s, the nature of parent–school partnerships had been irrevocably changed. The 1986 Education Act (DES, 1986) increased parental representation on governing bodies and required the governing body of each school to deliver an annual report for parents and to hold an annual meeting of parents to discuss that report. Although it is a path being followed elsewhere, the education system in England may have moved further than in many other countries to mobilise parental support for school improvement. This type of partnership has now been formulated into a formal agreement. All schools are required by the Department for Education and Employment (DfEE) to prepare a written home–school agreement and associated parental declaration (DfEE, 1998). These agreements must contain a statement of the school's aims and values, a definition of the responsibilities of both the parents and the school together with a statement of the school's expectations of its pupils. Governing bodies must consult parents before changing any part of this agreement. Once the agreement was finalised, schools 'invited' parents to sign it. This all had to be in place as soon after September 1999 as practicable – a year after the guidance to schools was published (Hood, 1999). The rationale for this development is that parents are the first and most enduring teachers of children and they play a crucial role in helping their children to learn. It is based on the belief that children are more successful when schools and parents work together and this can happen most effectively if parents know what the school is trying to achieve. The issue now is whether such a partnership based on a legalistic agreement is the best way of establishing an appropriate form of home–school relationship. Even if this is the way forward, how can such an agreement be enforced? The development of this form of partnership marks a change in emphasis in the role of parents from that of passive consumer through that of consumer exercising choice within the educational marketplace to that of participant, willing or coerced, in the educational enterprise itself. It is clear that one of the significant factors driving this particular approach to partnership is the extent to which schools strive to improve pupil performance.

Ng (1999) suggests that in many countries parents are no longer regarded by teachers as troublemakers or ill informed. Parent–school relationships in Hong Kong are similar to those in many other countries. These partnerships, he argues, are typified by collaboration but collaboration of a limited kind. He points out that parents can play a complementary role in educating children through their personal, social and academic development. Parents can provide volunteer help for schools and even be elected to governing bodies, thereby playing a direct part in school governance. It should be noted, however, that much of the literature on this form of partnership acknowledges that the relationships on which they are based are characterised by an imbalance of power in favour of the teachers (Vincent, 1996). Perhaps the solution to this problem lies in accelerating the process of empowerment of the weaker partner to ensure that the development of the partnership is not carried out through a process of teacher domination and on the basis of the teachers' agendas (Ng, 1999). Increasingly, however, these agendas are driven, not by parental interests, but by a focus on pupil achievement.

The impetus for such new partnerships in education is often linked to the development of strategies for school improvement by harnessing the new partners to improvement strategies linked to enhancing pupil performance (Ng, 1999). The most radical forms of parental partnership in education can be found in charter schools in the USA. Here parents are able to found or co-found schools which are governed by boards of directors composed primarily of parents (Yancey, 2000). More typically, however parental involvement in education is heavily bounded by the visions and desires of professional educators who largely determine what parental participation in schools should be (Yancey, 2000).

Parents may provide additional practical or supervisory support for teachers by working more closely with their children as part of the educative process. More frequently, however, these partnerships are related to an ideological position based on the introduction of market forces into education and the concomitant decentralisation of decision-making (Crozier, 1998; Linder and Rosenau, 2000). As McNamara et al. note:

> the ideological move to construct education as a market place holds both systemic and economic implications for schools, teachers, children and parents and may involve policies . . . based on 'educational' values being marginalized in favour of those lodged in market imperatives. Significant amongst them is the necessity for schools to promote a positive image of themselves in terms of performance indicators of product/output. (McNamara et al., 2000: 475)

Within this context contradictions are inevitable. For example, many parents focus on what is best for their own children. What matters is what their children are doing as individuals. Teachers, on the other hand, are more concerned with aggregate notions of school performance and improvement, and attempt to involve parents in the quest to achieve improved aggregate goals (McNamara et al., 2000).

Thus, the focus on school improvement and an emphasis on competition between schools fragments provision whereas partnership fosters commitment and collective responsibility. In the context of the educational market and the partnerships that it generates, this commitment and responsibility is based on that individual self-interest which is necessary to ensure that cost is minimised and benefit is maximised from the product available. This interaction between partnership and benefit is often expressed at a societal rather than an individual level. In many parts of the Asia-Pacific region the close connection between education and economic development is widely recognised and a significant number of improvement initiatives have been introduced to strengthen the contribution of education to economic growth. In Malaysia the entire education system is being reviewed in order to meet the workforce requirements of the knowledge-based economy and a system of lifelong learning is being promoted to ensure that workers can continuously upgrade their skills and knowledge (Third Outline Perspective, 2001). School–parent partnerships, therefore, are grounded in relatively high-level benefits, benefits that may accrue at a societal, regional, local community or even school level. Most parents, however, are concerned about the benefits that pertain to their own children as individuals within the education process. Such different perceptions of the benefits from these partnerships can lead to tensions within them. Nevertheless, policies that locate educational benefits largely at the highest levels can be identified in a significant number of countries:

> In Korea, the Presidential Council . . . announced the 'Education Reform Plan' . . . to improve their education system and to address the new challenges . . . In Singapore, significant education reforms were introduced after the Report of the Economic Committee . . . demanded substantial educational expansion and improvement to meet the needs of Singapore's economic development in a very competitive environment . . . The recent educational developments in South East Asia provide strong evidence to support the . . . assertion that educational reform is the major means of supporting the economic, political and cultural development of a society. (Cheng, 1999b: 3–5)

The recognition of the close links between education and the economy is not restricted to Asia. In Australia, students' mathematical capability must be improved to enable the economy to grow and be competitive (Kemp, 2000). The tertiary and higher education system in New Zealand must contribute to economic development by providing more graduates for science-based occupations (Gould, 2001). In Germany the emphasis is also on the link between the knowledge-based economy and the central importance of education to economic development (Bulmahn, 2000). In England it has been argued that: 'Our future prosperity as a nation depends on how well our schools, in partnership with parents, prepare young people for work' (Department for Education, 1994: 25). This new orthodoxy focuses on improving national economies by tightening the connection between schooling, employment and productivity and by enhancing student outcomes, employment-related skills and competences (Carter and O'Niel, 1995). The implication of this is that both students and parents are partners in the educational enterprise. As a result, parents who were once regarded at best as passive supporters have changed into active participants. They have now been further repositioned as informed consumers in the educational marketplace.

Thus, the nature of this partnership has now shifted from parents as passive or active consumers to one in which the total mobilisation of resources in support of the educative process has sought to transform parents into productive partners and places a responsibility on all stakeholders, including parents, for the success or failure of the educational enterprise. Such partnerships involve the sharing of both responsibility and risk. The responsibility for the attainment of pupils in any school, both collectively and as individuals, has now been broadened to include parents. This, of course, shifts some of the burden of responsibility away from teachers. Nevertheless, the extent to which schools succeed is determined by measures of pupil performance, and it is against these that school–parent partnerships will be evaluated.

In some partnerships the principle of subsidiarity posits a hierarchical relationship between partners. This is the case in education. The parents are not equal partners in determining desirable outcomes, the nature of the tests for those outcomes, or the levels that determine success. These remain located either within the sphere of the professional educators or of politicians. What is required is that parents take on a mediating role to the extent that they play a significant part in helping to implement the academic policy of the school by controlling and influencing their children. It is possible, however, that a dependency relationship may develop in which teachers are unable effectively to fulfil their functions without parental support. This will happen if substitution is either implied or takes place. Substitution is where one partner replaces all or part of the function of another such that parents take on the role of teachers.

It has been argued that home-school partnerships are really a control or accountability mechanism in another guise. As Crozier puts it:

> Partnership then, within the educational context, becomes something more than . . . support for schools. It is argued here that partnership as a part of this process of accountability is a device for surveillance. However, this surveillance is not one way: as well as the accountability of teachers through surveillance, school relationships have been underpinned . . . by some form of surveillance and social control of pupils . . . and parents. (Crozier, 1998: 126)

Such partnerships may challenge teachers' professionalism and mark a further erosion of teacher autonomy. At the same time, in order to achieve a partnership in which the school's aims are realised, teachers need to persuade parents to adopt the school's definition of what it means to be a 'good' parent and a 'good' pupil. This can often mean the imposition of an entire value system on parents for, as Crozier (1998) notes, the development of partnership is carried out through a process of teacher domination and on the basis of the teachers' agenda. Thus, while parents and external educational agencies may monitor the work of teachers, teachers are using home–school partnerships to monitor parents who monitor pupils.

It can be seen, therefore, that the fundamental question raised about the nature of such partnerships is the one identified by Kagiso (2000). As part of his artistic and architectural work in South African townships he recognised that collaborative partnerships can provide a structural framework within which participants can take responsibility for the shape and internal working of the partnership and its relationship with the outside world. Within such partnerships the participants are free to establish both the structure of the partnership and the nature of the relationships within it. Often, such partnerships with parents throughout Africa are focused on obtaining resources for schools. More often, however, partnerships intended to implement aspects of social policy tend to be arranged in such a way that all aspects of the relevant relationships are predetermined and controlled. This raises questions about the nature and purpose of any particular partnership. Who benefits from it, what new forms of organisational and management relationships are established to implement such partnerships and by whom? These questions are particularly pertinent in the case of school–parent partnerships.

Partnerships with the private sector

In many countries the alliance between education and commercial organisations is based on the need to find non-governmental resources to support either the basic provision of education or its improvement. In China, for example, local officials and school administrators are forced by circumstance to engage with groups outside the education system in fund-raising endeavours to support the provision of some schooling (Lo, 1999). The concern here is to absorb the impact of the market economy in such a way as to be able to raise adequate funds to keep teachers in schools and colleges, and to maintain facilities. This is partly achieved through linking business closely to schools through the establishment of school factories which provided important supplementary income for many schools. As Bush et al. point out: 'School-run businesses are a particular feature of Chinese education and relate in part to the emphatic view that education and work must be closely linked if China is to sustain its economic growth' (Bush et al., 1998: 139). Indeed, Coleman (1999) argues that the relationship between education and industry in China has become almost symbiotic. Schools and colleges have developed entrepreneurial activities including factories and farms as well as service industries to such an extent that virtually every type of school has embraced the idea of school-run enterprises as a source of additional funding. This is an example of a collaborative partnership where the symbiotic relationship between the partners benefits both of them.

In Malaysia the links between education and commercial agencies take a somewhat different form. Here the government: 'is keen that the private sector plays an active part in supplementing the provision of higher education, especially in technical and vocational education, which can be very costly' (Lee, 1999: 95). This has resulted in a significant element of tertiary and higher educational provision in that country being provided either by the private sector acting independently, rather than in partnership with the public sector, or by entrepreneurial institutions from abroad. Here, partnership is based on the collaboration between private sector providers of education and government agencies who benefit from that provision as well as seeking to regulate it. This results in a complex set of relationships that revolve around the extent to which the government acts as the client and the private sector organisation as the provider and how far this can be compatible with governmental regulation of privately provided education and its concomitant demands for compliance from the private sector. The constraints on each partner stem from the nature of the relationship between state and private organisations when they seek to coexist as both providers and consumers.

It has been argued (Linder and Rosenau, 2000) that more formalised partnerships based on an alliance between educational institutions and organisations in the private sector will enable all parties to escape from the constraints of the public–private dualism that can be found in many areas of social policy in most countries. That may be why many countries throughout the world are now experimenting with extra-institutional public–private partnerships in education (Linder and Rosenau, 2000). Such partnerships are based on establishing formal or informal co-operative relationships between educational agencies at national, regional or institutional levels on the one hand, and profit-making and non-profit-making organisations or specific groups of interested parties such as parents, on the other. These new forms of partnership are intended to facilitate or support the management of schools and colleges. Partnership in this context refers to the formation of co-operative relationships, the purposes of which include the implementation, but rarely the formulation, of policy or the provision of additional support for existing policies through empowering one or more of the partners to play a more active role or take more responsibility. These partnerships are a new departure in many countries and mark a change to the situation in which governments have defended their spheres of influence from incursion by private sector organisations. Governments are now more willing to shift at least some of the responsibility for educational provision into the private sector in order to keep public spending under control and to avoid tax increases. The rationale for this, of course, is that partnerships with the private sector reduce costs although the evidence for this is, at best, mixed and at worst contradictory (Linder and Rosenau, 2000).

A significant example of state sponsored extra-institutional partnership in education is the development of Educational Action Zones (EAZs) in England. While these are not found elsewhere in the world in this form, they do illustrate some significant general issues in relation to the role of business and commercial partners within education, as can be seen below. Educational Action Zones have evolved from the Educational Priority Areas of the 1960s which focused on improving pupil performance in basic subjects in deprived areas. They encapsulate the requirement for the state to shift at least some of the burden of financing education to the private sector, the opening up of education to influence from the private sector and the deployment of resources to facilitate school improvement. The EAZs provide opportunities for action where schools and/or LEAs are not proving to be sufficiently effective in raising standards in both urban and rural areas of deprivation. Educational Action Zones normally cover two or three secondary schools and their feeder primary schools. They are led by a Forum which provides an action plan as part of the bid for the EAZ. This plan might include an application to the government to modify the National Curriculum or to operate outside the national pay and conditions arrangements for teachers. Money is allocated by a competitive bidding process based on submissions which include a clear statement of the level of disadvantage being addressed and the roles that will be played by LEAs, schools and other partners from industry and commerce in establishing ways to raise standards. Educational Action Zones depend for their success on partnerships with industry and commerce. They are firmly located within an educational policy framework derived from the school effectiveness movement and are intended to have a far-reaching impact on the work of teachers in schools and classrooms (Bell, 1999).

This conceptualisation of partnership was intended to create a set of relationships based on the involvement of community, industrial and business groups that would move the educational agencies more rapidly towards the achievement of general educational policy objectives and to the attainment of specific levels of pupil performance in tests and examinations. In some cases, LEAs retained a leading role in the EAZ partnerships, but in others substitution of LEA functions and responsibilities by private sector partners has taken place (Lissaur and Robinson, 2001). At the same time, all EAZ partnerships were intended to bring in additional resources through private sector sponsorship. Yet few EAZs have been successful in achieving the desired level of private sector contributions, i.e. £250,000. It may be that this lack of private funding is a product of the location of the EAZs in areas of disadvantage. The level of private sector funding for EAZs reflects that for other initiatives, city technology colleges, for example. It is more likely, therefore, that the private sector, while it may be willing to take some of the responsibility for achieving policy objectives, is not prepared to accept extensive financial commitments. The benefits that may accrue to private sector organisations who become involved in such partnerships are, at best, indirect and limited and, at worst, non-existent. It is clear, on the evidence of EAZs, therefore, that the type of partnerships that the private sector is willing to accept are limited and specific. The nature of partnerships, in these cases, is largely determined by the perceptions of the major partner, the business partner, rather than the policy aspirations of government.

Conclusion

Partnerships in education now seek to impact on activities in the classroom that influence pupil performance as much as on the school and the regional administrative structure. They are both broad in scope and detailed in application. They are increasingly concerned with helping schools to achieve specific and measurable performance targets. This phase of educational policy-making, therefore, appears to be strongly post-Fordian (Bottery, 1998). Policy-making and implementation is becoming increasingly centralised. Specific criteria for success are determined by central policy-makers while a variety of providers are encouraged to identify new ways of meeting those criteria. The agenda focuses on raising standards but the standards to be attained are determined centrally. In the UK the responsibility for achieving those standards is clearly defined. In schools it rests with the headteacher, but schools must receive specific support from LEAs. Equity is now defined in terms of meeting those standards while social justice is expressed in terms of fostering civic virtues such as employability and productiveness. Those that are believed to be failing will lose their autonomy. In Hong Kong, Singapore and New Zealand schools are now required to employ similar new forms of partnerships with parents in order to ensure that their targets are met and their autonomy retained.

Many of the educational partnerships considered in this chapter, in England and New Zealand for example, are more or less located within the framework of an overarching philosophy which has as one of its central tenets the operation of market forces within education as a process for decision-making, choice and resource allocation. Each set of partnership arrangements is tasked, directly or indirectly, with supporting an explicit or implicit school improvement process. The model on which these processes rest contains a number of significant flaws, not least of which is its characterisation of the education enterprise itself as narrow and restrictive both in terms of the nature and scope of the curriculum and the related measures of performance. This is partly because the emphasis in many countries, Malaysia, Hong Kong and Singapore for example, on national economic competitiveness and the links made between educational, social and economic development, produce an excessively utilitarian approach to education that leads to an inappropriate narrowing of educational objectives and processes (Kam and Gopinathan, 1999). Consequently younger children must become proficient in the basic skills of literacy and numeracy while their older siblings need to enhance their skills through an emphasis on information technology, science and mathematics. In tertiary colleges and universities the focus shifts to that of the knowledge-based economy and lifelong learning to respond to the changing demands of the work place (Bassey, 2001). Within this discourse, a concern for values, equity and social justice has diminished. This need not be the case. The social capital approach to education is not the only alternative. In Denmark a Ministry of Education policy statement emphasises the importance of education in shaping the values that will influence the future direction of society (Vestager, 2001) while Bulmahn (2000) argues that those who consider education from the perspective purely of national economic self-interest are short-sighted and will be unable to develop long-term policies for the future. Indeed, the present global emphasis on developing partnerships within a market or economic development paradigm can be counterproductive. As both Ball (1999) and Bassey (2001) recognise, the overriding emphasis on the role of education in contributing to economic competitiveness derives from a set of pedagogical strategies linked to a narrow conceptualisation of school improvement and effectiveness that ultimately are antithetical to the demands of a high skills economy. Ng (1999) has pointed to the extent to which the narrowing of the focus of education in Singapore, for example, has helped to create an education system that produces students who are excellent at passing examinations but very limited when it comes to creative thinking and the development of enterprise.

At the same time, school improvement as currently conceptualised locates leadership and, therefore, power almost entirely in the hands of educators and especially school principals. This leads to the development of extremely limited forms of parent–teacher collaborations, such as those found in Hong Kong or to those intended to facilitate the implementation of government policy, in England for example. These forms of partnership are based on an under-conceptualising of leadership itself and often fail to recognise the complexity of school organisation and marginalise many important management processes (Chong and Boon, 1997). As Dimmock and Walker (2000) have reported, both the processes of education and the outcomes of that process, are influenced significantly by culture and religion. This failure fully to consider educational partnerships in the wider context, including the economic situation and the nature of power relationships within a country, has allowed researchers and, more especially, politicians to deduce simplistic solutions to complex problems and to seek to develop partnerships within education systems that serve a very narrow purpose. The partnerships that are now emerging to facilitate the achievement of policy objectives in these education systems contain tensions and conflicts that derive from the fundamental assumptions about the nature and purposes of the educative processes in those societies.

Further reading

Coleman, M. (1999) 'Working with employers and business', in J. Lumby and N. Foskett (eds), *Managing External Relations in Schools and Colleges*, London: Paul Chapman Publishing.

Hall, V. (1999) 'Partnerships, alliances and competition: defining the field', in J. Lumby and N. Foskett (eds), *Managing External Relations in Schools and Colleges*, London: Paul Chapman Publishing.

Vincent, C. (1996) *Parents and Teachers: Power and Participation*, London: Falmer Press.

References

Ball, S. J. (1999) 'Labour, learning and the economy: a "policy sociology" perspective', *Cambridge Journal of Education*, 29 (2): 195–206.

Bassey, M. (2001) 'The folly of the global phenomenon of economic competitiveness as the rationale for educational development', *Research Intelligence*, 76, July: 30–6.

Beare, H., Caldwell, B. and Milliken, R. (1989) *Creating an Excellent School*, London: Routledge.

Bell, L. A. (1999) 'Back to the future: the development of educational policy in England', *Journal of Educational Administration*, 37 (3 and 4): 200–28.

Bottery, M. (1998) ' "Rowing the Boat" and "Riding the Bicycle" – metaphors for school management and policy on the late 1990s', paper presented to the 3rd ESRC Seminar, Redefining Education Management, Open University, Milton Keynes.

Bulmahn, E. (2000) *Address to the American Association for the Advancement of Science*, www.bmbf.de/reden.htm

Bush, T., Qiang, H. and Fang J. (1998) 'Educational management in China: an overview', *Compare*, 28 (2): 133–40.

Carter, D. S. G. and O'Niel, M. H. (1995) *International Perspectives on Educational Reform and Policy Implementation*, London: Falmer Press.

Cheng, Y. C. (1999a) 'The pursuit of school effectiveness and educational quality in Hong Kong', *School Effectiveness and Improvement*, 10 (1): 10–30.

Cheng, Y. C. (1999b) 'Recent educational developments in South East Asia', *School Effectiveness and Improvement*, 10 (1): 3–30.

Chong, K.C. and Boon, Z. (1997) 'Lessons from a Singapore programme for school improvement', *School Effectiveness and Improvement*, 8 (4): 463–70.

Coleman, M. (1999) 'Working with employers and business', in J. Lumby and N. Foskett (eds), *Managing External Relations in Schools and Colleges*, London: Paul Chapman Publishing.

Crozier, G. (1998) 'Parents and schools: partnership of surveillance?', *Journal of Educational Policy*, 13 (1): 125–36.

Davies, L. (1997) 'The rise of the school effectiveness movement', in J. White and M. Barber (eds), *Perspectives on School Effectiveness and School Improvement*, London: University of London, Institute of Education.

Department for Education, (1994) *Our Children's Future, the Updated Parents' Charter*, London: HMSO.

Department for Education and Employment (DfEE) (1998) *Home School Agreements: Guidance for Schools*, London: Stationery Office.

Department of Education and Science (DES) (1967) *Children in their Primary Schools* (The Plowden Report), London: HMSO.

Department of Education and Science (DES) (1986) *The Education Act*, London: HMSO.

Dimmock, C. and Walker, A. (2000) 'Developing a cross-cultural approach to comparative school leadership, management and policy: some considerations of methodology', paper presented at the American Educational Research Association Annual Meeting, New Orleans, Louisiana, 24–28 April.

Education Commission (1997) *Education Commission Report No 7*, Hong Kong: Hong Kong Government Printer:

Education Department (1994) *Home–School Cooperation Research Report*, Hong Kong: Hong Kong Government Printer:

Gould, B. (2001) 'Science graduates in New Zealand,' *Times Higher Education Supplement*, 13 April: 34.

Hall, V. (1999) 'Partnerships, alliances and competition: defining the field', in J. Lumby and N. Foskett (eds), *Managing External Relations in Schools and Colleges*, London: Paul Chapman Publishing.

Hood, S. (1999) 'Home–School agreements: a true partnership?', *School Leadership and Management*, 19 (4): 427–40.

Hopkins, D. (1994) 'School improvement in an era of change', in P. Ribbins and E. Burridge (eds), *Improving Education: Promoting Quality in Schools*, London: Cassell.

Kagiso, (2000) *The Skeleton House Project*, New York: Guggenheim Museum.

Kam, H. W. K. and Gopinathan, S. (1999) 'Recent developments in Singapore', *School Effectiveness and Improvement*, 10 (1): 99–118.

Kemp D. (2000) *Australian Ministry for Education*, www.detya.gov.au/archieve/Ministers/kemp/may00

Lareau, A. (1996) 'Assessing parental involvement in school: a critical analysis', in A. Booth and A. F. Dunn (eds), *Family and School Links*, Hillsdale, NJ: Lawrence Erlbaum Associates.

Lee, M. (1999) 'Education in Malaysia', *School Effectiveness and Improvement*, 10 (1): 86–98.

Linder, S. H. and Rosenau, P. V. (2000) 'Mapping the terrain of the public–private policy partnership', in P. V. Rosenau (ed.), *Public–Private Policy Partnerships*, Cambridge, MA: MIT Press.

Lissaur, R. and Robinson, P. (2000) *A Learning Process; Public–Private Partnerships*, London: Institute for Public Policy Research.

Lo, L. N. K. (1999) 'Raising funds and raising quality for schools in China', *School Effectiveness and Improvement*, 10 (1): 11–54.

McNamara, O., Hustler, D., Stronach, I., Rodrigo, M., Beresford, E. and Botcherly, S. (2000) 'Room to manoeuvre: mobilising the "active partner" in home–school relations', *British Journal of Educational Research*, 26 (2): 473–90.

Ng, S.-W. (1999) 'Home–school relations in Hong Kong: separation or partnership', *School Effectiveness and Improvement*, 9 (4): 551–60.

Sammons, P., Thomas, S., Mortimore, P., Owen, C., Pennell, H. and Hillman, J. (1994) *Assessing School Effectiveness: Developing Measures to Put School Performance in Context, for the Office for Standards in Education*, London: University of London, Institute of Education.

Stoll, L. and Mortimore P. (1997) 'School effectiveness and school improvement', in M. Baker and J. White (eds), *Perspectives on School Improvement*, London: Bedford Way Papers.

Teddlie, C. and Reynolds, R. (eds) (2000) *The International Handbook of School Effectiveness Research*, London and New York: Falmer Press.

Third Outline Perspective (2001) *Plan 2001–10 Malaysia*, April, paras 5.27–5.29.

Vestager, M. (2001) *Ministry of Education*, www.uvm.dk/eng/publications/value

Vincent, C. (1996) *Parents and Teachers: Power and Participation*, London: Falmer Press.

Yancey, P. (2000) *Parents Foundation Charter Schools: Dilemmas of Empowerment and Decentralization*, New York: Peter Lang.

Section VII
Managing Quality in Education

17
Managing Change to Improve Learning
Hugh Busher

Introduction

Change can be either imposed by external authorities or events or generated by the internal actors in a situation, although the final outcomes of a process of change usually reflect a negotiated compromise between the internal and external perspectives. When change is imposed too heavily by external agencies, internal actors tend to become demoralised. In England and Wales in the late twentieth century, Simkins et al. (1992) chronicled the impact of central government imposed curriculum change on schoolteachers. Helsby and McCulloch (1996) pointed out that these changes were alienating for teachers and support staff because it led to senses of disempowerment or loss of control. Busher and Saran (1995) discovered that many support staff were complaining about the extra duties these changes brought and the worsening of their conditions of service. Earley (1998) showed the extent to which these changes were focused through particular agents of central government, such as inspectors, and how stressful this was for staff in schools. Thrupp's work (1999) in New Zealand echoed this view, also showing how it had a deleterious effect on students' attitudes to learning in schools serving socially disadvantaged areas.

Leaders have an important mediational function for their school or college's members between the external contexts and the internal processes, helping staff colleagues and students to understand and cope with externally imposed changes (Busher et al., 2001). They need to perform this function effectively to avoid staff feeling disempowered and resistant to, or alienated from, the changes proposed by themselves or by external agencies. Glover et al. (1998), among others, refer to this as a bridging and brokering function. Middle leaders perform a similar function within a school or college, explaining and interpreting the views of senior staff or external agencies to their departmental colleagues, in part to try to avoid their colleagues and themselves being perceived as resistant or incompetent. They also put forward their departmental colleagues' views to senior staff to try to influence the strategic policy of their educational institution. Bradley and Roaf (1995) describe this function as advocacy.

However, as Grace (1995: 2) points out, 'there are paradoxes and contradictions in the constructs of school leadership currently held by different interest and ideological groups'. Work in Australia by Gronn (2000) shows that some of these contradictions can be addressed if leadership in schools is viewed and analysed as distributed throughout the staff and not just as an attribute of an elite: the senior staff. By implication, teachers should be considered as leaders, too, since that is their function with students, a stance argued by Wilkinson and Cave (1988) from their work in Northern Ireland.

Teacher-generated change arises out of the values and ideologies held by teachers and school leaders about the appropriateness of particular teaching, learning and pastoral care processes, practices and outcomes for educational organisations (Frost et al., 2000). These views are strongly influenced by school members' preferences for particular workplace cultures and particular teaching and learning practices in given subject areas. Siskin's (1994) research in the USA showed that the epistemological frameworks of different subjects have a considerable impact on what teachers construe as appropriate approaches to teaching and learning and to organising their subject departments.

This view resonates with that of Foucault (1980) in France, who explored how the power which socially constructed epistemological structures assert shapes social processes and individual people's identities in organisations. This implies that senior and middle leaders wanting to promote change, such as reflective action planning (Frost et al., 2000) by teachers, need to work with and understand teachers' own subject-based epistemological frameworks. It also implies that the appropriate parameters for evaluating teachers' work rigorously have to take account of the values and beliefs about teaching and learning embedded in the practices of each subject area, including special educational needs (SEN).

Contexts that interact with leaders' and teachers' strategies of change

Teaching and learning are social processes carried out in socio-political contexts. In order to understand more clearly how teachers and their leaders at middle and senior level can bring about changes in teaching and learning, it is important to be aware of the influence which various socio-political contexts have on education, constraining certain strategies of action and promoting others. These contexts can be summed up as national and local or regional government policy; the residential communities which schools and colleges serve; the organisational cultures which school and college leaders construct through their interactions with staff and students; and the views and values held by individual members of a school or college. The epistemological contexts of teachers' subject knowledge are considered in a separate section.

National and local government policies significantly affect not only the background values within which teachers have to work but their detailed practices too. Taylor et al. (1997) pointed out how the policies of national and regional government in Australia represented an attempted enactment of particular values and ideologies, or belief systems, which affected how schools were organised. Gewirtz et al. (1995) argued that the emergence of market-oriented ideologies in education in England and Wales in the last quarter of the twentieth century altered understandings of appropriate relationships between leaders in and of schools and their staff colleagues, pupils, parents and governors. These policies are imposed on schools through central government agencies, such as the Office for Standards in Education (Ofsted) or the Qualifications and Curriculum Authority (QCA) in England and Wales, that organise centralised inspection systems or national tests. These materially affect how teachers teach and what changes to teaching they can make (Earley, 1998). In many countries, such as Turkey and Saudi Arabia, teachers have to use set textbooks which are prescribed by central government, and are given strong central guidance on the lessons they have to teach. Policy contexts at local or regional authority level affect how schools operate, the size of classes which teachers have to teach, which affects the teaching strategies they can use, and even whether schools stay open (Busher et al., 2001).

The residential communities that a school serves powerfully influence the culture within it as O'Connor (1997) indicated when reporting the attitudes of students from different ethnic backgrounds to schooling in the USA. Osler et al. (2000) note the impact of students' home and community backgrounds on the disciplinary frameworks which teachers and school leaders can construct and implement successfully. It emphasises the importance of inclusive education for all young people in education (Clark et al., 1999) and elaborates this into a series of school or college policies that stretch well beyond the management of the formal curriculum and the classroom. For example, it will influence the range of extra-curricular support activities teachers might choose to implement, such as breakfast clubs, homework clubs and classes, or outreach work for parents.

To bring about effective change, school leaders at senior and middle level and teachers need to look at schools from the perspectives of their students. Students in schools are often sharply and critically aware of the success of teachers' work (Rudduck et al., 1996) as a result of their lived experiences as people in complex socio-political circumstances of family, school and community (Howard and Gill, 2000). Wallace et al.'s (1997) work in the USA suggests involving students actively in the process of creating effective learning communities a view endorsed by Marsh (1997) in London, UK. Krechevsky and Stork (2000), in a study comparing successful teaching strategies in Italy and the USA, noticed the impact of local cultures on the quality of work which students produce.

What changes can be introduced to improve learning and how they are introduced are also influenced by an educational organisation's culture (Schein, 1992), and the sub-cultures within it of different formal and informal groups of staff and students. These have a considerable influence on how teachers, students and school leaders relate to each other and work together (Ribbins, 1992). These cultures are expressed in the language, customs and rituals used by each group, be it a subject department in the formal organisation of a school or a group of disaffected students (Willis, 1977), and are an expression of that group's work-related and social identity. It incorporates how members perceive themselves, individually and collectively, and how they think they are perceived by other people inside and outside the school or college.

Leaders, teachers and students need to work together to create a positive culture towards learning that enacts particular values and practices that promote success and maintains social cohesion between all members of a school's staff and students (Hopkins et al., 1994). In Anglo-American and Australasian schools and colleges this culture is said to be collegial in nature. Such a culture sets high standards of performance, welcomes change, encourages risk-taking in pedagogy, and offers support to people developing their professional practice (Stoll and Fink, 1996). Work by Blase and Blase (1994), in the USA, established that leaders' trust encouraged teachers to be proactive in improving their teaching. However, Hargreaves (1994) argues that collegiality is often false or constrained by leaders holding effective power, whatever claims they make about consulting staff when taking decisions. These latter approaches to leadership and management tend to lead to staff becoming cynical about their degree of involvement in decision-making (Busher and Saran, 1992).

In bringing about change, teachers and school level and middle level leaders need to work with people as individuals, as well as working with groups of people. Schools and colleges are socially constructed organisations made up of individual members and external stakeholders, although the distinction between these two categories is blurred. Each has different personal perspectives, encompassing different values and beliefs, on how the organisation should be run (Greenfield and Ribbins, 1993) and how successful teaching and learning should be undertaken. These conflicting perspectives need to be reconciled if members and leaders of a school or college are to work together successfully. So, leadership is as much a moral undertaking (Hodgkinson, 1991) as a functional or technical exercise.

School or college leaders, then, have to help staff and students to balance the competing demands of their educational organisation and their work-related or professional needs and interests (Busher, 2001) in ways that are perceived as valuable to the individual people involved and to the school as an organisation (Busher, 1990). Interests are here considered to include aspects of teaching and learning – which topics people prefer to teach (or learn) and how to teach them; work-related social processes – which student groups teachers prefer to teach, which teachers students prefer to work with, or how a subject area is managed; and social activities that people enjoy, be they extra-curricular clubs or sports, or out of school or college events. Leithwood et al. (1999) suggest that these conflicts can be resolved through helping people create personal goals that subsume them. To be effective for each person these goals have to be achievable but demanding; concrete and clear (e.g. beginning lessons effectively); and are short term but understood within a longer-term developmental context.

Adapting to changing understandings of knowledge

Leaders and other staff in schools and colleges work with students, and per-haps parents, too, to help them process and acquire knowledge. Teachers are members of particular knowledge or discourse communities, which are usu-ally defined by the subjects they teach (Siskin, 1994) although Nias (1999) points out that primary school teachers often define their work-related iden-tities in terms of the age-group of the students whom they teach. Middle and senior leaders in secondary schools often use such definitions to shape their roles as well as their work-related identities.

In these discourse communities (Foucault, 1980), knowledge is constantly changing, although the rate of change is variable. New knowledge takes many forms. First, it may concern the content knowledge of a subject area, perhaps derived from new research made public through subject association confer-ences or publications. Second, it might focus on pedagogy, considering the range of approaches available for teaching and learning a subject for different pupils and groups of pupils of different ages and abilities from different socio-economic backgrounds. Third, it may be about various aspects of the curricu-lum: syllabus construction, public examinations, assessment processes. Fourth, it might focus on government prescribed processes of regulation, inspection or staff appraisal that offer particular definitions of effective teaching. Fifth, it may result from changes in the resources available for the curriculum, in what-ever medium they are published. For example, new information and commu-nication technologies, because of the access to knowledge that they require and permit, offer the opportunity to alter the ways in which people teach and learn (Comber et al., 1998).

School and college leaders at various levels are the mediators of these epis-temological horizons to their staff colleagues, as research in England (Busher et al., 2001) and in the USA has discovered (Siskin, 1994). Teachers mediate these same horizons to their students. Together, school staff and students have to weigh how new knowledge can be adapted and implemented to meet exist-ing and preferred educational values, the resources and equipment available through the school or college, the skills held by the teachers and the learning needs of students. They also have to consider how to change existing practices to meet the demands of new knowledge frameworks, especially when these are generated by powerful sources, such as central government changes to the curriculum. Such evaluation of practice, so long as it is under professional control, is said to be empowering of teachers and other staff, and likely to raise their morale, as they take responsibility for improving their own practice (Somekh, 2000). However, MacBeath (1999) suggests there is a need to achieve a balance between internal institutional evaluation and external inspection of practice to ensure rigour in teachers' evaluations of their practices as leaders, managers and instructors.

To develop classroom processes, teachers and their leaders have to collaborate in analysing rigorously how learning and teaching is currently carried out and to what extent it meets the needs of students (Frost et al., 2000). Evaluation can be carried out in many ways. The Office for Standards in Education (Ofsted, 1998) offered guidance on how schools can carry out self-evaluation of their work. Action-research encourages teachers to develop their own rigorous means of evaluating teaching, learning and management practices (Frost et al., 2000; Lomax and Parker, 1995). As a matter of professional practice, many teachers regularly if informally evaluate their lessons with specific students or groups of students. They are examples of the self-critical practitioners with whom Smyth (1991) worked in Australia, who theorise practice in common-sense language to discover ways of improving their students' learning opportunities. As Goodson pointed out: 'Whilst [teachers] may say that they are uninterested in research, nevertheless in their own lives and in their teaching they constantly reflect upon and refine their practice' (Goodson, 1997: 40).

Bringing about change

To bring about changes in teaching and learning, school and college leaders at all levels have to work with staff colleagues, students, parents and governors. Day et al. (2000) discuss the levers for change that are used successfully in the schools in their study. Successful change involves leaders not only understanding the functionalist or managerial aspects of leadership, but also the cultural and (micro) political aspects (Grace, 1995) and the contexts in which change takes place. Busher and Harris (1999) suggest that the arenas in which leaders need to operate can be summarised as:

- an awareness of context and the creation of professional networks
- bridge and brokering between different levels of authority
- using power to support particular educational values and ideologies
- creating social cohesion
- mentoring staff development.

In addition, middle leaders need to be perceived as modelling successful practice, if they are to have the respect of their staff colleagues and students

(Busher, 2001), since teaching is a practical activity as well as a managerial one. Wilkinson and Cave (1988), in Northern Ireland, explored the centrality to effective teaching of teachers being successful managers.

There are various ways in which the need for change can become visible. One of these is through rigorous evaluation of current practice, as has already been discussed. This is the exploratory step in an action research or action planning cycle (Frost et al., 2000). Writing in Hong Kong, Fung (1996) suggested that another means was through leaders raising awareness with staff and students that change is needed. Morrison (1998) perceives this as a form of force field analysis for deciding what are the pressures for and against change in particular directions. Work in Canada by Fullan (1992) suggests that only when people are engaged with the nature and shape of a problem can leaders and colleagues begin to initiate and implement changes. Somekh (2000) and Lomax and Parker (1995) describe this as noticing conflicts between preferred values and actual practices of teaching and learning (or managing) and consider that such analysis is an essential first step for teachers, albeit with the help and support of senior or middle leaders (Hutchinson, 1995), trying to devise more successful practices.

However, choosing to implement a particular course of action involves teachers making decisions about conflicting values and priorities as well as about opportunity costs (Busher et al., 2001). The use of resources – time and money, as well as more visible factors in schools such as books, materials, rooms and staff – for one student or group of students means that other uses of these resources have to be forgone, even if that is detrimental to the education of other students. Such decisions, then, are value laden (Simkins, 1997) rather than technicist, involving choices between competing sets of social and educational values and priorities. To resolve this, teachers and school leaders need to first develop and then project a coherent vision for action, as Gronn (1996) discovered in his work in Australia.

The strategy for implementing action can be expressed through a plan, the development of which involves consulting all the relevant staff and students and, if necessary, parents and governors of a school or college too. At a simple level, development plans involve leaders and their colleagues deciding how they are going to act, how they are going to implement action, and how they are going to monitor and evaluate the success of that implementation. Hopkins and MacGilchrist (1998) discuss how plans need to be broken down into manageable targets and these assigned as practical tasks to individual members of the team trying to implement change. In addition to planning how to act, and how to resource that action, the sequence and timing of the change process need to be located by critical path analysis: members of the team need to carry out particular tasks by particular times if the proposed change is to be implemented by a chosen time. The implementation of the changes needs to be monitored against predefined targets or indicators, including preferred and underpinning social and educational values, to allow its success to be evaluated and to give guidance to what further and future actions need to be taken.

However, all leaders, whether of schools and colleges or of students in classrooms, encounter resistance, whether trying to implement change or maintain the status quo. Wolcott's (1977) research in the USA led him to describe this resistance as a continuum that ranged from disinterest in a project or lack of enthusiasm for it to open opposition to its implementation. Plant (1987) outlined a number of reasons why people resist change – fear, lack of confidence, lack of skill, particular beliefs – which leaders have to understand to help staff accommodate change.

To resolve conflicts of views between members of a school or college, for example, over the possible exclusion of a student, leaders have to try to negotiate a solution which benefits everybody if the change is to be implemented successfully (Bennett, 1995; Busher, 1990). Such negotiations illustrate clearly the processes of transactional leadership which complement those by which transformational leaders try to build cohesive cultures in work groups (Leithwood et al., 1999). More successful leaders seem to be those who are able to overcome resistance either through persuasion, or through assuaging people's fears, or through cajoling people to act in ways they prefer. These leaders are more astute politically and know how to apply a variety of strategies to the people and situations involved (Ball 1987; Busher, 2001). Altrichter and Salzgeber (2000) argue that such micro-political processes are the vehicle by which people in organisations create different types of consensus out of potential or actual conflict.

Helping teachers to cope with and instigate change

In order to bring about change, then, leaders need to help their colleagues and students to cope with change. A key means is through leaders promoting the professional development of their colleagues to meet the needs of their students better (Moyles et al., 1998). Hopkins et al. (1997) suggest that this can best be achieved through pedagogic partnerships: groups of teachers working together inside and outside the classroom to bring about improvements in teaching and learning. It may also involve middle leaders arguing with senior staff for adequate resources for staff development and training in their subject or pastoral areas, and allocating in-service opportunities equitably among their colleagues (Busher et al., 2001).

Middle leaders can approach this process of staff development in four different ways, Lomax (1990) argues:

● a research perspective, as an extended professional approach, which requires teachers to consider their practice in its policy, institutional and personal professional contexts

- a political perspective which defines staff development as a means to meet national and local policy agendas, regardless of the relevance of particular developments to improving learning
- a managerialist perspective which emphasises the importance of a school's corporate goals and needs with little regard for teachers' individual professional needs
- a restricted approach which focuses only on working in classrooms.

Only the first encourages staff to think critically about their work in order to improve it. The second and third options prioritise organisational needs (corporatism) over individual work-related needs, while the fourth is underpinned by a technicist perspective that tries to ignore the impact of contexts on teaching and learning processes.

For practitioners, whether teachers, subject leaders, senior staff or school or college governors, to reflect critically on practice in a rigorous manner requires help from other people, such as experienced colleagues, who can act as critical friends (Golby and Appleby, 1995). The Ofsted criteria for effective teaching (Ofsted, 1999) provide useful benchmarks for thinking about how teaching and learning can be developed effectively. Experienced colleagues can act as critical friends or mentors in a number of different ways. Moyles et al. (1998) suggested five key functions:

- professional supporter – who encourages and reassures their colleagues in their actions
- professional trainer – who coaches colleagues and helps them to clarify what situations need
- professional educator – to encourage colleagues to reflect critically on an evidence base of their actions
- professional assessor – to offer an evaluation of performance according to agreed criteria
- professional sponsor – able to help colleagues negotiate the organisational structures
- personal friend and counsellor.

In order to carry out many of these five aspects, mentors need to gain access to their colleagues' teaching rooms in order to observe, first, how their colleagues are teaching and, later, to monitor what changes are taking place as a result of mentoring work. This is an uncomfortable experience for many teachers, especially the first time they experience it. The fact that they are observed and their practice monitored on a daily if informal basis by dozens of students and any visiting classroom assistants and stray visitors to a school seems to make no difference. Hopkins et al. (1997) suggest some useful procedures to facilitate the process of classroom observation. These include leaders and colleagues defining the agenda for observation before observation takes place, deciding how records will be made and kept, and agreeing how discussions will be conducted after a period of observation. It creates a negotiated and transparent framework within which people can work.

Dealing successfully with such sensitive work with staff and students requires middle and senior leaders to develop a variety of interpersonal and work-related skills. Moyles et al., (1998) suggested that these are

- flexible in their style of working with staff
- to use a wide range of interpersonal skills effectively
- effective communication
- sound professional practice
- sound professional knowledge involving a wide range of pedagogic and analytical skills
- negotiative and enabling skills
- fostering self-esteem
- patience.

The need for such careful support of teachers in their work in classrooms is succinctly summed up by Frost et al. (2000), who points out that school improvement can only be maintained if teachers' leadership of classroom-based innovation is sustained by more senior staff in a school.

Teachers as the leaders of learning

It is teachers who are the leaders of students in the classrooms, laboratories and workshops. The importance of teachers' leadership of learning is acknowledged in the career entry profile for newly qualified teachers in England and Wales (Teacher Training Agency, 1997: 18). It lists four main areas, three of which relate directly to core functions of leaders and managers:

- knowledge and understanding
- planning teaching and class management
- monitoring, assessment, recording and accountability
- other professional requirements.

Mortimore (1993) suggests that the types of knowledge and understanding that teachers require to be successful in the classroom are not only subject knowledge, but also social knowledge about the dynamics of students and student groups in their social contexts, psychological knowledge about how students learn and organisational knowledge about how to lead and manage lessons in their particular schools and colleges. The last encompasses an understanding by teachers of the micropolitical processes of their schools and colleges, so they are able to influence decision-making at subject area and whole-school level and promote the interests of the students they teach (Ball, 1987; Busher, 2001), as well as an understanding of the social dynamics of the communities from which their students are drawn.

Like successful leaders at other levels in schools and colleges, teachers need to be able to project a vision that excites students and inspires their enthusiasm for a topic or activity, as well as planning carefully the learning opportunities that students are to experience in each lesson. To be successful, teachers need to be transformational and transactional leaders (Gunter et al., 2001) with their students. In drawing up lesson plans that establish a developmental sequence of topics and skills and draw on a variety of different resources and activities to maintain student engagement with the tasks, teachers need to take account of the various learning and social needs of each of the students they teach for each lesson. That alone is a mammoth task for a teacher in most schools in England and Wales, given classes that are often in excess of 30 students.

In addition, as the Teacher Training Agency (1997) suggests, successful teaching also involves teachers in effective monitoring of student performance, as well as of their own practice, to assess how best to help students develop their further learning. Although such monitoring can be carried out by observing and coaching students during times when they are undertaking individual or group work during a lesson, more formal reviews of learning also need to take place quite frequently. These can be carried out in a great many ways. Both formal and informal monitoring of students' work is carried out in order to explore how to develop students' better understanding of a topic and to avoid students becoming disaffected with lessons because they have misunderstood some of the work and so can no longer make sense of the topic being studied. For those students who are having particular difficulties with a subject, teachers might need to develop individual learning programmes that are monitored in discussion with students on a lesson by lesson basis.

At least as important as their leadership of the technical curriculum processes of students' learning, is teachers' leadership of students' social processes in classrooms and schools. This is not merely a matter of maintaining discipline and imposing school sanctioned rules of behaviour, but of creating social cohesion in each class so that students support each others' learning and reject behaviour that mitigates against that, as Marsh (1997) describes. Maintenance of effective discipline, then, is dependent on teachers building shared norms with their students, of whatever age, about what is acceptable behaviour that will positively sustain learning. Those same factors which are said to define effective and collegial cultures in schools and colleges also apply to their sub-units, the classrooms: a clear vision and programme for development by the teacher leader; care for students as individuals; trust between leaders and students; clear high expectations of behaviour and standards of work; support for risk-taking; appropriate support from the leader for students' work-related development.

It is no surprise then that the research of Wragg et al., (2000: 55) into incompetent teachers in England and Wales highlights what are, essentially, the qualities that might be expected of incompetent leaders and managers:

- low expectations of pupils
- not ensuring adequate pupil progress
- poor planning and preparation
- poor classroom discipline
- inability to respond to change
- poor relationships with pupils
- poor management of classroom resources
- inadequate monitoring and assessment of pupils' performance.

If change is to be brought about successfully in schools and colleges, it has to focus on the improvement of teaching and learning. The key people in such improvement are the teachers who lead and manage the student groups and the learning of the students, individually and in groups. This views students as the creators and constructors of learning, rather than as just the imbibers or consumers of it, and of their school or college as an organisation, under the leadership of their teachers as well as formally promoted leaders within the organisational framework of a school or college.

It is for school leaders at middle and senior level to facilitate improvements in teaching and learning by helping teachers to engage in a critical way with their current practice to explore how it can be improved, i.e. meet more successfully the needs of all the students in their institution. However, what changes can be brought about in any one school or college to improve learning will be strongly influenced by the socio-political contexts in which the institution is embedded. Thus, improving teaching and learning is a complex process that occurs through the interplay of internal and external forces in a school or college and the agency of individual staff and students engaged in it (Giddens, 1984). To be successful it requires the active engagement of staff and students in implementing preferred changes that enshrine individually and locally important values and beliefs while meeting nationally required goals and targets.

Further reading

Frost, D., Durrant, J., Head, M. and Holden, G. (2000) *Teacher-Led School Improvement*, London: Routledge/Falmer.

Gunter, H. (2001) *Leaders and Leadership in Education*, London: Paul Chapman Publishing.

Wragg, E. C., Haynes, G. S., Wragg, C. M. and Chamberlin, R. P. (2000) *Failing Teachers?*, London: Routledge.

References

Altrichter, H. and Salzgeber, S. (2000) 'Some elements of micro-political theory of school development', in H. Altrichter, and J. Elliott (eds), *Images of Educational Change*, Buckingham: Open University.

Ball, S. J. (1987) *The Micro-Politics of the School*, London: Methuen.

Bennett, N. (1995) *Managing Professional Teachers: Middle Management in Primary and Secondary Schools*, London: Paul Chapman Publishing.

Blase, J. and Blase, J. (1994) *Empowering Teachers: What Successful Principals Do*, Thousand Oaks, CA: Corwin Press.

Bradley, C. and Roaf, C. (1995) 'Meeting special educational needs in the secondary school: a team approach', *Support for Learning*, 10 (2): 93–9.

Busher, H. (1990) 'Micro-political processes: negotiating the implementation of change in schools', in R. Saran, and V. Trafford (eds), *Research in Education Management and Policy: Retrospect and Prospect*, Lewes: Falmer Press.

Busher, H. (2001) 'Schools, effectiveness and improvement, a political analysis', in N. Bennett, and A. Harris (eds), *School Effectiveness and School Improvement: Searching for the Elusive Partnership*, London: Cassell.

Busher, H. and Harris, A. (1999) 'Leadership of school subject areas: tensions and dimensions of managing in the middle', *School Leadership and Management*, 20 (1): 99–112.

Busher, H. and Saran, R. (1992) *Teachers' Conditions of Employment: A Study in the Politics of School Management*, Bedford Way Series, London: Kogan Page.

Busher, H. and Saran, R. (1995) 'Managing with support staff', in H. Busher, and R. Saran (eds), *Managing Teachers as professionals in Schools*, London: Kogan Page.

Busher, H., Barker, B. and Wortley, A. (2001) *School Leaders and Organisational Change in Turbulent Times*, Occasional Papers in Education, Leicester: University of Leicester, School of Education.

Clark, C., Dyson, A., Millward, A. and Robson, S. (1999) 'Theories of inclusion, theories of schools: deconstructing and reconstructing the "inclusive school" ', *British Educational Research Journal*, 25 (2): 157–78.

Comber, C., Lawson, T. and Hargreaves, L. (1998) 'From familiarisation to adaptation: teachers' responses to the introduction of communications technology in the classroom', paper presented at IN-TELE 98, Strasbourg, University Louis Pasteur.

Day, C., Harris, A., Hadfield, M., Tolley, H. and Beresford, J. (2000) *Leading Schools in Times of Change*, Buckingham: Open University Press.

Earley, P. (ed.) (1998) *School Improvement after Inspection? School and LEA Responses*, London: Paul Chapman Publishing.

Foucault, M. (1980) *Power/Knowledge: Selected Interviews and Other Writings 1972–1977*, New York: Pantheon Books.

Frost, D., Durrant, J., Head, M. and Holden, G. (2000) *Teacher-Led School Improvement*, London: Routledge/Falmer.

Fullan, M. (1992) *The Meaning of Educational Change*, London: Cassell.

Fung, A. (1996) 'Management of educational innovations: the "Six - A" process model', in Wong Kau-Cheng and Cheng Kai Ming (eds), *Educational Leadership and Change: An International Perspective*, Hong Kong: Hong Kong University Press.

Gewirtz, S., Ball, S. J. and Bowe, R. (1995) *Markets, Choice and Equity in Education*, Buckingham: Open University Press.

Giddens, A. (1984) *The Constitution of Society*, Cambridge: Polity Press.

Glover, D., Gleeson, D., Gough, C. and Johnson, M. (1998) 'The meaning of management: the development needs of middle managers in secondary schools', *Educational Management and Administration*, 26 (3): 181–95.

Golby, M. and Appleby, R. (1995) 'Reflective practice through critical friendship: some possibilities', *Cambridge Journal of Education*, 25 (2): 149–60.

Goodson, I. (1997) 'Trendy theory and teacher professionalism', in A. Hargreaves and R. Evans, (eds), *Teachers and Educational Reform*, Buckingham: Open University Press.

Grace, G. (1995) *School Leadership: Beyond Educational Management: An Essay in Policy Scholarship*, London: Falmer Press.

Greenfield, T. and Ribbins, P. (1993) *Greenfield on Educational Administration*, London: Routledge.

Gronn, P. (1996) 'From transactions to transformations: a new world order in the study of leadership', *Educational Management and Administration*, 24 (1): 7–30.

Gronn, P. (2000) 'Distributed properties: a new architecture for leadership', paper presented at Sixth Quadrennial BEMAS Research Conference, Robinson College, Cambridge, UK.

Gunter, H., McGregor, D. and Gunter, B. (2001) 'Teachers as leaders: a case study', *Management in Education*, 15 (1): 26–8.

Hargreaves, A. (1994) *Changing Teachers, Changing Times: Teachers' Work and Culture in the Postmodern Age*, London: Cassell.

Helsby, G. and McCulloch, G. (1996) 'Teacher professionalism and curriculum control', in I. Goodson, and A. Hargreaves (eds), *Teachers' Professional Lives*, New York: Falmer Press.

Hodgkinson, C. (1991) *Educational Leadership: The Moral Art*, Albany, NY: State University of New York Press.

Hopkins, D. and MacGilchrist, B. (1998) 'Development planning for student achievement', paper given at the 11th International Congress for School Effectiveness and School Improvement, Manchester, 7 January.

Hopkins, D., Ainscow, M. and West, M. (1994) *School Improvement in an Era of Change*, London: Cassell.

Hopkins, D., West, M., Harris, A., Ainscow, M. and Beresford, J. (1997) *Creating the Conditions for Classroom Improvement*, London: David Fulton.

Howard, S. and Gill, J. (2000) 'The pebble in the pond: children's constructions of power, politics and democratic citizenship', *Cambridge Journal of Education*, 30 (3): 355–78.

Hutchinson, B. (1995) 'Learning action research and managing educational change: improvement in careers education', *Educational Management and Administration*, 26 (4): 379–93.

Krechevsky, M. and Stork, J. (2000) 'Challenging educational assumptions', *Cambridge Journal of Education*, 30 (1): 57–74.

Leithwood, K., Jantzi, D. and Steinbach, R. (1999) *Changing Leadership for Changing Times*, Buckingham: Open University Press.

Lomax, P. (ed.) (1990) *Managing Staff Development in Schools: An Action Research Approach, BERA Dialogues 3*, Clevedon: Multilingual Matters.

Lomax, P. and Parker, Z. (1995) 'Accounting for ourselves: the problematic of representing action research', *Cambridge Journal of Education*, 25 (3): 301–14.

MacBeath, J. (1999) *Schools Must Speak for Themselves*, London: Routledge.

Marsh, M. (1997) 'In conversation with Janet Ouston', in P. Ribbins (ed.), *Leaders and Leadership in the School, College and University*, London: Cassell.

Morrison, K. (1998) *Management Theories for Educational Change*, London: Paul Chapman Publishing.

Mortimore, P. (1993) 'School effectiveness and the management of effective learning and teaching', *School Effectiveness and School Improvement*, 4 (4): 290–310.

Moyles, J., Suchitsky, W. and Chapman, L. (1998) *Teaching Fledglings to Fly: Report on Mentoring in Primary Schools*, London: Association of Teachers and Lecturers.

Nias, J. (1999) 'Becoming a primary school teacher', in J. Prosser (ed.), *School Culture*, London: Paul Chapman Publishing.

O'Connor, C. (1997) 'Dispositions towards (collective) struggle and educational resilience in the inner city: a case analysis of six African-American high school students', *American Educational Research Journal*, 34 (4): 593–629.

Office for Standards in Education (Ofsted) (1998) *School Evaluation Matters*, London: HMSO.

Office for Standards in Education (Ofsted) (1999) *Guidance on the Inspection of Secondary Schools: The Ofsted Handbook*, London: HMSO.

Osler, A., Watling, R. and Busher, H. (2000) *Reasons for Exclusion from School: Report to the DfEE*, London: DfEE.

Plant, R. (1987) *Managing Change and Making It Stick*, London: Fontana.

Ribbins, P. (1992) 'What professionalism means to teachers', paper given at the British Educational Management and Administration Society Fourth Research Conference, Nottingham, University of Nottingham.

Rudduck, J., Chaplain, R. and Wallace, G. (1996) *School Improvement: What Can Pupils Tell Us?*, London: David Fulton.

Schein, E. (1992) *Organisational Culture and Leadership*, 2nd edn, San Francisco, CA: Jossey-Bass.

Simkins, T., Ellison, L. and Garrett, V. (1992) *Implementing Educational Reform: Early Lessons*, London: BEMAS/Longman.

Simkins, T. (1997) 'Managing resources', in H. Tomlinson (ed.), *Managing Continual Professional Development in Schools*, London: Paul Chapman Publishing.

Siskin, L. (1994) *Realms of Knowledge: Academic Departments in Secondary Schools*, London: Falmer Press.

Smyth, J. (1991) *Teachers as Collaborative Learners: Challenging Dominant Forms of Supervision*, Buckingham: Open University Press.

Somekh, B. (2000) 'Changing conceptions of action research', in H. Altrichter, and J. Elliott (eds), *Images of Educational Change*, Buckingham: Open University Press.

Stoll, L. and Fink, D. (1996) *Changing our Schools: Linking School Effectiveness and School Improvement*, Buckingham: Open University Press.

Taylor, S., Rizvi, F., Lingard, B. and Henry, M. (1997) *Educational Policy and the Politics of Change*, London: Routledge.

Teacher Training Agency (1997) *Career Entry Profiles for New Teachers*, London: HMSO.

Thrupp, M. (1999) 'A decade of markets and managerialism in New Zealand schools: views from the front line of reform', paper given at the British Educational Research Association Annual Conference, Brighton, University of Sussex.

Wallace, R., Engel, D. and Mooney, J. (1997) *The Learning School: A Guide to Vision-Based Leadership*, Thousand Oaks, CA: Corwin Press.

Willis, P. (1977) *Learning to Labour: How Working Class Kids Get Working Class Jobs*, Farnborough: Saxon House.

Wilkinson, C. and Cave, E. (1988) *Teaching and Managing: Inseparable Activities*, London: Croom Helm.

Wolcott, H. (1977) *Teachers Versus Technocrats*, Ann Arbor, MI: Centre for Education Policy Making, University of Oregon.

Wragg, E. C., Haynes, G. S., Wragg, C. M. and Chamberlin, R. P. (2000) *Failing Teachers?*, London: Routledge.

18

External Evaluation and Inspection

Brian Fidler

Introduction

There has been a trend to greater accountability in most educational systems and at most levels and stages within those systems. This has been a spur to the development of evaluative practices. The main focus of accountability has been of giving an account to those outside the educational system. This has implications for the evaluative processes which provide that account.

The chapter examines the reasons for this increased interest in accountability and highlights the tensions between evaluation for accountability and evaluation for improvement. It details different approaches to evaluation and examines their contributions to evaluation at system and institutional levels. Finally, it analyses two different recently designed approaches to school evaluation. One highlights evaluation for system and institutional accountability by inspecting all schools, whilst the other emphasises institutional development and review.

Reasons for accountability

The reasons for increased attention to accountability are many and varied and undoubtedly there has been much 'policy borrowing' by some systems from those that were first in the field. The range of reasons which have been adduced are:

- Economic competitiveness. Nations have been increasingly concerned about their international competitiveness in business and commerce and they have regarded the performance of the educational system as a way of preparing students to become economically productive. This effect has been particularly marked in countries where economic performance has been a cause for concern.
- Financial stringency. Meeting the costs of providing public services has become an issue in all countries. Whilst one element has been the overall proportion of national production consumed by public expenditure, an

equally important effect has been the distribution of spending. There have been rising claims from services such as care for the elderly and health. This has led to pressure on educational spending and a concern to obtain value for money for whatever is spent on the educational system.

- Equality of opportunity. This has three aspects. In addition to the general social and political concern that all citizens in a democracy receive equal access to public services there has been increasing recognition that certain groups either have not profited from their educational opportunities or have dropped out. These groups have particularly included the socially disadvantaged and ethnic minorities. This is an especially insidious effect as the proportions of these groups in education decrease in the more advanced sectors, particularly higher education. Two consequences of this have been recognised. Without educational qualifications such groups are unable to escape their social deprivation as they grow older and they cannot contribute to national economic performance to their true potential. Even in successful school systems such reasons direct attention to the performance of schools for all their students including those groups for whom, in the past, they were less successful.
- Decentralisation. For a variety of reasons many countries have begun to decentralise their educational systems and devolve increasing degrees of decision-making to lower levels in the system. This has led to greater diversity in schooling and less knowledge centrally of what is going on at institutional level. In devolved systems there is a developing feeling that the counterpart of greater freedom at institutional level is an increased need for accountability to show how such freedom is been used (OECD, 1995b).

Whilst these have operated to some degree in all educational systems, the priority accorded to particular reasons has varied as have the resulting policy decisions. A number of factors have influenced the outcomes in different countries, including the degree of satisfaction with the educational system, its status and the degree to which it is being used as a vehicle for social and economic change. In addition to these political issues, there may also be structural factors.

Levels and sectors affected

These issues have affected all levels and sectors of the educational system but the intensity has varied by country and by sector. Levels refers to levels in the administration of education – national, upper intermediate, lower intermediate, institution – whilst stages means the various age ranges of students in educational institutions – pre-primary, primary, lower secondary, upper secondary, post-compulsory, higher education (OECD, 1995a). Correspondingly the particular evaluation machinery has differed by sector. In this chapter the major preoccupation will be with accountability and evaluation in the school sector since this is by far the largest sector and has generally been subjected to the greatest degree of accountability and evaluation in most countries (OECD, 1995b).

A general trend in educational reform has been for power to be concentrated at the level of central government and in institutions. Other levels have generally had their power and influence limited so the analysis of evaluation within the school system will concentrate on the effects on the centre and on institutions.

Increased attention to accountability and evaluation has not been confined to education. Power (1997) has drawn attention to the extent to which societies have begun to identify audit and evaluation as at least part of the solution to any problem. He refers to this trend as the 'audit society'.

Public and private sectors

Whilst the main emphasis here will be on public sector institutions – those wholly financed by public resources and controlled by public bodies – over the last 10 years there has been an increase in wholly or partially private institutions (OECD, 1995a). The wholly private are those financed and governed by private individuals or corporations. A large growth area has been of institutions that receive some public funding in addition to their private income. The state has generally regulated this sector in a variety of ways and this may include some element of evaluation. Although increased accountability in the public sector has raised awareness of such pressures on the private sector, governments have not generally intervened. Italy is an exception since it assesses private schools as part of the certification process whenever they apply to be acknowledged by the state (Hopes, 1997).

Purposes of evaluation

Institutional evaluation, like staff appraisal, is generally held to have two main purposes – accountability and development. Whilst these two ideas are linked, combining them in the same process has its tensions. Whilst accountability is intended to be made public, this is inimical to an honest assessment of performance, particularly where there may be deleterious consequences of not receiving a favourable report. Thus, particularly in a competitive situation, there is a great incentive to disguise or suppress any shortcomings and to appear to be performing well. The higher the stakes, the greater the incentive. This, however, is not consistent with the kind of assessment which would be needed as the basis for improvement (Fidler, 1997). This needs to be an accurate assessment of current performance so that any shortcomings can be accurately diagnosed and a realistic improvement plan formulated. Thus an assessment for the purposes of improvement would need to be carried out privately so that there was no incentive to put on a show.

For either accountability or improvement the ideal is an accurate assessment of current strengths and weaknesses. This will be least likely where there are adverse consequences of a poor assessment and where the assessment is carried out in an adversarial spirit.

Much rhetoric appears to treat accountability as an end in itself rather than as a means to an end. Here it will be assumed that the desired ends involve policy-making and action at some level in the educational system which lead ultimately to improvement of some kind. Once the self-evident value of evaluation for accountability is questioned, its value changes with the type of assessment which is carried out, and the level within the system where the results are assessed. Further, the consequences of accountability depend on the type of accountability which is operating. These factors will be explaining in the following section of this chapter.

Evaluation for accountability

Although accountability is the most often cited reason for external evaluation, this often means little more than the assessment of institutional performance is in the public domain. The potency of this rather depends on the consequences which follow from a performance assessed as poor. Where a small number of institutions are publicly pilloried for poor performance, then the impact may be substantial – not necessarily helpful, but substantial. However, where a large number of complicated and technical assessments are made public at the same time, the impact on each institution may be quite small. So some analysis is needed of mechanisms for accountability.

Kogan (1988: 25) takes as his definition of accountability 'a condition in which individual role holders are liable to review and the application of sanctions if their actions fail to satisfy those with whom they are in an accountability relationship'. He recognises that any definition of accountability may be contested but he differentiates accountability from more general forms of pressure and feelings of moral responsibility.

He accepts the analysis of Becher et al. (1979) that in schools a teacher has three kinds of accountability:

- to one's clients (moral accountability)
- to one's colleagues (professional accountability)
- to one's employers or political masters (contractual accountability).

However, he detected an emerging further type – market accountability. This was where clients have a choice of institution that they might attend. Whilst the other forms of accountability could be seen to bear directly on an individual, this further form was mainly directed at the institution rather than an individual teacher. As Hirschman (1970) has suggested, there are two expressions of market accountability; 'exit' for those entering or leaving an institution and 'voice' for those who remain. The analysis of market accountability has tended to focus on the former since some degree of choice of institution is a hallmark of a competitive arena whereas working with existing clients, and having some form of accountability to them, is a more general feature of educational systems. If market forces are to be used to drive up standards and influence consumer choice, any evaluative information must be available to them in a form which they can comprehend.

Where the performance of an individual teacher is assessed the locus of accountability is relatively clear. I qualify the clarity because an assessment is needed as to whether the task which the teacher is performing in a particular context is one that a competent practitioner should be expected to demonstrate to an acceptable standard (Fidler and Atton, 1999). Where this condition is satisfied then the teacher is accountable for his or her own performance. However, when it is the institution which is the unit of assessment, and this is the general trend (OECD, 1995b), the situation is more complex.

When the institution is the unit of accountability an analysis is first needed of the sanctions which can be applied *to* the institution and then a separate analysis of the sanctions which can be applied *within* the institution, resulting from an adverse evaluation.

Professional and moral responsibility may bear heavily on individuals, be the most substantial motives to deliver a high-quality service to clients and be potent spurs to improvement. However, within the tight definition given by Kogan (1988), they do not meet the test of involving explicit sanctions if the performance of an individual is found wanting. Hence the analysis here will concentrate on forms of accountability which do meet Kogan's test. This should not be taken to mean that professional and moral responsibility of an individual for his or her performance are unimportant, only that they cannot be enforced if the performance does not meet expectations.

Accountability at the institutional level   The following are accountabilities which could incur sanctions for the whole institution:

- statutory non-educational requirements – these include employment legislation and health and safety requirements
- statutory educational and financial requirements – these include curricular requirements and publication of student performance data
- statutory arrangements for the control and direction of the educational institution

- market accountability – this includes any consequences of clients choosing to study in a competitor institution.

Within the institution   The main enforceable accountability operates on individual staff through their contract of employment. This contract takes account of the statutory arrangements for the control and direction of the institution.

Thus performance within the institution is overseen by the governance and leadership of the institution in the large number of educational systems where the institution has a corporate entity. In countries such as Germany, where the accountability is directly on the teachers (OECD, 1995b), school supervisors deal with such issues.

Evaluation for improvement

Evaluation is intended to report on the current performance of individuals and institutions and be a spur to improvement either in preparation for the evaluation or as a result of the evaluation. The basis of this may be different for each accountability system and for institutions which are evaluated at differing standards of performance.

A further issue on which systems differ is the provision of advice and support following evaluation. It is generally recognised that to improve following the diagnosis provided by an external evaluation, further advice and support will be needed. In some educational systems this is combined with evaluation, in others there is a separate support function whilst in others it is the responsibility of the institution to seek out and fund its own advice and support (OECD, 1995b).

Means of evaluation

The four principal means of formal evaluation are

- external inspection
- external audit or review
- performance indicators
- self-evaluation (OECD, 1995b).

These are not mutually exclusive and are actually likely to be interrelated. The value of performance indicators as the sole data or as adjutants to other mechanisms should be noted. Observers generally see rather greater potential for performance indicators than has been achieved at the present time (OECD, 1995b; 1995c).

Which of these is the principal mechanism varies by sector within a particular country and between countries. The unit of accountability also changes between countries. With much delegation of decision-making to school level there has been a corresponding concentration of evaluation and accountability at the level of the school. However, this depends upon the educational system of a particular country.

As a recent Organisation for Economic Co-operation and Development (OECD, 1995b) report suggests, the methods used for evaluation, and the consequences of evaluation, reflect the satisfaction of the country with education, its national culture and the esteem with which teachers are held.

External inspection   This involves some external professionals visiting the institution to collect data. Usually this involves the observation of teaching performance. Inspection may involve explicit criteria for data collection and describe the various levels of performance against which teaching and other activities are to be judged. Whilst some educational systems demonstrate this more systematic approach, others rely on the professional judgement of inspectors using more implicit criteria, e.g. Germany. A case study of the English school inspection system is presented later in this chapter as other countries are watching this experiment with interest (OECD, 1995b).

External audit   External audit or review involves external evaluation but acts mainly as a check on an internal evaluation of performance which has been made against previously formulated institutional priorities. Thus although the range of aspects to be evaluated may be common across institutions, the priority accorded to different areas varies by institution. The assessment which is made is against individual institutional priorities and what is being assessed is the degree to which internal evaluation has made a valid assessment of performance against these priorities. Later in this chapter, a case study of school review in Victoria, Australia, illustrates extensive use of performance indicators to inform an internal assessment by school staff which is validated by an external verifier.

Performance Indicators (PIs)   For the purposes of evaluation of institutional performance Gray (1995), following Gray and Jesson (1991), has suggested the following requirements of PIs:

- central to process of teaching and learning
- cover significant parts of a school's activities
- reflect a range of competing educational priorities
- capable of being assessed
- allow meaningful comparisons to be made (over time and between schools)
- be capable of change by the school
- be few in number (three or four are suggested).

They suggest three areas:

- academic progress
- student satisfaction
- student–teacher relationship.

The measure of academic progress would be calculated using a value added methodology which examined the difference between the exam or test scores when the student leaves compared to the test scores when the student arrived (Willms, 1992). Those schools ensuring that their students make more progress than a typical school would be high added-value schools.

Performance indicators can be of two kinds – outcome and process. Evaluative performance indicators tend to be outcome indicators but for institutions to improve they need some indication of the processes by which other institutions achieved better results. A combination of outcome and process indicators may help identify other organisations for benchmarking (Fidler, 1999).

There are problems in trying to evaluate performance in multi-indicators systems unless the relative weightings of the various outcome indicators have been specified in advance. As Mayston and Jesson (1988) point out, improvements in one indicator may be achieved at the expense of another, so, unless the trade-offs are known or specified, higher performance may be ambiguous. A further issue to be considered in using performance indicators for institutional evaluation is that, as 'higher stakes' assessments are made, there is an increasing risk that those who provide the data will feel pressurised to massage or falsify the information as a form of institutional protection against adverse consequences. The risks of untrustworthy data should not be underestimated.

Self-evaluation This may have different forms and may be highly structured with areas to be assessed, and even have means suggested for collecting data to make the evaluation, but the judgement is an internal one. Issues raised concern the extent to which valid comparisons can be made by those intimately involved in the activity and the extent to which unpalatable judgements will be made. Beyond that there are issues of the ability and will to make changes, particularly where they may be radical and may have deleterious consequences for the teachers involved (Clift, 1982).

How the evidence is used

As Wilcox (1992) has noted, the means by which evidence is assessed to yield judgements is not well understood and yet it is critical for valid assessments. For improvement it is important both that any evaluation should be a valid one and also that those within the institution accept the assessment as valid. This latter requirement is particularly difficult if the assessment is a negative one since there is an inevitable tendency for those involved to deny the results and to rationalise such denial as resulting from an assessment which is not valid (Earley, 1997).

The requirements for a valid assessment involve the following stages:

(1) common, defined criteria for the collection of evidence and judgements
(2) collection of representative and valid data
(3) the comparison of these data with explicit norms for other schools
(4) judgement about the meaning of differences emerging from the previous stages.

Comparison is the main mechanism by which informed judgements can be made. The different forms of comparison are:

- comparisons of one institution's data over time
- comparison with all institutions
- comparison with similar institutions
- examination of the profile of responses (Glogg and Fidler, 1990).

Difficulties arise at the third stage, particularly for qualitative judgements. The norms are likely to be implicit and be derived from the accumulated experience of the inspector. At a minimum this implies some requirements for prior experience to form these implicit norms. Both this and the final stage are judgemental and depend to differing degrees on personal opinion (Fidler et al., 1998).

There are well-known psychological biases in decision-making which arise from biased comparisons. These include:

- heightened recollection of the most recent experience
- high-profile examples dominate
- a search for consistency – good or bad (Fidler, 2002).

In the management literature (Hammond et al., 1998) these and others are well-known potential biases but they have not been widely discussed in education, nor have procedures been suggested to lessen them in the evaluation of institutions.

Evaluation at differing levels in educational systems

Evaluation can be considered at the following levels:

- system
- institution
- teacher.

The purpose of evaluation at different levels

At the system level, national data provide evidence of school standards and their change over time. Evaluation data can provide evidence on the progress of school reforms, the compliance of schools with national requirements and the responsiveness of schools to parental and societal demands. Such data facilitate an analysis of value for money and are part of general democratic accountability (OECD, 1995b). In a study of inspection in European Union countries, the tracking of school reforms was the least used outcome compared to institutional or individual evaluation (Hopes, 1997).

At the institutional level, evaluation identifies strengths and weaknesses which may aid school improvement. Schools with very poor performance are identified for support. Institutions may be encouraged to engage in self-evaluation in preparation for external evaluation and new ways of working may be encouraged. Student performance should benefit.

At the level of the individual teacher, evaluation identifies their strengths and weaknesses and may aid their improvement. External inspection can provide an independent assessment which can be compared to internal school judgements of teacher performance. Very poor teaching performance can be identified.

The contribution of different mechanisms of evaluation at different levels

System level   External inspection can make a substantial contribution to knowledge of what is happening and the standards reached in each institution. This can be achieved either by inspection of each institution on a regular cycle or by inspecting a representative sample of institutions. Where all institutions are being inspected over an extended period, then the results for any particular year will depend on the findings from the institutions inspected in that year. If the sample is biased by the overrepresentation of certain types of institution then this will distort estimates of the performance of the system. For example, in the case of England, where in the first year of the new inspection regime those schools likely to have problems were scheduled for inspection in greater numbers than would have been representative, this gave an overly negative picture of school performance. Such schools were scheduled for an early inspection as a way of speeding up their recognition and improvement (Ofsted, 1999). In this case raising individual school performance was chosen as an overriding priority rather than achieving an accurate picture of system performance.

External review makes a more limited contribution to knowledge of the system because each institution is being judged according to its own mandate and priorities. Although these can be recorded as part of the review evidence they are more difficult to conflate and summarise at system level.

Performance indicators make a major contribution to knowledge of system performance but only on the areas covered by quantitative indicators.

Institutional self-evaluation plays almost no part in assessing system performance since the judgements are made by a large number of different individuals on differing bases and the people making the judgements have a vested interest in the result.

Institutional level   The relative contributions change at the level of the individual institution. Whilst external inspection and performance indicators continue to make major contributions by comparing the performance of the institution with that of others, external audit and self-evaluation make greater contributions. External audit compares the performance of an institution with its own set priorities in a systematic way and gives it external legitimation. This may involve some comparison with other institutions where there are common criteria.

Institutional self-evaluation engages staff in making an assessment of the performance of their institution. Although they may have a vested interest in the result, if the assessment involves comparison of data with other institutions it will be an assessment which takes account of prevailing standards of performance elsewhere. The range of areas of an institution's activities which are evaluated can be wider than other forms of evaluation and can be chosen because of institutional priorities for improvement.

Teachers   Teachers have been included to demonstrate that, with the move to concentrate on institutional assessment, the performance of an individual teacher has become more peripheral to the evaluation process. Teachers may be assessed as part of external inspection but each teacher will be seen so little that any assessment will be very slight.

The performance of teachers can be inferred from examining the progress which their students make in a year when they have been tested at the start and end of the year but, as the number of students in a class is not large, the errors involved in making such an assessment mean that only exceptional performance – good and bad – stands out. The use of such statistics is also the only way in which the performance of individual students could be tracked.

Figure 18.1 summarises the impact of different forms of evaluation.

Case studies

Two case studies give details of two very different approaches to inspecting schools. One uses external inspection as the principal mechanism and operates

Level	Ext inspection	Ext audit	PIs	Inst self-evaluation
System	++	+	++	0
Institution	++	++	+	+
Teacher	++	0	+	+

Figure 18.1 The contribution of different mechanisms of evaluation at different levels

in a competitive school environment – this is the case of England. The other uses external verification of an internal audit using a large number of performance indicators – this is the case of the state of Victoria in Australia.

School inspections in England under the Office for Standards in Education

This is a scheme to inspect all state schools which began in 1993. Over four years all 23,500 state schools have been inspected. Major modifications have been made to the scheme on a number of occasions and a number of the original criticisms have been met – data collection before the inspection has been streamlined, brief feedback to teachers after they have been observed has been instituted, developments on which schools are already working are recognised, briefer inspections have replaced standard inspections for those schools which appear to be making good progress, ongoing training has been provided for inspectors, inspectors with a poor record have been dismissed and an appeals procedure has been put in place. The changes make it quite difficult to provide research evidence on the working of the scheme because some of the research evidence becomes outdated when the scheme is modified. However, where it is appropriate, evidence will be cited.

The particular features of this inspection scheme include the following:

- systematic external inspection of all schools on a six-yearly cycle
- separates advice and inspection
- published criteria for inspection – content and process
- reports are made public
- high-stakes consequences for poorly performing schools
- independent inspectors operating under contract
- presence of a lay inspector
- comprehensive account of a school's performance
- systematic classroom observation and aggregated assessment
- action plan required from school afterwards.

The scheme is administered by a specially created Office for Standards in Education (Ofsted). In principle this is independent of the central government education department. This office organises but does not conduct the inspections. It created an explicit set of criteria and set of protocols for inspections and these were published and sent to schools. Thus for the first time schools were aware of the inspection criteria and arrangements and could prepare for inspection.

The inspections are carried out by inspectors who have been accredited by Ofsted following a short period of training and assessment. The inspection of a school is carried out by contract. A range of organisations tender for inspection contracts and of those which have passed a quality threshold; the lowest cost tender is accepted. The successful contractor is then responsible for organising the inspection and submitting a report afterwards. Contractors include LEAs, non-profit-making organisations and commercial firms.

All except the lay member of the inspection group are expected to have relevant professional experience in schools and to have appropriate subject expertise. Research has shown that this is quite difficult to ensure. Initially there was a shortage of inspectors with primary teaching experience and, because of the scheduling of inspections, inspectors are brought into teams at short notice and may not have the exact subject match for the role they are undertaking. Many inspectors do not have recent teaching experience and a number are retired teachers (Ferguson et al., 2000). A small number of inspectors are full-time teachers or headteachers in other schools. This can be particularly developmental for those individuals who report that they take a more analytical view of teaching in their own school and also are able to see the detailed working of other schools that they are inspecting.

The new inspection regime was intended to divorce inspection from advice and involve a fresh examination of a school. Thus inspectors identify strengths and weaknesses in teaching and the general operation of a school but do not give direct advice on how to improve and have no continuing relationship with the school after the inspection (Ferguson et al., 2000). Some schools have taken the opportunity to employ inspectors afterwards to help them make changes, but that is a school decision and a school expense. Inspectors were also intended to have no recent prior knowledge of the school they were inspecting so that their evaluation would be unbiased by any previous experience at the school. This has proved quite difficult to operationalise when it is contractors who organise the inspection and may need to make changes to planned inspection teams through the unavailability of some members (Ouston et al., 1996). The inspection of some 5,000 schools per year, when these inspections have to take place in a limited number of weeks in the school year, is a huge logistical operation.

The inspection involves a number of inspectors visiting a school over a number of days to observe teachers teaching, to sample student work and to interview other interested parties. There is a simple parental satisfaction questionnaire which is sent to all parents and there is a meeting of parents held by the lead inspector at which parents can air their views of the school. The inspection group have previously had access to a great deal of

303

documentation from the school and its performance indicators. For a small primary school three inspectors might spend three or four days inspecting, whilst for a large secondary school up to 10 inspectors might spend up to a week in the school.

The inspection team are expected to sample between 10 and 20 per cent of the lessons taught in the period they are in the school, although this may involve only partial lessons. They are expected to grade each teacher on the teaching that has been observed and give brief feedback. Both inspectors and teachers report dissatisfaction with the brevity of the feedback and the pressured circumstances in which it is conducted (Ferguson et al., 2000). All these data from observation and all other sources are systematically aggregated and used as the basis for making qualitative judgements about the performance of the school and its teachers. All these data, typically comprising some 2,000 pages for each inspection, are stored on a huge database overseen by Ofsted and which is used to make authoritative statements about the working of the educational system.

The inspection team are required to make corporate judgements on four areas of a school's work:

- the quality of education provided by the school
- the educational standards achieved by the students
- the efficiency with which resources are managed
- the spiritual, moral, social and cultural development of the school.

The results of the inspection, including strengths, weaknesses and areas for improvement, are fed back to senior school staff at the conclusion of the inspection and a full written public report is issued within six weeks. This is available on the Internet, is distributed to newspapers and other organs of publicity, and a summary is sent to each parent at the school.

As part of the inspection regime a group of schools was defined for the first time. The worst schools (about 2 per cent of all schools) are deemed 'in need of special measures' or, more colloquially, 'failing schools'. These are schools which have a range of weaknesses. Usually these weaknesses involve poor examination or test results, a low proportion of satisfactory teaching, poor student attendance and other weaknesses (Ofsted, 1999). Whilst these schools are disproportionately in deprived inner city areas, this is not always the case. Some schools have failed because children were not making sufficient progress and the teaching was of too low a standard (Ferguson et al., 2000).

More typical schools are required to formulate an action plan for improvement, but there is no systematic monitoring of progress on this plan until the school's next inspection. The original design was for inspections every four years but this has been lengthened to every six years for typical schools, although schools causing concern may be inspected more frequently.

Since the year 2000 about 30 per cent of schools which have good performance indicators have shorter inspections where not all staff are observed teaching. However, expectations for these schools are very high and so shorter inspections do not appear to have lessened the stress on teachers which inspection has induced.

The publication of inspection reports has been part of an experiment with the whole school system in England (OECD, 1995b). That inspection has been accepted as readily as it has, is in no small part due to the experience and judgement of the initial group of inspectors who had to operate the system and the explicit criteria on which the inspection was to be conducted. There have been many criticisms of the new regime. A trenchant one concerns the lack of demonstrated validity of inspector judgements following observation of teaching (Fitz-Gibbon, 1997). A voluntary comparison of grades between inspectors has demonstrated a fair measure of agreement but the use of volunteers almost certainly makes the result unrepresentative (Matthews et al., 1998).

Undoubtedly this form of inspection has engendered a great deal of stress in teachers and inspectors (Jeffrey and Woods, 1998). A more insidious concern is the extent to which the inspection criteria dominates teachers' discourse and set up an orthodoxy (Maw, 1996). However, a House of Commons (1999) investigating committee was not persuaded that this was a sufficient danger to suggest major changes to the inspection regime. They noted that headteachers in surveys have reported that inspection has been to varying degrees developmental for their school and led to improvement (Ouston et al., 1996).

Public knowledge of the working of the educational system is much greater and more soundly based than previously. This is aided by external public testing and end of school examinations at 16, which apply comparable standards to each school and from year to year. However, improving performance indicators and improving inspection results from schools as a whole do not seem to have lessened politicians' concerns about the performance of schools.

The small number of poor schools are now public knowledge and action is being taken, often in very difficult circumstances. Informed professional opinion considers that these schools have been in this state for some time and it is the new inspection regime which has exposed them rather than created them (Watling et al., 1998).

Finally, it should be remarked that increased research interest in inspection brings effects to light which would otherwise be unknown. It would be surprising if similar effects are not operating in other inspection regimes.

School review in Victoria, Australia

A very different approach to school review has been taken in the state of Victoria in Australia. This framework makes far greater use of performance indicators, including a good deal of data specially collected by each school, and examines each school's progress against its charter of priorities. The scheme began in 1996 and all 1,600 state schools have been reviewed over a three-year cycle (Ferguson et al., 2000). There are two main purposes of the framework: 'to satisfy legitimate expectations of government about accountability for the outcomes of schooling, and to assist schools and teachers to improve standards of student learning' (Office of Review, 1998: 4).

Particular features of this scheme are:

- audited self-evaluation of progress against an individual school charter every three years
- presence of an external verifier
- extensive use of comparative data
- school data used in addition to specially collected data – some mandatory and some at the school's discretion
- specially written computer software to facilitate school comparisons of data over three years
- analysis of student level data
- staff involvement in interpreting data
- results incorporated in the next school charter.

General inspections of schools had ceased some 20 years previously and so, in devising this new system, much attention was paid to what was happening in other countries and the following were some guiding principles which influenced the design:

- external evaluation is more effective in improving school performance when schools have well developed internal processes
- school self-evaluation without some external component lacks the rigour necessary to effect real and lasting improvements in school performance
- evaluation processes should assist schools not only to analyse their performance but also to improve the effectiveness and efficiency of their management practices (Office of Review, 1998: 4).

This is a regime overseen by a specially created section of the State Education Department, the Office of Review (the Accountability and Development Division since 1999). It set up the system and oversees its operation, and is a good deal simpler and less costly than Ofsted. There are no inspectors.

Schools review themselves by comparing their collected data against that of other schools, particularly 'like schools'. These are schools within a similar band of free meals and proportion of children whose first language is not English.

The sole external contribution to the review is the presence of a verifier at a review meeting at the school towards the conclusion of the process. Ten organisations have verifier contracts and supply a person to act as verifier to each school review. The task of the verifier is to ensure that data have been collected appropriately and that the results have been professionally considered by teachers at the school for their implications for school performance and, finally, that improvement targets emerge from the process.

The whole process revolves around a school's charter. This is the set of priorities which are set up by the school in conjunction with its parents for the next three years. Each year for the following two years the school collects data on a range of criteria and compares its results with state averages and with those from like schools. Either this process, or new state mandates introduced during the year, provide developmental targets for the following year. In the third year there is a cumulative examination of the data and appropriate comparisons. The results of the review are expected to inform the school's next three-year charter (Gurr, 1999a).

The range of areas on which data are collected fall into two groups. First, there are data which are collected routinely by a school as part of its record-keeping on student and staff activities. Second, there are data which are specially collected by surveys for the purposes of review:

- parental satisfaction
- staff satisfaction.

The data are stored on computer and specially written software facilitates the display of data for comparison purposes.

As these data are presented and compared with other schools, a substantial number of inferences and questions arise. These include questions about classroom teaching even though there has been no classroom observation. An approach such as this can identify areas in need of further scrutiny in a very discriminating way.

In Victoria market mechanisms are weaker than in England and, so, in addition to any professional and moral responsibility to improve, it is the bureaucratic accountability of schools to the central office which is a sanction which could be used if schools did not take the self-review seriously and formulate challenging improvement targets. The verifier role is a crucial one in assessing the extent to which this has been done. A dissatisfied verifier could write a note of dissent following the review process which would be sent to the central office.

Some evaluative data on the working of the accountability framework is available from a report by the Victorian Auditor General's Office (1997) and one commissioned by the Office of Review from verification panel members (Gurr, 1999b). These indicate an improvement in planning and reporting by schools and more active involvement by schools in the review process:

> the framework presents an integrated programme that works at two levels: school planning and development, and system accountability. It is this dual utility that is the key to success. Schools value the framework for it provides them with a helpful developmental tool . . . the Victorian Accountability Framework is primarily an integrated school development framework, but one which also meets government accountability needs. (Gurr, 1999b: 10)

Whilst I consider that the assessment of school involvement in the improvement process can be substantiated, I am rather less convinced about the extent to which system-wide performance is evaluated. The centrally collected data provide some benchmarks against which progress in state schools can be assessed – attendance, examination results and student destinations after school. However, the only state-wide measure of student progress is the school-leaving examination at 18, although there are voluntary tests at other ages. Most of the data on student performance is provided by individual teachers in schools and with little cross-moderation. However, there are process data on the curriculum covered and much attitudinal data.

The curriculum data do provide evidence of the effectiveness of policy developments. For example, recent curriculum changes have required a 'Language other than English' (LOTE) to be taught in each school. Curriculum reviews have identified which languages have been chosen including the reasons. This has revealed the availability of language teachers to be an issue for primary schools.

The results of the review are available to parents in each school but are not publicly available. Thus they play a greater part in 'voice' rather than 'exit' (Hirschman, 1970). The main pressure for improvement comes from the state education department and its local offices.

Conclusion

The reasons for evaluating institutions need to be clearly specified. These should influence the choice of evaluation method and how it operates. Combining evaluation for accountability and evaluation for improvement involves tensions and compromises. There is also a further tension between system-level requirements and those of individual institutions. These tensions are illustrated in the two case studies and the design choices which were made in setting them up.

A systematic process which covers all schools is needed both to enable valid statements about the performance of the system and so that poor schools can be identified. Doing this once provides a sound benchmark against which any future data can be compared. The two case studies illustrate different approaches to this systematic process.

Educational systems without such a regime can have no certainty about the number and location of schools with very poor performance. However, identifying such schools is only the precursor of a very difficult improvement process. Such schools often have a long history of poor performance which has become institutionalised, and such organisations are not easy to change. The introduction of the new inspection regime in England was used as an opportunity to set up procedures to tackle 'failing' schools as they were discovered, whilst in Victoria the existence of this group of schools has emerged as a result of the review process.

Valid inspection requires clear published criteria so that the evidence base and the basis for judgements are known both to inspectors and those inspected. However, running any evaluation regime for too long unchanged will cause it to lose impact because schools operate to the expectations of that evaluation regime. There is some evidence of Ofsted criteria being used in school self-reviews and hence reinforcing an orthodoxy.

The collection of data for performance indicators by schools has a number of advantages. The data are more neutral than judgements presented by inspectors, and teachers can be expected to accept the data and make their own inferences about their meaning. An extensive range of indicators is needed to give a rounded picture of each institution's performance. The Australian experience demonstrates both the extent to which data can give a comprehensive view of a school's performance and also the degree to which staff accept and examine the implications of the data.

If the assessment is perceived as 'high stakes', steps are needed to ensure that the data on which the evaluation is being made are valid and accurate since there will be increasing pressure on schools to massage the data to avoid adverse consequences for the institution. There are some indications that this is happening in England because the data are made public and may have serious consequences for a school.

An external dimension to this process is needed both to ensure that valid data are being collected and used and that appropriate inferences are being made. Using performance indicators could have the effect of familiarising teachers with the value of data and making them more reflective about using evidence to guide their practices. The English and Australian experiences demonstrate different ways of achieving this. In Victoria, a key role is played by the verifier as the sole external participant in the process.

Whilst performance indicators can be of value to good and typical schools, poor schools exposed by them need further help and support to improve. It is probably in such cases that teams of inspectors visiting the school can help confirm in greater detail the nature of strengths and weaknesses and help formulate priorities for improvement.

Further reading

Earley, P. (ed.) (1997) *School Improvement after Inspection? School and LEA Responses*, London: Paul Chapman Publishing.

Ferguson, N., Earley, P., Fidler, B. and Ouston, J. (2000) *Improving Schools and Inspection: The Self-Inspecting School*, London: Paul Chapman Publishing.

Organisation for Economic Co-operation and Development. (OECD) (1995b) *Schools under Scrutiny*, Paris: OECD.

References

Becher, T., Eraut, M., Barton, J., Canning, T. and Knight, J. (1979) 'Accountability in the middle years of schooling: an analysis of policy options', final report of the East Sussex LEA/University of Sussex Research Project, Brighton: University of Sussex.

Clift, P. (1982) 'LEA schemes for school self-evaluation: a critique', *Educational Research*, 24 (4): 262–71.

Earley, P. (1997) 'External inspections, "Failing Schools" and the role of governing bodies', *School Leadership and Management*, 17 (3): 387–400.

Ferguson, N., Earley, P., Fidler, B. and Ouston, J. (2000) *Improving Schools and Inspection: The Self-Inspecting School*, London: Paul Chapman Publishing.

Fidler, B. (1997) 'The school as a whole: improvement and planned change', in B. Fidler, S. Russell and T. Simkins (eds), *Choices for Self-Managing Schools: Autonomy and Accountability*, London: Paul Chapman Publishing.

Fidler, B. (1999) 'Benchmarking and strategy', in J. Grant (ed.), *Sharing Experiences: Value for Money in School Management*, York: Funding Agency for Schools.

Fidler, B. (2002) 'Strategic leadership and cognition', in K. Leithwood and P. Hallinger (eds), *Second International Handbook on Educational Leadership and Administration*, Dordrecht: Kluwer Academic.

Fidler, B. and Atton, T. (1999) *Poorly Performing Teachers in Schools and How to Manage Them*, London: Routledge.

Fidler, B., Earley, P., Ouston, J. and Davies, J. (1998) 'Teacher gradings and Ofsted inspection: help or hindrance as a management tool?', *School Leadership and Management*, 18 (2): 257–70.

Fitz-Gibbon, C. T. (1997) 'Ofsted's methodology', in M. Duffy (ed.), *A Better System of Inspection?*, Hexham: OfSTIN.

Glogg, M. and Fidler, B. (1990) 'Using examination results as performance indicators in secondary schools', *Educational Management and Administration*, 18 (4): 38–48.

Gray, J. (1995) 'The quality of schooling: frameworks for judgement', in J. Gray and B. Wilcox (eds), *'Good School, Bad School': Evaluating Performance and Encouraging Improvement*, Buckingham: Open University Press.

Gray, J. and Jesson, D. (1991) 'The negotiation and construction of performance indicators', *Evaluation and Research in Education*, 4 (2): 93–108.

Gurr, D. (1999a) *From Supervison to Quality Assurance: The Case of the State of Victoria (Australia)*, Paris: International Institute for Educational Planning.

Gurr, D. (1999b) *School Review Evaluation*, Melbourne: Office of Review.

Hammond, J. S., Keeney, R. L. and Raiffa, H. (1998) 'The hidden traps in decision making', *Harvard Business Review*, September–October: 47–58.

Hirschman, A. O. (1970) *Exit, Voice and Loyalty: Response to Decline in Firms, Organizations and States*, Boston, MA: Harvard University Press.

Hopes, C. (1997) *Assessing, Evaluating and Assuring Quality in Schools in the European Union*, Frankfurt am Main: Deutsches Institut für Internationale Pädagogische Forschung.

House of Commons (1999) *The work of OFSTED*, Education and Employment Committee (Fourth Report of the Committee, Session 1998–99), London: The Stationery Office.

Jeffrey, B. and Woods, P. (1998) *Testing Teachers: The Effects of School Inspections on Primary Teachers*, London: Falmer.

Kogan, M. (1988) *Education Accountability: An Analytical Overview*, 2nd edn, London: Hutchinson.

Matthews, P., Holmes, J. R., Vickers, P. and Corporaal, B. (1998) 'Aspects of the reliability and validity of school inspection judgements of teaching quality', *Educational Research and Evaluation*, 4 (2): 167–88.

Maw, J. (1996) 'The handbook for the inspection of schools: models, outcomes and effects', in J. Ouston, P. Earley and B. Fidler (eds), *OFSTED Inspections: The Early Experience*, London: David Fulton.

Mayston, D. and Jesson, D. (1988) 'Developing models of educational accountability', *Oxford Review of Education*, 14 (3): 321–39.

Office for Standards in Education (Ofsted) (1999) *Lessons Learned from Special Measures*, London: Ofsted.

Office of Review (1998) 'Building high performance schools: an approach to school improvement', paper presented at the national seminar on School Review and Accountability, Hobart, Australia, April.

Organisation for Economic Co-operation and Development (OECD) (1995a) *Decision-Making in 14 OECD Education Systems*, Paris: OECD.

Organisation for Economic Co-operation and Development (OECD) (1995b) *Schools Under Scrutiny*, Paris: OECD.

Organisation for Economic Co-operation and Development (OECD) (1995c) *Measuring the Quality of Schools*, Paris: OECD.

Ouston, J., Fidler, B. and Earley, P. (1996) 'Secondary schools' responses to OFSTED: improvement through inspections?', in J. Ouston, P. Earley and B. Fidler (eds), *OFSTED Inspections: The Early Experience*, London: David Fulton.

Power, M. (1997) *The Audit Society*, Oxford: Oxford University Press.

Victorian Auditor-General's Office (1997) 'Schools of the future: valuing accountability', Special Report No. 52, December, Melbourne, Australia.

Watling, R., Hopkins, D., Harris, A. and Berisford, J. (1998) 'Between the devil and the deep blue sea? Implications for school and LEA development following an accelerated inspection programme', in L. Stoll and K. Myers (eds), *No Quick Fixes: Perspectives on Schools in Difficulty*, London: Falmer.

Wilcox, B. (1992) *Time-Constrained Evaluation*, London: Routledge.

Willms, J. D. (1992) *Monitoring School Performance: A Guide for Educators*, Lewes: Falmer Press.

19

Understanding Quality

John West-Burnham

The purpose of this chapter is to explore the contribution that the concept of total quality has made to our understanding of educational management and leadership. The chapter will first discuss the evolution of the concept of quality and quality management and will then explore the problems in developing a definition of quality in the context of education management. The actual experience of educational organisations in implementing total quality approaches will then be explored and will be related to other models of education management. The chapter will end with a discussion of some of the objections to the total quality approach and a consideration of possible future developments.

One of the key underlying issues in this chapter is the way in which educational management, like all other theoretical perspectives of organisations, is susceptible to changes in fashion. Prevailing orthodoxies change in response to a range of complex variables. Government policy, the publication of a particular text, and trends in the design and delivery of academic programmes have all influenced what might be described as the dominant hegemony in educational management. Although this hegemony will be continually challenged and will never achieve full implementation, any attempt to analyse the impact of a particular model has to recognise the importance of the status and credibility attached to a model and the extent to which it achieved the status of an orthodoxy.

The development of management theory often resembles the machinations of the medieval Christian church with schisms, alternative creeds, heretics and apostates all claiming to be true and denying the validity of other perspectives. There is little doubt that quality management in education became a movement with prophets and disciples (and heretics), and suffered from the zeal of the convert. This chapter will seek to balance dogma with analysis to provide a systematic review of the contribution of the quality movement to our understanding of educational management.

The genealogy of quality management

The first significant text on the place of quality in education management is probably Plato's *Republic*. In describing the ideal education system, Plato was

313

working from a clear and well-developed philosophical model which argued, in essence, that quality is an absolute, a metaphysical entity, that can only be understood by an elite, the philosopher-kings (a status still aspired to by many in educational management and leadership), and then translated into actual practice. Plato's influence on education systems, notably the British, will be discussed in the next section but his important and pervading notion was that of the possibility of defining and achieving a 'gold standard'. This notion of perfectibility, central to all the world's great religions, is a crucial underpinning to most debates about quality.

A second strand, far more prosaic, is to be found in the European enlightenment and industrial revolution. The scientific revolution produced, for the first time, the possibility of accurate measurement which could be replicated. It is easy to underestimate the impact of the standardisation of time, units of length and weight. The possibility of accurate measurement created the potential to replicate, and this was seized on by such pioneers as Josiah Wedgwood in the eighteenth century and Henry Ford in the twentieth century. The mass production of goods to a consistent standard introduced a new component, the notion of measurable quality.

The use of measurement to ensure consistent standards of production reached its apogee during the Second World War when the American munitions industry used a technique known as Statistical Process Control (SPC) to ensure consistent standards in the mass production of weapons. One of the key advocates of SPC was W. Edwards Deming and his role in the evolution of quality management is now legendary. The SPC technique was largely abandoned by American industry after 1945 but was enthusiastically adopted by Japanese industry with whom Deming worked as part of the post-war reconstruction.

The so-called Japanese economic miracle of the 1960s and 1970s is generally attributed to the evolution of total quality management – significantly inspired by Deming but with Juran and Ishikawa making important contributions to a management theory which had a substantial and profound impact on business practice. Importantly, the model had proven economic success, the dominance of Japanese industry in most areas of manufacturing was best reflected in the relative decline of those areas in most Western economies.

It is difficult to synthesise the components of total quality management succinctly but the key characteristics can be summarised thus:

- the centrality of the design process in order to ensure the product meets customer specifications
- the use of statistical process control to ensure compliance to specification in the manufacturing process
- the emphasis on prevention, 'right first time' rather than remediation
- the use of analytical and problem-solving techniques by the workforce to improve the process

- engagement with the customer to ensure continuous improvement of both product and process
- the creation of a team-based corporate culture with a high degree of consensus about organisational goals, purpose and processes.

Total quality management (TQM) thus combined elements of scientific management, a Zen-based belief in perfectibility and the sort of corporate thinking found in companies like IBM in the 1950s.

The 'secrets' of TQM were discovered in the USA in the late 1970s and there followed what can only be described as a scramble to subscribe to the new orthodoxy. The imperative to change was reinforced by the emergence of the excellence movement – best exemplified in Peters and Waterman (1982) *In Search of Excellence*. Total quality management and excellence offered broadly similar panaceas to the commercial ills of the Western economies and they were widely adopted and espoused by governments. It was only a matter of time before the evolutionary process saw the adaptation of TQM from manufacturing to service industries and from the private sector to the public sector.

The first significantly documented account of the application of the principals of TQM to education is probably Mount Edgecombe High School in Sitka, Alaska where the principal, Larrae Rochleau, introduced many TQM principles (Tribus, 1994).

The late 1980s and early 1990s saw an explosion of publishing on TQM in education. In Britain, Murgatroyd and Morgan (1992), West-Burnham (1992), Sallis (1993) and Greenwood and Gaunt (1994) all produced books whose titles were permutations of total quality, education and schools. Significantly, all of these studies were essentially normative, each advocated a model of total quality for use in schools as an alternative paradigm – justified by moral imperatives rather than any research base.

The second tranche of publications, Doherty (1994), Parsons (1994), Lomax (1996) and Davies and West-Burnham (1997) all offered case studies of the implementation of total quality in schools and colleges in the English-speaking world. But these were largely self-selecting studies; all reported success in varying degrees and they tended to be written by the champions of the total quality approach in the school or college. There was no research base, no empirical survey and, crucially and fundamentally, no evidence that a total quality approach was in any way causally related to improvements in the school, college or system – however such outcomes might be defined.

The anecdotal evidence from industry in the USA and Britain was that total quality initiatives failed in 60 per cent of companies – no such evidence is available for education. It is therefore very difficult to draw any meaningful conclusions about the status of total quality in education, or indeed in management generally. The relative decline of the Japanese economy has raised doubts about the overall efficacy of the model in business. There is less activity in education in Britain and the USA with alternative models, such as school effectiveness and school improvement, becoming dominant. However, the fact that this chapter has been commissioned indicates that the issue of quality in education remains significant: how significant will be discussed in subsequent sections.

Defining quality

The central tension in defining quality is best encapsulated in the philosophical divergence between Plato and Aristotle. Plato argued for quality as an absolute as discussed above, Aristotle by contrast defined quality in terms of behaviour. This captures the tension that permeates most writing about quality in education, the historical notion of quality as an ideal in contra-distinction to quality as a relationship. A good example of the former perspective lies in the use of phrases such as 'gold standard' to describe the British Advanced Level examination – it is at the pinnacle of the system. In this context quality is always perceived in a hierarchical way – everything is judged in the extent to which it shares the characteristics of the ideal. Hence much of the criticism of improving educational standards – they are only getting better because the ideal has been compromised.

Another example of the enduring impact of the Platonic model is the continual reliance in many educational systems of league tables, ranked measures of performance using quantifiable outcomes. This hierarchical and absolutist approach reinforces the notion of quality as a non-negotiable entity, of almost metaphysical status, which individuals and organisations can only strive to approach.

The quality movement, by contrast, has always rejected the notion of quality as an abstract entity. A number of aphorisms have emerged as the common perspective:

- 'Quality is what the customer says it is.'
- 'Quality is fitness for purpose.'

When elaborated in the various models, these precepts represent the profound shift that the total quality movement introduced – the notion that quality is defined by the customer's satisfaction rather than the supplier's intentions. It is difficult to overstate the profound conceptual leap that this represents; it is probably one of the reasons why the total quality movement has never really flourished in Anglo-Saxon societies. This approach challenges the perceived superiority of some universities and the status usually accorded private schools over state schools; it questions the notion that mastery of a prescribed curriculum equates to a quality education.

The quality approach argues that a quality lesson is one which children or students understand rather than one which teachers feel meet *their* criteria. A quality lesson, school or college, curriculum etc. is delivered in terms of fitness for purpose, i.e. it starts with the learner rather than an abstract view of how things should be. There cannot be an absolute in terms of the quality of a car, a restaurant, a museum, a holiday or a novel. For each, individuals make a choice to suit their needs, wants and values. The enthusiastic advocates of the gold standard in education would doubtless be distressed if they had to accept somebody else's gold standard in their own lives.

This tension reveals one of the main paradoxes in the application of total quality principles to education. People do have a choice in buying cars, going to restaurants etc.; the majority do not have such a choice in education. In most countries, developed and developing, choice in education is a direct product of family wealth and/or social status. Universal, free education is still an elusive aspiration for most of the population in many countries. In most developed countries it is possible for the wealthy to buy privileged access to education, the same is true in many developing countries. A genuine choice does not exist in most education systems, the ability to choose is usually a function of the ability to pay. In this respect education is no different to any other aspect of consumer-based societies but it could also be argued that education is such a fundamentally important social process that it should be prescribed and defined, and not left to individual whim or wealth. Equally, children are not fully formed and informed customers, and so any attempt to define quality in terms of their expectations will inevitably be compromised and inhibited.

In many ways, this debate has been rendered marginal by the systematic educational reform that has taken place in most education systems in recent years, i.e the standards-driven reform programme. The increasing specificity of government policies and the introduction of performance-based accountability has limited the amount of discretion available to schools to implement quality-based approaches. In most respects, quality is defined by educational policy – and there is no example yet of a national government working to the principles of total quality. In reality the rhetoric of consumer choice is usually limited to constrained options within a system rather than guaranteed access and entitlement to educational provision which has parity of esteem.

Total quality in education

There is no consensus as to what constitutes a suitable model for total quality in education. One of the characteristics of the writers listed above is that they have all produced idiosyncratic models, although their pedigree is very obvious and the differences are matters of nuance. Thus West-Burnham (1992) tends to place greatest stress on the values basis of management; Murgatroyd and Morgan (1992) place significant emphasis on the techniques of quality management and Greenwood and Gaunt (1994) stress the importance of statistical process control.

However, the consensus view would include the following factors in any model of total quality in education:

- shared values, common purpose, i.e. mission
- a strategic perspective
- an emphasis on leadership
- team-based structures
- a focus on training and development
- clear articulation of standards and expectations
- systematic monitoring and measurement
- the use of techniques for problem-solving and decision-making
- integration of clients/customers into processes.

Expressed like this, there is nothing really distinctive about this list as it replicates many other prescriptions and formulations for educational management and leadership. It closely resembles long-established models emerging from the school effectiveness and school improvement movements, and there is nothing in the list that could not be broadly subscribed to by the most fervent anti-managerialist. However, this list represents only the warp of total quality – it is the weft that makes quality approaches distinctive and this can be summarised as:

- the 'total' approach, everybody involved in every aspect, all the time
- the emphasis on prevention, working to prevent rather than correct mistakes
- the importance attached to continuous improvement
- the holistic and integrative nature of the model.

It is this last point that marks a crucial difference to other models, management in schools is often a noun, describing a minority group. In the total quality philosophy, it is the activity of everybody. Quong and Walker, in describing a case study of a school in Hong Kong which adopted total quality management, argue:

> Total Quality Management then is a philosophy of management for schools that requires them to change both how they think and how they are. It is all about empowering the people closest to the client to make decisions about how best to improve . . .
>
> Total Quality Management in schools involves examining and changing traditional structures and empowering groups of teachers to make real decisions about the purpose, process and product. (Quong and Walker, 1996: 224)

Significantly, the changes described by Quong and Walker focus on structure and roles as the key to improvement. The school they describe was a private, fee-paying institution – working outside the constraints of national policies and prescriptions. Although the evidence base is limited, it is possible to summarise a number of practical outcomes, reported by educational institutions involved in the quality movement, in the study outlined above:

- a new focus on values and strategic thinking, usually expressed in the formulation of mission statements, strategic planning and a greater emphasis on being 'values driven'
- increased emphasis on monitoring and review with greater use of quantitative data to inform analysis and decision-taking; this applies particularly to student progress and attainment
- standardisation of key processes to ensure consistency and adherence to defined best practice, e.g. admissions procedures and programme design with students applying to further education colleges
- the use of team-based structures for both staff deployment and the organisation of student learning
- greater involvement of students and parents through satisfaction surveys and the use of the outcomes of such surveys to inform policy-making, e.g. a middle school regularly sampling pupil satisfaction with subject teaching
- the use of external 'kite marks' to benchmark best practice, e.g. ISO 9000, Investors in People, Basic Skills Agency in the UK and the School Excellence Award in Singapore.

It is the emphasis on prevention that has perhaps been the most difficult area to come to terms with in education. Quality control and quality assurance are both well understood in the manufacturing context; it is easy to spot and reject a badly made widget – the same does not apply in the classroom. It is in this respect that the wholesale application of total quality to education becomes problematic. The early 1990s saw great enthusiasm for the international quality assurance standard now known as ISO 9000. However, it was usually only applied, often successfully, to management structures – not to relationships in the classroom. The notion of developing strategies to prevent failure in teaching and learning seems beyond any system – indeed, failure is often perceived as a necessary part of learning.

The issue typifies a key problem with TQM. It can be used to address the supportive infrastructure in schools and colleges but it has not been used to address the core purpose of education – the nature of learning and teaching. It is relatively easy to apply total quality principles to administrative systems, and this has validity. Many colleges of further education have applied the discipline of ISO 9000 to their support services with a significant improvement in efficiency and satisfaction. However, the movement from student records to student learning is a significant conceptual leap. Perhaps the greatest challenge facing any management structure is its ability to deal with those aspects of organisational life which are not amenable to reductionist and instrumental definitions. In this context TQM may have the potential to offer a better understanding of the importance of processes, i.e. relationships, in the design and operation of schools and colleges.

In reporting the impact of the Next Generation School Project (NGSP) in Georgia, USA, Weller (1997) shows how schools involved in the project, using total quality principles, achieved significant improvements in student learning outcomes. In the project schools the number of students passing all subjects at the end of a year was significantly higher than for groups not using the strategy. There were similar improvements in terms of improved attendance and a fall in the number of reported disciplinary incidents: 'Seventh grade teachers emphasised personalised and small group instruction and continuous improvement. Students were told they could and would succeed . . . teachers had high expectations of success for each of their students' (Weller, 1997: 202).

It would be wrong to claim a precise causal relationship between the introduction of TQM and the improvement in results; there is a real possibility of a 'Hawthorne effect'. However, results did improve dramatically in the project classrooms and did not in others. It could also be argued that the changes in teacher behaviour were not exclusive to TQM approaches, the strategies are recognised good practice in any context. The issue is that change, and improvement, were the result of a quality management initiative. Weller is appropriately cautious about the long-term impact of the project but concludes: 'the application of TQM principles is showing positive results as schools are adopting TQM as a reform and restructuring process' (Weller, 1997: 204).

Difficulties with total quality in education

As far as can be established, there are no examples of schools or colleges which have adopted and sustained a total quality approach. Many have successfully incorporated aspects of total quality (see Davies and West-Burnham, 1997; Doherty, 1994; Lomax, 1996 and Parsons, 1994) but there remains the issue of the extent to which it is possible (let alone desirable) for educational institutions to adopt the approach.

There are a number of significant caveats about total quality in education:

- the tension between government policy-making and institutional autonomy
- consensus and professional autonomy
- managerialism
- the appropriateness of industrial models in education.

Although subject to the law, commercial organisations are largely autonomous when it comes to determining their management philosophy, even shareholders do not have to be consulted. This never has been the case with educational organisations. They are subject to a wide range of external requirements which inhibit their ability to make significant choices. A pertinent example of this is to be found in England. A major bank, Lloyds TSB, introduced an important quality initiative in 1999. Based on the European Foundation for Quality Management (EFQM) model of quality, it represents a systematic resource for schools in developing a quality approach (www.qualityineducation.co.uk). Over 2,500 schools have been involved. However, it could be argued that the model will always be constrained by the policy context that schools in England have to operate in.

For example, a key component of the model is leadership. The ability of an individual school in England to develop its own model of leadership will always be compromised by the National Standards for Headship and the National Professional Qualification for Headship. In the same way, other components of the model, policy and strategy and processes, will inevitably be constrained by national initiatives such as the Literacy and Numeracy Strategies and the Key Stage 3 Strategy. This is not to argue that any of these strategies are hostile to quality but rather that they compromise the institutional integrity of the school or college – and such autonomy is fundamental to most models of total quality. The most significant compromising factor is that school self-assessment using the EFQM model will always be compromised by the national model of school inspection and by the use of national league tables. This diminishes the potential of the model as external inspection is in complete contradiction to any definition of quality management. Another example from England, although it is used in many other educational systems, is the imposition of a national scheme of performance-related pay – a concept not found in most total quality companies. It could be argued that total quality is impossible in the public sector unless a government adopts total quality – and that is close to an oxymoron.

The second area of concern is the perceived tension between the notion of professional autonomy in teaching and the insistence in total quality theory on high degrees of consensus, acceptance of organisational goals and working in teams. Leaving aside the moot point as to the professional status of teachers, there is obvious tension between the corporate alignment required by total quality and the historic autonomy of teachers. How defensible that autonomy is remains problematic as is the extent to which it is still true in times of increasing prescription about the curriculum, assessment and teaching strategies. On the one hand, total quality can be seen as anti-democratic, on the other hand, this is not unique to the quality movement. Once we move beyond the debate about real or contrived collegiality, every model of organisational effectiveness assumes a high degree of what Senge (1990) calls 'alignment' – indeed, it is difficult to envisage an organisation which does not require acceptance of values, core purpose and operating procedures. The perceived tension between the nomothetic and the idiographic, between organisational and individual imperatives, is probably at its strongest in education. Indeed the claim to professional autonomy is often seen as one of the defining features of the concept of the educational professional, not least in higher education. While this can be seen at one level as a debate about academic freedom, it is also a pragmatic issue – how are those aspects of organisational life which are common to be organised?

Managerialism in this context is taken to mean excessive concern with systems and structures to the detriment of the core purpose of the organisation. The bureaucratic imperative is often cited as one of the main objectives to quality management strategies, and it is easy to see why. Thick folders of standard operating procedures seem far removed from the joy of learning and the creativity of teaching. The use of ISO 9000 undoubtedly led some schools and colleges into the rationalistic fallacy – if it is defined and documented then it will happen. In fact every educational organisation has always had standard operating procedures – curriculum documents and schemes of work, the staff handbook, etc. What often happened was that schools and colleges focused on quality assurance and neglected the other components of the total quality model. It is much easier to manage routine procedures than to provide the leadership to create a culture of continuous improvement.

The issue of culture is central to any debate about the application of TQM to education. Not only is there the issue of transfer across sectors there is also a major concern with what might be described as a new form of cultural imperialism. In discussing educational change in Thailand, Singapore and Hong Kong, Hallinger and Kantamara argue that:

> An ever-expanding array of western management innovations are traversing the globe and finding their way into traditional cultures. Not unlike the response of a living organism to a virus, the instinctive response of many organisations is to attack with self-protecting mechanisms. Thus, even as policy makers embrace foreign educational policy reforms, change engenders more suspicion than enthusiasm. (Hallinger and Kantamara, 2000: 202)

It may well be that the only way that the principles of total quality will be fully incorporated into educational systems is through systemic cultural change, which is exactly the same principle as applies in commercial organisations. The example cited above from Georgia, USA, is a good example of this. Perhaps the most powerful illustration of this approach is to be found in Singapore with the School Excellence Model. The model is clearly value driven, giving practical expression to the principles of the national vision 'Thinking Schools, Learning Nation'. The key areas of the model, organisational effectiveness, student all-round development, staff well-being and teaching and learning, provide a systematic and integrated approach with clear criteria to be applied within a review framework. The model meets many of the criteria for a quality approach but is distinctive in that it fits within an overarching national strategy, which is unique, and has been developed to fit specific cultural requirements; it has not been 'taken off the shelf'. Most importantly it has created a coherent vocabulary which is capable of informing action. It has status and significance and has the potential to deliver sustainable change.

Future developments

It is highly unlikely that the total quality approach will ever be seen as the panacea for all the ills that assail educational systems and institutions. Indeed, there is a major issue in debating the extent to which one approach is possible or desirable. The increasing specificity of government policy throughout the world points to a political confidence that it is possible to identify and promulgate the 'one best way'. However, in societies which are, at least ostensibly, pluralist and where the nature and purpose of education remain contentious, there may be validity in debating the nature of educational management as well as that which is to be managed. In this debate total quality offers a distinctive perspective which is derived from an explicit concern with translating values into concrete experience and stresses the status and significance of the perceptions of the customer or client.

The most significant issue facing educational institutions of all types is the extent to which the way they are currently organised, managed and led is 'fit for purpose'. This is perhaps the most powerful axiom of the quality movement in that it raises the issue of the relationship between form and function. It is worth questioning the extent to which roles, structure and processes in schools and colleges are actually fit for the purpose of educating young people to live adult lives in a world which, by any criterion, is going to be very different to the one in which the current patterns of schooling and educating were laid down. If nothing else, the quality movement offers a distinctive perspective and alternative criteria which might contribute to a complex and highly significant debate.

Further reading

Doherty, G. (1994) *Developing Quality Systems in Education*, London: Routledge.
Parsons, C. (1994) *Quality Improvement in Education*, London: David Fulton.
West-Burnham, J. (1997) *Managing Quality in Schools*, 2nd edn, London: Pitman.

References

Davies, B. and West-Burnham, J. (1997) *Reengineering and Total Quality in Schools*, London: Pitman.

Doherty, G. (ed.) (1994) *Developing Quality Systems in Education*, London: Routledge.

Greenwood, M. S. and Gaunt, H. J. (1994) *Total Quality Management for Schools*, London: Cassell.

Hallinger, P. and Kantamara, P. (2000) 'Educational change in Thailand: opening a window onto leadership as a cultural process', *School Leadership and Management*, 20 (2): 202.

Lomax, P. (1996) *Quality Management in Education*, London: Routledge.

Murgatroyd, S. and Morgan, C. (1992) *Total Quality Management and the School*, Buckingham: Open University Press.

Parsons, C. (ed.) (1994) *Quality Improvement in Education*, London: David Fulton.

Peters, T. and Waterman, P .(1982) *In Search of Excellence*, London: Harper and Row.

Quong, T. and Walker, A. (1996) 'TQM and school restructuring: a case study', *School Organisation*, 16 (2): 224.

Sallis, E. (1993) *Total Quality Management in Education*, London: Kogan Page.

Senge, P. M. (1990) *The Fifth Discipline*, New York: Doubleday.

Tribus, M. (1994) 'The application of quality management principles in education at Mt. Edgecombe High School', in G. Doherty (ed.), *Developing Quality Systems in Education*, London: Routledge.

Weller, D. (1997) 'TQM: Georgia's approach to educational reform and school restructuring', in B. Davies and J. West-Burnham (eds), *Reengineering and Total Quality in Schools*, London: Pitman.

West-Burnham, J. (1992) *Managing Quality in Schools*, Harlow: Longman.

Subject Index

Author Index

Adams, J.E. and Kirst, M.W. 233
Adler, N. 71
Aedo-Richmond, R. and Richmond, M. 174, 180
African National Congress 135
Ainley, P. and Bailey, B. 254
Alexander, R. 157, 160
Altrichter, H. and Salzgeber, S. 282
Anderson, L. 209, 213
Ansoff, H.I. and McDonnell, E.J. 92
Argyris, C. and Schön, D.A. 65
Arnott, M.A. 227, 230
Audit Commission 199, 217
Audit Commission/Ofsted 217
Auala, R. 243

Babyegyega, E. 244
Badat, S. 28
Balazs, E. 104
Ball, S. 9, 10, 22, 269, 282, 285
Ball, S., Bowe, R. and Gewirtz, S. 244, 251
Barth, R.S. 54
Bass, B.M. 51, 52, 53–4
Bassey, M. 268, 269
Beardall, J. 122
Beare, H., Caldwell, B. and Millikan, R. 27, 89, 90–1, 139, 259
Becaj, J. 17, 19–20
Becher, T., Erault, M., Barton, J., Canning, T. and Knight, J. 294
Beer, M. 122–3
Bell, L. 4, 25, 86, 208, 260, 267
Bennett, N. 282
Bennis, W. 52
Bentley, T. 172–3
Berg, R.V.D. and Sleegers, P. 66
Berka, W. 188
Bishop, P. and Mulford, B. 22
Blackmore, J. 137
Blair, M. 141
Blair, T. 36
Blake, R.G. and Mouton, J.S. 52, 55, 56, 79
Blandford, S. 211

Blasé, J. and Blasé, J. 278
Blatchford, P. and Martin, C. 214
Bolam, R. 107, 113–4
Bolam, R., Dunning, G. and Karstanje, P. 104, 105, 106
Bolam, R., McMahoon, A., Pocklington, K. and Weindling, R. 114
Bolman, L. and Deal, T. 3–4, 5, 16, 28, 29, 55, 56
Bond, K. 77
Bottery, M. 225–6, 235, 268
Bradley, C. and Roaf, C. 275
Bray, E. 138
Brookfield, S. 164
Brundrett, M. 22
Bruner, J. 166
Bryk, A.S. 41
Bryk, A.S., Sebring, P.B., Kerbow, D., Rollow, S. and Easton, J.Q. 41
Bullock, A. and Thomas, H. 37, 38–9, 44, 199, 208, 231, 232
Bulmahn, E. 263, 268
Burton, L. 147
Bush, T. 5, 6, 8, 9, 12, 16, 17, 18, 20, 22, 23, 26, 28, 114, 120, 208, 210, 213
Bush. T. and Anderson, L. 28
Bush, T. and Jackson, D. ix, 5
Bush, T. and Qiang, H. 29, 70, 78
Bush, T., Coleman, M. and Glover, D. 23
Bush, T., Coleman, M. and Si, X. 17, 21, 29, 70, 175
Bush, T., Qiang, H. and Fang, J. 8, 265
Busher, H. 278, 280, 282, 285
Busher, H. and Harris, A. 280
Busher, H. and Saran, R. 275, 277
Busher, H., Barker, B. and Wortley, A. 275, 277, 279, 281, 282

Caldwell, B. and Spinks, J. 11, 35, 36, 39, 42, 44, 208
Campbell, R.J. and Neill, S.R.StJ. 105
Campbell, P. and Southworth, G. 21
Cardno, C. and Piggot-Irvine, E. 73, 129

327